Community and Conscience

Community and Conscience

THE JEWS IN

APARTHEID SOUTH AFRICA

Gideon Shimoni

University Press of New England

HANOVER AND LONDON

Brandeis University Press
Published by University Press of New England,
37 Lafayette St., Lebanon, NH 03766

Printed in the United States of America
5 4 3 2 1

Published in South Africa in 2003 by David Philip Publishers,
an imprint of New Africa Books (Pty) Ltd,
PO Box 46962, Glosderry 7702, Republic of South Africa.
ISBN 0–86486–620–8 (David Philip paperback)

Library of Congress Cataloging-in-Publication Data

Shimoni, Gideon.
Community and conscience : the Jews in apartheid South Africa / Gideon Shimoni.
p. cm. — (The Tauber Institute for the Study of European Jewry series (Unnumbered))
Includes bibliographical references and index.
ISBN 1–58465–329–9 (cloth : alk. paper)
1. Jews—South Africa—History. 2. Jews—South Africa—Politics and government. 3. Zionism—South Africa—History. 4. Apartheid—South Africa—History. 5. South Africa—Race relations. 6. South Africa—Ethnic relations. I. Shimoni, Gideon. Jews and Zionism. II. Title. III. Series.
DS135.S6S527 2003
968'.004924—dc21 2003004623

Grateful acknowledgment is made for the financial support
of the South African Jewish Trust.

A note from the author regarding figure 2: Every reasonable effort has been made to trace the photographer or copyright holder of this image. However, this has proven impossible. The author and publisher will be glad to receive information leading to more complete acknowledgment in subsequent printings of this book and in the meantime extend their apology for any omission.

The Tauber Institute for the Study of European Jewry Series

Jehuda Reinharz, GENERAL EDITOR
Sylvia Fuks Fried, ASSOCIATE EDITOR

The Tauber Institute for the Study of European Jewry, established by a gift to Brandeis University from Dr. Laszlo N. Tauber, is dedicated to the memory of the victims of Nazi persecutions between 1933 and 1945. The Institute seeks to study the history and culture of European Jewry in the modern period. The Institute has a special interest in studying the causes, nature, and consequences of the European Jewish catastrophe within the contexts of modern European diplomatic, intellectual, political, and social history.

GERHARD L. WEINBERG, 1981
World in the Balance: Behind the Scenes of World War II

RICHARD COBB, 1983
French and Germans, Germans and French: A Personal Interpretation of France under Two Occupations, 1914–1918/1940–1944

EBERHARD JÄCKEL, 1984
Hitler in History

FRANCES MALINO AND BERNARD WASSERSTEIN, EDITORS, 1985
The Jews in Modern France

JEHUDA REINHARZ AND WALTER SCHATZBERG, EDITORS, 1985
The Jewish Response to German Culture: From the Enlightenment to the Second World War

JACOB KATZ, 1986
The Darker Side of Genius: Richard Wagner's Anti-Semitism

JEHUDA REINHARZ, EDITOR, 1987
Living with Antisemitism: Modern Jewish Responses

MICHAEL R. MARRUS, 1987
The Holocaust in History

PAUL MENDES-FLOHR, EDITOR, 1987
The Philosophy of Franz Rosenzweig

JOAN G. ROLAND, 1989
Jews in British India: Identity in a Colonial Era

YISRAEL GUTMAN, EZRA MENDELSOHN, JEHUDA REINHARZ, AND CHONE SHMERUK, EDITORS, 1989
The Jews of Poland Between Two World Wars

AVRAHAM BARKAI, 1989
From Boycott to Annihilation: The Economic Struggle of German Jews, 1933–1943

ALEXANDER ALTMANN, 1991
The Meaning of Jewish Existence: Theological Essays 1930–1939

MAGDALENA OPALSKI AND ISRAEL BARTAL, 1992
Poles and Jews: A Failed Brotherhood

RICHARD BREITMAN, 1992
The Architect of Genocide: Himmler and the Final Solution

GEORGE L. MOSSE, 1993
Confronting the Nation: Jewish and Western Nationalism

DANIEL CARPI, 1994
Between Mussolini and Hitler: The Jews and the Italian Authorities in France and Tunisia

WALTER LAQUEUR AND RICHARD BREITMAN, 1994
Breaking the Silence: The German Who Exposed the Final Solution

ISMAR SCHORSCH, 1994
From Text to Context: The Turn to History in Modern Judaism

JACOB KATZ, 1995
With My Own Eyes: The Autobiography of an Historian

GIDEON SHIMONI, 1995
The Zionist Ideology

MOSHE PRYWES AND HAIM CHERTOK, 1996
Prisoner of Hope

JÁNOS NYIRI, 1997
Battlefields and Playgrounds

ALAN MINTZ, EDITOR, 1997
The Boom in Contemporary Israeli Fiction

SAMUEL BAK, PAINTINGS
LAWRENCE L. LANGER, ESSAY AND COMMENTARY, 1997
Landscapes of Jewish Experience

JEFFREY SHANDLER AND BETH S. WENGER, EDITORS, 1997
Encounters with the "Holy Land": Place, Past and Future in American Jewish Culture

SIMON RAWIDOWICZ, 1998
State of Israel, Diaspora, and Jewish Continuity: Essays on the "Ever-Dying People"

JACOB KATZ, 1998
A House Divided: Orthodoxy and Schism in Nineteenth-Century Central European Jewry

ELISHEVA CARLEBACH, JOHN M. EFRON, AND
DAVID N. MYERS, EDITORS, 1998
Jewish History and Jewish Memory: Essays in Honor of Yosef Hayim Yerushalmi

SHMUEL ALMOG, JEHUDA REINHARZ, AND ANITA SHAPIRA, EDITORS,
1998
Zionism and Religion

BEN HALPERN AND JEHUDA REINHARZ, 2000
Zionism and the Creation of a New Society

WALTER LAQUEUR, 2001
Generation Exodus: The Fate of Young Jewish Refugees from Nazi Germany

YIGAL SCHWARTZ, 2001
Aharon Appelfeld: From Individual Lament to Tribal Eternity

RENÉE POZNANSKI, 2001
Jews in France during World War II

JEHUDA REINHARZ, 2001
Chaim Weizmann: The Making of a Zionist Leader

JEHUDA REINHARZ, 2001
Chaim Weizmann: The Making of a Statesman

CHAERAN Y. FREEZE, 2002
Jewish Marriage and Divorce in Imperial Russia

MARK A. RAIDER AND MIRIAM B. RAIDER-ROTH, 2002
The Plough Woman: Records of the Pioneer Women of Palestine

EZRA MENDELSOHN, 2002
Painting a People: Maurycy Gottlieb and Jewish Art

ALAN MINTZ, 2002
Reading Hebrew Literature: Critical Discussions of Six Modern Texts

HAIM BE'ER, 2002
The Pure Element of Time

YEHUDIT HENDEL, 2002
Small Change: A Collection of Stories

THOMAS C. HUBKA, 2003
Resplendent Synagogue: Architecture and Worship in an Eighteenth-Century Polish Community

UZI REBHUN AND CHAIM I. WAXMAN, 2003
Jews in Israel: Contemporary Social and Cultural Patterns

GIDEON SHIMONI, 2003
Community and Conscience: The Jews in Apartheid South Africa

To the memory of Hanns Saenger,
refugee from Nazi Germany, South African,
Jewish community leader,
friend of the Hebrew University of Jerusalem

Contents

Preface

This is a study of the Jews in a particular community of the Jewish Diaspora. Its vantage point is that of a historian specializing in the contemporary history of the Jews: contemporary being understood roughly as the period of time coextensive with generations of people still largely active in society. This book, however, does not purport to provide a comprehensive account of the contemporary Jewish community in South Africa. It focuses specifically on the Jewish experience as part of a privileged white minority that dominated a society based upon a system of legalized racial discrimination. This was certainly a poignantly unusual experience in the light of the painful record of racist victimization suffered by Jews in modern times.

The historical record of South African whites in general remains an indelible stain on mankind's moral conscience even after the redeeming transformation of South Africa and its negotiated reconstruction as a nonracial democracy. Yet, I am governed by the professional opinion that neither indictment nor apologia belongs to the task at hand. The historian should not presume to be a moral judge. Rather, he should aspire to the presentation of as objective, balanced, comprehensive, and empirically documented an account as possible. This might then form a sound basis for value judgments by each and every reader who chooses to make them, universal agreement on such complex issues being unlikely in any case.

The structure of this book is chronological, beginning with an introduction that recounts the most apposite aspects of the Jewish community's origins, character and experience in South African society prior to 1948. I have also incorporated some revised sections of an earlier work, *Jews and Zionism: The South African Experience (1910–1967)*, published in 1980 by Oxford University Press, Cape Town. This book has long been out of print and copyright has reverted to me as author. The last chapter of the present book deals with the Jewish community's comportment in the period of South Africa's negotiated transformation and the institution of a nonracial democracy. Only in a section of chapter 2, in which I attempt to analyze the factors that went into the making of Jewish radicals and liberals who joined the struggle against apartheid, is the narrative's chronological sequence partly broken. This analysis necessitated the inclusion of data relating to activities extending chronologically beyond the heyday of the apartheid program in the 1950s and 1960s and into the period of reformed or modified apartheid that ultimately culminated in its complete dismantling.

A few words about the system of footnoting are called for: the primary sources of this study are predominantly derived from the records held by the South African Jewish Board of Deputies in Johannesburg. Although these provide a vast treasure-house of invaluable documentation, they do not constitute an organized archives such as historians conventionally rely upon. Not only have the records undergone changes in filing classification over several decades of my research, but also they have been rearranged since completion of this book. Consequently some of the book's endnotes of necessity indicate only the general classification of the documents, e.g., BD, Public Relations Files. Although their specific location will have been reclassified, future researchers wishing to check or make new use of these sources should be able to retrace them via this general classification.

I wish gratefully to acknowledge the help of several persons and institutions. Sadly, the foremost of these, Hanns Saenger, is no longer with us. He passed away a few months before completion of the manuscript. In his capacity as chairman of the South African Jewish Trust, he urged me to undertake this work and provided generous funding for research conducted during a series of visits to South Africa over a period of four years. In order to protect my academic freedom, a condition of my undertaking was that neither any sponsor of the project nor any person holding a position of authority in any of the Jewish community's institutions would be shown the manuscript before publication. Regretfully, Hanns therefore never saw the product of the project he so enthusiastically initiated.

I am profoundly indebted to David Saks, who placed his fine scholarly talents at my disposal as a research assistant on the spot. He has since been appointed senior researcher at the South African Jewish Board of Deputies. Situated as I am so far away in Jerusalem, I could never have written this book without his splendid assistance and steadfast devotion to the task. I also wish to thank Seymour Kopelowitz, former executive director of the Jewish Board of Deputies; former librarian Sylvia Tuback; current library consultant Professor Reuben Musiker; archivist Naomi Musiker; and the Board's staff members Hamilton Nare and Sonnyboy Rashoalane. All provided me with every consideration and assistance throughout all my research visits. I especially appreciate Reuben Musiker's help in locating photographic illustrations. I also wish to thank Jeanne Cope for her painstaking preparation of the index.

I am grateful for the cooperation of innumerable former and present leaders in the Jewish community who allowed me to conduct a large number of oral interviews, not all of which have been cited in this book. I also wish to thank the Isaac and Jessie Kaplan Centre for Jewish Studies and Research at the University of Cape Town for assistance rendered while I worked in Cape Town, and its librarian, Veronica Belling. I am especially grateful to its director, Professor Milton Shain, for giving me the benefit of his comments after reading parts of the manuscript. Of course I alone bear responsibility for any errors or faults that remain.

My thanks go out to Brandeis University president Jehuda Reinharz; Sylvia Fuks Fried, executive director of its Tauber Institute; Phyllis Deutsch, executive editor at University Press of New England; and production editor Lisa Sacks for their concern and care in seeing to the publication of my manuscript.

Above all, words fail to express the depth of my feelings for the steadfast help of Toni, my partner in life and in work. She truly shares with me in the making of this book.

Jerusalem, 2002 G. S.

Community and Conscience

INTRODUCTION

The Jewish Community in South African Society

A fundamental and conspicuous fact underlies this study: the Jews of South Africa have shared in the status of the privileged in a society based upon a system of legalized racial discrimination. Viewed in the broad context of Jewish history this was a highly unusual situation, even if not entirely unique. What was the Jewish experience in these circumstances? What was the political behavior of Jews as members of the dominant and domineering white minority? What were the perceived implications of Jewry's moral heritage and historical experience? How did Jewish leadership, lay and religious, seek to reconcile these implications with its responsibility for the safety and welfare of its own community? These are the primary questions to be addressed in the chapters that follow. Consciously attendant upon the empirical record to which this inquiry aspires is the sensitive evaluation of the relation between community and conscience in the modern Jewish experience. Was this a community with a conscience? Does the record show a community that acted upon its conscience, or a community that failed to so act: a community with a bad conscience?

Our inquiry focuses on the period, roughly 1948 to 1994, in which the South African political and social order was infamously epitomized by the term "apartheid." However, the rudiments of that order prevailed long before the term became current, and a Jewish presence in South Africa long preceded the apartheid era. Comprehension of the Jewish situation therefore requires the recounting at least of the most apposite aspects of the Jewish community's origins, character, and experience leading up to the advent of officially espoused apartheid.

Formation of the Jewish Community

The formation of a Jewish community in South Africa was the outcome of emigration from Great Britain and Europe. It began in the course of the nineteenth century as an incidental offshoot of British Jewry, was greatly consolidated from the 1880s to 1930 by a broad wave of immigration from eastern Europe, and capped by a small wave of German Jewish refugees in the 1930s.[1] It has been estimated that in the thirty-year period from 1880 to 1910 some 40,000 Jewish immigrants entered South Africa. Another 30,000 had come by 1948. This figure includes about 3,600 who fled from Nazi Germany in the years 1933 to 1937 and constituted the final immigrant augmentation, the major flow from eastern Europe having been stemmed by a new immigration law enacted in 1930. The first census of the Union of South Africa was held in 1911. It showed 46,919 Jews in South Africa (3.7 percent of the 1,276,242 whites). In 1936 there were 90,645 Jews (4.5 percent of 2,003,857), and by 1946 the number had reached 104,156 (4.4 percent of 2,372,690).[2]

The society into which these Jews entered was one in which an ascriptive attribute, race (signified by skin color), was the primary determinant of people's lives. Socially, it was stratified by what might be described as caste-like divisions between various racial groups of which the white group was in every respect dominant. The subordinate groups were designated collectively as "non-Europeans," comprising Africans (at various times labeled Natives, Bantu, or blacks), Asiatics (mainly Indians), and mixed-race persons designated as "Coloureds."[3] Politically, for the white inhabitants it was a parliamentary democracy on the Westminster model, while for all the other inhabitants it was a white oligarchy. Culturally, it was markedly heterogeneous: not only were there major cultural differences between blacks, Asiatics, and whites, but even the white racial group was further segmented into an institutionalized duality of Afrikaans and English culture. Yet, economically it was already on the path of inextricable interdependence between the whites and the other racial groups.

When the eastern Europeans began to arrive in large numbers, there were already some 4,000 Jews who had come from Britain. Most were born in Britain, some in Germany. This was the Jewish population core that laid the foundations of the community's institutional structure, beginning in 1841 with the founding of the first synagogue congregation in Cape Town and continuing with various community burial and benevolent aid societies, a federation of Zionist societies in 1898, and a Jewish Board of Deputies by 1912. The latter was a representative type of Jewish organization, modeled wholly on the Anglo-Jewish prototype of the same name in London. Its objects were to "watch and take action in all matters affecting the Jews in the southern portion of the continent of Africa." Membership was open to any congregation or burial society "having bona fide continuous and organized existence," as well as any other Jewish public body or institution "duly recognized by the Board for the purposes of representation."[4]

Although Anglo-Jews took the lead in the various communal institutions well into the first decades of the twentieth century, Jews of eastern European birth or parentage gradually displaced them. The overwhelming majority of the eastern Europeans were "Litvakes,"[5] a term or nomenclature in Yiddish speech, folklore, and literature that connoted Jews from the northwestern region of the Pale of Settlement to which the Jewish population of the Russian empire was confined in terms of copious restrictive laws and regulations.[6] The remarkable Litvak homogeneity of the immigration to South Africa led the Zionist leader Nahum Sokolow (who visited South Africa in 1934, during his tenure as president of the World Zionist Organization) to call the Jewish community in South Africa "a colony of Litvak Jewry." It is further noteworthy that a high proportion of the immigrants came from Kovno Province, which became the heart of the independent state of Lithuania established in 1919, towns such as Kovno, Ponevez, Riteva, Plungian, Yanoshek, and Shavli featuring prominently as hometowns. Ties between immigrants from such towns formed the basis for a number of mutual help associations known as *landsmanshaften* within the South African Jewish community. It is estimated from czarist Russian statistics that some 33,800 emigrated from Kovno Province from 1896 to 1914. It appears that a considerable proportion of these headed for South Africa.[7]

Of fundamental importance for the future socioeconomic prospects of these Jewish immigrants in South Africa was the fact that they had the status of being Europeans, that is to say, whites. From the outset the Jewish immigrant entered into the dominant, caste-like white sector and lived thereafter within its confines. At best, relations with "non-Europeans" (at worst also called "kaffirs"[8]) were limited to employer-employee or domestic master-servant spheres. Indeed, for most Jews, as for most whites, blacks were almost invisible in social terms. To be sure, as we shall have cause to note in the pages that follow, this privileged white status of Jews did not go entirely unchallenged over the years, but in the final analysis it was sustained in all major respects. South Africa offered Jewish immigrants civic freedom in all essentials, as well as upward economic mobility and ultimate prosperity.[9] At the same time acculturation took its toll in erosion of Jewish religious observance and linguistic-cultural identity. In South Africa it was overwhelmingly the English segment that served as the reference group for acculturation.

South African Jewry thus came to have much in common with other New World Jewish communities. Yet in comparative perspective, a number of factors converged to confer a distinctive character upon the South African Jewish community. One of these factors was the nature of its religiosity—a direct outcome of the extraordinarily homogeneous Litvak composition of the community. It is important to note not only the absence of reform Judaism in the Litvak region but also that it was the heartland of the *misnagdi* tradition in orthodox Judaism, that is, the tradition of opposition to the mystic and sectarian manifestations of Hasidism. By and large, the Litvak immigrants had a traditionalist religious upbringing before coming to South Africa, although secularization had already made considerable inroads. But the historical record shows a tremendous lapse from religious observance after arrival in South Africa largely because the exigencies of making a living in that socioeconomic environment made Sabbath observance difficult.[10] The outcome in South Africa was a blend of Litvak *misnagdi* religious orthodoxy, in rather lax fashion, with Anglo-Jewry's already acculturated United Synagogue form of synagogue ritual. This issued in a normative mode of religiosity that has been characterized as conservative traditionalism and also as "non-observant orthodox," an apt description of the reality notwithstanding the apparent oxymoron.[11] It has as well been described as the "pouring of Litvak spirit into Anglo-Jewish bottles."[12]

A related and even more significantly distinctive consequence of the Litvak predominance in South African Jewry was the highly self-affirmative ethnicity that characterized the community. It should be noted that the ethnicity of the Jews in the Russian Pale of Settlement was at its most cohesive in the Lithuanian region. This was largely because they experienced very little acculturation to their immediate social and cultural environment, the indigenous Lithuanian population being predominantly of the peasant class. The culture and even the language of the Lithuanian ethnic majority exerted no magnetism. Litvak Jews tended to acculturate, if at all, toward the Russian language and attendant cultural institutions (or, toward German in the Baltic coast region)—hence, the deeply ingrained Jewish ethnic identity of Litvak immigrants to South Africa.[13]

Moreover, the ethnicism of the Jews produced several competing political movements with nationalist programs of varying intensity, including the liberal Folkspartey (People's Party) and the socialist Yiddisher Arbeter Bund (Jewish Workers' Organization). But the paramount political movement within Lithuanian Jewry was Zionism, and in no country was Zionism more firmly entrenched than in interwar independent Lithuania.[14] Therefore it is not surprising that Zionism was already deeply ingrained in the normative mode of Jewish identity, whether religious or secularized, that characterized successive generations of Litvak arrivals in South Africa. Zionism was integral to their ethnic identity as Jews. Furthermore, in contrast to the situation in the United States and also, although to a lesser extent, in Britain, this Zionist orientation did not come into conflict with an established mold of reform Judaism, with its attendant antagonism to Zionism. Indeed, reform Judaism (later officially called progressive Judaism) was not introduced into South Africa until as late as 1933, and might never have been able to make headway had its founder, Rabbi Moses C. Weiler, not been one of the minority of American-trained reform rabbis who strongly identified as a Zionist. By dint of his influence, from the outset progressive Judaism adopted relatively moderate reforms and was no less Zionist in orientation than orthodox Judaism.[15]

If ethnic cohesiveness expressed in strong Zionist sentiment might be described as a genetic inheritance of the Litvak Jews who came to South Africa, one should add that the social environment of the host society nurtured and enhanced this heritage. Nature and nurture were at one in this case owing to the compound ethnic segmentation of South African society. Since the privileged white segment was in itself culturally dualistic and of inchoate national identity, the circumstances were highly conducive to the preservation of a sense of Jewish ethnicity that found expression in Zionism. It is indicative of the pivotal role that Zionism played in the history of South African Jewry that the community's first countrywide organization was the South African Zionist Federation, founded in December 1898 as a comprehensive framework for all Zionist societies and activities. Judged by almost any criterion—membership, prestige, fund-raising capacity, publicity, press resources—the Zionist Federation became the preeminent institution in the life of the community.

It might be said that the Zionist movement enjoyed a form of hegemony in the life of the organized Jewish community. Viewed in the comparative perspective of

Jewish communities in Britain and the New World countries, South African Jewry generally held the record for formal membership in the World Zionist Organization as measured by the percentage of Jews who purchased the "shekel" membership certificate (for which men and women over eighteen years of age were eligible) entitling one to a vote in the elections to the World Zionist Congress. In mid-1946, when the first postwar Zionist election took place, no less than 39,945 of South Africa's 104,156 Jews were shekel holders, and of these 28,876 cast their votes. Two years after the creation of the State of Israel, out of a population of 110,000 Jews, 50,000 were shekel holders.[16]

As elsewhere in the world, political party divisions and also youth movements, in most cases affiliated to the parties, developed in South African Zionism. However, in contrast with Zionist federations in many other countries, the South African federation encompassed all these parties and youth movements. A constitutional change in 1943 vested control of the Federation's executive in the hands of the parties, but this became a point of ongoing controversy after the creation of the State of Israel. Settling in Israel, an act termed *aliya* (the Hebrew word for "ascent" to the Land of Israel) was always integral to the program of Zionism, especially emphasized in the youth movements, but never a sine qua non for membership of the Zionist Organization. In general, for Jews in South Africa, no less than in America, confidence in the continued viability of Jewish life in the New World lands of the Diaspora imparted a vicarious quality that enabled them to identify with the idea of a return to Zion without necessarily regarding it as applicable to themselves. Hence, outside of the youth movements, the idea of *aliya* was not posed as an ideological imperative. At best, it was perceived as an act of altruistic service to the cause, or as an idealistic act of personal fulfillment.

In day-to-day practice fund-raising was the axis around which revolved the commitment of Jews who considered themselves to be Zionists. In this respect the record of South African Jewry was extraordinary. Indeed, per capita the contribution of this small community was unequaled in the world. From 1921 to 1939 its contribution, even in absolute figures, to the Zionist Organization's major fund-raising instrument, known as the Keren Hayesod (Hebrew for "Foundation Fund," initiated in 1921), was second only to that of United States Jewry.[17] Since the main method of contribution to the campaigns was by bank order, that is, a printed instruction signed by the contributor to pay the amount of his donation in regular installments, Zionist fund-raising came close to being a permanent system of voluntary taxation.

The communal hegemony enjoyed by the Zionist movement and the integral role of Zionism in the normative identity mode of Jews owed much to the legitimacy and sympathy accorded to Zionism by South African political leaders. Foremost of these was Jan Christiaan Smuts, who led the political camp that advocated Afrikaner-British conciliation for much of the period from the creation of the Union in 1910 until the fateful postwar elections of 1948. Prior to the 1930s also the Afrikaner nationalist camp of South African politics evinced sympathy for Zionism and approvingly acknowledged its importance for local Jews.[18] In sum, Zionism as an integral manifestation of Jewish identity was recognized by the consensus of

South Africa's political elite, whether in power or in opposition. At best it was regarded as fully compatible with a conciliatory (white) South Africanism; at worst it was taken for granted by those Afrikaner nationalists who assumed that the Jews were indeed an unassimilable alien nation—a negative view that, as we shall see, became increasingly prevalent after 1930.

Accommodation to South African Race Relations

Given the conduciveness of South African society to Jewish ethnicity, successful integration and upward socioeconomic mobility of the Jews stood, by and large, in no perceived contradiction to their strong Zionist sentiments. But the main impetus in the life and work of Jewish immigrants was not preservation of Jewish ethnicity; it was integration into the host society. In general, the Litvak immigrant generation was too preoccupied with basic concerns of livelihood, social adjustment, and coping with new languages to be concerned with the rights and wrongs of the regnant system of race relations and exploitation in the country. Gauging by the adaptability of Jews from eastern Europe to the codes of behavior underlying the caste-like separation of the races and the norms, legal and customary, of white domination, it is doubtful whether their own experience of discrimination and persecution in the Russian Pale of Settlement had as ennobling an effect upon them as might be imagined. Indeed, most Jewish immigrants soon became accustomed to regarding blacks as inferiors fit solely to be servants and unskilled laborers. In the words of the amateur historian and Yiddishist (that is, activist for preservation of Yiddish culture) Leibl Feldman, who was speaking from his observations as a part of this generation of Litvak immigrants: "Immediately upon their arrival they were, thanks to their white skins, taken into the ruling section of the population. . . . One accepted the privileges 'with both hands' and one allowed oneself to be served by the Africans just as all other whites did."[19] Perhaps the most contorted of all accommodations to racist social norms was to be found among, and in relation to, Jews who worked in the "eating houses"—shamelessly called "kaffireatas"—catering to blacks along the gold-mining reef of the Transvaal. No white racist contempt could be more acute than that reserved for low-class whites who served blacks. Hence the "kaffireatniks," as those employed there were contemptuously labeled, became pariahs, trapped between the caste-like strata of the social system, simultaneously the victims and the perpetrators of ugly racism.[20]

Yet, alongside this overwhelming pattern of conformity, a deviant tradition that balked at the established social order is also traceable in the history of South African Jewry. One outstanding early manifestation was related to the struggle for relief from the disabilities suffered by the Indian population from 1906 to 1914. During this campaign the legendary Mohandas Karamchand Gandhi developed his doctrine of active nonviolent resistance, named by him satyagraha and employed years later with empire-shaking effect in India itself. The closest of Gandhi's white associates were in fact Jews, notably Henry Polak, who had come from England, Hermann Kallenbach, who was Litvak-born but had come to South Africa from Germany where he had qualified as an architect, and Sonia Schlesin, a young Litvak immigrant who served faithfully as Gandhi's secretary.[21] Moreover, their actions resonated in perhaps the earliest incidence of a publicly aired controversy over the moral implications of Jewish complicity in the South African system of racial discrimination. Polak averred that he had been drawn into the Indian satyagraha struggle "as a Jew who has tried to remember that Judaism is a matter not only of belief but also of action." Drawing a parallel with discrimination against the Jews in czarist Russia, he complained that, "either in ignorance or by design, Jews have lent themselves to, or at least not openly dissociated themselves from, racial persecution." The only consolation he found as a Jew was "that those non-Indians who have taken a leading part in the effort to expose and do away with this persecution are most of them members of our faith."[22]

This observation and others, aired in an ensuing exchange of views in the columns of *The Jewish Chronicle* of London during 1911, bear a remarkable similarity to controversies on the Jews and race relations that, as we shall see, became current some fifty years later in South Africa of the apartheid era. Polak's views elicited an indignant response from another Jew, one D. Greenberg, who invoked a consideration that went to the core of the Jew's dilemma in South Africa: "The action of the Jews in Africa, who are an insignificant minority, is in keeping with the entire white population," he wrote. "I wonder if Mr. Polak has ever thought what would be the feeling of the white population in Africa towards the Jews if they . . . threw in their lot with the Indians."[23]

The record shows that the Jewish community certainly did not throw in its lot with the Indians' cause, not even when there was an incidental convergence of Jewish and Indian concerns. Such a convergence occurred in 1902–3, for example, when proposed immigration legislation sought to disqualify any immigrant who was unable to write in a European language. Although primarily aimed at stopping Indians from coming to South Africa, this legislation also stood to hamper the free flow of Jewish immigration on the grounds that Yiddish was not a European language. In pursuit of the interests of the Jewish community its representatives were at pains to dissociate their case from that of the Indians by proving that Yiddish was indeed a European language.[24]

The involvement of some Jews in Gandhi's struggle was not the only manifestation of liberal political attitudes evinced by individuals belonging to the relatively well-acculturated stratum of the Jewish public. Another major example was Morris Alexander, a distinguished parliamentarian who was at the same time arguably the foremost Jewish communal leader of his time. In Cape Town during the first three decades of the twentieth century, also Alexander's wife, Ruth (daughter of the famous scholar Rabbi Solomon Schechter, president of the Jewish Theological Seminary in New York), was at the center of a circle of what might be described, however paradoxically, as a liberal-cum-leftist deviation from white supremacist norms, initially associated with the renowned writer Olive Schreiner.[25] However, the most consequential strains of deviant Jewish political behavior emanated from working-class circles in the Yiddish-speaking immigrant public.

The upward socioeconomic mobility of Jewish immigrants over the long run, which shaped South African Jewry into a predominantly prosperous middle-class community by the mid–twentieth century, should not blind the historian to the fact that quite apart from the numerous ethnic-based *landsmanshaft* mutual aid associations, there was significant class-based activity that at times divided Jewish workers from Jewish employers. Indeed, at the turn of the twentieth century in Cape Town, Jewish workers pioneered the forming of craft unions of Jewish tailors, bakers, and carpenters. The Jewish craft unions were, in turn, in the forefront of efforts to unite all workers, not excluding coloreds.[26]

Against this background it is not surprising that some Jewish trade union activists rose to prominence in the South African trade union movement. Whereas British-born trade unionists were preeminent in the major mining, engineering, and building unions, the Jewish trade unionist was ubiquitous in the new generation of smaller trade unions following the growth of secondary and tertiary industries, in efforts to create federated or united trade union frameworks, and in attempts to organize non-European workers.[27] One famous example was the Lithuanian-born Emil (Solly) Sachs in his role as general-secretary of the (white) Transvaal Garment Workers' Union. Dramatically leading a series of strikes with extraordinary organizational and negotiating skill, he bettered the appalling conditions in the garment trade.[28] Some Jews were also prominent in the Labor Party. That party's race relations policy rested in essence on protection of the interests solely of white workers. However, the justice and wisdom of this policy did not go unquestioned over the years, and Jews in the Labor Party's leadership generally were numbered among the proponents of a color-blind policy. As this failed to gain acceptance, several major players moved politically leftward.

Even more than in the South African labor movement, Jews were prominent in the development of radical socialist groups. A striking early exemplar was Yeshaya Israelstam. Born in 1870 in Waksne, Lithuania, Israelstam wandered to the United States at the age of sixteen. There he acquired a fair command of English and became an enthusiast of Daniel DeLeon's school of socialism. Coming to South Africa in 1900, Israelstam soon threw himself into a variety of radical socialist activities. He opposed the racial discrimination that was countenanced in the early labor movement and castigated Jews in political life for being party to this when "they should know that they themselves belonged to a persecuted race."[29] Israelstam was a leader of the Society of Friends of Russian Liberty, formed in 1905. This was the first manifestation identifiable with the Jewish socialism of the powerful socialist workers' movement in Russian Jewry, the Yiddisher Arbeter Bund, founded in Vilna in 1897.

Friends of Russian Liberty, however, was merely a support group for the Bund rather than a branch of the movement in the sense of a body aiming at the sectional organization of Jewish workers aligned within a broader social democratic movement.[30] In South Africa Jewish workers had neither the critical mass nor the ideological drive for attaining the program of Yiddish cultural autonomy that underlay the Bund's development in eastern Europe. Although the continuous flow of Jewish immigrants included some individuals who had formerly been active members of the Bund in eastern European countries, these directed their radical energies directly into the local labor movement or the International Socialist League (ISL). Indeed, Jews rallied to the league on a scale sufficient to warrant the creation within it of a recognized "Yiddish-Shprechende Gruppe" (known in English as the "Yiddish-Speaking Branch").[31] Formally founded in Johannesburg in August 1917, it commanded a following of a good few hundred members and fellow travelers. The ISL was a major player in the founding of the united Communist Party of South Africa, which duly became an affiliated section of the Communist International.

Thus a self-defined Jewish group was intimately involved in the formation of a communist party from the outset—the only political party that opened its ranks to blacks. Once the party was created the Jewish group dissolved itself, but individual Jews continued to constitute a remarkably high proportion of its active white membership.[32] It is an index of the prominence of Jews in the leadership core of the party that, when directives from the Moscow Comintern forced the South African Communists to adopt the slogan—considered by some party leaders as disastrously unrealistic—of a "Native Republic, with minority rights for the Whites," and to launch a campaign against an alleged danger of right-wing deviationists, both the main fomenters and the victims of the purge-like expulsions that ensued were Jews.[33] The main Comintern dogmatists who evicted the defaulters in 1931 were Douglas and Molly Wolton and Lazar Bach. Douglas was a Gentile from Yorkshire, but his wife Molly was a Lithuanian-born Jew whose maiden name had been Zelikowitz. Bach was born in Latvia where he had already been active in the communist underground before coming to South Africa in 1929. On the strength of this he was regarded in the party as an authoritative communist ideologist and tactician.[34] The purge victims who favored "democratic equality" over a "Black Republic" included Solly Sachs, Ben Weinbren, and Sidney Bunting, a Gentile who had been the founding leader of the party, and his Jewish wife, Rebecca.

The prominence of Jews in the leadership of the Communist Party continued to be an obvious fact of which the authorities were only too well aware. Thus, a police report delivered to Prime Minister Smuts, listing sixty active leaders, secret and open, of the Johannesburg District of the Communist Party of South Africa in February 1946, contained twenty-three Jewish names, one of which was the chairman Michael Harmel.[35] Paralleling the highly disproportionate involvement of individual Jews in the Communist Party, leftist sentiments and affinities continued to be manifest in the framework of cultural activities conducted by a Yiddisher Literarisher Farein that had been founded in 1912 and in an ephemeral socialist-Zionist group of Yiddish speakers formed in 1919, which also participated in the founding of the Communist Party. Assuming the name Poalei Zion (Workers of Zion), it identified with the socialist-Zionist movement of that name, which was an ascendant political force in the world Zionist movement.[36]

The political ambience of the 1930s, sharply polarized between fascist and communist impulses emanating from Europe, was conducive to a revitalization of the Yiddishist left in South Africa. This found expression in the founding in 1929 of the Yiddisher Arbeter Klub (Jewish Workers' Club) in Johannesburg.[37] By 1937, when the club was at its peak, it had a membership of about 250, but its activities, conducted mainly in its own hall in the predominantly Jewish suburb of Doornfontein, frequently attracted a much wider audience of Yiddish-speaking sympathizers. The Arbeter Klub might be described as a fellow traveler of the Communist Party of South Africa. It rendered valuable assistance to the party and gave financial support to the leftist organ *The Guardian.* The columns of its own *Die Proletarishe Shtimme* rang out with orthodox communist phraseology—calls for proletarian unity across the color line, and condemnation of the evils of capitalist exploitation. The cover drawing of *Die Proletarishe Shtimme*'s issue of November–December 1932 epitomized the club's spirit. It depicted a giant image of Lenin above a thronging mass of whites and blacks brandishing the banners "Defend the USSR" and "A Native Republic, A Workers' and Peasants' Government!" In relation to the inner affairs of the Jewish community the club declared that it "conducts a relentless struggle against Zionism, national chauvinism and social-fascism in the Jewish street." Religion was treated with demonstrative contempt, the holiest day of the Jewish year, Yom Kippur, serving as an occasion for picnics.[38]

However, the Arbeter Klub's ideological milieu ran contrary to the upwardly mobile socioeconomic trend of the Jewish population. A statistical survey of Johannesburg Jewry showed that by 1935 about 39 percent of all males over fifteen years of age were engaged in commercial, financial, and insurance occupations and a little over 8 percent were professionals. Artisans constituted barely 10 percent of the gainfully employed.[39] By 1948 not a few of the Arbeter Klub's own members were on the way to becoming well-to-do employers. Yiddish too was rapidly receding before English as the home language of Jews. According to government census statistics, in 1936 only 19 percent still spoke Yiddish at home. By 1951 the proportion of Yiddish speakers had dwindled to 9 percent.[40] In 1948 the Arbeter Klub came to a sudden inauspicious end after a fire, the cause of which remained unknown, broke out in its Doornfontein meeting hall.

Concurrently with the small Arbeter Klub's activities, and partly overlapping with these, a far broader leftist movement made its presence felt in the late 1920s and in the 1930s. It devolved from the project sparked within the Soviet Union for the promotion of Jewish colonization on the land in the Soviet Union, a project that captured the imagination of diverse leftist circles throughout the Jewish Diaspora.[41] In 1932 the project's supporters resolved to declare themselves an organization under the name of Afrikaner Geserd.[42] The Geserd's purpose was "to render effective material and moral support towards Jewish socialist reconstruction in the Soviet Union and particularly in Birobidzhan" (the territory designated by the Soviet government for autonomous Jewish settlement).

In sum, a small radical tradition existed in South African Jewry, undergoing several organizational transmutations throughout the first half of the twentieth century. As we shall see, the ideological milieu generated by these groups, and their critical marginal-outsider position in relation to the general social order and the Jewish community alike, proved to be the nursery for not a few Jewish radicals who joined the struggle against apartheid. Yet the main picture must not be obscured—this leftist strain in all its variety was minor and peripheral to the normative sociopolitical attitudes and behavior of South African Jews.

On the whole, the pattern of political involvement of the Jews reflected their acculturation primarily to the English-speaking segment of society and their conformity with the established social system. Most of the Anglo-Jews involved in politics at the municipal and parliamentary levels, both before and immediately after the creation of the Union of South Africa in 1910, were attached to the pro-British imperial parties. At that time, when people spoke of the "race question" they usually meant the conflict between Boer (later Afrikaner) and Briton. Within that context, by the 1920s Jews tended to identify mainly with the centrist South African party led by the former Boer generals Louis Botha and Jan Christiaan Smuts. They favored this party's policy of conciliation between the Afrikaners and the English speakers and its attempt to mold a united, bilingual (white) South Africanism. In addition, Jews held Smuts in particularly high regard, thanks to his consistent support of Zionism.

Also the still race-bound Labor Party enjoyed a measure of Jewish support throughout the years, and some Jews were numbered among its leaders. In 1924 an alliance of labor with J. B. M. Hertzog's National Party, which represented mainstream Afrikaner nationalism, won the general election. Hertzog became prime minister and retained this position after a second electoral victory in 1929 and again after a major political realignment that took place in 1934 when he combined forces with Smuts to form the "fused" United Party. Without doubt, this became the party most favored by Jews, especially after a more militant segment of the Afrikaner nationalists, led by Dr. Daniel François Malan, deviated from Hertzog's course to form what was called the Gesuiwerde (Purified) National Party.[43]

Emergence of the "Jewish Question"

Almost nothing is known about the attitude of blacks toward Jews throughout the period surveyed above. It seems unlikely that blacks perceived Jews in any significant degree as a category of persons other than whites in general. As for the Jews, on the whole, their sole frame of reference was the culture, society, and politics of the whites of South Africa. "Non-Europeans" were simply not part of the field of forces that determined their status and situation, except, of course, in the economic spheres of life and these too were subject to the control of whites. Changes in the attitude of the white population, however, profoundly affected the situation of Jews. This became critically evident in the year 1930, when the South African parliament enacted a new immigration law that effectively reduced the flow of Jewish immigrants from eastern Europe to a mere trickle.[44] The word Jew was not mentioned, but only the politically blind could fail to see that Jews were the main target of restriction. Introducing the bill to parliament, the minister of the interior Dr. Malan explained that it was motivated by "the desire of every nation in the world to maintain its development on the basis of its original composition" and to avoid the problems created by "an undigested and unabsorbable minority."[45] Malan averred that the Quota Bill met "the desire of a very large majority of the people." Gauged by the parliamentary opposition's approval of its main principles as well as the support of almost the entire spectrum of the press, English not much less than Afrikaans, Malan was not mistaken.[46]

The widespread support throughout the white public for a law aimed at stopping the further entry of Jews, and in its wake the escalating animosity evinced by Afrikaner nationalists toward Jews already in the country (a subject to which we shall return anon), raises a major historical question concerning the roots of antisemitism in South Africa. The illuminating research of Milton Shain has provided a persuasive answer to this question.[47] Shain has demonstrated the prevalence of potent, multilayered antisemitic stereotyping and traced its roots to the very beginning of a substantial Jewish presence in the nineteenth century. His findings attest to the ubiquity and tenacity of antisemitism within European cultures even as transplanted in the most distant of regions and climes. Seeds transmitted from the European legacy of antisemitic prejudices easily struck root and sprouted anew in forms and image constructions fitted to the local South African social environment. The most puissant of these were encapsulated in the opprobrious epithets "Peruvian" and "Hoggenheimer." The etymology of "Peruvian" remains obscure; the most common conjecture attributes it to an acronym somehow derived from the terms "Polish and Russian." What is clear is its stereotyped representation of the poorer class of immigrant Jew, typically described as a "pettifogging Peruvian," who "presents the apparition of a slovenly, unkempt and generally unwashed edition . . . of the wandering Jew."[48] The complementary, and more sinister, antisemitic epithet "Hoggenheimer" is traceable back to a stage character in a West End musical comedy of 1902 that toured South Africa shortly after the Boer War.[49] The obese, thick-lipped, hook-nosed Hoggenheimer stereotype, popularized particularly by the cartoonist D. C. Boonzaier, represented the quintessential Jew-capitalist; an image as avaricious and guileful as it was ugly and repulsive. Shain found plentiful evidence that even before these stereotyped images became prevalent, the itinerant Jewish trader known as a "smous" (another term of obscure origin), who peddled his wares among the rural Boers, was depicted as devious, manipulative, and dishonest.[50]

Paralleling patterns known in Britain and other Western countries, the "Bolshevik scare" that erupted in the wake of the Russian Revolution conflated Jews with communist subversion, a stereotypical embellishment that could draw richly on the factual prominence of Jewish names in the ranks of leftist radicalism in South Africa. Shain shows that, in the 1920s, to this antisemitic imagery was added a potent layer of nativist discourse, heavily peppered with eugenic notions privileging "Nordic stock" races and decrying the Jews as irredeemably alien and "unassimilable." All of this, when highlighted in the context of the grave socioeconomic problem of the "poor whites" whose cause was ardently taken up by Afrikaner nationalists, renders comprehensible the broad white consensus that welcomed the Immigration Quota Act of 1930. Of course, the Jewish leadership objected to this legislation, but to no avail. The foremost Jewish communal leader and member of parliament, Morris Alexander, denounced it as a measure that "places a blot on our national honour and upon our individual self-respect."[51]

The Quota Act and its aftermath inaugurated the politicization of South

Africa's already formidable legacy of publicly expressed antisemitism. All the same, political antisemitism might not have developed beyond nativist-style opposition to Jewish immigration as evinced in the Quota Act itself, were it not for the influence of German national socialist ideas after Hitler's rise to power in 1933.[52] The downpour of Nazi propaganda material from Germany fell on fertile soil in South Africa.[53] Local Afrikaner groups of national socialist character mushroomed. Foremost among these was a paramilitary organization commonly called the Greyshirts, founded in October 1933 by Louis T. Weichardt, an Afrikaner of German stock. At its peak it claimed some two thousand members.[54] The Greyshirts and the various satellite organizations that mushroomed were thoroughly antisemitic on the German Nazi model, except for their emphasis on Christian religion—*Christelikheid*. Greyshirt propaganda taught that the Jews were not a European but an Asiatic race; they were anti-Christian, and the fomenters of a worldwide conspiracy using both communism and capitalism as their instruments. Addressing "the Jewish Menace," the Greyshirts' political program advocated the treatment of all Jews merely as temporary guests in accordance with the provisions of an "Aliens Statute."

Although Malan as leader of the Gesuiwerde National Party distanced himself from Greyshirt ideology, his party increasingly found it expedient to take advantage of the resonating appeal of Greyshirt agitation over the "Jewish Question." It was, above all, the acute reemergence of the immigration issue that propelled the Gesuiwerde nationalists toward adoption of antisemitism as a political instrument. Malan had expected the Quota Act to put a stop to Jewish immigration, but an unanticipated loophole in the quota formula developed after the rise of Hitler. Germany was one of the nonrestricted countries, and it was now precisely from Hitler's clutches that refugees were fleeing. Between 1933 and 1936, 6,132 German immigrants entered the Union: 3,615 of these were Jews, 2,549 of whom arrived in 1936 alone.[55] Greyshirt agitation against Jewish immigration crested, and Malan's Gesuiwerde Party was quick to jump onto the bandwagon.[56] In late 1936 widespread public opposition rose to a crescendo surrounding the arrival of a ship carrying Jewish would-be immigrants, the *Stuttgart*, which had been chartered by the Council for German Jewry in London.[57] Prominent among the protesters was Dr. Hendrik F. Verwoerd, a professor at the University of Stellenbosch destined to become prime minister of South Africa and the foremost architect of apartheid.

Submitting to public pressure and the entreaty of South Africa's most important diplomatic representative in Europe, Eric Louw, who warned that Jews now blocked from entry into all other countries would flood the country, Hertzog's government relented and introduced a new Aliens Bill in 1937.[58] This bill abandoned the quota system and reverted to the principle of selective immigration on the criterion of the "desirability" and "assimilability" of each individual applicant.[59] Although in practice the new law effectively stemmed further Jewish immigration, its form still failed to satisfy Malan's party. In the parliamentary debate on the bill, he openly admitted that he was advocating discrimination against Jews. "I have been reproached," he said, "that I am now discriminating against the Jews as

Jews. Now let me say frankly that I admit that it is so. . . . There are too many Jews here, too many for South Africa's good and too many for the good of the Jews themselves."[60]

Although Malan was still resistant to the national socialist ideology of the Greyshirts, as far as the Jewish question was concerned his own party's differences with the Greyshirts were negligible by 1937.[61] The Transvaal branch of the party was even more at one with the Greyshirts on the Jewish question. As its leader, Johannes G. Strijdom, who was one day to succeed Malan as prime minister of the Union, said: "The different shirt parties divide the Afrikaner. This is a pity because they are not our enemies. They aim at the same things as we do, but go about it in the wrong way."[62] At their congress in October 1937 the Transvalers demonstratively resolved that Jews were disqualified from membership of the party.[63]

At about that time a thorough exposition of the Gesuiwerde National Party's attitude to the "Jewish problem" was provided by Verwoerd, who had moved from Stellenbosch University to become the first editor of the party's new organ in the north, *Die Transvaler*. Appearing in the paper's very first issue, Verwoerd's exposition purported to explain the party's policy sociologically, in terms of objective factors.[64] Acknowledging quite unashamedly that "events in Germany and the development of organizations here that got their inspiration from that country" helped to make the Afrikaner realize the nature of the Jewish problem, he denied only the charge of racial motivation. The issue, he contended, was purely a conflict of interests. Afrikaners driven to the towns by economic necessity since the Great War had come face to face with a situation in which Jews with doubtful business practices dominated commercial undertakings and stood in the way of the Afrikaner's well-being and national aspirations. Verwoerd suggested a quota system by which, henceforth, licenses would be refused and expired ones not renewed, so that Jews would be barred until the stage when they occupied no more than 5 percent of the country's commerce and industry.

When the white electorate again went to the polls in 1938 the National Party conducted its election campaign on an avowedly anti-Jewish platform. After the United Party attained a resounding victory, *Die Burger* featured a cartoon in which the English "imperialist press" was seen leading Hertzog and Smuts to victory, while they both carried on their shoulders a stereotyped caricature of the Jew "Hoggenheimer."[65] If further evidence was needed that the nationalists were fostering a strain of racist antisemitism, it came in the new parliament in January 1939. Eric Louw, the former ambassador, now a National Party member of parliament, introduced—unsuccessfully—a private member's bill with the full backing of his party. It bore the unmistakable marks of crass Nazi antisemitism. Stating categorically that "no applicant who is of Jewish parentage shall be deemed readily assimilable," it went on to define a person of "Jewish parentage" as "that person whose father and mother are or were either wholly or partly Jews, whether or not they professed the Jewish religion."[66]

The question whether South Africa should stand by Britain and enter the war rent asunder the United Party's "Fusion" government in September 1939. Smuts favored entry whereas Hertzog opposed it. By a narrow parliamentary margin Smuts brought South Africa into the war. He replaced Hertzog as prime minister while a segment of the Afrikaner supporters of Hertzog recombined with Malan's party in 1941 to form the Herenigde (Reunited) National Party. This was the party of Afrikaner nationalism that was to introduce apartheid after winning the elections of 1948, make South Africa a republic in 1961, and secede from the British Commonwealth.

Opposition to the war greatly increased the receptivity of Afrikaner nationalists to Nazi German influence; the shortest path to a restored Afrikaner republic seemed to lie in the prospect of an understanding with a victorious Germany. This affinity to Germany and hostility to Britain found its most powerful expression in the movement known as the Ossewa Brandwag (Oxwagon Sentinel). Emerging out of the popular nationalist fervor in celebration of the centenary of the Great Trek at the end of 1938, it began as a cultural-nationalist mass movement but assumed a paramilitary and authoritarian character under its formidable second Kommandant-General, Dr. (Hans) J. F. J. van Rensburg. The Ossewa Brandwag owed its mass-based membership—300,000 at its peak—to its rather loose ideological content and strong appeal to Afrikaner *volkseenheid* (national unity), its rejection of participation in the war on Britain's side against Germany, and its advocacy of a republic.[67] German national socialist influence was clearly evident in its symbols, although it also adhered to a characteristically local "*Christelik-Nasionale Lewensbeskouing*" (Christian national outlook). It was all too apparent that when the Ossewa Brandwag spoke of the "elimination of nationally harmful [*volksdadelike*] and liberal attitudes," it was referring above all to the Jews.[68] It was openly contemptuous of British parliamentary democracy and formed a militant unit known as the Stormjaers, which engaged in sabotage activities, such as the cutting of telegraph wires and bombings, all in an effort to demonstrate popular opposition to the South African war effort. Among those of its members who were consequently interned by the government during the war was Balthazar Johannes Vorster, later to become prime minister of South Africa.

In 1940 another group of antidemocratic Afrikaner nationalists came into existence inside the framework of the National Party itself—Die Nuwe Orde (The New Order), founded and led by Oswald Pirow.[69] It was the most sophisticated of all the antisemitic groups in South Africa. Priding himself on original thinking within the national socialist world outlook, Pirow purported to reject crude antisemitic diatribes. Although he had no compunction about declaring, "I am openly and outspokenly anti-Semitic," he disdained propaganda based on "arguments of blood and race interlarded with whispering about ritual murders and shock references to the Protocols of the Elders of Zion." In his view, this was an "inefficient form of anti-Semitic propaganda which continually plays directly into the hands of the Jewish Board of Deputies." He said his New Order would make a distinction between three categories of Jews: first, a small group that had assimilated with the Afrikaners and would therefore be entitled to full citizenship rights; second, Jews who had come to South Africa prior to the First World War—they would be disenfranchised but could remain if they behaved well; third, Jews who entered after 4 August 1914—they would be regarded as illegal immigrants and would have no right of residence.[70]

Research into South African archival sources by Patrick Furlong has confirmed that the boundaries between the radical right and Malan, already blurred by the late 1930s, were hardly visible in the first few years of the war, especially on the "Jewish Question."[71] To be sure, research in German archives has not revealed significant intrigue between the Third Reich and the National Party under Malan's leadership. What it has shown, however, is that only when it came to antisemitism was there unqualified German willingness to come to the aid of those Afrikaner intellectuals and politicians who advocated adoption of the national socialist model in South Africa.[72]

In the final analysis it is evident that Malan and the mainstream National Party held back from importing or copying German national socialism, seeing it as too foreign and alien to Afrikaner tradition. Recognizing the threat posed by the radical right to its hegemony over the camp of Afrikaner nationalism, Malan's party asserted itself and outmaneuvered the Ossewa Brandwag politically, a victory facilitated by the turn of the tide of war against Germany. Yet, it is a matter of key significance for comprehending the fears and concerns of South African Jews that throughout this intra-Afrikaner ideological conflict, antisemitism, so far from being a bone of contention, was a central point of consensus, if not the very linchpin of accord between the adversaries. The Jews felt themselves well advised to heed Dr. Malan's warning, delivered at the Transvaal party congress in December 1940, that the Jews had best not forget "they were guests in South Africa."[73]

Throughout the entire period of antisemitic activity surveyed above, the collective response of the Jews as a community was vested by consensual convention in the body known as the Jewish Board of Deputies, whose foundation and function was mentioned earlier in this chapter. The logic of the political constellation after 1933 had inexorably polarized the political forces in South Africa. In consequence, the Board of Deputies, not to speak of many of its leaders in their personal capacities, found itself cooperating in one way or another with those political forces that were in the forefront of the fight against the National Party.[74] The rationale for this strategy was officially crystallized at its congress in May 1945, when the executive announced a "Nine Point Programme" to combat antisemitism. The first point stated: "The fight against anti-Semitism is part of the defence of democracy and of freedom; and only if the larger victory is won is there hope of eliminating (or mitigating) anti-Semitism." The editorial article in the Board's monthly organ, *Jewish Affairs,* of January 1948 included the following comment: "It is doubtful whether there can be a specific Jewish viewpoint, but something, nevertheless, can be expected of the Jew. On racial issues he should take as liberal a view as possible. He should be profoundly sensitive to injustice arising from discrimination based on race or caste. He can and must be progressive."[75]

Liberal expressions such as these have been cited as proof that after the National Party's victory of 1948 the Board made a hypocritical volte-face.[76] However, the Board's liberal utterances must be weighed against its no less frequent statements that it was not a political body and that its resistance was restricted only to the antisemitic aspect of Afrikaner politics. The Board's general-secretary, Gustav Saron, said as much in explication of the Board's "Nine Point Programme." Referring to the Board's opposition to the Afrikaner nationalist organizations, he emphasized that "insofar as these groups have anti-Semitism, in one form or another, integral to their ideologies, the position of the Jew is directly bound up with the democratic forces in their struggle against these totalitarian and reactionary doctrines." However, Saron went on to qualify this as follows:

> We should not, however, simplify the situation. The causes of tension and conflict in this multi-racial South Africa are very complex. It is a mistake to believe that all racial problems here can be treated on the same level. . . . There can be no question whatever that a democrat must work strenuously for the progressive amelioration of the lot of the non-Europeans. But when one is dealing with so delicate and so difficult a subject as the social Colour Bar for instance, I do not think it at all helpful to say (as some do say) that one must oppose the Colour Bar because it may lead ultimately to discrimination against Jews.[77]

In the final analysis, although the policy of the Board of Deputies in this period dictated a new practice—involvement in support of the liberal, democratic sector in politics—it yet remained faithful to its traditional premise, namely, noninvolvement in politics except where Jewish interests were implicated. Hence, it ought not to be a matter of surprise that the alliance with liberal political forces turned out to be a temporary linkup based on convergence of interests, rather than a permanent alliance based on principle.

CHAPTER 1

The Jewish Community and the Afrikaner Regime

Advent of Apartheid

In the global annals of the twentieth century, the image of the Afrikaner nationalist regime that came to power in South Africa in May 1948 is notoriously symbolized by the race relations policy that came to be known by the term "apartheid." The apartheid system was the new government's panacea for the problems and dangers in the post–World War era that threatened the supremacy of the whites, now, at long last, led by the representatives of their own Afrikaner *volk*. But, as has been emphasized in the introductory chapter of this book, the underlying social order that the apartheid policy was meant to defend and bolster was not the preserve of Afrikaners. White supremacy, racial discrimination, and social separation of the races were rooted also in British colonial policies and in the practice of English-speaking South Africans. The innovatory thrust of the new Afrikaner nationalist government lay not in invention of the system but rather in its ideological rationalization, its reinforced legislative institutionalization, and the implementation of massive social engineering to fortify it against the winds of change in Africa.

The apartheid idea itself was never static. After its entrée into political usage in the mid-1940s it underwent a process of ideological refinement. At its crudest level it was a racist rationale and affirmation of white domination (*baasskap*) in all aspects of South African society. Although apartheid ideology never freed itself entirely from racist elements, at its most refined level it postulated a regulated system of race relations as a strategy for guaranteeing white self-preservation while at the same time providing parallel so-called "separate development" for all of the racial groups comprising South African society. As such, it purported to be a unique conception of race relations commensurate with the unique race relations problems of South Africa. Its proponents claimed that notwithstanding the apparent ethical deficiencies in its current implementation, in the final analysis it was the only just alternative to the inevitable black domination that would result from racial integration.[1]

The literature on the apartheid system is vast, and the limited focus of the present study allows for only the briefest of surveys.[2] As a program of action, apartheid meant reinforcing white domination of the entire political and economic order of the country. It also meant bureaucratic systematization of social separation between the various racial groups. Adjusting to circumstances as well as in order to placate international censure, the practitioners of the apartheid system began to construct frameworks, institutional and territorial, for the purported separate development of each racial group. Accordingly, measures were taken to remove some of the remaining irregularities in the political system, such as the long-standing entrenched right enjoyed by coloreds in the Cape to vote for parliament on a common voters' roll with whites. Legislation was passed to systematize the division of the population into rigid statutory racial categories and to prevent miscegenation and even social fraternization. Similarly, segregation was more stringently enforced in public places and public services such as railways, buses, and parks. Residential segregation of the racial groups in urban areas was systematically implemented by the terms of the Group Areas Act. Members of racial groups other than the ones designated for a particular urban area were uprooted and forced to move to other areas designated for them. Controls over black migration to the towns were strenuously tightened and harsh measures enforced to deal with blacks present in the towns without legal permission. Job reservation for the racial groups was systematized, and separate industrial conciliation machinery was instituted. In the field of black education, control was transferred from Christian missions and from provinces to the government, and the implied policy was to withhold from blacks such education as might prepare them for positions in society that they were in any case not allowed to hold. Similarly, the Separate Universities Act denied blacks access to the few universities that had previously admitted them together with whites. Instead, it decreed the establishment of separate universities and colleges for the various races and ethnic groups, all under strict governmental supervision.

At the same time, the government began long-term planning for the consolidation of certain historically tribal areas into projected "Bantu Homelands." The stated intention was eventually to grant them far-reaching independence. All urban blacks were ultimately to hold citizenship and political rights in the respective homelands of their particular ethnic tribes, rather than in the white state of South Africa. The government also invested considerable resources in the removal of old black slum "locations" in the cities and the creation of new segregated areas of housing such as the enormous Soweto (acronym for South-Western Townships) complex near Johannesburg.

The boundless inequity, disruption, distress, and suffering resulting from these measures aroused bitter opposition. This is not to say that manifestations of opposition to the South African political and social order had been lacking before the National Party's accession to power. A long and varied history of opposition antedated 1948, most notably by the African National Congress and the South African Indian Congress. There were whites too, although not many in number, who had long been involved in resistance to the social order, whether as liberal reformists operating through the existing constitutional machinery in order to ameliorate the conditions of the underprivileged and incrementally develop an open multiracial society, or as leftist radicals, especially communists, aiming to overthrow the entire socioeconomic system.

The enforcement of the apartheid policy almost immediately sparked a desperate conflict. On one side were the Afrikaner nationalists, grimly determined to consolidate their political and economic empowerment and use it to ensure the conservation of white supremacy over the entire social order of South Africa. On the other side, ranged against the new regime were an array of black, Indian, and colored political movements supported by a small but ardent minority of white liberals and radicals, struggling, some to reform, others to overthrow that social order. In the course of the 1950s, opposition to the new government's policies swelled to unprecedented proportions. While remaining essentially nonviolent, it gave rise to waves of widespread black unrest enjoying the support of the small minority of radical and liberal whites. The first major wave was the Defiance Campaign of 1952, in which protesters openly violated apartheid laws and allowed themselves to be arrested; the second led to a "Congress of the People" in 1955, constituted by an alliance of the African and Indian Congress movements together with the white Congress of Democrats. It adopted the famous "Freedom Charter" calling eloquently for freedom and equality in a nonracial, democratic South Africa. The fateful Sharpeville demonstration of March 1960, in which the police opened fire, killing 67 blacks and wounding 186, was the tragic climax of the third wave.

To this public unrest and nonviolent political opposition the government reacted with an escalating series of repressive legislative and police measures. The kingpin of these measures was the 1950 Suppression of Communism Act, which defined communism in the most sweeping terms, to include "any doctrine or scheme . . . which aims at bringing about any political, industrial, social or economic change . . . by means which include the promotion of disturbance or disorder." Subsequently augmented by various amendments, this legislation invested the authorities with enormously wide powers to ban organizations that even in the remotest sense could be deemed to be furthering the aims of communism. As belief in racial equality was one of the aims of communism, it became possible to ban persons who were in fact avowed ideological opponents of communism but advocated racial equality. The legislation also empowered the authorities to impose bans on persons, publications, and gatherings. There was no recourse to the courts against banning orders, whose terms varied from person to person, but usually involved restriction to a magisterial district and reporting in person to the police at fixed intervals. Banned persons were forbidden to communicate with each other, to attend any gathering of persons above a specified small number, to speak in public or write in any newspaper or other published form. To quote a banned person became a punishable offense. Other repressive measures not subject to the rule of law included house arrests, banishments, and deportations. By a law of 1963 police officers could arrest without warrant and detain for a period of up to ninety days any person deemed a suspect for any political offense. This procedure could be repeated immediately after the person's formal release. In many cases detainees were subjected to cruel solitary confinement.

By the late 1960s almost every form of overt political resistance to the policy of apartheid and separate development had been legislated out of existence and crushed. Organizations such as the African National Congress, the Pan-Africanist Congress, the South African Indian Congress, and the (white) Congress of Democrats had been banned, while most of their leaders had been arrested or had fled the country. Yet a variety of still legally defensible, and at times quite formidable, acts and expressions of liberal opposition to apartheid persisted in the all-white parliament, in provincial and municipal councils, in some of the universities, and, above all, in the press. At the same time residual multiracial radical resistance perforce went underground.

Legacy of the "Jewish Question"

Having emphasized the importance of apartheid and its consequences for South African society and the country's international image it must nevertheless be noted that, within the actual political context that brought the National Party into power, apartheid policy was not nearly as prominent as might be imagined. The purely intrawhite political context in which the elections of 1948 took place should not be overlooked. As may be seen from the main political events traced in the previous chapter, Dr. Malan's party was, first and foremost, waging a nationalist battle aimed at gaining political hegemony for the Afrikaner. The struggle, in essence, was less to keep the black man in his place, so to speak, than to get the country back for the Afrikaner *volk.*[3] It was in this primary context that the Jews in the country fitted into the picture because, as we have seen, Afrikaner nationalists perceived the Jews as a major obstacle to the fulfillment of their aspirations. Against the background of the Afrikaner nationalists' marked antisemitic record, not only Jews but also many liberal-minded Gentiles feared the worst when the [Herenigde] National Party won the watershed election of 1948. The historian Arthur Keppel-Jones gave eloquent expression to these fears in his satirical peep into the future, *When Smuts Goes,* which appeared in 1947 on the eve of Dr. Malan's electoral victory. Keppel-Jones predicted an anti-Jewish pogrom by 1955. His description of that year included the following passage:

> The "pogrom" of 1955 did not eject any Jews from the positions they already occupied, but in effect deprived the younger generation of all hope of a career. Most fathers therefore felt it their duty to take their families away. The Jews were too familiar with the recent history of Germany to be deceived as some Gentiles were by . . . friendly and tolerant speeches. . . . It was clear to them that worse was to come.[4]

In light of such predictions, it is hardly surprising that a cold shiver of shock and anxiety ran through the Jewish community of South Africa when the sensational news of the National Party's victory was announced. The Jewish community expected the worst. Yet Keppel-Jones's pogrom never came to pass. Quite to the contrary, as shall be shown in this chapter, Dr. Malan's ascent to power inaugurated a gradual process of rapprochement between newly empowered Afrikaner political and intellectual circles and the Jewish community.

Only in retrospect may one discern undercurrents of change in policy toward the Jews even before the fateful elections of 1948. During 1947 two Jewish individuals, Isaac Frank and Joseph Nossel, who obviously identified with Dr. Malan's policies other than on the Jewish Question, tried to elicit from him and some other party leaders a renunciation of their party's antisemitic record and claimed that they had received an encouraging response. They said that it was now up to the Jews to show that they appreciated the change.[5] The Jewish leadership, however, regarded these self-appointed intercessors with some distaste. Not only did their behavior seem injurious to Jewish dignity, but also their claims appeared to be wholly implausible since Eric Louw was at that very time avowedly reaffirming his party's antisemitic policy.[6]

The archival papers of Dr. Malan and Eric Louw respectively make it evident that a serious difference of opinion had developed between them over the Jewish Question. It seems that Malan had decided to phase out the antisemitic plank in the party's platform, and to that end he wished to issue a moderate statement in the form of questions and answers on the Jewish Question. Louw not only considered that this would be interpreted as a repudiation of his own stance in the matter, but held it to be contrary to the party's established policy and a serious political error to boot. He earnestly appealed to Malan not to go ahead with this decision: "What will you achieve with such a clarification," he asked, "except for conceding to the challenge of the Jews?... Our policy stands in our Programme of Action for all to read! ... Do you really believe that we shall gain any Jewish votes with it, except for a few here and there who are today strongly against Britain because of the Palestine business?" Arguing that the antisemitic plank of the party was a valuable political asset, Louw said that Malan's proposed statement would only serve to disappoint "ten thousand Nationalists" and alienate the Greyshirts, who were worth two or three seats for the party in the coming elections.[7]

However, Dr. Malan overrode Louw's fervent objections, and on 30 October 1947 the statement he had prepared appeared prominently in *Die Burger,* ostensibly as an interview with the party leader. Asked whether the National Party was "anti-Jewish," Dr. Malan replied that if the question meant were there antisemites within the party, the answer was "yes" but no more so than in Smuts's United Party; yet as far as "stated party policy" was concerned, the answer was "no." The kernel of the interview, described as "the most important question," was: "Does the National Party aim at internal discrimination against established Jews?" To this Dr. Malan replied that as far as its "declared policy" was concerned, the party did not stand for legislative measures that discriminated between Jew and non-Jew. "I have expressed my opposition to it, time and time again, although I warned openly at the same time that if the flocking in of Jews were not put to a stop in good time, it would not be possible to withstand the demand for internal protective measures." Of talk that the party would deport Jews, Malan declared that this was "evidently the product of an inflamed imagination."[8]

At the time, the suspicion and trepidation of South African Jews were far from being allayed by these words. The legacy of Afrikaner antisemitism cast a long shadow over the Jews of South Africa and darkened their vision. The purpose uppermost in the minds of Jewish communal leaders, charged with looking after the interests and welfare of their own community, was elimination of all vestiges of the Jewish Question from the South African political scene. In their eyes, Jews still appeared to be potential victims of the new government, although of course not in anything like the monstrous way that "non-Europeans" were the objects of victimization. Casting the lot of Jews with that of "non-Europeans" was absolutely inconceivable for the mind-set of all but the tiniest minority of Jewish communists who had long been alienated from Jewish identification and were peripheral to Jewish affairs.

What the future held in store for Jews was still shrouded in uncertainty for several months after the elections. But the leadership of the Jewish Board of Deputies braced itself and, taking the bull by the horns, asked for an interview with the new prime minister in the hope of ascertaining his intentions. In July1948 Dr. Malan received a deputation, consisting of the Board's president, Bernard Arthur Ettlinger, its chairman, Simon Kuper, and its general-secretary, Gus Saron. It submitted to the prime minister that as "considerable disquiet exists in various quarters regarding the attitude of the Government, specifically in relation to the Jewish community," the Board wished to obtain clarification. Dr. Malan replied that he looked forward "to the time when the so-called Jewish Question will disappear altogether from the life of this country and its politics." However, he tellingly added this caveat: "Apart altogether from the question of immigration, we believe that there must be no discrimination in regard to the Jews who are in South Africa."[9]

It could not be said that Malan's answer was entirely to the satisfaction of the delegation. His pointed reservation about Jewish immigration remained a source of deep concern. Indeed, to avoid creating more Jewish anxiety the Board afterward saw to it that Dr. Malan's unequivocal reservation regarding immigration was left out of official news reports of the interview.[10] However, fortune had provided Dr. Malan with a unique opportunity to prove his goodwill to the Jews, for he had come to power at a point in time almost exactly convergent with the establishment of the State of Israel. He knew only too well that the overriding concern of South African Jewry was to help the embattled new Jewish state. Had he wished to pursue his former anti-Jewish policy he could have frustrated the community's efforts or even raised the specter of dual loyalty. But he did neither of these things. Instead, in what could only be regarded by the community's leaders as a gesture of reconciliation, Dr. Malan's new government closed its eyes even to the continued dispatch of Jewish volunteers to fight in Israel.

To be sure, Dr. Malan did not hasten to extend de jure recognition to the State of Israel. This had to wait another year, until 14 May 1949,[11] but he responded sympathetically and obligingly to the first delegation from the Zionist Federation, which came to him on 12 July 1948. He agreed to its request for renewal of the special permission given by the previous government for transfer to Israel of sterling, food, and clothing as well as nonoffensive war materials such as trucks, helmets, gas masks, and wireless equipment. Reporting back to the Zionist Federation, the delegation said that the reception was "very friendly, courteous and cordial," and that the Federation "could hardly expect anything more from the Prime Minister."[12] There could scarcely have been a better way to prepare the ground for elimination of the Jewish Question from South African politics and for reconciliation between Afrikaner nationalists and Jews.

The die-hard antisemites in the Transvaal branch of the National Party, however, did not yield easily to Dr. Malan's new course. This was evident when a congress of the National Party held in November 1948 failed even to debate the question of removing the ban on Jewish membership in the Transvaal. The Board of Deputies was very disappointed. "If the Government and the National Party are genuinely anxious to convince South African Jews and the community as a whole that they have turned their backs on anti-Jewish discrimination," stated *Jewish Affairs* editorially, "they must find a way out from the present equivocal situation and demonstrate beyond any doubt where the party really stands."[13]

The upholding of the Transvaal ban on Jewish membership did not deter a handful of Jewish sympathizers with the National Party, whose activities had already begun in the run-up to the 1948 elections. One of them, Joseph Nossel, had become a member of the party in the Cape and now not only made approaches to the government on matters affecting Jews independently of the Board of Deputies, but even attempted to establish an organization of Jewish supporters of the National Party. In the view of most leaders of the Board of Deputies his behavior was undignified and reprehensible. Moreover, his activities derogated from the status of the Board as the Jewish community's representative organ and contradicted its policy on political matters. Max Melamet, of the Cape committee of the Board, censured Nossel's pretensions, and the chairman of the Board's executive council, Simon Kuper, issued a full statement declaring:

> The Board of Deputies takes no part whatever in the party-political struggle. Party politics are entirely beyond its province. The Board is concerned only to protect the Jewish community against discrimination or any interference with their rights as citizens. The position of the individual Jew is, of course, entirely different. As a citizen it is both his right and his duty to play his part in the political life of the country, in terms of his own viewpoint and party affiliation.[14]

It is noteworthy that it was thus in response to Nossel's pro–National Party activities rather than to Jewish opponents of the government that the Board initially enunciated, or to be more precise reiterated, its traditional policy of noninvolvement in political matters. On this policy *Die Burger* commented caustically: "The Board obviously still maintains its attitude that the individual Jew has an unquestioned right to choose which political party he will support—as long as it is not the National Party!"[15]

The atmosphere exemplified by *Die Burger*'s comment prevailed for several years after the National Party's election. Yet it was far better than the Jews had feared in 1948. The Board of Deputies welcomed what it described as the "abatement in the public life of our country of what has been called the Jewish Question," but could not be sanguine knowing that one of the new government's first acts was the lifting of Smuts's ban on Ossewa Brandwag members joining the civil service. Former pro-Nazi, Afrikaner Broederbond leaders appeared to be on the rise in the National Party.[16] One was Nico Diederichs, who later became a cabinet minister and state president; another was Piet Meyer, who was appointed head of the South African Broadcasting Corporation in 1959. Indeed, particularly disturbing for the Jewish community was the government's rehabilitation of the notoriously antisemitic Greyshirt leader L. T. Weichardt, who had been interned in late 1944 by Smuts's government for security reasons. He climaxed his political career under Strijdom's government as an appointed member of the South African Senate. Other antisemites who were rehabilitated included the notorious pro-Nazi Robey Leibbrandt, and Eric Holm, the man behind wartime radio broadcasts of Nazi propaganda to South Africa. Another avowed antisemite and fascist, Johannes Strauss von Moltke, emerged as leader of the National Party in South-West Africa, which in 1950 received six seats in the South African House of Assembly. B. J. Vorster, the former member of the Ossewa Brandwag's militant Stormjaer organization who had been interned on suspicion of subversion during the war, was elected to parliament in 1953 on a National Party ticket. When Verwoerd became prime minister in 1958, Vorster was included in his government. He served as minister of justice from 1962 to 1966 and rose to be prime minister (1966 to 1978) and state president until he retired in 1979. In 1968 he appointed his close former Ossewa Brandwag associate, Hendrik van den Bergh, to head the newly created Bureau of State Security.

It was the unification of Dr. Malan's Herenigde National Party with its coalition partner, Dr. Havenga's Afrikaner Party, in late 1951 that resolved the problem of the Transvaal ban on Jewish membership. The Afrikaner Party regarded itself as the true successor to Hertzog's broader Afrikaner nationalism and had remained open to Jewish membership. Since the unification agreement provided that existing members of the separate parties would automatically become members of the new party, maintenance of the Transvaal ban was in effect rendered untenable. Both *Die Vaderland* and *Die Transvaler* gave explicit prominence to the announcement that "Jews can become members of the new party!"[17]

Far more significant was the continuing transformation of Dr. Malan's public views on the Jewish Question during his period in office as prime minister. Local political considerations and confidence that the problem of Jewish immigration had been resolved by the creation of Israel no doubt played a part in this change. But quite apart from these factors, the revision of his former views appears to have been mediated by a genuine admiration for the courage and achievements of the young State of Israel. Indeed, in 1953 he visited Israel, becoming the first head of government in the world ever to do so while in office. Although it was officially described as a private visit to the Holy Land in fulfillment of Dr. Malan's lifelong ambition as an ordained minister of the church, he was cordially received by the prime minister, David Ben-Gurion, and officials of the Tel Aviv office of the South African Zionist Federation accompanied him on his tour of the country. Deeply impressed by what he saw, Malan began to speak in a manner reminiscent of his former arch-opponent, Jan Smuts. He described "the restoration of Palestine to the Jewish race as their national home" as "one of the most important and significant events in modern history."[18]

In a number of further statements Dr. Malan expounded a pluralistic conception of [white] South Africanism and of the place of the Jews in it, very different from the references to Jewish unassimilability that he had voiced in former years. When, on their private initiative, Joseph Nossel and a group of his pro–National Party associates honored Dr. Malan in 1955 by inscribing his name in the Golden Book of the Jewish National Fund,[19] he praised the Jews for the tenacity with which they maintained their group identity in words quite the same as those used by Smuts in earlier years. "The national and the international are not with the Jew, as in truth they need not be, two irreconcilable opposites, but a sound basis supplementary to each other," he affirmed; "accordingly, the Jew can, and does often, become a good national as well as a good Jew . . . a good South African as well as a true son of Israel."[20]

Exposure to the old-new Land of Israel had a deep impact not only on Dr. Malan himself but also on groups of Dutch Reformed Church ministers and various Afrikaner journalists who, with the encouragement of the Zionist Federation, visited Israel in the 1950s.[21] The Calvinist Old Testament religious heritage of the Afrikaner resonated with exposure to revived Jewish statehood. As one journalist who accompanied Dr. Malan to Israel explained: "The key to an understanding of the Afrikaner's feeling" was that a visit to Israel was "an emotional experience, which no other land in the world could offer to the Afrikaner. He felt at home there in a revealed history which, in an important sense, was also his own." Indeed, the journalist frankly admitted that it was almost in spite of themselves and of the recent record of animosity toward Jews that Afrikaners identified with Israel. It was, he said, as if they "had no choice; their sympathy was with the Jews in Jerusalem." Commendation of Israel as a model for the Afrikaner became commonplace. "As the Afrikaner nation drew inspiration in the past from the history of ancient Israel so it ought to now heed the example of the new Israel," wrote the editor of *Die Volksblad* in a typical comment.[22]

This role of Israel as catalyst, and the example of Dr. Malan in relinquishing the former antisemitic line, paved the way for what may aptly be described as a dialogue of rapprochement. It took the form of addresses by important Afrikaner journalists to Jewish gatherings and a spate of articles on Afrikaner-Jewish relations in Afrikaans and Jewish newspapers and journals.[23] The contributors to this dialogue frankly examined what had gone wrong with Afrikaner-Jewish relations in the 1930s and 1940s and aired expectations and hopes for a new era of Afrikaner-Jewish understanding. A particularly forthright formulation of the Afrikaner viewpoint in this dialogue came from the pen of S. W. Pienaar, assistant editor of *Die Burger*.[24] He asserted that in the final analysis it was the Afrikaner more than the Jew who was the injured party, for the Jews had joined the English in usurping the Afrikaner's rights. Pienaar did not deny that Hitler had wielded an influence on the behavior of the Afrikaner nationalists. As a result they "did foolish things and said still more foolish things." But, he claimed, "it would also be foolish to judge their national behavior in terms of Hitler's influence. . . . The essential fact in the situation was, that the Jews abandoned the National Afrikaner before the National Afrikaners abandoned the Jews." He advised against delusions: "At the moment," he said, "we have reached the stage that we do not want to strike one another with the fist." This was progress but it was not enough. In his view, one requirement for restoration of good relations between Jews and Afrikaners was that a reasonable section of the Jewish community should identify itself with the Afrikaner.

Max Melamet, at the time chairman of the Cape council of the Jewish Board of Deputies, offered a no less candid response, featured simultaneously in three Afrikaans newspapers.[25] He asserted that it was the Jews who were the injured party and denied that Jews had ever been against the Afrikaner. If they had been drawn toward the English culture this was not a matter of choice but of objective circumstances, for as town dwellers engaged in commerce and trade, they were bound to be attracted to the English culture. But, argued Melamet, this did not mean that Jews were out of sympathy with Afrikaner cultural and national aspirations. Melamet asked Afrikaners to consider how Jews viewed the Nazi-dominated world around them in the 1930s. He admitted that under those circumstances he and other Jews had worked hard against Dr. Malan's party, and said he would do so again if the same circumstances were to reappear. He acknowledged that Jewish anxiety was being dispelled as the government was seen to be honoring its promise to remove the Jewish Question from public life and showing friendship to Israel. This did not mean that Jews necessarily supported the National Party politically. However, it did mean that they no longer judged political parties by their respective attitudes toward the Jews, but rather "by the programmes of the various parties as policies for the welfare of South Africa as a whole."

Although the very fact that frank dialogue was taking place betokened improved relations, it was all too obvious from the great differences in interpretation that there was still a considerable credibility gap. Even in regard to the attitude toward Israel, which, as we have said, served as a catalyst for dialogue, there were some curious conceptual distortions at play. Initially Afrikaner identification with Israel grew out of what was regarded as its plucky struggle against Britain, compounded by admiration for its internal achievements. However, as the Afro-Asian diplomatic offensive against South Africa became more acute and Soviet influence penetrated into Egypt under Nasser's rule, a dimension of geopolitical identification with Israel was added, and Afrikaner—and indeed also English—newspapers frequently drew a parallel between Israel as an important bulwark against communist penetration in the north and South Africa in the south.[26] However, from this geopolitical identification Afrikaner commentators jumped to quite another dimension of identification in terms of social purposes. References to the Jews and to Israel as if they were the epitome of apartheid became commonplace. Thus, for example, Professor L. J. du Plessis could advocate the idea of ultimate "division of southern Africa amongst its racially based nations," as opposed to the idea of one multiracial society, by holding up "Jewish apartheid" and Israel as an example. Citing biblical sources on the separation between Abraham and Lot, Isaac and Ishmael, he claimed that "apartheid is amazingly inherent in the Jewish ethos," and that "the Jews everywhere practised apartheid in all possible forms up to this day, when they were finally reconstituted as a national State."[27]

Jews had mixed feelings about the prevalent comparisons between Israel and South Africa. On the one hand, they were comfortable with the improved attitude toward Jews that these comparisons connoted. They could also readily agree that there was a common geopolitical interest between Israel and South Africa. On the other hand, most Jews demurred at the spurious thesis that Judaism and Israel were embodiments of the apartheid principle. It was after all not the Afrikaner's right to preserve his distinctiveness—as did Jews—which was morally at issue, but the means by which he was attempting to do so; means that involved denial of political rights to the majority of the population, racial discrimination, coercive social engineering, and cruel suppression of all opposition. Refuting the notion that Israel was founded on apartheid, the *South African Jewish Chronicle* argued:

> Even though Israel is a Jewish island in an Arab sea, that island is inhabited by Jews whose complexions are as varied as the countries of their origin; they run the whole gamut of colour from the blonde to the darkest of brunettes. . . . One wonders whether *Die Burger* appreciates that the Arabs of Israel have the same political rights as the Jews and that there are Arab members of the Knesset.[28]

No Jew engaged Afrikaner thinking more compellingly on this issue than Henry Katzew, a leading journalist associated with the *Zionist Record*. For over fifteen years, in his regular *Zionist Record* column under the pseudonym Karl Lemeer, as well as in articles for the Afrikaans press and in two books, Katzew conducted a passionate dialogue with Afrikaners on the explicit basis of his Jewish and Zionist consciousness.[29] His premise was: "I am a Jew; I want my group to survive. What I seek for my group, I cannot deny to another group. Therefore I support the Afrikaner in his survival struggle." However, he argued with equal conviction that as a Jew he had to repudiate the techniques manifested in apartheid by which the Afrikaner sought to ensure his survival. "The Afrikaner cannot ask the Black man to pay the price for his survival. He has to pay it himself," asserted Katzew. The means he was using—discriminative legislation, pass laws, job reservation, suppression, banning, and so on—were injurious to human dignity, unjust, and abhorrent. He commended to Afrikaners the thinking of one of their own great intellectuals, N. P. van Wyk Louw, who in his book *Liberale Nasionalisme* (Liberal Nationalism) had pleaded for "righteous survival." At the same time Katzew drew upon the experience of Zionism. He explained that Jews had found that the prerequisites for their survival in modern times were voluntary regeneration through self-labor and the restoration of a national-cultural center in their homeland. Katzew quoted the aphorism he had heard from the lips of Ben-Gurion: "A nation that doesn't do its own dirty work commits suicide."

On the basis of these ideas Katzew suggested that the Afrikaner begin to think about a center-Diaspora or "sanctuary-dispersion" solution, according to which South Africa would ultimately be divided into two parts. One part, formed by an idealistic volunteer movement, would evolve into a white homeland, possibly in a segment of the Cape Province. It would be based on white self-labor and would provide for the cultural, social, and political fulfillment of Afrikaners and other whites, as Israel did for the Jews. The other, and larger part would become a multiracial society in which South Africans of all groups and colors would live in full equality. For Afrikaners it would be the equivalent of the Jewish Diaspora.

From the retrospective perspective of the 1990s transition years that culminated in the new democratic South African state, Katzew's ideas appear intriguingly prescient because at this time a group of die-hard Afrikaner patriots staked a claim, however unsuccessfully, to something very similar as a last stand for residual Afrikaner independence. At the time when Katzew first expressed his views, however, his proposals were generally adjudged simplistic, naive, or unrealistic. His expressions of empathy, though, did enjoy an appreciative reception in the Afrikaans press and struck a responsive chord among a number of Afrikaner intellectuals. His exposition also went some way toward correcting the facile comparisons Afrikaners were inclined to make between themselves and the Jews in Israel.

As for the attitude of Jews to Katzew's philo-Afrikaner sentiments, there can be no doubt that the conscience of most morally sensitized and politically aware Jews was troubled, if at all, not by the Afrikaner's plight but by that of the underprivileged and oppressed black majority. This, then, brings one to the question—how did the Jewish community's representative body, the Jewish Board of Deputies, cope with this conscience?

Accommodation to the Apartheid Order

Jewish individuals were extraordinarily salient in the various forms of opposition to the regime of apartheid mustered by whites, an important phenomenon to which we shall return shortly. But the conventionally recognized representative organ of the Jewish community, the Jewish Board of Deputies, steered away as far as it could from any engagement whatsoever with the political struggle against the government's apartheid program. Deep-seated fears underlay this behavior. In a very real sense the Jews as a community felt themselves to be hostage to Afrikaner nationalist goodwill. Precisely because government circles and the Afrikaans press were offering rapprochement, adoption of any adversarial stance in relation to the government seemed out of the question. Quite to the contrary, the unquestioned priority was reciprocation of cordial relations with the Afrikaner public. Notwithstanding some sensitive ambiguities that we have noted, on the whole steady progress toward this objective was being made.

Dr. Malan's new course in relation to the Jews was maintained by his successors, J. G. Strijdom, H. F. Verwoerd, and B. J. Vorster. Of these three Afrikaner leaders,

Verwoerd was the one whose ascent to the premiership was viewed by Jews with the most circumspection on account of his prominent role in the anti-Jewish agitation of former years. It will be recalled that in 1936 Verwoerd had led the protest against the arrival of German Jewish refugees in the *Stuttgart,* and it was he who, as the first editor of *Die Transvaler,* had blatantly set forth the nationalist policy of quotas against the Jews in 1937. But when a delegation of the Board of Deputies came to him not long after he became prime minister in 1958, Verwoerd was at pains to allay their doubts. He himself raised the issue of his former record and assured them that it "all belonged to the past," and that he intended to maintain the cordial policy toward South African Jewry and Israel shown by his predecessors. To be sure, he did not acknowledge that he had ever been motivated by antisemitism but rather sought to justify the former conflict in objective sociological terms, much as he had done in his 1937 *Die Transvaler* article. The delegation did not hesitate to demur at this interpretation, pointing out that the agitation against Jews had a pro-Nazi coloring and had continued even after Jewish immigration had been restricted by legislation. Although this brief exchange hardly convinced the delegation that Dr. Verwoerd's subjective attitude toward the Jews had undergone real change, it left with the impression that as a matter of public policy, Verwoerd was indeed intent on continuing with the new course set by Malan.[30]

In these circumstances, the communal Jewish leadership, for its part, was anxious not to do anything that would hinder that course. The Board's executive was quick to formulate a policy of scrupulous noninvolvement in politics, and the community's premier organization, the Zionist Federation, enjoying adequate representation within the Board's councils, was satisfied to leave to it the steering of this policy. The Board went about this in innumerable statements issued throughout the 1950s and 1960s, stating, defending, and elaborating its attitude. Typical of the resolutions passed at its biennial congresses was the following:

> Congress reaffirms the view expressed at previous congresses of the Board of Deputies—namely that Jews participate in South African public life as citizens of South Africa and have no collective attitude to the political issues which citizens are called upon to decide. . . . Jews share with their fellow citizens of other faiths and origins a common interest in and responsibility for our country's affairs and participate in them according to their individual convictions.[31]

On the one hand, such reaffirmation bore witness to the consistency and perseverance with which the Board stuck to its policy. On the other hand, the fact that it was necessary to reiterate its position with such frequency reflected the public pressures to which it was relentlessly subjected and the intense moral strains inherent in its stance.[32]

The Board of Deputies consistently deplored appeals to Jews qua Jews whether issued for or against the government's policies. "It has been the accepted policy of the community," repeatedly stated the Board, "that neither the Board of Deputies, as its representative organization, nor the Jewish community as a collective entity, can or should take up an explicit attitude in regard to specific policies in the political field."[33] The explicit justification most frequently offered for this position was that it was impossible to formulate a collective political viewpoint since, objectively, it simply did not exist. The implicit justification, more rarely enunciated, was that even were it possible to arrive at a single viewpoint, this would be undesirable if not downright dangerous to the interests and safety of the community. In the incipient formulations of this policy the phrase used in this connection was "party-political": "The Board takes no part whatever in the party political struggle. Party politics are entirely beyond its province."[34] This reflected the intrawhite struggle between the United Party and the National Party, which, as we have noted, was the initial context of political concern. Gradually, however, the context widened to include issues that transcended intrawhite party politics. The burning question became whether one supported or opposed a social order based on racial discrimination. Hence the Board's affirmations of noninvolvement increasingly referred to "political issues" or "racial issues," or even were stretched to encompass "controversial issues of national policy" in general. Thus in January 1958, *Jewish Affairs* stated:

> Racial issues form the very warp and woof of party politics in South Africa, and it has been a long-standing principle of the Jewish community that there is not and should not be a Jewish vote on controversial questions of national policy. The only possible exception to this rule is where the rights and status of Jews themselves as citizens may be directly threatened.[35]

Implicit in this formulation of policy was the denial that Judaism or Jewishness dictated any absolute imperative on the question of how a society such as South Africa's ought to be politically and socially ordered. There being no single authoritative viewpoint stemming from Judaism, "each citizen must act according to his individual insight," reasoned the Board's formula, adding, as if in parentheses, "and that insight we may hope, will be influenced by each person's understanding of what the Jewish traditions and the teachings of Jewish history demand of him."[36] The problem was, of course, that the dilemmas presented by the South African societal system extended beyond both intrawhite and interracial politics into moral spheres concerning basic human dignity and rights. The question whether, as the acknowledged representative body of the Jewish community, the Board of Deputies at least ought to say something about those fundamental moral issues that transcended formal party politics was hotly debated at every congress. Some argued that the Board had no business whatsoever making statements on any controversial issue not directly affecting Jewish rights. Others asserted that the agreed principle of noninvolvement in politics did not preclude some statement against racial prejudice and in affirmation of fundamental human rights. Not only the public pressure of liberals, Jewish and gentile, but no less the presence among the Board's leaders of individuals of pronounced liberal persuasion, such as Arthur Suzman, who headed the important Public Relations Committee in Johannesburg, or Dr. Ellen Hellmann, a leading figure in the Institute of Race Relations, called for some expression of Jewish ethos. Also international and American Jewish bodies were frequently critical of South African Jewry in this respect. Hence, from time to time, the Board found it necessary to explain, somewhat apologetically, that its policy was "not due to any indifference but because it is not its function to enter into the political arena other than in matters of specific Jewish concern."[37] Hence, too, resolutions were periodically passed giving expression to a Jewish ethos sufficiently generalized to be politically innocuous. The earliest such resolution was passed at the congress that took place in September 1955. It stated:

> Congress repeats its conviction that the welfare of all sections of the population depends on the maintenance of democratic institutions and the enjoyment of freedom and justice by all. It believes that the elimination of inter-group conflict and the abatement of racial prejudice are vital for the national good and urges support of efforts directed to these ends.[38]

In this way the Board delicately trod its precarious path between nonembroilment in the political thicket on the one hand and the impulses of moral conscience on the other hand.

By 1956 the policy of the Board of Deputies was well crystallized. Responding to growing public awareness of, and Afrikaner reaction to, the prominence of individual Jews in the opposition to apartheid, the Board declared: "Every individual Jew has the right to his own political views and actions." But it cautiously added the caveat, "of course within the framework of the law." At the same time, it stated: "The Jewish community does not seek, nor is it able, to control the political freedom of the individual Jew, but neither can it accept responsibility as a community for the actions of individuals." Finally, in terms that were politically innocuous, the Board again urged every Jewish citizen "to make his individual contribution in accordance with the teaching and precepts of Judaism towards the promotion of understanding, goodwill and cooperation between the various races, peoples and groups in South Africa and towards the achievement of a peaceful and secure future for all inhabitants of the country, based on the principles of justice and the dignity of the individual."[39]

In the final analysis, this communal policy of political noninvolvement was a function of the Jews' collective interests as perceived by the leadership of the Jewish Board of Deputies. It may be said that it was a characteristic minority-group phenomenon, better understood in sociological terms as a function of self-preservation than in ideological terms as a function of Judaism. One might ask: What were the stakes involved in this perception of self-preservation? Only with historical hindsight might it be said that they were not the prospect of being subjected to active persecution. Punitive sanctions probably would not have gone much beyond public expressions of hostility, allowing antisemites a freer rein, and administrative hindrances to free existence of a Jewish communal life in which Zionism occupied a central place. But this was not the perception of Jewish leaders at the time. The record of antisemitism in the two decades preceding 1948 left little cause for sanguinity in the 1950s and 1960s, the high tide of the apartheid regime's repression of almost every form of resistance to the system.

This is not to say that moral issues and dilemmas of conscience were of no account. They certainly were major factors in the experience of the foremost Jewish communal leaders, especially since they included persons who held membership in the Liberal and Progressive Parties and high-profile personages such as advocate Israel Maisels, who led the defense of the accused in the great Treason Trial of the late 1950s (a subject to which we shall return later). But the very fact that even those who in their personal lives were known to be strongly opposed to apartheid affirmed the policy of communal noninvolvement was indicative of the basic consensus on the subject. Given this consensus, there remained the struggle with conscience over what could nevertheless be said on a purely moral plane, in the light of Judaism and Jewish historical experience, and this without undermining the stance of political noninvolvement. The chairman of the Board's Public Relations Committee throughout most of this period, Arthur Suzman—himself a supporter of the Progressive Party in his personal capacity—wrestled repeatedly with this profound dilemma in his addresses to successive congresses of the Board. But he was driven regretfully to the conclusion that "though we may rightly be expected to speak with one moral voice—to do so without entering the political arena appears to be a well-nigh insuperable task."[40] Hence, the Board could but urge Jews as individuals to draw their own conclusions and determine their actions on the basis of their own understanding of Judaism. The golden mean between self-interest and principles to which the Board aspired remained exasperatingly elusive. For in the realities of the South African situation, opponents of the existing social order were bound to construe the Board's policy as pious lip service, while government supporters saw it as covert political involvement.

Although the collective noninvolvement policy of the Board of Deputies precluded any social action, this self-restriction did not apply to one of its major affiliates, the Union of Jewish Women. No discussion of the Jewish community's collective behavior in relation to the underprivileged black majority would be complete without mention of the Union's manifold activities. Its founder and first leader was Toni Saphra, who had been a social worker in Germany and member of the Deutsche Jüdischer Frauenbund before immigrating to South Africa. In 1931 she gained the support of the Jewish Board of Deputies for the creation of branches of a Jewish women's organization dedicated to work both in the Jewish and the general community and duly affiliated to the International Council of Jewish Women. By 1936 the various branches that had emerged were consolidated nationally in the Union of Jewish Women of South Africa, and by 1975 it had seventy-one branches throughout South Africa and Rhodesia with a total membership of 10,600.[41]

The Union of Jewish Women engaged Jewish women extensively in educational programs aimed at strengthening and deepening Jewish identity. Its feminist activities were moderate, although it did lobby and agitate continuously for improvement of the rights of Jewish women in Jewish religious law (*halakha*). This endeavor was to little avail and aroused sporadic communal dissonance. During the Second World War years the Union had been very active in a wide range of home front work. In the 1950s it began to conduct a women's section of the United

Communal Fund and partnered with the Jewish Board of Deputies in establishing Hillel Houses for Jewish students at South African universities. Other activities later included provision of kosher mobile meals for elderly Jews and Passover parcels for Jewish men in the military.

Extending its work beyond the Jewish community and across the color line, the Union of Jewish Women founded mothercraft welfare centers for Africans, crèches (day care programs) in the colored community, and soup kitchens in hospitals. One of its most important projects, founded in 1950, was the erection and maintenance of the Entokozwene crèche for blacks in the Alexandra Township of Johannesburg. The Union also undertook a project called Ken Mekaar (Getting to Know Each Other) in 1979 together with an Afrikaans women's organization, Kontak. The Union also sponsored bursaries (scholarships) for study, notably the Toni Saphra Bursary inaugurated in 1949 to help underprivileged women of any race to study nursing. It was to be awarded to a woman student irrespective of race, creed, or color whose proposed course of study would fit her more adequately to render some form of social service to the community.

While pursuing its extensive humanitarian social work, implicitly in a spirit at odds with the discriminatory social system of apartheid, the Union of Jewish Women nevertheless adhered to the Board of Deputies policy of nonpolitical involvement. It carefully refrained from making statements that might be construed as explicit opposition to the government's policies. In a typical statement of credo, the Union's president in 1964, Mrs. Sylvia Silverman, wrote: "It is for us to share the legacy of our Jewish heritage, which has its origins in a culture many thousands of years old, a legacy which prompts us to accept the premise that the welfare of young and old *of all sections of the population* [emphasis in the original] shall be our concern."[42] In this sense the Union of Jewish Women served as the unofficial arm of the Board of Deputies for practical social action both within and beyond the Jewish community.

Thus far we have considered the delicate position of the Jewish Board of Deputies. But what of the rabbinate? Since concern with moral issues affecting society was universally recognized as the legitimate province of the clergy, rabbis potentially enjoyed considerably more latitude in responding to the moral implications of apartheid. These advantages of clerical prerogative were not overlooked by the Board of Deputies, which, ostensibly at least, tended to shift to the rabbinate responsibility for providing guidance on the moral ethos of Judaism. Yet, knowing full well that the gentile public was unlikely to separate the statements of rabbis from the views of Jewry at large, the Board was reluctant wholly to relinquish its discretionary influence. Typical of this ambivalence was a statement it issued in 1960. On the one hand this affirmed, "Members of the Jewish ministry have the right, and indeed, the duty of speaking to the community on the relevance of Jewish religious and ethical principles to the problems of today." But on the other hand it cautioned, "At the same time the Board has emphasized the duty which rests upon all to deal with those important matters in moderate and sober language and with a due sense of public responsibility."[43]

For all but a handful of the rabbis serving in South Africa—to whose views we shall return—this caveat was hardly necessary since, by and large, they concurred with the Board's views and felt bound by the very same considerations and constraints. Their consequent abstention from any political involvement was in marked contrast to the actions of a number of Christian clergymen who opposed apartheid from the outset with the utmost conviction and courage. However, they too were very much the exception rather than the rule for the Christian clergy as a whole.

The Christian churches had multiracial adherents in South Africa, but congregational segregation had long been the rule in the land and the Afrikaans-speaking Dutch Reformed Churches virtually became theological pillars of apartheid policy.[44] The Anglican, Catholic, and other English-speaking church denominations, although also segregated by long-established custom at congregational and parish level, did demur at the theological and institutional implications of apartheid or, in some cases, objected to them outright. On the whole these churches rejected racial discrimination in principle but were very inhibited and divided in regard to involvement in political action against apartheid policy. However, when government policy directly affected the work of the churches, confrontation was unavoidable. The first clash was thus precipitated when black education was largely withdrawn from church control in terms of the Bantu Education Act of 1953. A few years later, in 1957, the Anglican bishop of Cape Town, Geoffrey Clayton, and the Roman Catholic archbishop of Durban, Denis Hurley, fought the government's attempt to bar blacks from attending churches in residential areas reserved only for whites.

The Anglican priest Father Trevor Huddleston was foremost among the clergymen who not only defied and challenged the apartheid system theologically but also actively identified with the resistance movement of the African National Congress and the Congress of the People, which produced the Freedom Charter of 1955. He had thrown himself selflessly into the unavailing resistance to the removal of the black township of Sophiatown in Johannesburg, which the government bulldozed in accordance with its notorious Group Areas Act. His classic attack on apartheid as unchristian doctrine and practice, *Naught for Your Comfort,* appeared in 1956. But Father Huddleston's struggle was far from representative of the average churchgoing Christian, and his order recalled him to England in 1956. There he continued to lead in the international crusade against apartheid. Like Huddleston, most other clergymen who offered defiant resistance during the first two decades of apartheid rule held aliens status in South Africa. This facilitated the government's ability to rid itself of such rebellious presence simply by refusing renewal of residential permits. A foremost example was Ambrose Reeves, the Anglican bishop of Johannesburg, who took a strong stand against apartheid and had to leave the country.

An important milestone in church criticism of the government's apartheid policy was the conference convened by the World Council of Churches at Cottesloe in Johannesburg in December 1960 in the wake of the Sharpeville massacre. The participants were primarily from the English-speaking denominations but included Afrikaans church clerics along with some black delegates. The consensus reached, although not unequivocal in regard to the purported "separate development" principles of apartheid, challenged some basic tenets such as racial segregation in the church and the prohibition of racially mixed marriages. But under indignant pressure from Prime Minister Verwoerd, the Nederduitse Gereformeerde Kerk (NGK) afterward repudiated the Cottesloe statement. One remarkable cleric, the Reverend Beyers Naudé, moderator of one of the NGK's regional synods, courageously refused to fall in line with his church's proapartheid position, and in 1963 he launched the ecumenical Christian Institute of Southern Africa, which became an unrelenting foe of apartheid racism and a thorn in the side of the Dutch Reformed Churches. By the time the government finally cracked down on the Christian Institute in 1977, it had gone so far as to support international economic sanctions against the regime, conscientious objection to military service, and demands that the government remove the ban on the African National Congress and enter into negotiations for a new South Africa.

Against this background, a balanced evaluation of the record of the rabbinate on the question of apartheid in South Africa ought to take into account the fact that, unlike the major Christian churches, Judaism had no adherents outside the white population of South Africa. Consequently, the rabbinate was never answerable to, or responsible for, a black membership suffering directly from the apartheid system; it never had to formulate theological or practical principles either justifying or denouncing discrimination among its own members. On the other hand, rabbis had very much to contend with the vulnerable minority-group status of Jews within the white racial group. They were all too aware that the white majority public did not differentiate between the statements and actions of rabbis and the position of the Jewish community. A primary sense of responsibility for the safety and welfare of the Jewish community inhibited even those few rabbis whose consciences were deeply perturbed by the acute moral issues that apartheid placed at their door. This constraint was most marked in the peak years of apartheid implementation—the 1950s and early 1960s—when the leadership of the Jewish community was most intimidated by the government's assertive Afrikaner devotees.

Rare were the occasions when a rabbi adopted a stand of unequivocal opposition to the whole apartheid system, and when it did happen, the response within the Jewish community was anything but enthusiastic. A striking illustration may be found in the extraordinary case of André Ungar. Ungar was born in Budapest and came to South Africa in 1955, at the age of twenty-five, to serve as rabbi of the reform congregation in the city of Port Elizabeth. He found apartheid utterly appalling, and it did not take long before he began vehemently to say as much, both from the pulpit and from public platforms. Protesting audaciously against the government's refusal to issue a passport to a black youth who had been offered a scholarship to study in America, he said the government's refusal was made by "arrogantly puffed up little men in heartless stupidity." Citing Ungar as having said that "race hatred is an atrocity and the Group Areas Act is a despicable atrocity," *Die Transvaler* called this "a savage attack on the Group Areas Act."[45]

The reaction that followed was instructive not only of the government's method of dealing with such opposition but also of the policy of the Board of Deputies and the attitude of the average Jew. Ungar was not yet a South African citizen. Hence it was no problem at all for the authorities to get rid of him. In December 1956 the minister of the interior duly sent notice to the secretary of his congregation withdrawing his permit of residence, and he was ordered to leave the country. It so happened that Ungar had already notified his congregation that he intended leaving South Africa, a fact that released it and the community as a whole from the necessity to defend his right to stay. This was much to their relief because his actions were, in fact, an acute source of embarrassment.[46] As became evident in a spate of correspondence in the Port Elizabeth newspapers, opinion in the local Jewish community was divided over Ungar. One of his defenders wrote:

> All people in South Africa who live by the word of the Book and who are prepared to see justice done to all people irrespective of colour, creed and race will miss him. . . . For here was a man who was prepared to live his religion, who was prepared to castigate his own people . . . and to stimulate them, not only to read the holy word of God but to apply the principles of the word in their lives.

But there were also Jews who rejected and resented Ungar's behavior, as was evident in another letter:

> As a member of the Port Elizabeth Jewish community I would like to record my indignation at the abuse of the freedom of the press by the non-desirable visitor to South Africa, Rabbi Ungar. . . . He lacks the sense of responsibility and dignity of a responsible leader of a community. . . . The Jewish community of Port Elizabeth should pronounce the traditional Hebrew blessing of "*Boruch sheptoranu,*" i.e., "Thank God we are getting rid of this rabbi."[47]

Ungar himself contended that since the authorities must have known of his intention to leave South Africa at the end of January 1957, their purpose in sending notice of his undesirability was to intimidate the Jewish community. He argued that the government sought to bully the Jews "if not into active conformity, then at least into a fearsome silence."[48] But the communal leadership, far from rallying in support of Ungar, was anxious to dissociate itself from him. The local Eastern Province Committee of the South African Jewish Board of Deputies issued a statement arguing that Ungar had spoken "neither for his own congregation nor for South African Jewry as a whole." It refuted Ungar's contention that the Jewish community regarded the government's withdrawal of his temporary permit as an attempt to intimidate Jewish citizens.[49]

The national executive of the Jewish Board of Deputies found itself in accord with the Port Elizabeth leaders. When it discussed the matter at a meeting of the executive council in December 1956, it was unanimously agreed that

> There is no occasion for the Board to intervene or make a statement. Action was not taken by the government against Rabbi Ungar because he was a Jewish minister. The rabbi did not confine his utterances to the pulpit but went on to the political platform and must therefore bear the consequences as an individual. As we have repeatedly asseverated, an individual Jew has the right to take whatever line is dictated by his private conscience and the Jewish community can take no credit or accept any blame for the individual's utterances.[50]

Notwithstanding this attempted justification of the Board of Deputies' set policy, it cannot be denied that it failed utterly to apply even that policy with true conviction and impartiality. At the least it might have said a word in principled defense of a rabbi's right outspokenly to voice his interpretation of Jewish religious imperatives.[51] No incident better illustrates the fearful and timorous mind-set of the Jewish communal leadership, lay and religious, during the first two decades of National Party rule, the period that might be called "high apartheid." Most telling of all is the fact that even the chief minister of the United Progressive Jewish Congregation, Moses Cyrus Weiler, refrained from taking a public stand in support of Ungar. Obviously Ungar's behavior discomfited Weiler no less than the community's lay leaders. One might surmise that he thought Ungar got his just desserts because, sensing the provocative temperament of the young rabbi, he had already warned Ungar of the dangers when he inducted him in January 1955. In his induction speech Weiler had stressed the virtue and courage of restraint, and warned: "A rabbi who was not at one with his congregation . . . was a failure." In replying, Ungar had undauntedly averred that a minister's ultimate responsibility was to God alone.[52]

Weiler himself had formulated his own guidelines in relation to political issues and the welfare of the underprivileged in South Africa. It was his view that Jews ought to give expression to their religiously rooted ethical concerns primarily through welfare and educational action. Hence, already in 1945 he had encouraged the Women's Sisterhood of the Progressive Congregation to set up an elementary school with attached health and scholarship facilities in the poverty-stricken Alexandra Township of Johannesburg. This school, whose name honored Rabbi Weiler, became perhaps the most impressive individual project for the benefit of the black community ever maintained by a Jewish organization. The sisterhood also adopted a high school in Pimville Township, establishing a library in the school and helping to add classrooms. Similar activities were undertaken in Durban. On occasion, Weiler also associated himself with Christian clergymen in protest against specific acts that he regarded as arguably outside the sphere of party politics. Thus he was a signatory to a protest by civic and clerical leaders against segregation at the universities, and he spoke out against the forced removal of nonwhites from certain areas and townships in Johannesburg. There can be no doubt that Weiler found apartheid wholly repulsive. However, remaining ever mindful of his responsibility to the collective safety of the Jewish community, he explained his policy thus:

> The fact is . . . that my attitude to the non-European section of South Africa's population is not political. . . . As a rabbi I do not engage in political activities, but participate (with some other members of the Jewish community of diverse political affiliations) in work for the welfare of non-Europeans. Furthermore, I do so not in my private capacity but as a rabbi, motivated by tenets of prophetic Judaism.[53]

Weiler's successor, Arthur Saul Super, who was chief minister of the progressive congregation in Johannesburg from 1965 to 1976, when he too settled in Israel, became far more active in opposition to apartheid. He frequently joined Christian leaders in protest against specific measures of the government that infringed basic human rights. Summing up his position in an article written in 1972, Super was categorical in regard to Judaism's belief that all men are created equal in the image of one God. "There can be no basic division of the human race whereby it is asserted or assumed that one human being is to be preferred to another by virtue of a differentiation in race, colour or creed." But he added that he did not think it appropriate for rabbis to engage in translation of this principle into precise lines of political policy. He allowed that "there may be decent, conscientious Jews who believe that a scheme for separate development might be a vehicle whereby the recognition of equality of all human beings could be implemented in practice." But he made it clear that he did not share this view and said it was incumbent on Jews to scrutinize "with a thousand eyes any policy that is put forward to be sure that it is not a rationalization or an attempt to disguise the perpetuation of a system which leads to inequality."[54] All the same, he too adhered to the view that the synagogue as such could have no part in the political life of its members and should not make pronouncements on political or other public issues outside the immediate province of Jewry.

By and large the orthodox rabbinate adopted much the same attitude. Some rabbis maintained utter silence on the implications of apartheid society from the point of view of Judaism, while others occasionally spoke out from the pulpit on Judaism's incompatibility with racist beliefs or the practice of racial discrimination. However, out of a sense of responsibility for the Jewish community's position, almost all remained careful not to spell out the implications in terms that categorically impugned the government's apartheid program. Chief Rabbi Israel Abrahams of Cape Town was particularly cautious and compliant, especially when Israel's international stand against South Africa in the early 1960s provoked strong government resentment. On one auspicious occasion, the centenary celebration of the Gardens synagogue (the "mother synagogue" of South African Jewry) in December 1963, he conspicuously omitted the customary prayer for the safety of Israel and the *Hatikva* anthem. This was obviously in cautious deference to the anticipated resentment of high-ranking government personages who were in attendance. Although he always identified himself as a Zionist and indeed chose to live out his retirement years in Israel, this timorous posture aroused considerable criticism in the Jewish community and even the anxiety of Israel's consul general in Cape Town.[55] On the other hand, since Abrahams, in common with Chief Rabbi

Rabinowitz of Johannesburg, was also a university professor of Hebrew studies, he spoke out from time to time in defense of academic freedom and participated in protests against the enforcement of segregation in the universities. Both chief rabbis also joined church leaders in some of their public protests against specific government actions such as forced removal of people resulting from Group Areas legislation.[56]

Chief Rabbi Rabinowitz's demeanor was quite the opposite of Abrahams's. By temperament far less repressible, he never wavered in demonstration of his ardent Zionism (he was a foremost supporter of Revisionist Zionism) and, at the same time, tended to make his opposition to apartheid increasingly explicit. Indeed, he champed at the bit of the lay leadership's policy of noninvolvement. On several occasions he expressed dissatisfaction with the Board of Deputies' stance insofar as it implied a denial of any collective view even on the purely moral dilemmas inherent in South African society. "Our concern is with the doctrines of Judaism, not the views of individual Jews," he said, "and we betray these doctrines if we do not proclaim that Judaism teaches, without equivocation, the absolute equality of all men before God." He pleaded that there surely *was* a specifically Jewish attitude toward discrimination based on race or creed and that "it was as unreasonable to suggest that it was wrong to denounce discrimination because Jews favoured it, as it was to suggest that it was wrong to denounce theft because some Jews are thieves."[57] In his sermons he protested against the deportation of Bishop Reeves, declaring: "It was the sacred duty of all religious leaders to speak out clearly on the ethical aspects of social problems."

As might have been expected, Rabbi Rabinowitz's outspokenness and occasional participation in protests alongside Christian clerics drew fire from some of the Afrikaans newspapers. He was also the recipient of anonymous hate mail and threats.[58] The antisemitic, progovernment *South African Observer* warned that in "using the synagogue to intrude Judaism's doctrine of 'absolute equality' into South Africa's political affairs," the rabbi was treading on dangerous ground, because it gave the sanction of Judaism to the activities of liberal and communist Jews."[59] On the other side of the political barricades, Rabinowitz drew some praise from radical opponents of apartheid. In November 1959, for example, a bulletin of the South African Congress of Democrats commented on the welcome significance of his Yom Kippur sermon "for those who have given up all hope of seeing organized Jewry express anti-racialist opinion."[60]

Taking stock of his fifteen-year-long ministry on the eve of his departure to settle in Israel, Rabinowitz retroactively criticized "the caution which the Board has shown in refusing to declare a Jewish ethical attitude on the vexed problem of race relations." He said that it could be "variously interpreted according to one's views as either admirable discretion or reprehensible timorousness," and had inevitably meant "the abdication of any claim to give a lead in these matters."[61] He also severely criticized the Jewish press of South Africa. "With rare unanimity they sedulously and completely refrain from publishing one single word by any prominent Jew which can be construed as criticism of the Government," he wrote, adding that he had ascertained that no such directive had ever been issued to the press by the

South African Jewish Board of Deputies. "It is only in the national press that extracts from the sermons of a Rabbi, which are critical of the racial policy of the Government, find a place," noted Rabinowitz, "and, on the other hand, what prominence is given to a speech or an address by a Rabbi which can be interpreted as being favourable to the Government! With what joy and adulation is it hailed, and how he is lionized."[62]

Behind the scenes there were a number of sharp exchanges between Rabbi Rabinowitz and the executive of the Board of Deputies, which indignantly denied that it had ever interfered with his right to speak and act according to the principles of Judaism.[63] Even the prominent liberal Ellen Hellmann thought his criticisms were too harsh, while veteran Jewish journalist Edgar Bernstein challenged his interpretation. "What Rabbi Rabinowitz mistakes for fear of political repercussions to his statements is, in fact, mistrust of his sagacity in making them," he argued. "His right 'to speak out' has not been denied him: what is questioned by his challengers is whether he exercises due responsibility in using it."[64]

Much as outspoken Christian clergymen were criticized by some of their flock, Rabinowitz faced criticism from not a few fellow Jews. Even some rabbis were disconcerted by the lead Rabinowitz appeared to be giving. When, on one occasion, he asked for prayers to be said in all synagogues under his jurisdiction, not only for the peace and security of South Africa, but also on behalf of political prisoners, another prominent rabbi, Dr. Michael Kossowsky (who was also a leader of the Mizrahi Zionist party) publicly dissociated himself from Rabinowitz's actions. "I thoroughly disapprove of involving the Synagogue and the Jewish community as a whole in activities which in any way bear a political character," he said in a sermon delivered to his own congregation. "No political labels must be stuck onto our holy prayers. The pulpit as well as the Synagogue must be kept out of the political struggle."[65] In balance, there can be little doubt that most of the rabbinate inclined toward Kossowsky's view rather than that of Rabinowitz. Something of Rabbi Rabinowitz's dilemma can be gathered from a letter he wrote to *The Jewish Chronicle* of London explaining the South African Jewish situation and his own position in it:

> In an atmosphere such as this the position of the rabbi becomes one of peculiar difficulty, which is well nigh intolerable. No matter how rigidly he confines himself to the purely ethical and religious implications of the prevalent racial policy, the moment he utters a word which can be construed as a criticism of that policy he is immediately charged with "preaching politics." . . . The official policy of the South African Jewish Board of Deputies, which is that the Jewish community as such cannot express any view on the political situation since Jews belong to all parties, generously concedes the right of the rabbi to speak on its ethical aspects. In effect, however, this is widely interpreted not only that he should confine himself to pulpit utterances, but that such pulpit utterances should not receive any publicity outside the pulpit. When, therefore, as often happens, the daily press finds a sermon on the political situation of sufficient general interest to warrant publication, there is a vague feeling that the rabbi has gone too far.[66]

In one of his Yom Kippur sermons Rabbi Rabinowitz gave vent to his anguish and frustration in a frank outburst:

> The most lamentable failure of Judaism to make its impact upon our lives lies not in the failure to observe, but in the almost complete absence of any specific Jewish ethical standards which mark us out from the community in which we live. What do we do to loosen the bonds of wickedness, to undo the bonds of oppression? . . . There are some Jews in the community who do attempt to do something . . . and when, as a result, they fall foul of the powers that be, the defence put up by the Jewish community is to prove that these are Jews only by name, that they do not belong to any synagogue. . . . Have Jewish ethics ever descended to a more shameful nadir? . . . I have practically abandoned all hope of effecting any change in this matter. The power of fear and of the possibility of security being affected is too strong. . . . Do not think that I am proud of my record in this matter, that I do not squirm inwardly at the thought that on many occasions I have been infected with that same fear and that same cowardice and have failed to rise to the level which my calling demands of me. But when from time to time a blatant, glaring case of injustice occurs, and it is one in which there is a hope that my intervention may possibly have a salutary effect, then no power in the world can prevent me giving expression to what I conscientiously believe to be the authentic voice of prophetic Judaism.[67]

Notwithstanding this dilemma of conscience, in the final analysis even Rabbi Rabinowitz did not seriously enter the lists in the battle against apartheid. If ever there was a rabbinical personality powerful enough to make an attempt to lead the Jewish community into such a battle, it was Louis Rabinowitz. That he did not do so is in itself evidence of the constraining power of the Jewish sense of vulnerability in the heyday period of apartheid. He too was not prepared to risk the consequences for the Jewish community.

Overall, remarkably little reflective thought was applied by the rabbinate in South Africa to the question whether Judaism provided definitive imperatives in relation to the reality of race relations in the South African context. In a rare examination of the question from a purely *halakhic* (Jewish legal) point of view, even Rabbi Rabinowitz found himself unable to conclude anything more than the following: "The reply of *Halakha* as to whether apartheid is admissible seems to be as follows: If apartheid is just and non-discriminatory as the supporters of the Bantustans say; if, in other words, it offers all racial groups the same rights and development, then it is in accordance with *Halakha;* otherwise it is against the *Halakha*."[68] In the harsh reality of the South African scene, however, this was a far cry from the provision of unequivocal guidance for believing Jews. Of course, in the light of his many statements on the subject, Rabinowitz himself clearly did not consider apartheid to be offering "the same rights." He regarded both the theory and practice of apartheid as an abomination. But Prime Minister Verwoerd and other ideologists of apartheid were insistent that apartheid was a fundamentally moral solution to South Africa's problems, which did offer ultimately equal but separate development for all of its racial groups, and there were Jews willing to adopt this interpretation.

One of South African Jewry's most intellectually distinguished rabbis, Dr. Solomon Rappaport, did, at one stage, make a serious attempt to adduce a Judaic view on the basis not of the strict letter of the *halakha,* but of an examination of rabbinical sources in general. In a booklet titled *Rabbinic Thoughts on Race,* Rappaport concluded that "there is no justification for basing collective consciousness of racial group superiority on Biblical teachings," and that "an unbiased examination of Jewish sources bears out the thesis that the doctrine of a biologically justified supremacy of one group over the other is incompatible with the leading thoughts of Rabbinism." The validity of this conclusion was compounded by consideration of what the Jews had suffered at the hands of Nazi racism. All considered, he thought it self-evident that "the Jewish people should scrupulously refrain from becoming accessories to any acts of oppression, injustice or humiliation, committed in the name of race."[69] But even this conclusion was far from unequivocal in the context of South African realities, for among Afrikaners a *verligte* (enlightened) ideological interpretation of separate development was evolving which denied that it was motivated by racist criteria. Sensing the complexity of the situation, Rappaport himself found it necessary to note: "It is hardly practicable to apply directly rabbinic views on race and colour to the baffling realities of a multiracial society with varying standards of education such as exists in the Union of South Africa. The intricate problem of interracial adjustment, resulting from difference in colour, is a comparatively new experience in Jewish life." Indeed, disillusionment with the chaos, violence, and dictatorship that accompanied the birth of many independent African states later led Rappaport himself to amplify his reservations about the direct applicability of *Rabbinic Thoughts on Race.* In 1965 he went on record to the effect that liberal spirits in South Africa had been shaken by developments in other African states. "Judging by the seeming irrefutable evidence of current experiences in Africa," he wrote, "the chance for such an ideal solution is so remote and the risks so enormous that the present state of affairs [in South Africa] with all its manifest imperfections, is far preferable and serves the best interests of the country as a whole." He cautioned any rabbi who contemplated coming out to South Africa that he "will be unable to allay the anxieties of his flock by delivering sermons on the Fatherhood of God and the Brotherhood of Man," and noted that "while Jews wanted to keep their community separate, they could not deny this same right to the Afrikaner."[70]

Rappaport's view elicited statements of disagreement from a number of quarters, including Rabbi Rabinowitz writing from Israel, and also his successor, Chief Rabbi Bernard Casper. They reminded him of what he had once written in *Rabbinic Thoughts on Race* and deplored his apparent change of attitude. He was, however, defended by Edgar Bernstein. "In my long experience as a journalist and a communal worker," wrote Bernstein, not without credibility, "it is my observation that the overwhelming majority of South African Jewry shares the realistic appreciation of South Africa's position which Rabbi Rappaport's letter reflects." In responding to his critics, Rabbi Rappaport said there was nothing wrong in modifying one's outlook. "I refute the liberalism of irresponsibility," he declared, "social problems cannot be solved merely by good intentions . . . the last years have taught me that some of our cherished beliefs about the way of ordering South African society in a just and lasting manner were illusions."[71]

One of those who upbraided Rappaport for bending to such views was a young South African–born rabbi, Benzion (Ben) Isaacson. If one might speak of someone approximating to a rabbinical counterpart of the daring Christian clerics—the like of Father Huddleston and Bishop Ambrose Reeves—who fearlessly battled the apartheid system and also had to contend with objections from within their flock, this title would go almost solely to Isaacson.

Ben Isaacson came from a rather typical first-generation, moderately orthodox background. As a child Ben participated in the Bnei Akiva religious Zionist youth movement, and after matriculating in 1952 he studied at an orthodox yeshiva in the United States. Back in South Africa, he was a protégé of Chief Rabbi Louis Rabinowitz, who attached much importance to the nurturing of a South African–born generation of dedicated rabbis. Isaacson served as assistant rabbi to Rabinowitz, with particular responsibility for the youth congregation.

From the outset the young rabbi stood out as an outspoken critic of the apartheid system and of the quiescence of the official Jewish community. Very soon this aroused the anger of some of the congregants, who objected strongly to the "political" implications of this precocious young rabbi's preaching. The president of the congregation at the time was none other than Dr. Percy Yutar, the zealous attorney who later led the state's prosecution against apartheid's opponents in the famous Rivonia trial to which we shall return in the next chapter. Yutar took the young rabbi to task and attempted to have him dismissed, but Chief Rabbi Rabinowitz, who had a great fondness for Isaacson and set much store upon his prospects as a rabbi in his own mold, stood firmly by his protégé.

The first two pulpits occupied by Isaacson were in Jewish congregations situated within conservative Afrikaner social environments, the town of Krugersdorp near Johannesburg and, thereafter, Bloemfontein, capital city of the Orange Free State. This was anything but a deterrent for Isaacson. It was the stormy period of Dr. Verwoerd's ascent to the premiership, the fateful Sharpeville massacre, and its sequel of escalating repressive legislation aimed at crushing the opposition. Isaacson supported the Defence and Aid Fund for the Treason Trial accused and not only continued to be outspoken in sermons criticizing the government's racial policies but also associated himself with activists in the antiapartheid Congress of Democrats, among them Ben and Mary Turok. Moreover, he gave public prominence to his views explicitly as a Jewish religious minister in letters to the general press. In one such letter, for example, he refuted, as "one who has a knowledge of the original texts of the Bible," the so-called proofs for racial segregation, which protagonists of apartheid purported to derive from Old Testament stories such as the curse of Ham and the Tower of Babel or from what was spuriously described as the "religious apartheid" of the children of Israel.[72]

Edgar Bernstein, who apart from his work as a journalist was also active in the Jewish Board of Deputies, took Isaacson to task in a manner as patronizing as it was caustic. In a letter addressed to Isaacson but with copies to both his congregation and the Federation of Synagogues, Bernstein scolded the young rabbi for being derelict in his responsibility "to refrain from word and deed which might be prejudicial to the Jewish community." He told Isaacson: "Any letter you write to the press, any speech you deliver from a public platform, is taken to reflect, not simply your private opinion, but a Jewish point of view." Bernstein's own outlook was revealingly shown by his adding: "Judaism takes no position on the politics of apartheid. On the plane of man's relation to man, it is concerned with achieving a social justice that can be realised within an apartheid no less than within an 'integrated' society." Once more, Louis Rabinowitz vigorously took up the cudgels in support of Isaacson. He charged Bernstein with attempting to incite the lay leaders under whose authority a rabbi serves "in order to suppress his freedom of expression in matters of conviction." Bernstein subsequently apologized for not having limited himself to private correspondence, but he stuck to his contention that a rabbi had "a duty to ensure that his statements should not have repercussions on the Jewish community which it is his first responsibility to serve."[73]

It did not take long before Rabbi Isaacson's political involvement acutely embarrassed his Krugersdorp congregants. The cause was a police raid and search of the rabbi's home because he had taken under his care the children of the Congress of Democrats' general-secretary Ben Turok, who was in hiding from the police. Chief Rabbi Rabinowitz stepped in once again to arrange a new position for Isaacson, this time in Bloemfontein. It was not an easy appointment. An unknown self-described "action committee," in which officials of the Board of Deputies suspected that a Jew was involved, rained threatening letters on the Bloemfontein congregation. These demanded that the congregation withdraw its call to Isaacson and that he be "unfrocked" [*sic*] for his insidious political activities in the name of religion. "Let him go to Israel to preach for the oppressed Arabs," fumed one letter.[74] However, the lay head of the congregation, Henry Bradlow, in consultation with the Board of Deputies, was not deterred from inducting Isaacson as the Bloemfontein congregation's rabbi. Once installed there in 1962, the charismatic and energetic young rabbi succeeded in spiritually enriching the community. He took a particular interest in the local branch of the Habonim youth movement, becoming its official head, actively participating in the movement's camps, and serving on its national executive. Isaacson made a distinctive contribution not only to the Judaic content of the movement but also to another important aspect of its educational program, which aimed, however discreetly, to arouse critical awareness of the moral evils of South Africa's apartheid society.

The maverick rabbi continued to attract public controversy, not only on account of his "political" acts, but also for refusing to comply with a new prohibition issued by the Johannesburg Beth Din forbidding orthodox rabbis to participate in any activity, even of a secular nature, with rabbis or representatives of reform Judaism. In 1965 Isaacson decided to leave the congregation and settle in Israel. In a valedictory article he wrote for the *Jewish Times,* he stressed that his "*aliya* decision" derived from positive Jewish-Zionist motives but he was taking this step earlier than he had planned largely out of frustration with the Jewish community's comportment in regard to apartheid:

> It is my personal conviction that a society based on racial discrimination is immoral and in conflict with the ethical teachings of Judaism. But while we are told on the one hand, that the rabbi is free to discuss and even criticise the South African scene from his pulpit, my experience has pointed to the exact opposite trend. Criticism of racial discrimination . . . leads to outcries of "politics from the pulpit," "endangering the Jewish community," and even cries of "defrock him." On the other hand, those rabbis who defend the existing society are not accused of the above crimes. In such a situation, I feel myself stifled to the point of choking.[75]

Isaacson's departure for Israel in 1965 was not the end of his rabbinical career in relation to South Africa, but we shall have to return to its continuation in a later chapter.

Coping with Israel's Intrusion

Thus far we have focused on the chronic dilemma of the Jewish community's main lay representative organ and its rabbis in relation to the increasingly ruthless entrenchment of the apartheid policy on which revolved all of the country's internal politics. But as South Africa entered the second decade of National Party rule this dilemma was acutely compounded by an important development in the international crusade against apartheid that profoundly affected South African Jews, namely, Israel's increasingly active participation in the African alignment against white South Africa. This was to perturb South African Jewry and trouble the conscience of the community's leaders even more than the concurrent salience of Jewish radicals and liberals in the resistance to apartheid (a subject to which we shall return in the next chapter). Attention must now be turned to the implications of this important development.

Throughout the 1950s the foreign relations between Israel and South Africa developed cordially enough, although diplomatic representation remained low-key. Only Israel maintained a permanent diplomatic mission. Although by the late 1950s there were already signs that Israel was developing close relations with several African countries hostile to the South African white regime,[76] Prime Minister Verwoerd himself could comment in conversations with Israel's minister plenipotentiary, Katriel Salmon, that he appreciated Israel's restraint regarding the international crusade against South Africa. Verwoerd added pointedly that this contrasted with the difficulties he was experiencing with the Jewish community, whose members had disappointed him by mostly voting nay in the plebiscite on declaration of South Africa as a republic.[77] But as the chorus of international condemnation of South Africa grew louder and Israel was drawn deeper into the vortex of the antiapartheid campaign, progovernment circles began to react to Israel's participation with bristling sensitivity.

A crisis was precipitated in October 1961 when at the United Nations some African states launched an attack on the South African foreign minister unprecedented in its severity. He was none other than Eric Louw, well remembered by Jews as a foremost antisemite in the pre-1948 period. Amid the clamorous support of many of the African delegates, the Liberian representative moved that Louw's speech be struck from the record. Although this did not pass, the General Assembly did roundly censure Louw, and Israel voted in favor of this censure.[78] In white South Africa this news was received with much indignation. With the exception of Holland and Israel, all the Western states had abstained from voting or absented themselves from the debate. This made Israel's offense against white South Africa particularly conspicuous. The embarrassment and apprehensiveness felt by the leaders of both the Jewish Board of Deputies and the Zionist Federation became acute when Eric Louw proceeded, implicitly, to invite a response from South African Jewry. Broadcasting to South Africa from New York, he expressed his dismay at the stand taken by the Netherlands government but referred, by way of consolation, to telegrams he had received from a number of Dutch immigrant organizations in South Africa expressing resentment at the Netherlands' vote. He was sure, he said pointedly, that "South African citizens who have racial and religious ties with Israel" would also disapprove of "the hostile and ungrateful" action of Israel.[79]

Louw's statement made headlines in the press. The Jewish communal leadership was in a dilemma. To speak out against apartheid in principle was one thing, but to side with those who denied South Africa the minimal courtesy of freedom of speech was quite another matter and seemed wholly indefensible. The prevailing feeling was one of acute embarrassment at Israel's action and fear of its consequences for Afrikaner attitudes toward Jews. Anxious consultations were called between the honorary officers of the Jewish Board of Deputies and the Zionist Federation until a consensus was reached on the substance of a statement mildly critical of Israel.[80] Its gist was "that this was a case where the issue was a simple one: the question of freedom of speech in the international forum. In these circumstances Israel should have joined the western nations in abstaining from voting on the Afro-Asian motion of censure."[81] Their decision was not at all to the liking of Israel's diplomatic representative in South Africa, Simha Pratt, with whom it was customary for the Zionist Federation to maintain consultative liaison. Pratt wrote to his superiors in Jerusalem: "I saw before me panicky people, gripped by fear and without backbone." When Pratt held up for emulation the bold stand of Anglo-Jewry in the last years of the British mandate over Palestine, the Zionist Federation's chairman, Edel Horwitz, retorted that if Oswald Moseley had been in power in Britain then the Jews would have acted differently.[82]

This criticism of Israel, however oblique, served its purpose insofar as Afrikaner resentments indeed appeared to be mollified. Thus the moderate progovernment organ, *Die Burger,* welcomed what it described as the protest of "the stranger within our gates" against the attitude of his former fatherland. "We have seen how particularly Netherlanders and Jews . . . manned the barricades for the good name of South Africa."[83] But the incident reflected both basic Jewish conformity to white South African norms and lingering fears of Afrikaner nationalist antisemitism.

Not long after the Eric Louw incident, Israel took another step toward alliance with white South Africa's enemies at the United Nations. Whereas a clause calling for diplomatic and economic sanctions against South Africa met with the opposition of the United States, the United Kingdom, and other Western states, Israel again conspicuously aligned itself with those who voted in favor.[84] Within the Jewish community as a whole opinion was divided. Outright supporters of the National Party's policies were still rare. But conformity to the normative political belief in maintaining white supremacy was prevalent. Israel's turn to out-and-out support of the African threat to this fundament of the South African state was regarded by many Jews not only as disappointingly inconsiderate of the situation of fellow Jews in the Diaspora but also as wrong in principle. This view may be illustrated from a letter *The Jewish Times* journalist Edgar Bernstein took it upon himself to write to Israel's prime minister David Ben-Gurion. Bernstein said he was writing "in deep sorrow as a South African hurt and shocked" by Israel's vote in favor of sanctions. "I know that there are reasons why Israel is unable to support South Africa's colour policies," he explained. "Her non-support . . . would be understood," but to swing from a position of understandable abstention to support of sanctions—and against a state that had always shown friendship—was an "inexcusable action." "Are relations with African states which have no Jewish communities," he asked, "more important to Israel than the position of a proud and conscious Jewish community of 100,000 souls in South Africa which has never wavered in its Zionism?" Thus far Bernstein might be said simply to have been making an appeal for Israel to show consideration for the interests of Diaspora Jewry. However, he proceeded to show his true ideological colors in terms that might have been voiced by an Afrikaner apologist for apartheid theory. For he offered a defense of "what we in South Africa call Separate Development—the recognition that all peoples have the right to their own existence and must not be swamped by numerical majorities." He continued: "This was a recognition which is basic to your own government's refusal—in my opinion, entirely proper—to take back so-called Arab 'refugees.'"[85]

In contrast to these views, a few letters from antiapartheid activists reached the Board of Deputies complaining that the Board's statement was a hypocritical departure from the hallowed principle of noninvolvement in South African political issues.[86] One radical leftist opponent of apartheid, Jack Tarshish, wrote a letter in the *Rand Daily Mail* accusing the Board of Deputies that only when it suited itself did it "trot out its stock expedient of 'political neutrality' in order to evade its responsibilities to the Jewish community." "Is Mr. Louw's freedom of speech more important than Mr. Luthuli's?" he asked. He said that Jewish South Africans should be proud that Israel affirmed the basic democratic principle of racial equality and the biblical injunction "Thou shalt not stand idly by the blood of thy brother."[87]

At this point in our narrative one might appropriately pause in order to examine the considerations of the government of Israel for the policy that had precipitated this crisis for South African Jewry. Somewhat ironically, Israel's permanent representative at the United Nations in the critical period from 1959 to 1967 was Michael Comay, a South African–born Zionist who, after serving in the South African forces in the Second World War, had settled in Israel. There he had risen in the ranks of Israel's diplomatic service. It now fell to his lot to execute Israel's policy in the very votes against apartheid at the United Nations that so agitated white South African opinion. Comay deplored apartheid and felt that Israel should take a clear antiapartheid stand in principle. However, at times he considered that Israel's leeway in diverging from the Afro-Asian line at the United Nations was greater than Foreign Minister Golda Meir estimated, and he felt that at least the acerbity of Israel's embarrassment of South African Jewry could have been blunted by more restrained action.[88]

What were the considerations that determined the Israel Foreign Ministry's policy? There can be no doubt that Israel's overriding motivation was to gain the diplomatic support of African states as counterbalance to the chronic international hostility it had to face from the Arab states and the Soviet Union and its satellites. This interest was reinforced by moral repugnance for the racism that apartheid signified. At the same time foreign office officials also showed concern for the position of South African Jewry.[89] When the subject became a public issue in the press and the Knesset (Israel's parliament) in late 1961, the government defended its votes against South Africa on the convergence of three considerations: in Prime Minister Ben-Gurion's words, "the moral heritage of the Jewish people, the needs of our people in the Diaspora, and our international status."[90] Responding to critics from the opposition benches, Ben-Gurion lectured the Knesset on Judaism's incompatibility with racial discrimination, quoting extensively from biblical passages to prove this. "We have experienced the taste of racial discrimination for thousands of years," he said, "and are unable to be indifferent to a regime which practices such deplorable discrimination."[91]

In the final analysis, the government of Israel accorded precedence to the weaning of African goodwill and votes away from hostile Arab influence, over the interests of South African Jewry. It was implicitly assumed that no more than acute discomfort and embarrassment were at stake for South African Jewry. Retrospectively questioned on this point, Ben-Gurion said candidly: "We knew the Jews there wouldn't suffer very much. . . . If there would have been pogroms—or if their lives were in danger—then we would have abstained, but we would not have voted in favor, certainly not. A Jew can't be for discrimination."[92] One should not overlook the premises of Zionist ideology that inhered in the thinking of Israel's policy makers. The Zionist position implied the primacy of Israel as the embodiment of the collective Jewish fate. None was governed more firmly by this conception than Ben-Gurion himself. He plainly stated it thus:

> It was always my view that we have always to consider the interests of Diaspora Jewry—any Jewish community that was concerned. But there is one crucial distinction—not what they think are their interests, but what we regard as their interests. If it was a case vital for Israel, and the interests of the Jews concerned were different, the vital interests of Israel come first—because Israel is vital for world Jewry.[93]

We return now to our narrative of the effects of Israel's actions on the position of the Jews in South Africa. Before the year 1961 was out, the Jewish community was caught up in another public relations predicament. A newspaper scoop brought to light the contents of a private letter from Prime Minister Verwoerd in reply to a Jewish citizen, one S. A. East. The latter had presumptuously seen fit to express to the prime minister his regret at Israel's behavior and his identification with South Africa's hurt. The prime minister's reply contained what appeared to many as threatening innuendos. In a tone uncomfortably reminiscent of National Party statements in the antisemitic era of the 1930s and 1940s, it described the attitude taken up by Israel in the United Nations Assembly as "a tragedy" for Jewry in South Africa, implying that it might provoke local antisemitism. Verwoerd's letter left little doubt as to what he expected the Jews to do: "Fortunately the reaction of many Jews and Jewish organizations in South Africa was such," he commented, "that what might have been worse was relieved to a certain extent by this pro–South African reaction." These remarks in themselves were sufficiently disturbing to Jews. But Verwoerd's letter contained yet a further comment: "The fact that during the last election so many Jews had favoured the Progressive Party and so few the Nationalist Party, did not pass unnoticed." This smacked of intimidation.[94]

Verwoerd's letter to East dominated press editorials and letters to the editor in both English and Afrikaans newspapers throughout the country. The Afrikaans press was resentful of Israel, whose actions were regarded as a stab in the back. *Die Burger* commented that every South African nationalist wondered why "some South African Jews do not find it irreconcilable to combine a passionate survival politics in Israel with an enthusiastic capitulation politics for the Whites in South Africa." By contrast, the English-language press censured Verwoerd's letter as a calculated attempt to hold South African Jews hostage for Israel's behavior and to pressure them into the white South African *laager* (defensive encampment). *The Cape Times* challenged Verwoerd's facile equation of Israel with South African apartheid. It pointed out that Israeli Arabs had the vote just as Jews did, and that in Israel there were no color bars and no signs saying "Whites Only."

As might have been expected, the most resentful criticism of Israel came from a few Jews who actively identified with the National Party. Thus a certain Dr. Sam Fielding wrote a letter to *The Jewish Times,* a copy of which he sent to Dr. Verwoerd, charging that Israel's decision "constituted a total disregard for the important Jewish community of South Africa," which was "obviously expendable" in her eyes. "I for one, and there must be thousands like me," he declared, "must give my first allegiance to South Africa, the country of my birth, the country which gave safe domicile and sustenance to my parents and grandparents, all of whom are buried in this country."[95]

In contrast to these views, Jews and Gentiles of liberal or radical political persuasion were very gratified by Israel's behavior and, if anything, found fault with the leadership of the Jewish community for not applauding Israel. Thus, obviously inspired by some of its Jewish members, the militantly antiapartheid Congress of Democrats sent the Board of Deputies a memorandum expressing shock at what it considered that body's shameful behavior. It argued that the Board had contradicted its own constant protestations of noninterference in any matters of a political nature. "Our objection in this instance," it stated accusingly, "is not to the political involvement of the Board, but to its involvement on the wrong side, on the side of the advocates of racialism." The memorandum went on to warn that "the fund of [black] goodwill" that had accrued thanks to the part Jews were playing in "denouncing and fighting against apartheid" was at risk. Because the black majority inevitably would constitute the future nonracial government, reasoned the memorandum, the Board was well advised to reevaluate its attitude lest blacks "come to feel that the Board constitutes an antagonistic force."[96]

The public controversy over Dr. Verwoerd's ill-starred letter to Mr. East was certainly not doing any good for South Africa's already tarnished international image. As one Afrikaner newspaper editor pointed out: "Whatever the case may be, the Afrikaner cannot afford any enmity towards the Jews as a group. Further isolation is out of the question."[97] Nonetheless, when Israel's support of the abortive UN sanctions vote in November 1961 made it clear that Israel was going the whole hog with its assault on apartheid, the South African government decided to react. It chose to exert counterpressure on Israel via the Jewish community by withdrawing permission to transfer gift funds raised in South Africa for the Jewish Agency in Israel.[98]

Reporting to the honorary officers of the Zionist Federation, chairman Edel Horwitz said "this was the most severe blow which had befallen the Zionist movement in this country in the sixty years of its existence."[99] There was uncertainty as to how the community would react to the news that funds raised could no longer reach their destination. It was feared that contributions would drop drastically and that consequently the whole edifice of Zionism might collapse. When an anxious appeal was made to Minister of Finance Dr. Dönges, he commented sternly that after South Africa had gone to great lengths to be helpful to Israel, Israel had now "slapped South Africa in the face and ganged up with her enemies." He asked the delegation to imagine the South African public's reaction were the government to continue giving Israel privileges not granted to any other country. "This would have resulted in a wave of anti-Semitism," he suggested, adding, "which the Government did not want." Dönges did, however, hint that he would be happy to see the deputation again "if circumstances changed."[100] The intimation was clear—South African Jewry was expected to influence Israel to change its policy.

Since Israel continued to vote with the Afro-Asian bloc against South Africa, the repercussions upon South African Jewry were exacerbated. *Die Transvaler*, for example, said that the hostile behavior of Israel toward South Africa destroyed whatever compatibility had ever existed between the dual loyalties of the Jews in South Africa. "The Jews will thus now have to choose where they stand . . . with South Africa or with Israel. It can no longer be with both."[101] By late 1963 the South African Ministry of Foreign Affairs was deliberating over the question how to react to Israel's behavior. Since South Africa had never taken up reciprocal diplomatic representation in Israel, all it could do by way of punitive action was to expel Israel's delegation. But this would only add to South Africa's isolation. The prevailing perception was that the sole consideration now keeping Israel from withdrawing its legation was its link with the Jewish community. Taking its cue from a statement by Verwoerd in a speech made in the town of Roodepoort—"Ons gaan Israel nie help uit sy dilemma nie. Hy moet self besluit" (We shall not help Israel out of her dilemma. She must decide for herself)—the decision was not to give Israel the excuse it probably wanted in order to tell the Jews that it had no choice but to sever relations.[102]

Meanwhile, Israel was already reducing its diplomatic representation. In September 1963 it recalled Minister Plenipotentiary Simha Pratt, ostensibly for diplomatic reassignment elsewhere. In fact, as became quite obvious when he was replaced merely by a chargé d'affaires, this was a step in the downgrading of Israel's diplomatic relationship with South Africa. When Pratt made courteous parting visits to the prime minister and to the foreign minister he was received with bitterness. Verwoerd charged that Israel was "hypocritical" because Israel too refused to be a minority in an Arab sea. Louw even complained about the high percentage of Jews in the treasonable underground movements.[103] The cycle of indignant newspaper articles repeated itself. *Die Vaderland* was scornful of Israel's shortsightedness. It said Israel was bartering the goodwill of South Africa "together with our Jewish citizens who have contributed so enormously toward the upbuilding of the national home." But it was a dangerous bargain because the African states were bound to turn their backs on Israel sooner or later. *Die Burger*, reasoning in similar fashion, wrote: "For South Africa it is a bitter and tragic thing, this hostility of a predestined friend."[104]

This was the context in which the lay and religious leaders of the Jewish community continued to tread a precarious path in the 1960s. Their response to the crisis in Israel–South Africa relations was highly ambivalent. On the one hand they were disappointed, even offended, by the extremes to which Israel had gone in voting against South Africa. On the other hand many of them had unclear consciences on the substantive issue of South African apartheid, and they resented the tendency of progovernment South Africans to make them answerable for Israel's actions. Indeed, the conundrum of Israel–South Africa relations overshadowed even the grave dilemma of conscience over the Jewish community's compliance with apartheid itself. A series of policy and information guidelines was prepared by the Zionist Federation's general-secretary, Zvi Infeld, to equip Zionist workers with answers to the many embarrassing questions of a disconcerted Jewish public. The list of questions that formed the basis for the enlightenment program vividly mirrored the bewildered state of the Jewish public. It included the following:

> Why do we support Israel, which is the enemy of South Africa? Why give to Zionist funds when you can't get the money out? Is aliya not desertion of South Africa? How can people leave when South Africa is in danger, or alternatively, is it not our duty to stay and try to change conditions here? Israel does not care about us. She treats us as if we were dispensable. Therefore why should we care for Israel?[105]

Although the communal leadership contended publicly that South African Jewry had neither the right nor the ability to influence the foreign policy of Israel, delegations of the Zionist Federation visited Israel a number of times in order to meet government ministers and Foreign Ministry officials. In these discussions, the South Africans did not hide their anxiety over the deterioration of relations between Israel and their country. However, they refrained from entering into any discussion on the substantive issues involved: they neither contested Israel's foreign policy in Africa nor defended South Africa's internal policies.[106] After all, as avid Zionists, they shared Ben-Gurion's view that the fate of Jews everywhere depended upon the safety of Israel. "South African Jewry did not ask that its interests be put before those of Israel," a delegation stated in November 1963 at a meeting in Prime Minister Levi Eshkol's office, "but the question was being asked why Israel always had to be at the head of the queue in taking measures against South Africa." The delegation cautioned that if there were a continuation of unnecessary "pinpricks," South African Jewry "might be split into two sections, pro and against Israel, "and the Zionist movement might "grind to a halt." On one question only did they adopt a demanding tone. This was in response to Foreign Minister Golda Meir's intention to stop El Al airline's flights to Johannesburg in anticipation of Kenya's independence in December 1963. Arguing that Kenya's leaders would not permit landing rights in Nairobi for South Africa–bound flights, she asked why Israel should wait until it was ignominiously ordered off the Nairobi airport. This shocked the South African Jewish leaders into an irate response. They declared that it would be unforgivable if Israel were of its own accord to cut the lifeline of South African Jewry with Israel. Golda Meir relented and, as it happened, independent Kenya continued to permit landing rights for El Al.[107]

There was, to be sure, one important section of the South African Jewish community that would have preferred a more demanding posture vis-à-vis Israel—the Revisionist Zionist Party, whose foremost spokesman was Harry Hurwitz, general-secretary of the party and editor of *The Jewish Herald*. The Revisionists by no means endorsed apartheid, but they were critical of the lengths to which the Israeli government was going to toe the African line against South Africa. In Harry Hurwitz's view, Israel's policy was "unwarranted, unjustified and politically unrealistic." He gravely doubted the durability of African friendship for Israel. "Far too much stress is being placed on this mythical friendship," he wrote in October 1961. It did not seem to him wise that Israel should sacrifice the friendship of white South Africa for such doubtful gains.[108]

It is not unlikely that the Revisionist position came closest to representing the majority view among Jews. That there was a general atmosphere of embarrassment and discomposure among Jews is beyond doubt; that many Jews harbored resentment against Israel is also evident from the nature of the questions with which, as we have noted, the leadership had to contend. Yet very few Jews reacted by dissociating themselves from Zionist work of any kind. Only some 20 individuals out of nearly 17,000 contributors canceled their bank orders in explicit protest against Israel's actions. To be sure, by 1966 the number of contributors had dropped to about 12,600 and it had become difficult to persuade these to increase their contributions, but the cause was the knowledge that funds could not be transferred to Israel, rather than punishment of Israel.[109]

In sum, throughout the Verwoerd era—the peak years of apartheid implementation and legislative suppression—the issue of Israel's condemnations of apartheid compounded and, indeed, overshadowed the acute dilemmas of the Jewish leadership over the Jewish attitude to the apartheid order itself. However, these gravely trying times were to pass within a few years as the tide turned against Israel's relations with the states of Africa. The Six Day War of 1967 was the turning point in restoring normalcy for South African Jewry. Notwithstanding the strains in South Africa's relations with Israel, when Egypt's Abdel Nasser peremptorily ordered the compliant United Nations out of the Gaza Strip, moved his army into Sinai, and blockaded Eilat, a wave of public sympathy for Israel swept over white South Africa. Almost the entire South African press identified with what was perceived as a small country around whose neck a noose was being tightened by surrounding Arab states, while the United States and other Western powers, supposedly committed to Israel's security, equivocated. This was followed by wonderment and admiration as news came through of Israel's dramatic preemptive strike and decisive victory in the six days of battle that ensued.[110] Stirred to its core, first by deep anxiety harking back to the Holocaust era and then by relief and euphoria at Israel's victory, the Jewish community plunged into a massive effort to raise funds for the emergency needs of Israel in the wake of the war.

Encouraged by the positive press reaction, the leadership of the Jewish community decided to make a direct request to the government to waive its ban on the transfer of funds to Israel. To their great relief, Balthazar J. Vorster, who had become prime minister after Dr. Verwoerd's assassination in 1966, gave his agreement as a gesture of goodwill.[111]

CHAPTER 2

The Political Behavior of Jews

Jews in the Political System

As is evident from the events and issues discussed in the previous chapter, pro-government circles in general and the Afrikaans press in particular tended to relegate the Jews to the liberal pole of the white political spectrum, a position that was regarded as inimical to legitimate Afrikaner aspirations and the apartheid program, aimed at ensuring continued white supremacy. This in itself may be taken to attest to the fact that as a rule the minority Jewish sector of the white public was certainly more liberal than the Afrikaner sector. But were Jews in fact more liberal than other whites or, more pertinently put, than other English-speaking whites? This question is difficult to answer definitively on the strength of historical sources alone. Apposite sociological research conducted during the apartheid era does, however, cast some light on the general question whether the attitudes of Jews toward the nonwhites of South Africa differed from those of other whites. In 1959 Henry Lever, a sociologist at the University of the Witwatersrand, undertook a study into the "ethnic attitudes" of a sample of white high school children in Johannesburg.[1] Lever used a version of the Bogardus Social Distance Test requiring the respondents to indicate their first-feeling reactions toward the members of nine ethnic groups, including the three nonwhite groups—coloreds, Indians, and blacks. On the one hand, the study showed clearly the acculturating influence of the South African environment on the ethnic attitudes of Jewish youth, since they followed the characteristic pattern of South African whites, whether English- or Afrikaans-speaking, in assigning blacks to a relatively low position in the hierarchy of ethnic preferences. On the other hand, relative to other whites, Lever did find a significant difference. His conclusion was: "Jews are more favourably disposed towards Natives [Africans], Coloureds and Indians than are the members of any other White group. Jews were found to be consistently more tolerant than any other group in their attitudes to non-Whites." In the light of the first part of the finding, namely, the fact that the Jewish respondents also rated all the nonwhite groups low on the scale, perhaps it might more aptly be stated that Jews were found to be less intolerant than other whites in their attitudes to nonwhites. Another sociological study of

Johannesburg Jews, conducted by Dr. Allie Dubb in the late 1960s, found that the respondents considered themselves to be more tolerant than Gentiles toward the nonwhites. But Dubb found it noteworthy that "in the attitude scale, this tolerance was reflected in responses to items referring to so-called petty apartheid whereas items expressing more general political policies aroused a considerably less negative reaction."[2]

Findings such as these do not in themselves justify ascription of liberal political views to South African Jews in general.[3] Nor does it necessarily follow that ethnic attitudes were major determinants of political choice in elections. Some empirical studies conducted in the late 1960s and early 1970s indicated that the political preferences of Jews in South Africa tended to be much the same as those of English-speaking Gentiles of the same socioeconomic status. Factors such as the family income and level of education of Jews appeared to be more important determinants of political preference than the quality of their Jewishness.[4]

One specific, if limited, indicator of Jewish political preferences may be found in an examination of the party allegiance of Jewish candidates for election. It reveals that throughout the two decades following the 1948 elections the majority of candidates for the parliamentary House of Assembly, almost all successfully elected, belonged to the United Party. In the 1948 elections two Jews, and in 1953 one, still gained seats for the Labor Party in addition to seven and six respectively for the United Party. Thereafter the Labor Party faded out of the electoral scene, and in 1958 all five of the Jews elected to the House of Assembly were of the United Party. However, when the more liberal wing of the United Party split in 1959 to form the Progressive Party, two of the five Jews in the Assembly became Progressives. One of these, Helen Suzman, was reelected in 1961 and remained the sole Progressive member of the House of Assembly for the next three sessions of parliament, alongside five, two, and three Jewish United Party members elected in 1961, 1966, and 1970 respectively. In the elections to the provincial councils the affinity to the United Party of Jews seeking political office was even more observable. Until 1954 there were still a few Labor members of provincial councils who were Jewish. Thereafter, almost all the Jews successfully elected were of the United Party.[5] The pattern was similar in municipal elections but the party allegiance of candidates was more complex, since many stood as independents or as members of citizens' groups and ratepayers' associations.[6]

While these data clearly indicate that the United Party provided the most congenial home for Jewish political aspirants, this does not, of course, necessarily establish that the Jewish public actually voted for that party rather than for the Liberal or National or Progressive Parties. In this respect one may no more than infer that such was the tendency on the basis of the record in a number of specific constituencies known to have a high proportion of Jewish voters. In the 1958 elections, for example, a well-known local Jewish personality, Gerald Gordon, stood for the Liberal Party in the heavily Jewish constituency of Sea Point, Cape Town. But his gentile opponent, Japie Basson of the United Party, was elected with a resounding majority.[7] Similarly, a Jewish Liberal, Marion Friedmann, was unsuccessful in the considerably Jewish constituency of Houghton, Johannesburg.

That attachment to Britain no longer had special significance for Jews was evident when South Africa became a republic in 1961 and left the British Commonwealth. These events aroused no apparent anxiety in South African Jewry. Indeed, not a few Jews recognized them as the satisfaction of legitimate Afrikaner aspirations and felt that they would help to defuse historic intrawhite tensions.[8] Furthermore, by the mid-1960s, a number of knowledgeable commentators noted a rise in the respectability and credibility, if not the support, afforded by Jews to the National Party. As Max Melamet observed in a confidential Cape Board of Deputies memorandum: "There appeared on Nationalist platforms Jews who in 1948 or 1953, or even in 1958 would have shrunk from public acknowledgement of such an association." Likewise, the Jewish journalist Henry Katzew reported in 1965 that there was evidence that the Jews of South Africa were moving politically to the right. "It has sometimes been asked," he noted, "how a National Party candidate would fare in constituencies like Houghton, Orange Grove, or Sea Point. There is only one answer to that. It is that no-one would have put the question ten or fifteen years ago."[9]

Notwithstanding these general impressions, it remained clear throughout the 1950s and 1960s—the heyday of apartheid's entrenchment—that the occasional Jewish candidate who did stand for the National Party managed to gain only the most meager support from fellow Jews. Thus, when M. Levin stood as a nationalist candidate for the Johannesburg municipal council in Berea, a constituency that had a considerable Jewish population, he polled only 267 votes.[10] The only Jew who became a National Party member of parliament in this period was S. Frank, who in 1961 came in unopposed in a remote South-West African constituency, which had no Jewish electorate to speak of. In a few other cases of Jews standing as National Party candidates the upshot was a resounding defeat, irrespective of whether or not their constituencies contained many Jewish voters.[11]

By contrast, when the Progressive Party emerged in 1959 out of the more liberal wing of the United Party, it immediately attracted a considerable segment of Jewish supporters. This was evident not only in the fact, already mentioned, that a number of Jews came forward as Progressive candidates in the succeeding elections, but also in the repeated successes in the Houghton constituency of the most important of apartheid's parliamentary opponents, Helen Suzman. Moreover, where Jewish Progressive Party candidates did suffer defeat in constituencies known to have many Jewish voters, it was by narrow margins.[12] If the United Party still managed to hold its own against Progressives in constituencies with many Jewish voters, this was largely because it too put up Jewish candidates.[13] Yet in the 1970 parliamentary elections pundits could infer from the results in a number of constituencies containing a considerable Jewish electorate that the overwhelming majority of Jews still gave their support to the United Party rather than to the Progressives.[14]

In sum, to the limited extent that it is possible to discern a pattern of Jewish political behavior in the period between 1948 and 1970, it appears to have gravitated around the conservative center of the political spectrum, namely the United Party, with a tendency for a growing segment to move somewhat left of center to a position represented by the new Progressive Party. What did this trend of electoral support mean in terms of specific political advocacy in relation to the society and polity of South Africa? It must be noted that the United Party, although enjoying mixed English-speaking and Afrikaans-speaking support, was quite as committed to white supremacy as were the Afrikaner nationalists. At best, it tried—to no great effect—to counter the ideological dogmatism of apartheid with pragmatic adjustments "based on common sense and tolerance rather than ideological orthodoxy." Its vague mantras of "white leadership with justice," "enlightened leadership and guidance of the white group in the interests of all races," and a "race federation" translated into not much more than superficial modifications of the pre-1948 pattern of race relations. These were to include increased but still exclusively white representation of blacks in the all-white parliament; review of laws that discriminated with unnecessary offensiveness; and encouraging the growth of a "stable and responsible middle-class among the settled urban Black population," who should have freehold title to their homes in the black townships.[15]

Supporters of the Progressive Party (and its later incarnations as the Progressive Reform Party, thereafter the Progressive Federal Party) were expressing far stronger opposition to racial discrimination and willingness to progress, albeit in controlled stages, toward an ultimately nonracial, democratic dispensation. The Progressives promised to end the notorious pass laws and population influx controls, which destroyed family life, restricted the freedom of movement of blacks, and rendered them incapable of improving their economic position. Arguing that social relationships should not be regulated by laws but rather be left to conventions of society and the attitudes of individuals, the Progressives opposed compulsory segregation and called for repeal of the Prohibition of Mixed Marriages Act and Section 16 of the so-called Immorality Act, which made sex relations between whites and blacks a criminal offense. After the dissolution of the small Liberal Party in 1968 its adherents had no legally sanctioned alternative for exercising their vote other than casting it for the Progressive Party. This meant sliding back to the initial advocacy of a qualified franchise (on the basis of educational and economic criteria) rather than the universal franchise, which the Liberal Party had come to advocate by 1960. (It was not until about 1978 that the Progressives' program implied universal suffrage.) The Progressives were at pains to deny that the qualified franchise was merely a mechanism to perpetuate white political control. They claimed that their policy would ensure all people the opportunity to obtain the qualifications for the franchise, since it would provide free and compulsory education for children of all races up to the end of primary school at least, and remove all restrictions on earning capacity.[16]

These then were the respective policy preferences that the majority of Jews supported insofar as they were still voting for the United Party but beginning to veer more toward the Progressive Party by the 1970s. At the same time there appeared to be a grain of truth in the then current cynical quip that most Jews spoke like Progressives, voted for the United Party, and hoped that the National Party would remain in power.

So much for participation of Jews in conventional white South African politics and what can be surmised concerning the voting preferences of Jews. Turning now to the forces, legal and extralegal, that constituted the vanguard of opposition to apartheid on the part of whites, one cannot but be struck by the extraordinary salience of Jews. Two women, Ellen Hellmann and Helen Suzman, exemplified above all other persons the prominent involvement of Jews in the liberal opposition to apartheid, which functioned within the bounds of constitutional legality as laid down by white South Africans.

Dr. Ellen Hellmann, née Kaumheimer, was born in Johannesburg to Jewish parents who had come from Germany. She obtained her doctorate in social anthropology at the University of the Witwatersrand, specializing in research on the urban African. This led her into expanding social and political concern within the framework of the Institute of Race Relations. She served as its president in 1954–55 and took a leading part in numerous liberal activities such as the Johannesburg Citizens' Native Housing Committee, the board of management of a crèche in Soweto sponsored by the Union of Jewish Women, trusteeship of the defense fund in aid of the defendants in the great Treason Trial of the late 1950s, which will be discussed shortly, and the similar Defense and Aid Fund Committee in the mid-1960s. Politically, she associated herself mainly with the Progressive Party, serving on its executive committee in the 1960s and also standing for election to the Johannesburg City Council on that party's ticket in 1962. In all, Ellen Hellmann became one of the most prominent and academically authoritative liberal critics of South Africa's system of race relations. In the retrospective typological spectrum of the so-called "liberation struggle" she exemplifies those who worked primarily through the nonparty Institute of Race Relations, rather than through multiracial political agitation, and who have consequently been described by some observers as "social liberals."[17]

Helen Suzman, more than any other political personality, epitomized the white liberal opposition to the apartheid regime as much in the eyes of the world as in those of South Africans. She is undoubtedly the foremost exemplar of those who worked within the system and used it to attack apartheid intrepidly and relentlessly. In 1953 Suzman commenced her parliamentary career—thirty-six years in duration—as the successful United Party candidate for the Houghton constituency in Johannesburg. But before long she came to the conclusion that the United Party was too equivocal and ineffectual an opposition instrument in the face of Afrikaner nationalism's unshakable determination to institutionalize and fortify white racial domination. In 1959 she was part of the group that split to form the Progressive Party. However, the new party made precious little headway within the white electorate. For thirteen years, from 1961 to 1974, Helen Suzman was its sole member of parliament. In that solitary role she courageously battled each and every apartheid measure, often enduring not only general calumny but also anti-semitic taunts from the government benches. Yet occasionally there were also grudging acknowledgments of her political integrity and courage. Her parliamentary speeches were informed by a rationally articulated humanism. They were models of nondemagogic delivery, finely researched data, and sound reasoning.[18]

Although holding fast to her ideological convictions as a political liberal, Suzman also played a key role in rendering every form of legal, material, and moral succor to radicals who fell foul of the apartheid state's laws, whether the accused in the great Treason Trial or political prisoners such as Nelson Mandela and his comrades after they were incarcerated on Robben Island, off Cape Town. She retired from her parliamentary career in 1989, shortly before the great transformation of the South African political system, the essentials of which she had consistently and courageously advocated for so many years.

The forms of white opposition to apartheid that remained within the confines of formal legality ranged on a spectrum that included the work of the Institute of Race Relations, which conducted research and acted as a pressure group on the government; the Black Sash movement,[19] which mobilized women for protest and social action; the Christian Institute, an ecumenical organization founded in 1963 for promoting dialogue; the Liberal Party that existed from 1953 to 1968; and the Progressive Party, which at first coexisted with the Liberal Party and afterward succeeded it, in a sense by default. All these organizations were composed essentially of an English-speaking membership led by major public figures such as Alan Paton, or Margaret Ballinger and Patrick Duncan of the Liberal Party, or "renegade" Afrikaners such as Beyers Naudé of the Christian Institute. The role of Jewish individuals should not be exaggerated, although they certainly were involved in numbers disproportionate to the size of the Jewish population, and prominent almost emblematically Jewish assailants of apartheid such as the Liberal Party's Leslie Rubin or the Progressive Party's Helen Suzman were perceived in the Afrikaans press as thorns in the side of the positive forces upholding white supremacy.[20]

But this irritant was as naught compared with the glaring prominence of Jewish names in the radical opposition. Throughout the first two decades of National Party rule, Jewish names kept appearing in every facet of the struggle: in the lists of "named" communists and of persons banned from all public activity, detained without trial, or placed under house arrest; in the courts, whether as defendants or as counsel for the defense; and among those who fled the country to evade arrest or unbearable harassment. The public prominence of Jewish names was particularly marked in the course of the epic Treason Trial, which captured the attention of the news media throughout the second half of the 1950s. In a concerted effort to crush the antiapartheid resistance the police had dramatically swooped down upon well over a hundred suspects. When the trial opened in December 1956, 156 people belonging to all apartheid-defined racial groups were charged with treason in the form of a conspiracy to overthrow the state by violence in order to replace it with a state based on communism. The accused were mostly blacks, numbering 105, but there were also 21 Indians, 7 coloreds, and 23 whites. It was a glaring fact that more than half of the whites were Jews. They were Yetta Barenblatt, Hymie Barsel, Lionel (Rusty) Bernstein, Leon Levy, Norman Levy, Sydney Shall, Joe Slovo, Ruth (First) Slovo, Sonia Bunting, Lionel Forman, Isaac Horvitch, Ben Turok, Jacqueline Arenstein, and Ronald Press.[21] All had been associated with the Communist Party of South Africa at some time before it was banned in 1950, and some were in the clandestine reconstituted party (formed in 1953 and renamed the South African Communist Party). Most were overtly active in the South African Congress of Democrats and in other organizations associated with opposition to the apartheid regime such as the Society for Peace and Friendship with the Soviet Union and the Federation of South African Women.

The conspicuous disproportion of Jewish names in the list of accused was compounded by the prominence of Jews in the defendants' legal counsel. In the initial preparatory examination stage, the defense counsel included Maurice Franks and Norman Rosenberg. Jews were also prominent in the main fund-raising support effort within South Africa in behalf of the accused—the Treason Trial Defense Fund. Alongside author Alan Paton and Anglican bishop of Johannesburg Ambrose Reeves, seven of its initial twenty-two sponsors were Jews, as were also two of its four trustees—Dr. Ellen Hellmann and Alex Hepple. The trial was of unprecedented duration, the state repeatedly failing to establish its case, consequently dropping charges against more and more of the accused, and ultimately changing the indictment against the remainder. By August 1958 charges had been dropped against all but 92 of the accused. With (from the Jewish point of view) a twist of irony, however unintended, the trial was then resumed in a building known as "The Old Synagogue" of Pretoria, a synagogue that had fallen into disuse and been purchased from the local Jewish community in 1952.

To top it all, at the most critical stage in the trial the defense counsel was led by a prominent personality in the Jewish community, Israel Maisels, assisted by Sydney Kentridge (son of the notable parliamentarian and Jewish communal leader Morris Kentridge), while the prosecutor was none other than the former Nuwe Orde (New Order) leader Oswald Pirow. The juxtaposition was striking, and quite invidious from the vantage point of the Jewish community's public relations work: Maisels, the Jew, a prominent leader in both the Jewish Board of Deputies and the Zionist Federation, defending those accused of seeking to overthrow white supremacy; Pirow, the extreme Afrikaner nationalist and former assertive pro-Nazi, defending white supremacy. All in all the trial dragged on for four years and four months. In March 1961 the prosecution finally gave in, and all the remaining accused were released. It was a testimonial to the residual power of the formal rule of law, notwithstanding the fundamentally defective "democratic" polity of South Africa. As such, it was a most frustrating defeat for the governmental apostles of apartheid, who redoubled their efforts to legislate away such legal obstacles as far as was possible by deploying their parliamentary majority.

Prominence of Jewish names continued to glare in periodically issued government gazettes listing persons banned or restricted in various ways for falling foul of the increasingly sweeping repressive legislation. Sensitive to the implications for the public image of the Jewish community, the Board of Deputies monitored and filed such lists as they appeared in official gazettes and the press. One example is a particularly comprehensive list issued in November 1962, containing 437 names of persons who were suspected of being former officeholders, members, or active supporters of the banned Communist Party. According to a Board of Deputies memorandum, gauging by names alone at least 62 of the 132 whites listed were Jews. A later gazette dated 25 August 1967 listed persons (all white) who had been officeholders, members, or active supporters of the banned Congress of Democrats. Of the 37 names listed, 18 were identifiably Jewish.[22]

In terms of the Jewish community's image in the public eye, the exact numbers of Jews in such lists were really immaterial; what counted was the unmistakable impression that Jews were inordinately prominent in the ranks of those who were attempting to subvert the state. Indeed, the public image (and especially the image prevalent in security police ranks) associating Jews with antiapartheid agitation was so strong that gentile communists and liberals were often mistakenly identified as Jews.[23] Not surprisingly, a widespread Afrikaner public reaction ensued. The old charge, dating back at least to the 1930s, that Jews were unsympathetic to the Afrikaners' legitimate political aspirations was, as we have seen, still prevalent. Since, in Afrikaner eyes, the policy of apartheid was absolutely intrinsic to these aspirations, opposition to apartheid was ipso facto perceived as opposition to the Afrikaner national movement. As one letter to the editor of an Afrikaans newspaper expressed it:

> That the support of the Jews is readily granted to the powers which aim at the downfall of the Boer must be deduced from the behaviour of the Jews. When photographs appear in newspapers of resistance processions, or of joint singing and dancing with the "Africans," or of the "Black Sash"'s slander tableaux, the Jewish facial type is in the majority. When a book is published on the "bad conditions" in South Africa, the writer is ten to one a Jew. Under petitions protesting against the Boer's policy there always appear numbers of Jewish names. Jewish professors, lecturers, doctors, rabbis and lawyers fall over one another in order to be able to sign. Behind tables in the street collecting signatures against the Boer's policy a Jewish lady is usually enthroned. . . . The patience of the Boer must one day become exhausted.[24]

Throughout the first two decades of National Party rule the Afrikaans press bristled with ominous observations in this vein. In the 1950s even the identification of most Jews with the United Party was criticized, it being charged that Jews constituted the left wing, which sought to dominate the party. "It is interesting to note the list of names which indicates by whom the United Party is now actually represented in the Transvaal," commented the influential political columnist Neels Natte in August 1954, and he went on to enumerate the high proportion of "foreign" names in the "liberalistic left-wing" of the United Party: Woolf, Miller, Bielski, Weiss, Nestadt, Einstein, Emdin, Taurog, Kowarsky, Myer, Eppel, Fisher, and Sive. "Almost all of them [the Jews] make their political home in those parties which lean to the left," noted a typical letter writer to the editor of *Die Transvaler*, "the hearts of very few of them are with us. They themselves are the most exclusive apartheid people, yet they exert themselves here for integration." Another letter to the editor asked, "What would they say and do if it were Afrikaners who acted as saboteurs and inciters in Israel." Yet another correspondent wrote:

> We as Afrikaners would very much like to learn why the Jews work so conspicuously in every sphere against the government's apartheid policy, because their names appear most prominently as advocates for all agitation movements. . . . What do they aim at with their liberalistic policy of mingling between white and non-white? . . .

> Our Jewish friends work against apartheid in every field by indecent commiseration with the native, encouragement of intermingling, support of integration and advocacy of social leveling in city councils and Parliament. We see this everywhere in their dwellings and private cars, in which they do not scruple to travel together [with nonwhites]. . . . Why has not one of the leaders of the Jewish community yet openly stepped into the breach in support of the government's apartheid policy? We wish to bring to our Jewish friends' attention that these actions will not be observed without consequences by South Africans as a whole.[25]

Insinuations that the Jews were responsible for liberal trouble mongering and warnings of punitive consequences were not limited to letters in the progovernment press. Also parliament was not exempt from occasional outbursts in like vein directed against Jewish members such as Boris Wilson or Helen Suzman.[26] Also important Afrikaner personages periodically added fuel to the fire. Dr. C. F. Albertyn, at the time general manager of the powerful Afrikaans publishing company Nasionale Pers, for example, bluntly warned the Jews that "incitement of the Native against the White man endangered the future of the whole of Jewry in South Africa. The Afrikaner had to live or die in South Africa and would relentlessly eradicate everything and everyone who endangered his existence as a people before he himself went under."[27]

Replies by individual Jews or by the Jewish Board of Deputies, laboriously reiterating that "Jews do, in fact, belong to all parties," that "the Jewish community as a community does not and cannot adopt any political line," and that it was wrong to confuse "some" Jews with "all" Jews, were rather futile.[28] Nor were the critics satisfied by the policy of political noninvolvement, which, as we have seen in the previous chapter, was painstakingly enunciated by the Board of Deputies. Its much vaunted neutrality was mistrusted. Thus one commentator complained that Jewish publications meticulously avoided anything that had any semblance of approval of the government's policy. He was disturbed by their tone of "ice-cold neutrality" and by the deliberate manner in which their own people ignored the few pronationalist Jews. (The reference was to the like of Joseph Nossel in the Cape and Mendel Levin in the Transvaal.) "They are black sheep who are ostracized lest they give offence to the left-inclined flag wavers," he noted bitterly. "I am afraid," he concluded, "that the Afrikaner cannot rely on the good disposition of the Jews as a *volksgroep* [ethnic-national group] apart from a few exceptions amongst the *platteland* [rural] Jews."[29]

The undercurrent of distrust became increasingly ominous as the sorely battered opposition forces in South Africa retreated into underground activities and resorted to the use of violence. The turning point was the tragic Sharpeville massacre in March 1960. Police, faced with a menacing but unarmed crowd of antipass campaigners of the Pan-Africanist Congress, panicked and opened fire, killing sixty-nine people, many of them shot in the back. In the wake of Sharpeville the government declared a drastic state of emergency, banned public meetings, outlawed the African political organizations, and arrested hundreds of people.

In response to this near total suppression of nonviolent opposition, three main underground liberation organizations came into existence in the early 1960s. The major organization, Umkhonto we Sizwe [The Spear of the Nation] was an offshoot of the African National Congress in cooperation with the underground Communist Party. Another, Poqo ["pure" or "alone"], was founded at about the same time by members of the Pan-Africanist Congress. The third, the African Resistance Movement (ARM), was an amalgamation of some small incipient noncommunist groups—the National Committee for Liberation, the African Freedom Movement, and the Socialist League. Although aspiring to be multiracial in membership, the ARM consisted almost entirely of whites, both leftist radicals and liberals, many of them young students, who had despaired of the legal opposition's efficacy. During a three-year period beginning in December 1961, there was a wave of over two hundred separate acts of sabotage in South Africa. Most of these were targeted at communications, electrical power lines, and government offices, with the intention of undermining public order as a strategic prelude to anticipated eruption of guerrilla warfare, popular uprising, and the ultimate overthrow of white supremacy.

The government reacted to these acts of sabotage with emergency legislation and police measures of an even more drastic nature. It intensified bannings, prohibitions, and detentions of all kinds. As has been described earlier, particularly draconian was the "ninety-day clause" enacted in 1963, which provided for a period of ninety days during which any person could be held under arrest without the need of a warrant and without any recourse to the courts. By 1965, the state had successfully repressed all underground opposition. Many of its members had fled the country; others had been arrested, tried, and sentenced, and various forms of detention and banning neutralized yet others. Even the Liberal Party—which was multiracial and, since 1960, advocated universal suffrage but operated only within the limits of that which was deemed legal by the system—was constrained to disband in 1968 when faced by new legislation making any interracial political activity illegal.[30] The rump of the organized liberal opposition was made up of the small, wholly white Progressive Party and a few nonparty political institutions such as the Institute of Race Relations and the Christian Institute. White supremacy was, if anything, more entrenched and fortified than ever.

In this approximately five-year period between the emergence of violent opposition and its effective suppression, the prominent involvement of individual Jews was in the public eye even more than before. This was never more glaring than in the dramatic circumstances of the "Rivonia arrests." On 11 July 1963 the police raided the home of Arthur Goldreich at Lilliesleaf farm in Rivonia, near Johannesburg, where it captured the leadership cadre of the Umkhonto we Sizwe underground, apparently no less to its own surprise than to that of its captives. Seventeen people were arrested, including Walter Sisulu and Ahmed Kathrada, leaders respectively of the banned African National and Indian National Congresses, both in hiding from the police. Five of those arrested were whites, all of them Jews. They were Arthur Goldreich, Lionel Bernstein, Hilliard Festenstein, Denis Goldberg, and Bob Hepple.[31] At this time Umkhonto's major leader, Nelson Mandela, had already been arrested and was being held in jail. Those arrested in Rivonia together with Mandela and other white and black prisoners were charged with high treason and faced a possible death sentence in what became known as "the Rivonia Trial" of 1963–64. One of the white underground members arrested separately and included among the accused was another Jew, Harold Wolpe. Not having been present at Rivonia when the arrests were made, he had attempted flight from the country but was intercepted by the police. In the dock Mandela made his now famous indictment of the apartheid regime, and argued that it had outlawed every form of peaceful opposition, leaving its victims no alternative other than violent resistance. In the outcome, Mandela and seven of the accused were found guilty of sabotage, rather than high treason, and sentenced to life imprisonment. Mandela and the other black condemned were taken to Robben Island prison, where he was to be incarcerated for twenty-seven years.

A poignant twist was added to the public image projected by the trial when press reportage highlighted the role of the public prosecutor, deputy attorney general of Transvaal Province Dr. Percy Yutar. Yutar was an orthodox observant Jew, well known and respected within the Jewish community. He had served inter alia in the important position of president of the United Hebrew Congregation of Johannesburg and on the council of the United Hebrew Schools. At one level, the trial's proceedings highlighted the strikingly disproportionate role of Jews in subversion of white Afrikaner domination and apartheid. By contrast, at another level and with a twist of historical irony, the legal counsel engaged in the trial pitted the demonstratively patriotic Jewish prosecutor, Yutar, against a defense team headed by Abram (Bram) Fischer, scion of a famous Afrikaner family, grandson of a Boer prime minister of the Orange River Colony, and son of a judge-president of the Orange Free State supreme court. It was only a few years later that Fischer's secret identity as leader of the underground Communist Party came to light. While the role played by Yutar in a sense offset the prominence of so many Jews among those accused, it did not efface the overwhelming impression that Jews were in the forefront of the white radicals who were trying to overthrow the system of white supremacy in South Africa.

By all accounts, Percy Yutar's conduct of the prosecution in the Rivonia Trial was demonstratively zealous. But his overall comportment in the public service exemplified the conformity not only to law and order but also to South African racial mores that was the norm in the Jewish community. Born in 1917 in Cape Town to rather poor Litvak immigrant parents, he graduated in law on a scholarship at the University of Cape Town in 1933, and went on to gain academic distinction by gaining a doctorate in law. This made him, as one newspaper article once claimed "far and away the most qualified legal brain this country has ever possessed."[32] He did not, however, go into private practice, having at an early stage formed the aspiration to enter the government Department of Justice. His climb up the professional ladder did not come easily to him, because prejudice against Jews in the government bureaucracy was rife. At first he was able to get no more than a lowly appointment in the Post Office as a clerical assistant tracing defaulting telephone subscribers. It was not until March 1940 that he gained appointment as a fully fledged prosecutor. He was described as a "prosecutor with a mission." It seems that his sense of mission was informed by strong Jewish self-consciousness no less than professional ambition. As he once told a newspaper interviewer: "I am keen to serve the State in one of its most important functions, and the office of Attorney General is a laurel I would very much like to pluck. It has never been held by a Jew, and I feel it would not only be a tribute to me, but to the Jewish community." On this, the interviewer commented admiringly: "Percy meant every word of it. For he is not only a grand lawyer, but a grand Jew."[33] Ironically, this interviewer happened to be Bernard Sachs, brother of banned militant trade unionist Solly Sachs, one of apartheid's most vehement and renowned antagonists. But this was written in 1958, before the Rivonia Trial had badly tarnished Yutar's reputation, at least in the eyes of most liberal-minded Jews, including many of his Jewish colleagues in the legal profession. It was the impression of close observers of the trial that Yutar's zealous comportment seemed to be motivated not solely by professional duty but also by genuine identification with the state's case, abhorrence of the actions of the accused, and, not least of all, by a passionate desire to offset the negative image of Jewish disloyalty to white South Africa.[34]

Of course, Percy Yutar averred that his conscience was clear since he was merely performing his professional duty. As he reiterated upon his retirement from his elevated post as an attorney general in 1976: "I have my conscience to live with. I am an orthodox Jew and view life and my duty in a serious light."[35] Interviewed by journalist and author Glenn Frankel in 1988, Yutar also claimed that by opting to make the charge sabotage rather than high treason, he had with intent saved the accused blacks, including Nelson Mandela, from the death penalty. Instead, they were sentenced to life imprisonment in Robben Island.[36] More likely, the outcome of the trial was influenced by other factors—international pressure and the successful strategy adopted by the defense attorneys who, despite the prosecutor's argument, managed to prove that although Umkhonto's "Operation Mayibuye," involving guerrilla warfare, had been discussed, it had never actually been adopted.

In the Rivonia Trial as in the earlier mammoth Treason Trial and several later political trials, Jews were conspicuous among the young lawyers who selflessly undertook the defense of opponents of the apartheid regime. One of these was the attorney Joel Joffe; another was the barrister Arthur Chaskalson. In contrast to Percy Yutar, they exemplified the liberal conscience of many Jews, especially in the legal profession—Jewish South Africans who were not themselves politically active but found it unconscionable to desist from helping the victims of apartheid and governmental repression of apartheid's opponents. Characteristically, Joffe had not been involved in any political activity but was very sensitive to the evils of the society in which he had grown up, so much so that at the time of the Rivonia arrests he had made up his mind to leave South Africa. In his book *The Rivonia Story* he writes: "Life in South Africa with its injustice, its cruelty, its arbitrary resort to force . . . had become so intolerable to me that I could no longer face the prospect of living in it or of rearing a family in it. I was going to spend the few weeks I had left winding up my legal practice."[37] But when he was approached to act for the defendants by Hilda Bernstein (whose husband Rusty was one of the accused), after she had been turned down by other lawyers too wary to get involved, Joffe's conscience would not allow him to refuse. The same convictions of conscience prompted Arthur Chaskalson to join the defense team. He afterward created a vast legal aid network for victims of apartheid, a subject to which we shall return in a later chapter.

From the Jewish communal point of view, the impact of the Rivonia Trial bears comparison in some respects with the trial of Julius and Ethel Rosenberg in the United States of the early 1950s. The Rosenbergs were charged with conspiracy to commit espionage on behalf of the Soviet Union. There too the trial drama featured Jews on both sides, indeed even more markedly than in the South African Rivonia Trial. Judge Irving Kaufman, who sentenced the Rosenbergs to death, was a Jew, as was the prosecutor Irving Saypol. On the other side, yet another Jew, Emanuel Bloch, who was a known left-winger with a reputation for defending radicals, led the defense. The Rosenberg case had a deleterious effect on the public image of Jews and was an extreme embarrassment to major American Jewish organizations, especially the prestigious American Jewish Committee. It helped to make opposition to communism a normative tenet of the organized Jewish community in the United States.[38] When some Jews tried to save the Rosenbergs by pleading that they were victims of antisemitic vindictiveness, they met with strong opposition from American Jewish organizations. The intimidated comportment of South African Jewry in the wake of the Rivonia Trial's revelations concerning the involvement of Jews in subversion of the [white] state was not unlike that of American Jewish organizations in the McCarthy milieu.

The drama of the Rivonia arrests was exceeded only by its sequel: while awaiting trial in a Johannesburg prison cell, four men made a spectacular escape on 12 August 1963: two whites, Arthur Goldreich and Harold Wolpe (who was linked with the Rivonia conspirators but had been arrested independently), and two Indians, Abdullah Jassat and Mosie Moolla. Something of the characteristically stereotyped security police perception of the white renegades may be gathered from "wanted by the police" posters in some police stations: Goldreich was described as "Blanke man, Jood, 5' 10" . . . kleine neusie vir 'n Jood" (White man, Jew, 5' 10" . . . small nose for a Jew).[39] Notwithstanding an intensive police search, Goldreich and Wolpe managed to hide and make their way to Swaziland disguised as priests, whence collaborators flew them in a light aircraft across South African territory to Bechuanaland. A Dakota aircraft was to be sent from East Africa to take them and other refugees to Dar es Salaam. After one such aircraft was destroyed by fire and another crashed en route to them (apparently the work of South African security agents), on 8 September 1963 a light aircraft was privately chartered to fly Goldreich and Wolpe to Tanganyika whence they left for London. Wolpe settled in London, whereas Goldreich went on to settle in Israel.

If the escape of the four Rivonia Umkhonto captives showed the shortcomings of the police, the relatively easy crushing of the secret African Resistance Movement (ARM) in July 1964 revealed the amateurish secrecy and sabotage attempts of that organization.[40] The primary intention of the ARM's founders was to heighten protest to demonstratively threatening levels, thereby undermining the confidence of the regime and the white public in the possibility of perpetuating the apartheid system. This, they naively assumed, would pave the way to a change of heart and policy. They tried to avoid endangering human lives and limited their sabotage activities to damaging installations such as electric power pylons or railway signal cables. However, when one of their members, acting in unauthorized partisan fashion, planted a bomb in the concourse of the Johannesburg railway station on 24 July 1964, it resulted in the death of an innocent woman bystander and the injury of several others. The white public, of all political shades, was shocked and appalled. The perpetrator, a schoolteacher named John Harris, was arrested, convicted, sentenced to death, and hanged. The evidence brought to light in his trial and amplified in the press implicated several other members or helpers of the ARM, including a few with Jewish names, who had meanwhile managed to escape from the country.

Most of the ARM's founders and members were not Jewish; they included Randolph Vigne, Robert Watson, Edward Daniels (a "colored"), Denis Higgs, and Allan Brooks. However, in the course of police action and ensuing trials during 1964 the names of several Jews were brought to the fore in press reports. Montague (Monty) Berman, an ex-Communist and former executive member of the anti-apartheid Springbok Legion, was identified publicly by security police head, H. J. van den Bergh, as its major founder.[41] Berman and his wife, Myrtle, had by then fled the country after undergoing banning and detention. Bertram (Baruch) Hirson, whose name strikingly highlighted his Jewish identity, featured prominently in press reports of one of the trials. Hirson, at the time a physics lecturer at the University of the Witwatersrand, was an intensely ideological, leftist intellectual who had graduated from the socialist Zionism of the Hashomer Hatza'ir youth movement to cosmopolitan Trotskyism. He stood trial together with other arrested ARM members whose Jewish background was brought to the fore in press reports of the proceedings. One was Raymond Eisenstein. His mother gave evidence in mitigation, emphasizing that he was a child survivor of the Holocaust. He was born in 1936 in Warsaw, witnessed beatings and killings, escaped "selection" for certain death by being hidden in a laundry bag, and in 1943 the family escaped by the skin of their teeth through city sewers. They came to South Africa in 1955. Appealing for clemency, his mother claimed that contrary to the loyal political views of his parents he had been unduly influenced to join the ARM by an older man who had himself fled the country, leaving people like him to take the blame. Eisenstein was found guilty and sentenced to seven years in prison.[42]

Baruch Hirson's prison sentence was nine years. The only person acquitted in this trial was Frederick Prager, fifty-five years old and a photographer by profession, who told the court that he had been a social democrat in Austria before coming to South Africa, where he joined the Liberal Party. He was able to persuade the court that not he but his deceased wife, Rhoda Prager, had been involved in the ARM conspiracy. After his release he was placed under ban until he left the country on an exit permit.[43] In the Cape, among those associated with the ARM who managed get out of the country in time was a notable student leader, Neville Rubin, son of one of the Jewish founders of the Liberal Party, Leslie Rubin. Another was Michael Schneider, a major participant in the movement's sabotage ventures, whose narrow escape from imminent police arrest made dramatic news.[44]

He remained abroad and, turning to Jewish interests, eventually became a leading professional executive of the American Jewish Joint Distribution Committee in New York.

The Jewish personality who featured most sensationally in the media during the trials of the African Resistance Movement was Adrian Leftwich. Leftwich had been a prominent student activist at Cape Town University and served a term as president of the National Union of South African Students (NUSAS). He had joined the Liberal Party and in 1962 was recruited into the incipient National Committee for Liberation. Soon after his arrest and detention , Leftwich broke down under interrogation, turned state witness, and became, in the trials that ensued, the key witness against his own associates, gaining indemnity in return.[45] The Jewish angle of Leftwich's case was heightened when, after his release it was reported that he wished to settle in Israel. Rabbi Cyrus Weiler, founder and former head of the movement of progressive Judaism in South Africa and still its honorary life president, was at the time on a return visit from Israel. He made a rather gratuitous public statement to the effect that in his personal opinion as an Israeli and former Jewish leader in South Africa, Leftwich had no right to seek a home in Israel. Weiler said Israel's Law of Return was meant for those seeking a Jewish haven and for idealists, not for a saboteur turned state's witness: "He should stay in South Africa expiating his sins and leave Israel alone." Weiler's views prompted a flurry of controversy aired in the Jewish and general press, which served to further highlight the prominence of Jews in the radical resistance to the apartheid regime.[46]

The South African security police went on successfully to infiltrate the rump of the underground Communist Party and immobilize it. The main leader now apprehended in September 1964 was none other than the eminent advocate who had led the defense at the Rivonia Trial and scion of distinguished Afrikaner forebears—Bram Fischer. In January 1965 Fischer jumped bail and went into hiding. It took nearly a year until the police recaptured him in November 1965. Meanwhile the trial had proceeded against another thirteen accused persons. The Jewish background of four of them, Eli Weinberg, Esther Barsel, Hymie Barsel, and Norman Levy, was conspicuously highlighted in the press by some of the statements they made from the dock. Latvian-born Eli Weinberg, for example, was reported to have declared in court that having himself experienced racism as a Jew in eastern Europe, where members of his family had been killed in concentration camps, he was opposed to all forms of racism in South Africa. Similarly, Hymie Barsel told the court that he had grown up in a Jewish family deploring all bigotry and racism.[47] Weinberg was sentenced to five years in prison, Levy and Esther Barsel each to three years, and only Hymie Barsel was found not guilty. The extraordinary Afrikaner nemesis of white supremacy, Bram Fischer, was sentenced to life imprisonment and died of cancer in 1975 while still under that sentence.

After a number of other persons had been arrested in the wake of Fischer's capture, it was revealed that they included two Jews, David Ernst and Victor Finkelstein, who were implicated in helping Fischer. Both were former members of the Habonim Zionist youth movement.[48] The Jewish background of Ernst, who was found guilty and sentenced to three years in prison, was particularly conspicuous since he was the son of Sam Ernst, the director of Hebrew education in Natal. Ernst and Finkelstein were imprisoned together with Rowley Israel Arenstein, a high-profile antiapartheid activist. He was an attorney, had been a Communist Party organizer in Durban before 1947, and was active in the Congress of Democrats in the 1950s, but came to adopt a Maoist ideological outlook and was opposed to the Umkhonto founders' resort to the strategy of sabotage. Nonetheless, Arenstein was convicted in 1966 on a charge under the Suppression of Communism Act and jailed for four years, after which he was banned from practicing law and placed under house arrest.

Given the legacy of Afrikaner mistrust of the Jewish minority, it was not surprising that Jewish prominence in the lists of banned and detained persons and in events associated with the Rivonia Trial and its sequels provoked bitter reactions from progovernment circles. Both houses of parliament witnessed hostile comments from National Party representatives. Typical was the threatening jibe of one senator: "We know that a large percentage of a certain population group devote themselves to undermining activities." Apropos the Rivonia arrests, another nationalist member of parliament declared that the five Jews who led the arrested blacks were a scandal to South African Jewry. To this a United Party representative retorted with the question: "Why had the honorable member not mentioned that the prosecutor was also a Jew?"[49]

Outbursts of innuendo implying that Jews were sabotaging white survival punctuated the Afrikaans press. Characteristic was the cynical comment in one series of newspaper articles that focused on the English-language universities as dangerous "breeding places of liberalism": "Presumably the parents of the Slovos, the Hepples and the Wolpes, when they sent their children to these universities, did not at all expect that their children, at the end of their university careers would degenerate into complete traitors or enemies of the people."[50] A particularly sharp exchange was sparked in late 1962 by a spate of letters signed with the pseudonym "Nabob" that appeared in the Cape Town newspaper *Die Burger*. The writer stated that the whites in South Africa were "fighting for their lives," but there were people "who do not recognize our right to survival." The charges he made against the Jewish community included "the exceptionally high percentage of Jewish names that appear among the members of the Congress of Democrats and other Leftist organisations, which aim at the downfall of the white man in South Africa," the bad press that Jewish journalists gave South Africa, and the bad influence of Jewish students at the universities. "If anti-Semitism ever takes on serious proportions in South Africa it will be the Jews' own fault," Nabob warned, "and that because they have not stood actively on our side in our hour of crisis."[51]

Responding editorially to these allegations and threats the *Jewish Times* tried rather speciously to deny that Jews predominated in the leftist factions. More plausibly, it said that the Board of Deputies had no authority to tell Jews how to conduct themselves politically and that Jews would object or would ignore the Board if it tried to exercise such authority. Furthermore, "every citizen has the inalienable right to choose his political course according to his lights. Anything that diminishes this right, savours of totalitarianism and its browbeating tactics." After a further challenge by *Die Burger*'s political columnist "Dawie," a second *Jewish Times* editorial titled "Jews and Leftists" contended that leftists were a fringe phenomenon to be found in every racial group, even if "it may be that the Jews have more Don Quixotes in their midst than the others." To Dawie's insinuation that it was the duty of the Board of Deputies to take action, the *Jewish Times* retorted: "But what action can the Board take against Jews who have left the fold, and are ready to face bannings and other discomforts?" As an aside, it added: "Incidentally, the Jewish leftists find Jewish spiritual values as repugnant as Afrikaner nationalism."[52]

After the escape of Goldreich and Wolpe, *Dagbreek en Sondagnuus* engaged in an ongoing exchange with the Board of Deputies. It bluntly put certain questions to the Jewish Board of Deputies: "Why is it that such a high percentage of whites who are detained under the 90-day clause of the General Law Amendment Act are Jews?" "Is it an indication that Jews are not happy in South Africa," it asked. "What is the official Jewish standpoint about the actions of people such as Goldreich and Wolpe?"[53] In responding to challenges of this sort the Board's policy makers were at pains to adhere consistently to the policy of noninvolvement in "politics." They were careful neither to condemn nor to condone any Jewish radicals by name. To be sure, assertions that such Jews were in fact alienated from Judaism and hostile to any positive Jewish identification were occasionally voiced in the Jewish press and by some community leaders speaking as private individuals, but never in official statements of the Board of Deputies. At the same time, there was a complete consensus in the Board's executive that under no circumstances could acts of sabotage and violence be condoned. "The Jewish community condemns illegality in whatever part of the population it might manifest itself," declared the Board unequivocally: "if individuals break the law, they expose themselves to the penalties of the law."[54]

Meanwhile, against this background of mistrust and recrimination, there was a disturbing reactivation of antisemitic manifestations, harking back to the Greyshirt atmosphere of an earlier period. Several of the unrepentant antisemites spawned in the 1930s and 1940s got a new lease on life. Foremost among these was R. K. Rudman of Pietermaritzburg, Natal, the self-styled Kommandant-General of the rabidly racist Boerenasie organization. Another was Johan Schoeman of Broederstroom, Transvaal. To be sure, neither the presence of such hard-core antisemites nor the scurrilous nature of their propaganda activities was unique to South Africa. They belonged to a genre examples of which were to be found in Britain, the United States, Canada, and most Western countries. The lion's share of the propaganda material disseminated in South Africa was imported or copied from stock antisemitic forgeries such as the notorious "Protocols of the Elders of Zion"; from material produced by Aner Eiberg, the Swedish arch-antisemite; and from hate literature traceable to Gerald L. K. Smith and Lincoln Rockwell of the United States or Colin Jordan and A. K. Chesterton of England.[55]

Also the actions of such antisemites followed a pattern not unique to South Africa: periodic swastika daubings, bluff telephone threats that synagogues were about to be blown up, and dissemination of slogans and leaflets offensive to Jews, some ranting against "the lie" that six million Jews were murdered by the Nazis, others raising the specter of a Jewish "world plot." During the worldwide rash of antisemitic incidents of 1959, a considerable number occurred in South Africa too. In January 1961 an explosion caused some damage to the Great Synagogue in Johannesburg, and in June 1962, while the Eichmann trial was much in the news, a bomb blast damaged the Jewish War Monument in the Johannesburg Jewish cemetery. Again, in September 1965 some tombstones in the Jewish section of a Pretoria cemetery were desecrated, and in April 1966, on the anniversary of Hitler's birth, two synagogues in Johannesburg were daubed with swastikas.[56]

A particularly malevolent manifestation of antisemitic hate literature was a publication called *Boomerang* that began to appear in 1965. *Boomerang* purported to be the official organ of the "Patriots Society for Race Friendship," whose aim was to fight the "international world dictatorship through the study of the International Conspiracy." It propagated the myth of a Zionist conspiracy against white South Africa as part of a plot to dominate the world.[57] Also reflective of the groundswell of antisemitism was the hostility revealed by an organization called the Inter-Church, Anti-Communist Actions Commission (Anti-Com). It published a bilingual newsletter, which fostered the notion of a conspiratorial tie between Jewry and communism.[58] Anti-Com was particularly menacing, for it ostensibly enjoyed the responsible auspices of Afrikaner churches. Its views were from time to time echoed in the important organ *Die Kerkbode*.[59] Yet protestations by the Board of Deputies to the Anti-Com committee were of little avail. It responded that in the light of "the high percentage of Jewish names amongst the listed Communists," the Jewish community should declare where it stood in "the fight against Godless Communism."[60]

The bogey of "Jewish Communism" surfaced prominently in September 1966 when an "International Symposium on Communism" was organized in Pretoria by the Council to Combat Communism. In an address to this conference, Major General van den Bergh, chief of South Africa's security police, made offensive remarks coupling Jews with communism. Referring to the 1963 police raid in which Goldreich, Goldberg, and other Jews had been arrested, he allowed himself the mocking quip: "You know when a Jew gets scared he gets very scared!" It was left to the conference's American guest, Professor Possony of the Hoover Institution on War, Revolution, and Peace, to discredit the prevailing antisemitic undertones and to warn that antisemitism in fact harmed the fight against communism. After coming under attack from Jewish spokesmen and in parliament, van den Bergh retracted. But the incident was indicative of the prevailing atmosphere in the country.[61]

The grave deterioration in Israel's relations with South Africa after 1961, examined in the previous chapter, greatly compounded the public indignation that was being aroused by the plenitude of Jewish names in the radical opposition. Antisemitic publications increasingly fused these two issues in their recriminations against the Jewish community. Particularly virulent was an English-language promoter of the National Party's apartheid policy, the *South African Observer*, edited by the known antisemite S. E. D. Brown. He condemned Israel's attacks on South Africa, questioned the loyalty of the local Jewish community, and railed against "the audacity of the Harry Oppenheimers, Helen Suzmans, Joel Mervises [editor of *The Sunday Times*], as well as the[ir] co-racials . . . playing leading parts in liberal and progressive and all far-left organizations in South Africa."[62]

This telescoping of two stereotyped images of the Jew, as disrupter of white supremacy from within and as supporter of Israel/betrayer of South Africa from without, was not limited to these blatantly antisemitic publications. In both the English and Afrikaans press, letters to the editor periodically appeared coupling the two charges—that Jewish liberals were undermining white survival and were sending money to Israel, which used it "for cutting my country's throat,"[63] and adding that the Jews would be the first to abandon the sinking ship and flee to Israel.

Perhaps the most disturbing of all the verbal altercations of the 1960s into which the Jewish Board of Deputies was pushed by Afrikaner critics was its dispute with Dirk Richard, the editor of *Dagbreek,* whose newspaper brazenly headlined the question "Where does the Jew stand in the white struggle for survival?" He submitted frankly that in Afrikaner eyes the Jew was under suspicion: "The view of the average Nationalist is that the Jews are not well disposed to this party and its policy of separate development, that they are even hostile to it . . . so that he cannot rely on the Jew at a time when his country has to be defended to the last ditch." The suspicion was kindled, Richard claimed, by the numerous Jewish names appearing among leftists, student leaders, and others who were seeking to undermine white survival. "When one is suspicious of a group," he warned, "one judges it facilely by the deeds of its most extreme members. Hence Goldreich and Wolpe become, in the first place, not saboteurs, but Jews who wish to undermine South Africa." The silence of local Jewry after Israel's voting for UN resolutions against South Africa, added Richard, only compounded Afrikaner mistrust of Jews. In the light of this situation, Richard called upon Jewry "to take a stand as a group."[64] But as we have seen, this is precisely what the leadership of the Jewish community was determined not to do.

Returning to the question posed at the beginning of this chapter, it is as well to draw a clear distinction between two facets of Jewish political behavior that characterized the Jewish experience in South Africa: on the one hand, extraordinary prominence of Jewish individuals in the radical and liberal streams of political opposition to the apartheid system; on the other hand, avoidance of association with these streams on the part of the vast majority of Jews, and their tendency to cluster around a position in the white political spectrum somewhat to the left of center. If it is thus correct to say that many white liberals and radicals were Jews, it is equally correct that not many Jews were liberals or radicals.

Accounting for Jewish Radicals

The disproportionate involvement and salience of persons of Jewish birth in the opposition to the apartheid regime, particularly in the radical resistance, is a highly conspicuous fact.[65] Equally evident is the fact that the convictions and actions of the radicals were deviant not only in relation to the white population but also to the Jewish community. This phenomenon begs explanation. Was there a significant relationship between their being Jews and their choice to go against the fundamental societal norms, conventions, and political policies of the regnant system of white domination and its rules of racial discrimination?

It needs to be noted that notwithstanding the government's constant sharpening of its instruments of suppression, a considerable spectrum of possible forms of resistance by ordinary white citizens remained. At one end was the simple exercise of the vote—available of course only to whites—and of expression through the media and literature in support of the small Liberal or Progressive segment of parliamentary and local governmental opposition to the National Party. In the middle were various civic actions such as protest demonstrations and cooperation with the victims of the apartheid system in ways antithetical to apartheid purposes. Examples are the actions of the Black Sash women's organization, the aiding of black trade union activity or demonstrations of defiance such as the bus boycotts and burning of passes[66] of the 1950s. At the other end of the spectrum were radical acts aimed at undermining the entire system of white domination—active defiance of the laws promulgated by the white government, underground agitation, and resort to violence.

In the discussion that follows the terms "radicals" and "liberals" will be used not in an ideological sense but simply as a serviceable, even if artificial, distinction between two categories of apartheid's white opponents. "Liberals" will serve as the label for those whites who sought to conduct their opposition, however vigorously, only within the parameters deemed legal by the regnant white polity. "Radicals" will be the label for those who joined or actively identified with parties, groups, or movements that, in the face of legislative and police repression, determined to go beyond those parameters. Most but not all of those who became radicals were communists. By the early 1960s, the apartheid regime having effectively suppressed everything and anything it chose to label communist, some liberals for whom communism was ideologically anathema became radicals too. There were also some Trotskyites who had no truck with the Soviet Union. But there can be no doubt that the Communist Party of South Africa (renamed the South African Communist Party in its underground phase from 1953) had become the most persuasive and compelling for white radicals not only by virtue of its ideological aura of seeming certainties but also because, of all apartheid's opponents, it was in fact the most unequivocal and uncompromising. Indeed, in postapartheid retrospect it would appear that the communist ideology served its adherents—even those who tenaciously held on to their passionate faith in Stalin—less as an end in itself than as a vehicle for the objective of abolishing white privilege and domination, and dismantling the entire edifice of apartheid. In the final analysis this objective was shared by liberals and communists despite the profound ideological divide between them. If today's postapartheid communists still enjoy intellectual respectability in South Africa even after the manifest moral and political collapse of Soviet communism, this is mainly because their heroic role in the defeat of the apartheid regime, enhanced by a spate of awe-inspiring autobiographical publications,[67] overshadows all the discredited ideological dogmas and blind worship of the Soviet system associated with communism in the public memory.

It should, of course, be noted that the phenomenon of disproportionate salience of Jews in radical political movements (and also, if rather less disproportionately so, in liberal parties) is not unique to the Jews of South Africa. In the modern history of most Jewish communities not only in Europe but also in countries of the New World, and not least of all in the United States, Jews have been ubiquitously prominent in radical leftist movements, particularly communism.[68] But consensus on an explanatory theory remains elusive. Some theorists have speculated that certain moral and social values inhering in the Jewish religion predispose Jews to liberal forms of social consciousness and, by extension, also to radical movements.[69] The supposedly pertinent values thus identified in Judaism include its this-worldliness and the attendant messianic belief in ultimate social perfectibility; emphasis on *tzedakah* (social charity) and mutual responsibility for the welfare of others that translates into social justice; and respect for learning, which promotes rationality in human affairs.

This theory, which might be labeled the "Judaic values" theory, has great mythic appeal for Jews in liberal Western societies because it serves, as it were, to give Judaism a good name. (By the same token, Jews in conservative, antiliberal societies might prefer to deny the theory.) It is characteristic that one finds Jews who celebrate the freeing of South Africa from apartheid, and at the same time wish to identify strongly as Jews, drawn to the "Judaic values" approach. This is evident in the reflections of even as critical and perceptive an inquirer as Immanuel Suttner, the editor of an invaluable anthology of interviews with Jews who were in one way or another prominently involved in the struggle against apartheid, interviews that partly form the basis for the analysis that follows in this chapter. Explaining what prompted him to produce this work, Suttner admits candidly that "by celebrating the activism of this minority and in claiming it as the positive manifestation of an essential Jewish preoccupation with 'making right' the world," he seeks to reassert his "own value as a Jew." In his thought-provoking afterword to the book, Suttner grapples sincerely with the question whether the phenomenon of Jewish radicals can be attributed to inherently Jewish values. Although he recognizes that the sociological position of Jews is an important factor in explaining the phenomenon, he yet reverts to attribution of "atavistic religious values." He suggests in particular that "the aspect of Jewish tradition they link up to is the tradition of nonconformism, rebuke, and solidarity with the underdog," going back to Moses killing the Egyptian overseer and the message of the prophets.[70]

But this explanatory theory rests on simplistic if not wholly faulty assumptions concerning Judaism itself because, as any serious student of Jewish history and religion knows, there can be no doubt that countervailing conservative values also inhere in Judaism, and with no less potential effect on the behavior of Jews.[71] Moreover, there is overwhelming empirical evidence of an unmistakably inverse relationship between orthodox religious adherence and political activism. In South Africa, as elsewhere, the more observant of orthodox religious precepts a

Jew was, the less likely he or she was to be found among even the moderate adversaries of the apartheid system, not to speak of its radical opponents. If the various forms of liberal opposition to apartheid have included some observant orthodox Jews, and even an occasional militant rabbi, these were clearly the exception rather than the rule. As for radical opponents of apartheid, without exception they were nonreligious Jews and, more often than not, self-declared atheists. One may plausibly suggest that, whether knowingly or not, such Jews do in fact reflect certain elements of Jewish religion and culture. But it would be nothing short of absurd to argue that people who are avowedly believing Jews and observant of Judaism's precepts, yet hold conservative political convictions, are a less authentic expression of Judaism than others who are liberals or radicals but reject Judaism's primary beliefs and precepts.

A more empirical theory explains Jewish liberalism and radicalism as a function of perceived interests rooted in the historical experience of Jews in the modern state. That is to say, it posits that Jews are historically conditioned to sense that their civic rights and welfare are best assured and advanced if liberal values prevail in the state.[72] In the case of South African Jewry this theory cannot be confirmed unreservedly by the record of the political preferences of Jews, whether as individual citizens or as a community. True, the Jews of South Africa qua Jewish community certainly wished liberal values to prevail as far as the white societal context was concerned. Indeed, whatever liberal proclivities Jewish immigrants carried over from their countries of origin in Europe were much reinforced in reaction to antisemitic emanations from the nonliberal forces in South Africa's white politics. Yet, as we have seen, they did not venture to extend their liberal preferences universally to the point where this would endanger their share in the benefits of white privilege. Because the Jews in South Africa were part and parcel of the privileged white minority, their welfare was unmistakably dependent on conformity with the white consensus. Within the parameters of that consensus, they were more liberal than most other whites. But to challenge the very foundations of the white consensus, which liberally allowed equal opportunities and rights for all whites but denied them to nonwhites, was perceived by most Jews—including many who deplored apartheid—as courting a clear and present danger. As is posited by one theory, inferred by Peter Medding from a wide-ranging comparative examination of Jewish political behavior, the determining factor for Jewish communities is less liberalism in itself than the realistically perceived political interests of Jews. Their major concern is always "to achieve a maximum degree of stability and security, irrespective of the nature of the regime."[73] It may be said that this generalization is borne out by the record of the Jews as a community in South Africa as well as what we know about those Jewish politicians and voters who retained a strong identification with the life of the Jewish community. However, it cannot be said to account for the behavior of the Jewish radicals—those individuals who, bent on enlisting the community in a broader universal cause, implicitly or explicitly did not care if it harmed the community's immediate self-interest.

Many of the Jews who joined the struggle for liberty in South Africa espoused a dogmatic communism and slavish obedience to the Soviet line, which commanded the disavowal of any Jewish identity and engendered a self-blinding indifference to the crushing of liberty for Jews in the Soviet Union. Yet, it is noteworthy that some of these Jews maintained a positive, self-accepting attitude toward their Jewish identity even while subordinating it to their identification with what they perceived as an infinitely more important universal cause. Albie Sachs, whose radical record included important roles in the Congress of Democrats, and afterward in the African National Congress in exile, during which time an assassination attempt perpetrated by the South African security police left him severely wounded, has explained it in these words: "We were Jewish, there was no doubt about it, it was never an issue."[74] He adds however that it was never a pivotal factor in his life. In like vein, he has also said: "To this day I never let a snigger or snide remark about Jews pass and, while I hated and still hate any denial of being a Jew or any attempt to ingratiate oneself or become invisible, I did not feel in my bones that the central and dominating feature of my existence was my Jewishness."[75]

In autobiographical accounts one finds evocations of Jewish historical experience as victims of prejudice, discrimination, and hatred, and especially the horrors of the Holocaust. In this context it is claimed by some, but not all, radicals that their rejection of discrimination, racism, and oppression and their striving to remake the world is somehow rooted in a humanistic Jewish ethos and in the Jewish historical experience of suffering. This is no doubt what another Jewish radical, Pauline Podbrey, meant when, having been asked to relate her Jewishness to her role in the radical resistance, said: "I've always felt very conscious of being Jewish, and that my Communist sympathies had their roots in Jewish ethics and Jewish morality." Adding that she was also deeply influenced by knowledge of the Holocaust, in which members of her family perished, she described it as "a living sore in her body." "I think that by not aligning yourself with the oppressed you are betraying the Jewish tradition," she averred.[76] In his autobiography, Baruch Hirson, a Trotskyist who was jailed for nine years, related that the interrogators of the security police arraigned him and the other prisoners at the Pretoria local prison, where at the time eight of the twenty-five (white) prisoners were Jews, with the question "Why are so many of you Jews?" He found the answer to be "neither simple nor easy." "We were non-Jewish Jews, Jews who did not accept the religion or even the customs of the Jewish people. Yet we had no reason to deny that we were Jewish and with my name, which I had adopted in 1940 [Baruch rather than Bertram] I proclaimed my Jewishness." Hirson then speculates: "The ethnic origin and classlessness, the studentship and professionalism, the political awareness and the presence in prison were not entirely disconnected, at least in my case, from being born a Jew. It was a Jewishness that denied many of its attributes, but there was a residue, harking back to some past that helped mark out the trajectory along which I journeyed."[77]

Clearly, what these persons refer to as Jewishness is not coterminous with Judaism as religion. For in most cases the autobiographical recollections not only of the South African–born Jewish radicals but even of those born in the far more intensely Jewish milieu of eastern Europe reveal exposure to only the most superficial and uninspiring Jewish religious experience. On the basis of the evidence, attributing a formative influence to "Judaic values" is scarcely credible. At best theirs is the consciousness of the "non-Jewish Jew" in the sense famously coined by Isaac Deutscher—a consciousness that has more to do with the position of Jews in society than with the Jewish religion, and that self-servingly reads into the Jewish tradition ideas generated within the modern milieu quite independently of Judaism. By the same token, a more adequate explanation of their proclivity for political radicalism may be posited in terms of social marginality, that is to say, being outsiders in relation to the vested interests of society's established state authorities, social classes, and dominant ethnic group or groups. Of course, the radicalizing potential of marginality is most acute when Jews are directly victimized, as was the case in czarist Russia for example. This cannot be said to have applied in South Africa, where Jews had full civic equality and enjoyed all the privileges of the dominant white population. Yet even there, the segmented social structure of white society and the long shadow of Afrikaner nationalist antisemitism rendered Jews outsiders to a degree sufficient to generate in many of them alienation from the established order, conventions, and ideological norms of society. This facilitated the adoption of counternormative attitudes and ideologies by a disproportionate number of Jews relative to other whites.

Even if one retains the doubtful assumption that social values inherent to Judaism somehow do go into the making of Jewish radicals, it is surely their position on the margins of society that prompts them to apply those values in criticism of that society. This is recognized in the highly nuanced multifactor attempt to account for Jewish radicals that was suggested by Percy Cohen, a British sociologist who happened also to be a Jewish South African. In a work titled *Jewish Radicals and Radical Jews,* he upheld the hypothesis that secularized Jews may imbibe from the Jewish tradition cultural traits that may lead to radicalism.[78] According to Cohen they then tend to give expression to these traits in the form of what he described as "fantasies" of remaking society and perfecting the world. Identifying with the underdogs of society and fighting injustice are ancillaries of such fantasies. However, Cohen concurs that it is the marginal status of such Jews in relation to the larger society that mediates this transmutation of Judaism's traditional social values into such secular social fantasies. This then attracts them to unconventional and innovative ideas of radical social and political change. Moreover, such Jews, having abandoned Jewish ethnic ties and religion, then find in the movements that embody these ideas the warmth and intimacy of a new surrogate home and family.

Let us examine the example of Joe Slovo, perhaps the most important personality in the entire pantheon of radical whites who committed themselves heart and soul to the struggle in South Africa. As a young boy of sixteen, he joined the Young Communist League in the early 1940s. By 1954 a ban on all political activity had been placed on him, and he was one of the accused in the abortive Treason Trial of the late 1950s. After nearly a decade of radical work, overtly as a lawyer and covertly in the banned Communist Party, he left South Africa in 1963 on an underground mission and remained abroad. There he went on to become, variously, chief of staff of the African National Congress's military arm Umkhonto we

Sizwe, the first white member of the ANC's national executive, and, as well, general-secretary of the South African Communist Party. After his return to South Africa in 1990 under the new dispensation and the ANC's victory in the first democratic election of 1994, President Mandela appointed him minister of housing. Slovo became a legend of the revolutionary struggle in his own lifetime. When cancer tragically took his life in 1995, he was given a hero's burial.

What Jewish substance went into the making of Joe Slovo as a radical? Even though he was born as Yossel Slovo in the small Lithuanian village Obelai in 1926, the attribution of his later radicalism in South Africa to specifically Jewish social values imbibed from his childhood education there would be tenuous. Witness Slovo's own uninspiring recollection: "The synagogue was our school and an ear-twisting sadistic rabbi forced whatever he could into our heads from the Hebrew version [*sic*] of the Old Testament, which was our only textbook."[79] Nor was there any Judaic substance to his adolescent life in South Africa. The poor social and economic situation of Slovo's family seems to have been a far more formative factor. He spent his youth in the Jewish-immigrant milieu of the Doornfontein and Yeoville suburbs of Johannesburg in the 1930s and 1940s. It was an ambience of economically struggling Jews, the first generation in South Africa, partly working-class (mostly artisans or unskilled employees) and partly lower-middle-class. Ten-year-old Yossel came to South Africa with his mother in 1936, having been preceded by his father. Soon after, his mother died in childbirth, and his father barely eked out a living variously as a shopkeeper or bread deliverer for the Jewish-owned Crystal Bakery and Delicatessen in Doornfontein. Much of the time they lived in a boardinghouse, and Joe had to find work as a dispatch clerk in the firm of Sive Brothers and Karnovsky at the cost of not completing his high school education. Slovo's elementary schooling was at the so-called Jewish Government School. But, notwithstanding the name, the school adhered wholly to the provincial government's curriculum and was devoid of any specifically Jewish content. More significant was the fact that being in a government school almost all of whose pupils were Jews bolstered the condition of marginality in relation to white society as a whole.[80]

It is the demonstrable situation of social marginality in relation to the white society of dual Afrikaner-British stock, rather than the influence of values presumed to inhere in Judaism, that fits the case of Joe Slovo, as also of most other Jewish radicals. This observation applies also to members of an earlier generation of Jewish radicals—Hyman Basner, for example. Born in Dvinsk, Latvia, and named Haim Meyer, he was taken at age seven, in 1912, to South Africa by his mother to join his father, who had opened a small dairy shop in Doornfontein, Johannesburg. His mother related to him in later years that she had encouraged his father to leave Russia because she feared the consequences of his incipient association with revolutionary workers in a local factory.[81] Basner's life and career were particularly marked by outsider individuality. After a stay during the 1920s in Los Angeles, where his sister lived and where he began to study law, his father's financial misfortunes obliged him to return to Johannesburg. Training as a lawyer with a legal firm that had a largely Indian and African clientele, he was drawn into communist circles. He joined the Communist Party of South Africa in 1933, and by 1937 he was its candidate, unsuccessfully, for a "natives' representative" seat in the South African Senate, the upper house of parliament. (In 1936 the small number of "natives," that is, Africans, who had the vote in the Cape were removed from the voters roll, and provision was made for natives throughout the Union to elect four white members of the Senate to represent them.) In 1942 Basner at last gained election to represent the natives of the Transvaal and Orange Free State, but by then he had fallen out with the party over Soviet policy in Europe. He followed an independent and lone course that led him to form a short-lived "Socialist Party." In 1947 he resigned from the Senate and, although he was politically inactive in the 1950s, still suffered detention and restriction of his legal work. In the early 1960s he left South Africa, going first to Tanzania and then to Ghana, where he became a confidante of Kwame Nkrumah, was imprisoned in 1966 by Nkrumah's deposers, and after his release spent a year in Israel before settling in Britain in 1968. There he lived in Herefordshire until his death in 1977. In the preface to a volume of Basner's memoirs, Tom Lodge, a noted historian of black liberation politics, perceptively comments: "Marginality of existence was an essential ingredient of Basner's upbringing. . . . Being an outsider may have helped to cultivate his capacity for social observation."[82]

In almost every case the outsider marginality of these Jewish radicals was a double marginality, that is to say, in addition to social marginality in relation to the established society of whites, also marginality in relation to the established Jewish community. One might spell out the specifics in the example of Joe Slovo as follows: in relation not only to institutionalized white society but also to the established upwardly mobile Jewish community of Johannesburg and its norms of religious and Zionist identification, Slovo's was a marginal and alienated social environment. It was economically poor, irreverently nonreligious, and steeped in the leftist sympathies and rhetoric—still oriented on the Old World and unrelated to the South African scene—that typified many of the post–Russian Revolution emigrants to the New World countries. Slovo himself described this ambience perceptively:

> My leaning towards left socialist politics was also formed partly by the bizarre and paradoxical embrace of socialism shared by most of the immigrants who filled the boarding houses in which we lived. I say bizarre because they tended to combine a passionate devotion to the Soviet Union with a Zionism and vicious racism towards the majority of the South African population.[83]

Notwithstanding Slovo's rigidly communist disaffection from Judaism and attendant rejection of Zionism, all who knew him attest to his unselfconscious Jewish behavioral traits, especially his buoyant flair for Jewish humor. But it would be fanciful to say that these attributes signify any supposed values of Judaism that could inspire a radical disposition. Judaism's putative liberal or radical values, if at all invoked, seem to have been retrospectively imagined and read into the lives of Jewish radicals, sometimes by themselves but more often by others. This is nicely illustrated in the eulogy of the writer and poet Lionel Abrahams for the "utterly non-sectarian" Barney Simon, whose innovative theatrical work flouted the racist taboos of South Africa: "I like imagining an invisible yarmulke on Barney's pate," wrote Abrahams.[84] In the specific case of Barney Simon it happens to be feasible to assume that he had indeed been exposed to "Jewish values" at least through the medium of a Zionist youth movement,[85] but in the case of Joe Slovo, Chief Rabbi Cyril Harris probably came much closer to a true description in his carefully worded funeral eulogy for this famous Jewish radical. Harris acknowledged: "There are two major motivations towards helping fellow human beings. One is religious. . . . The second motivation is humanitarian. This was Joe Slovo's way."[86]

The explanation for Jewish radicalism that is being suggested here takes cognizance of Jewishness, but in the sense of the social situation and attendant familial and ethnic-group environment that characterized a segment of the Jewish immigrant generation, rather than in the sense of religion. It is in terms of this social condition that one may best account for the relative facility with which Jewish persons were able to feel disaffected from the apartheid system devised and enforced by the established ethnic groups of the white society or their political and social elites. Although such disaffection was not unknown within the established elites themselves—the Communist Party leader Bram Fischer, scion of a famous Afrikaner family, is a striking example—it was certainly far more exceptional and unpredictable than the disaffection demonstrated by Jewish persons. Albie Sachs has offered this insightful explanation of the Jewish factor in the liberal or radical political proclivity of Jews such as himself:

> A sensitivity to suffering, to discrimination . . . I'm sure that was all facilitated by the Jewish background. So, yes, from that point of view, a broader sensitivity to discrimination and suffering and exclusion would have come through. But not through an organized sense of saying: "We are Jews. We've been discriminated against, we've suffered." It's more through the fact that you didn't automatically regard yourself as part of the ruling élite in the country where you were, in the school where you were, or in the society in which you lived.[87]

As has been suggested above, an ancillary of the social marginality theory arises from the observable correlation between involvement of Jewish persons in opposition to the established societal system and their personal alienation from the Jewish communal and religious framework or even repudiation of it.[88] Indeed, the autobiographical record of almost every Jew who became involved in the radical opposition in South Africa provides evidence of such alienation. To be sure, it is a compound alienation—usually an initial estrangement facilitates the person's deviation from Jewish community norms. This then provokes a reaction—embarrassment or dissociation or even hostility—from the institutional elites whether lay or religious, which in turn compounds the person's disaffection from Jewish institutional life, sometimes quite bitterly so.

The radicals' estrangement from the Jewish community does not, however, mean dissociation from other Jews. Indeed, a cluster of social association with other Jews within the ranks of radical parties is one of the most characteristic features of the record in South Africa. It is rather a case of Jews associating with like-minded Jews who, as it were, prefer not to associate with Jews. Together, they found a warmly embracing cosmopolitan home—a sense of belonging and dedication, social no less than political, that they could find neither in conventional white society at large nor in the sectarian Jewish community. For the generation that became politically active before 1948, participating in the defense of Jews and society as a whole against fascism in South Africa was a profoundly meaningful part of the struggle. The real and present danger of fascism receded thereafter, but waging the color-blind battle against apartheid and challenging its racial taboos by socializing across the color line continued to engender a virtuous and liberating feeling. These qualities of the radical political home were felt to be absent in the Jewish community, and they more than made up for the personal sacrifices and persecution that were the lot of the radicals' political and social heresy.

Of course, even if what one might now term, for want of a concise label, "the double outsider or marginality theory" is plausible, it accounts for little more than the potentiality of Jews to balk at the imposition of the apartheid system on the society in which they were expected to conform as privileged whites. But, clearly, relatively few Jews fulfilled this potentiality. Moreover, as described in the plenitude of memoirs and interviews that have seen publication, the great variety of paths taken by Jews to the radical camp in South Africa defies attempts to explain, fully or sufficiently, why some Jews took these radical paths whereas others did not. However, one almost regular pattern *is* discernible. This is the role of the parental home or of the immigrant generation's social environment. There is considerable evidence of transmission from one generation to the next, particularly in regard to communist sympathies or affiliation. The compound effects of outsider marginality in the broad sociological sense and role models in the home or its immediate social environs are observable, above all, in the lives of several important radicals who were born in Europe and were brought to South Africa by their immigrant parents. As has already been suggested, this kind of influence is evident in the life of Joe Slovo. In Slovo's case, generational transmission appears to have been not directly from his parents but rather indirectly from the immigrant social milieu of his childhood and adolescence. In other cases the direct influence of the parental home is more evident.

An example is Ray Alexander. She was born in Latvia in 1913 and came to South Africa in 1929, at age sixteen. Her autobiographical recollections point to the early formative influence of radical political consciousness in the home in Latvia. Her father was, as she recalls, "inclined to socialist ideas," and his social circle included a local teacher who was a communist and became something of a mentor to the young Rachel Alexandrowich after her father died when she was twelve years old. While she was still in Latvia her own early political inclinations shifted from contemplation of Zionism to ardent communism, so that she found her way to the local Communist Party very soon after her arrival in Cape Town.[89] She went on to become one of the resistance movement's most militant and colorful personalities. Ray Alexander's main field of activity was as trade union leader in the Cape, most famously with the Food and Canning Workers' Union founded in 1941. Her activities continued into the period of National Party rule and included the formation of the Federation of South African Women. Banning orders forced her resignation from both frameworks, and in 1965 she left South Africa together with her husband Jack Simons, also a leading Communist Party member, who was hounded with banning orders out of his teaching position in African studies at the University of Cape Town. After a long period of politically active exile in Lusaka and in England, Ray and Jack were among the first ANC and Communist exiles to return in 1990.

Pauline Podbrey is another example of a ready-made radical so to speak. She was born in eastern Europe and came to Durban, South Africa, in 1933 at the age of eleven. Appropriately titled *White Girl in Search of the Party*, her autobiographical book vividly describes her search for engagement with the forces of resistance to the kind of society in which she found herself in South Africa. This search was an emanation of the radical leftist predisposition she had already formed in Lithuania. Her father, who according to her recollections had a strong influence on her, was a supporter of the socialist Jewish workers' party known as the Bund. Pauline found what she was seeking in the Communist Party, became heavily involved in trade union activities, and in 1950 married H. A. Naidoo, an outstanding Indian trade union and Communist Party leader. In the wake not only of the Suppression of Communism Act but also the draconian prohibition of mixed marriages enforced by the National Party government after 1948, the couple went into exile from South Africa. This included a few years in communist Hungary of the early 1950s, where disenchantment with the practice of Soviet-style communism began to set in. By the time she returned to the new South Africa from her exile in England Pauline had lost faith in some of the political dogmas that had formerly enveloped her dedication to the struggle against the system of racial domination in South Africa.[90]

Most of the Jewish radicals had in common their growing to maturity with a marginal-outsider perspective on white South African society and an increasing alienation from the institutional life of the Jewish community, whether embodied in the synagogue or in Zionist activity. For some, a leftist nursery was available in the form of the Yiddish-speaking immigrant groups that were described in the introductory chapter of this book, particularly the Geserd organization of the 1930s and the Yiddisher Arbeter Klub that existed from 1929 to 1948 in Johannesburg. As we have seen, within the Jewish community itself these groups represented a countercultural leftist strain, small but persistently challenging of the conventional community.

Eli Weinberg exemplifies the type of Jewish radical whose leftist roots reached back to eastern Europe and who was later nourished by association with local leftist, Yiddish-speaking circles.[91] Born in Libau, Latvia, he came to South Africa in 1929, at age twenty-one, with sound communist credentials; he had already been a member of the communist underground in Libau and had even suffered arrest. At first he first worked in the small Orange Free State town Kroonstad as a photographer, a profession to which he was to return many years later, after being banned from union work. Moving to Johannesburg, he worked for a time as secretary of the pro-Soviet, Jewish Geserd Society. In that capacity he welcomed the Jewish socialist leader Gina Medem on her 1932 visit to South Africa. Meanwhile he had joined the Communist Party of South Africa. At the party's request, he then moved to Cape Town. In association with the work of the renowned trade unionist Solly Sachs in Johannesburg, Weinberg started a new Garment Workers' Union in the Cape. Working with both coloreds and whites he and Ray Alexander branched out into the creation of many other unions in industries such as sweet (candy) making, chemicals, and canning. In 1939 Weinberg moved to Port Elizabeth, where he did similar union work with much success. Back in Johannesburg, from 1943 until his banning in 1953 he was general-secretary of the South African Commercial Travellers' Union. He returned to his earliest work as a professional photographer but continued clandestinely to be involved in trade union work associated with the radical opposition to the apartheid regime. In late 1964 he was arrested and put on trial together with fourteen others including Bram Fischer. Weinberg was sentenced to five years in prison, and after his release in 1970 he remained under banning restrictions. In 1976 Weinberg finally went into exile, and in 1981 he died while in Tanzania.

The list of Jewish radicals whose leftist roots reached back to eastern Europe includes several husband and wife couples, for example, the Barsels and the Harmels. Esther Barsel's parents had emigrated from Lithuania and settled in the Yeoville suburb of Johannesburg in 1936 when Esther was thirteen years of age. Like a number of other radicals, she was a member of the Hashomer Hatza'ir Zionist youth movement, until she went to university in Cape Town, where she was attracted to the Modern Youth Society, an off-campus leftist group comprising a mix of university students and trade unionists that became the ideological nursery for several important radicals, notably Albie Sachs.[92] Her husband, Hymie Barsel, grew up in the Fordsburg and Doornfontein immigrant environment of Johannesburg. He became estranged from the religiosity of his family as he came under the influence of a charismatic leader of the Young Communist League, Dr. Max Joffe (a medical practitioner), who was a major role model in the lives of quite a number of Jewish radicals. Barsel suffered from epilepsy and was treated by Dr. Joffe, who ushered him into the late 1930s antifascist activities of the Communist Youth League. Thence he went on to become the organizer of a branch of the Friends of the Soviet Union in the 1940s. Both Barsels were severely harassed by the security police in the 1960s. At one point Esther went on a hunger strike to force her release from detention or a charge in court. She was ultimately sentenced to three years in jail, and even thereafter suffered banning orders—no attendance at gatherings, not to be quoted by anyone, not to leave her magisterial district without police permission. From 1963 to 1968 Hymie Barsel was subjected to banning orders and thereafter to house arrest. He died in 1987, but Esther witnessed the advent of the new South Africa.[93]

Ray Harmel was born in Lithuania, where at age sixteen she was already involved in leftist labor union activities and hunted by the Lithuanian police. She came to South Africa in 1928. Her husband, Michael Harmel, became a major communist ideologist in the South African party and was already under police surveillance in 1946 before the induction of the apartheid regime. He was at that time chairman of the Communist Party's Johannesburg branch. Under apartheid suppression, after being subjected to twenty-four-hour house arrest, Harmel fled the country in May 1963. Ray, who managed to leave with a one-way exit permit, joined him in England.[94]

Another radical couple was Ben and Mary Turok (she was not Jewish). Ben was born in Latvia and brought out to South Africa in 1934 at age seven. According to his recollection, his father was a Bundist and a member of the Yiddisher Arbeter Klub in the 1930s, although he afterward lost interest and, not untypically, became a well-off businessman.[95] Ben became a leading trade unionist, was served with a banning order already in the mid-1950s, was one of the accused in the Treason Trial, and held the key position of secretary of the Congress of Democrats before it was suppressed. Having gone underground during the 1960 state of emergency, in 1962 he was caught, convicted for involvement in the planting of an explosive device, and served a three-year jail sentence. Mary Turok had also been a prominent member the Congress of Democrats and later was arrested on a charge of aiding the banned ANC and sentenced to six months in prison. Ben Turok, having been placed under house arrest immediately after his release, managed to escape from the country and joined the exiled resistance. After returning to the new South Africa he was elected an ANC member of parliament.

Not all of the immigrant radicals came directly from the leftist nurseries of eastern Europe. There were leftist immigrant offshoots in the west. Hilda Watts (originally Schwartz), who came to South Africa from London in the 1930s (she went back and forth a few times in that period), was the young daughter of emigrants from czarist Russia to Britain and had grown up in an avidly communist home environment. Indeed, after the Bolshevik revolution, her father had returned to live in the Soviet Union, leaving his family behind.[96] In South Africa, Hilda soon became a stalwart in the local Communist Party. In late 1944 she became the party's first elected representative by an all-white electorate when she gained election to the Johannesburg City Council. In the apartheid years she was active in the Congress of Democrats and the Federation of South African Women, was subjected to banning and detention, and later played a major role in liaison and succor of imprisoned comrades. After escaping from the country in 1964 together with her husband, Rusty Bernstein, and returning to England, she produced several books that passionately told the story of the resistance movement and explored the exile experience of opponents of apartheid who had left South Africa and aided the struggle from abroad.[97]

Hilda Watts's second-generation British background was an exception. Most second-generation Jews in communist ranks and the trade union movement during the 1950s and 1960s grew up in the immigrant Jewish neighborhoods of Johannesburg and Cape Town. The twin brothers Leon and Norman Levy are an example. They were born in 1929 to parents who had come from Lithuania and associated with the Yiddisher Arbeter Klub in Johannesburg.[98] Leon and Norman joined the Young Communist League in the mid-1940s, were active in the Congress of Democrats, and were among the accused in the 1950s Treason Trial. Leon became a major trade union worker and served as president of the important multiracial South African Congress of Trade Unions (SACTU). He underwent banning and then was held in detention under the ninety-days detention law, until being allowed to leave the country on an exit permit in 1963. Norman had been a schoolteacher and active, together with the intrepid antiapartheid fighter Helen Joseph (who was not Jewish), in the African Education Movement, which tried to provide an alternative education for blacks who boycotted the government's "Bantu" education system. In July 1964 he was detained under the ninety-days detention law and suffered solitary confinement for fifty-four days. He stood trial together with Bram Fischer, Eli Weinberg, and twelve other accused and served four years in prison. After his release in April 1968, he left the country with his wife and two children. Joining his brother in London, he worked as educational officer for the ANC, helping to place South African political émigrés in universities on scholarships. On his return to South Africa in 1991 he headed the Centre for Community and Labor Studies at the University of Durban-Westville and was involved in affirmative-action programs.

The formative role of the parental home and its immediate social environs is evident in the political education of several other South African–born radicals. The formidable journalist and communist activist Ruth First is a striking case in point.[99] Her left-wing outlook and double sense of alienation from white South African and Jewish communal norms was undoubtedly engendered in her by her parents, Julius and Tilly, both of whom had been dedicated communists. Julius was born in preindependent Latvia and came to South Africa in 1910. He served a stint as chairman of the Communist Party of South Africa in the 1920s. Having built up a prosperous livelihood as a furniture manufacturer, he remained a supporter and benefactor of the Communist Party, whose ranks were joined by his daughter in her late teens. In the radical weekly press, Ruth First fearlessly penned acerbic investigative reportage on the cruel ravages of apartheid on farms, in prisons, and in the black townships. Repeatedly defying suppression, this diminutive but dogged press kept reappearing under different names. Ruth First was one of the accused in the great Treason Trial of the 1950s and later endured banning, detention without trial, and cruel solitary confinement (described in her book *117 Days,* published in 1965). After her release in 1964, she followed her husband, Joe Slovo, into exile, where they both continued their leading roles in the liberation movement. In 1983, while Ruth was working as research director at the Center for African Research in Maputo, a parcel bomb aimed at her by the South African security police took her life.

Denis Goldberg is another example of radicalism rooted in the home environment, but in his case quite independently of the local Jewish-immigrant milieu. Both his father and his mother were communists, born in London's East End to immigrant parents from eastern Europe. They came to South Africa in about 1929, where Denis was born in 1933 into a home that, in his words, "was open to anybody in the [Communist] Party, in the ANC, in the liberation movement." The Goldbergs, Denis adds, "were not in the mainstream of the Jewish community."[100] Goldberg senior had a little cartage contracting business, "so his truck was used as the platform for meetings." Denis attributed no part of his radical predisposition to Jewishness: "I grew up in a communist household and was aware of political relations and realities in South Africa from a very early age. By the time I left school and went to the university in 1950, at the age of 16–17, I realized that I had to decide whether these were my own views or views I had adopted because they were my parents'."[101] Denis studied engineering at the University of Cape Town. Together with his future wife, Esmé, he advanced from involvement in the formation of the Modern Youth Society at the University of Cape Town to work in the Congress of Democrats. After he was banned under the government's suppression of communism legislation, he had an important role in the Umkhonto we Sizwe underground, in part by virtue of his training as a civil engineer. When he was arrested at Rivonia in 1963 and placed on trial together with Mandela, Sisulu, and other major African National Congress leaders, he got the harshest sentence imposed on any of the accused whites—life imprisonment.

Goldberg was released from prison, after serving twenty-two years, through the efforts of an Israeli personage, Herut Lapid, who had made rescuing political prisoners his personal mission in life. Lapid was a member of kibbutz Ma'ayan Baruch, on which Denis's daughter Hilary was living at the time. Even so, Goldberg continued firmly to dissociate himself from Zionism and Israel and chose to live in London. In an interview published in 1997 he referred to his Jewish background in unaltered dismissive vein: "I'm Jewish because my grandparents and parents were. My grandparents were orthodox, my parents were atheists." He said he saw no need to explain things in Jewish terms of any sort.[102]

That the daughter of a radical as negative toward Jewishness as was Goldberg could choose to go to Israel is indicative of the ongoing interplay between cosmopolitan and ethnic-Zionist propensities in Jewish families. This interplay is evident also in some other cases, for example, the family of another important radical, Rowley Israel Arenstein in Durban. His daughter was active in the Zionist youth movement Habonim, and several members of that movement's Durban branch came under Arenstein's influence. One was David Ernst, son of the leading Jewish educator in Durban, who also became involved in resistance to the apartheid regime and suffered imprisonment. Arenstein himself attributed his early social consciousness to the influence of his mother, who had grown up in the Ukraine with a radical outlook of the Menshevik variety.[103] He was an attorney by profession but was prevented from practicing by the terms of various banning orders imposed on him over a period of thirty-three years from 1953 until 1986, longer than any other opponent of apartheid. Although he had been a member of the Communist Party, Arenstein later followed a very independent ideological line, which led to his expulsion from the covert Communist Party. Clinging to the strategy of gradually developing a mass-based resistance movement, he opposed the turn to armed underground resistance and remained in South Africa. He also sided with the Maoist position against that of the Soviet Union communists. In the 1980s he associated himself closely with the Zulu Inkatha Freedom Party leader Mangosuthu Gatsha Buthelezi rather than with the African National Congress. Arenstein lived to see the change in South Africa and died in 1996.

The formative influence of the home is also evident in many of the generation of radicals who were born or reached adulthood after the National Party came to power in 1948. An obvious example is Albie Sachs, the son of Lithuanian-born Emil Solly Sachs, the prodigious trade unionist who had been a Communist Party member until he was expelled for not toeing the party line in the early 1930s. Albie studied law at the University of Cape Town in the 1950s and afterward did much civil rights work as a lawyer. He suffered detention without trial for 168 days in 1963, after which he went into exile in England, where he gained a Ph.D. and taught law. Active all the while in the ANC, in 1977 he moved to Mozambique. As has already been mentioned, in 1988 a car bomb planted by agents of the South African security forces severely injured him. He lost an arm and the sight of an eye. His writings include a book on his remarkable recovery: *The Soft Vengeance of a Freedom Fighter.* Returning to postapartheid South Africa, he was appointed a judge in its new Constitutional Court.

Gill Marcus is another example of a homegrown potential radical of the post-1948 generation. She was born in 1949 to actively communist parents who were perhaps spared incarceration in South African prisons when they chose to leave with her for London in 1969. She reports growing up in an environment where she "was very aware of justice and human dignity."[104] In London she became an active worker for the African National Congress and headed the organization's information unit. Returning to South Africa in 1990, Marcus was elected to the ANC's executive committee, and after the formation of Mandela's government was appointed in April 1996 as deputy finance minister.

Yet the empirical evidence does not permit a sweeping generalization attributing universal formative influence to generational transmission of a radical proclivity via the home or immediate social environment. These appear to be less significant in the lives of several other radicals who grew to maturity in the post-1948 apartheid years than they were for their predecessors. Ronnie Kasrils, born in 1938 to first-generation South African parents who were not particularly leftist or politically involved, became perhaps the most prominent of all white radicals who grew to maturity in the post-1948 period. As was typical of the adolescent experience of Jews who grew up in the Yeoville suburb of Johannesburg with its many, mainly lower-middle-class Jewish residents, Kasrils also had a brief exposure to the Zionist youth movements. He has said that he felt very Jewish, flirted briefly with membership in various youth movements, and identified strongly with Israel's War of Independence. He recollects being strongly aware of the Holocaust and the history of Jewish persecution and says that he "drew an analogy with the suffering of black people in this country and racism."[105] Kasrils relates that it was only in 1961, after being shocked into action by the Sharpeville massacre, that he joined the liberation struggle in the ranks of the Communist Party. Whatever may have been the factors or role models that influenced him at that stage, they do not seem to have included significant generational transmission in the home.

Evading arrest, Kasrils left South Africa in 1963 and became a major figure in the overseas development of the exiled African National Congress. In the course of his twenty-seven years of exile in London, Lusaka, and Luanda, and in the ANC's training camps in Angola, he rose to become head of military intelligence for Umkhonto we Sizwe. When the ANC launched Operation Vula in 1990, which aimed at clandestine reinfiltration of exiled ANC leadership into South Africa to link up with the internal resistance, he returned. Operating underground, he successfully evaded arrest until he got indemnity in June 1991 as part of the new dispensation. In Mandela's first government he served as deputy minister of defense.

A liberal home environment does appear to have played some role in the political development of Raymond Suttner, who stands out as one of the foremost white radicals involved in the liberation struggle during the post-Verwoerd period of "reformed" apartheid. He was born in 1945 to South African–born parents who were liberals and Progressive Party supporters. His grandparents on his father's side came from Lithuania and on his mother's side from England. Having operated underground for the Communist Party and the ANC in the early 1970s, Suttner was detained without trial in 1975 and then sentenced to seven and a half years in prison. Released in 1983, he undauntedly resumed his antiapartheid activity, particularly in the work of the United Democratic Front. In the 1986 state of emergency he was again detained without trial, becoming the longest-serving white detainee, He served twenty-seven months, of which eighteen were in solitary confinement.

Interviewed concerning his Jewishness, Suttner has provided a particularly insightful account. He attested to a low Jewish consciousness, heightened only in the face of antisemitism experienced particularly when he was in prison and found that the security police were obsessed with his being Jewish. "For the people who detained me," he commented, "my being Jewish was an essential element of [communist] criminality."[106] He expressed doubt that there was in reality such a thing as uniform Jewish values, because he had found that among Jews in South Africa there were contradictory values. "I don't think there's a uniform Jewish ethic which has informed people," he opined. "If there is, it's been capable of a variety of different meanings, and some of these meanings have been interpreted in a very ethnic, egocentric way."[107] By his own account, Suttner, who was a university lecturer in law, had begun his university studies with homegrown liberal values but formed the conviction that these were insufficient "as a strategy for change in South Africa"; they were no more than "a way of preserving a sense of personal rectitude."[108] While furthering his studies in England from late 1969 to mid-1971, he had joined the Communist Party and the ANC, and on his return to South Africa he began to operate underground. In sum, it seems that not "Jewish values" but the influence of universal liberal values in the home and intellectual influences in the university environment were the major formative factors in the making of Suttner as a radical opponent of apartheid.

So far we have identified, as a common formative factor in the making of Jewish radicals, a situation of social marginality vis-à-vis both white society and the institutions of the Jewish community. Additionally, we have observed that this was usually conflated by some degree of ideological radicalism imbibed within the family or from the proximate social environment. It should now be noted that a secondary factor noticeable in the lives of some radicals was exposure to the Zionist youth movements. This is seemingly paradoxical, because these youth movements were something integral to the Jewish community from which Jewish radicals were so sharply alienated. But it seems that these movements provided a stimulus for political awareness and sometimes a training ground for radical activism, which were otherwise lacking in the adolescent experiences of most Jews. In a dialectical way they played some role in the ideological education of quite a number of Jewish radicals.

Sam Kahn was an early case of a communist of note who had strong roots in the Jewish community's youth societies, the organizational predecessors of the uniformed youth movements. He was born in South Africa and became very active in the Zionist "Young Israel" movement in Cape Town and later in the Students Jewish Association at Cape Town University, where he qualified as a lawyer. But alienation from the Jewish community set in with his joining of the Communist Party in 1930. By 1938 Kahn was on the central executive committee of the Communist Party of South Africa, and he went on to gain election in 1943 to the Cape Town City Council. In November 1948 Kahn was elected to parliament as a white representative of the Africans in the Cape Western District, becoming the first Communist ever to gain a seat in the House of Assembly.

In parliament Kahn was the most fearless and acerbic denouncer of South African racism and oppression. With biting sarcasm, he attacked measures such as the new racist apartheid legislation that prohibited marriage between any white and nonwhite. Kahn pungently described it as "the moral offspring of an illicit union between racial superstition and biological ignorance." He labeled the bill's advocate, Minister of the Interior Dr. Dönges, a "political misanthropist" who had discovered a new germ, "the bacillus blanc supremacoccus."[109] In consequence of the government's Suppression of Communism Act, he was ejected from parliament in 1952. After more than a decade of further banning and harassment, in 1960 Kahn made his escape from the country and went into exile with his family in Britain. In 1987, while on a visit to Israel, which he never ceased seeing through critical communist eyes, an automobile accident tragically took his life at the age of seventy-five.

The most striking testimony for Zionist youth movement influence as a stimulator of social awareness, which in turn could lead to radical activism against South Africa's racist society, may be found in the autobiography of Baruch Hirson. Hirson was born in South Africa in 1921 and grew up in the same 1920s and 1930s Jewish-immigrant milieu of the Doornfontein suburb of Johannesburg that was a nursery for so many other future radicals. But his account of his own home background reveals no particular sensitivities to the injustices and oppression that pervaded the surrounding society. Quite to the contrary, both home and school conditioned him to be a typical privileged white. It was outside of the home and its conventionally superficial Jewish religious observances and rites of passage that he formed a critical perception of the social evils around him. Hirson titled his autobiography *Revolutions in My Life,* and he clearly attributes to his intense involvement in Hashomer Hatza'ir, from late 1939 until late 1943, the adoption of the Marxist weltanschauung that constituted the major revolution in his life. The ideas that engaged him in the course of his experience in Hashomer Hatza'ir became a catalyst for the Trotskyism that eventually became his rigorous ideological dogma and led to his sharp rejection of Zionism and his dedication to promotion of the class struggle in South Africa. After he left Hashomer Hatza'ir, his political activities, which were for much of the period concurrent with his academic career as a physicist at the University of the Witwatersrand, became increasingly radical. Hirson was only one of several major radicals who issued from Hashomer Hatza'ir into the local struggle and paid the price of arrests, banning, and exile. Most were communists and active in the Congress of Democrats. Other noteworthy ex–Hashomer Hatza'ir radicals were Lionel Forman, Sid Shall, and Monty and Myrtle Berman. In his autobiography Hirson himself commented: "The number of people who left Hashomer Hatza'ir to join the political left (as it was then conceived) indicates that Hashomer Hatza'ir was a crucible of political development."[110]

The formative influence of early Zionist attachments is manifest in the activities of Arthur Goldreich.[111] Goldreich was born in 1929 in South Africa. His family was unusual in that, unlike almost all of his Jewish contemporaries in the radical resistance, not only did it stem from England rather than eastern Europe, but even his grandparents were born in England. Although his father and mother were born in South Africa, they too spent some time back in England. In Arthur's recollection, when he was a child his family considered itself part of a kind of elite Anglo-Jewish segment of the Jewish community. One of his grandparents had first come to South Africa as a soldier in the Boer War period and was a cousin of Samuel Goldreich, an early leader of the South African Zionist Federation. Another unusual aspect of Arthur's upbringing was the completion of his high school education in the Afrikaans language in the small town of Pietersburg, to which the family had moved in the 1930s. His family was traditionally religious in the Anglo-Jewish manner, and as a child Arthur was provided with a private Hebrew teacher. In the Afrikaans-language high school that he attended in Pietersburg, he was permitted to choose Hebrew rather than the usual German as a third required language. The family was also well disposed to Zionism, and the bright adolescent Arthur became the leader of the local Zionist youth association. In 1948 he joined a group of contemporaries in the Habonim youth movement who volunteered to help in Israel's War of Independence, and spent some time after the war on a kibbutz in Galilee. After returning to South Africa in 1954 he became active in the Congress of Democrats, and later, as a front man for the incipient communist underground, he took up residence in a farm estate at Rivonia on the northern outskirts of Johannesburg, which became the underground's secret center. It was there that the South African security police captured the leadership in July 1963 in a series of arrests that led to the incarceration of Nelson Mandela and other leaders of the Umkhonto underground. As has already been related earlier in this chapter, while detained in the Johannesburg Marshall Square prison, Goldreich, together with three other prisoners, made a dramatic escape, after which he settled in Israel.

Harold Wolpe, Goldreich's comrade and partner in the escape, settled in England, where he became a university teacher in sociology and continued his anti-apartheid work. It is noteworthy that Wolpe too had passed through a period of exposure to the Zionist youth movement. He had a conventional upbringing as the offspring of typical immigrant-generation parents and was educated at Johannesburg's Athlone High School, whose pupils were predominantly from the Jewish background of the Doornfontein and Yeoville suburbs. But as a boy, like many of his friends, he was for a time a member of Habonim, and when he became a university student, he participated in a project of the Zionist Socialist Youth for teaching in a night school for blacks.[112] In his recollection, it was at that time that his mind began to open up to the racist realities of South African society. He began to search for a passage to political engagement and was drawn into the Young Communist League. He became a close comrade of Joe Slovo and Ruth First and a major personality in the Communist Party and underground.

It is thus noteworthy that several autobiographical works of Jewish radicals and numerous interviews point to the role of exposure to the Zionist youth movements in raising sociopolitical awareness, even if only as an ancillary factor and in a somewhat dialectical way. This is true also of the generation of activists in the struggle against apartheid in the period of "reformed" apartheid, the 1970s and 1980s. One illuminating example is Taffy Adler, who in those years became an important figure in the formation and consolidation of the black trade union movement. Adler grew up in the relatively poor Judiths Paarl-Bezuidenhout Valley area of Johannesburg adjacent to Doornfontein. His home environment was infused with leftist political sentiment; his eastern European–born father had been a member of the Yiddisher Arbeter Klub, and the communist Ray (Adler) Harmel was an aunt. As an adolescent in the 1960s, Taffy was an active member of the Habonim youth movement, which was intensely Zionist in a socialist vein. But his university studies and exposure to the incipient black trade union movement, initially in a voluntary capacity with the Industrial Aid Society, led him by 1976 into full-time work for the trade unions. Taffy Adler retained a leftist political outlook, regarded himself as a nonreligious Jewish humanist, and became critical of the community's Zionist preoccupation with supporting Israel at the cost of opposition to apartheid. Yet his alienation from the Jewish community never became as severe as that of radicals belonging to earlier generations in South Africa. This difference appears to characterize several other members of the last generation of Jewish activists in the liberation struggle.[113]

A gut sense that Jews, having been the classic historical victims of racial persecution, should feel a moral imperative to oppose apartheid is evident in autobiographical writings of, and recorded interviews with, almost all Jewish radicals and liberals. However, whatever clues may be picked up from these sources as to the specific ideas and values that demonstrably shaped their political opinions and turned them against the South African social order, all point in diverse directions other than Jewish religion. If sociopolitical awareness was awakened in some potential radicals through a Zionist youth movement experience, in other cases it was stimulated in the course of being a school pupil. One influence that stands out is compassionate humanitarian sentiments and liberal political ideas communicated by some extraordinary teachers in certain English-language high schools and, more so, by role models, usually senior students, in the Universities of Cape

Town and the Witwatersrand. In some cases, exposure to these role models was a primary factor in the stimulation of antiapartheid convictions; in other cases, they merely reinforced tendencies already generated in the home (or in the Zionist youth movements) and redirected them toward involvement in the antiapartheid struggle.

It seems that Rusty (Lionel) Bernstein, a major personality in the communist segment of the liberation struggle, is an example of a pathway to radical convictions and activism barely touched by Jewish substance. Reflecting on his path to political awareness, Bernstein writes: "I have no ready answers. . . . I can give no explanation for the origins of my politics." He certainly could not trace them to his home. Born in South Africa in 1920, he was orphaned at the age of twelve and educated in Hilton College, an exclusive boarding school in Natal. But in his autobiographical book he does in fact relate how he was influenced by the antifascist convictions of a particular Hilton College teacher (whose subject, curiously, was Latin).[114] The struggle against fascism in the second half of the 1930s was the context in which he took his first political steps in the small Labor League of Youth in the late 1930s, but it was during his studies at the University of the Witwatersrand's School of Architecture that he became a convinced communist. He mentions in particular being inspired by "an extraordinary third-year student," Kurt Jonas: "It was at Florian's [a coffeehouse in Hillbrow frequented by leftists] via Kurt Jonas that I first learnt of the invisible world of black workers and their trade unions which existed on my own doorstep."[115] Jonas was a Jew, born in South Africa but educated in Germany, where he had qualified in law. Returning to South Africa when Hitler came to power, he switched to the study of architecture. He was a profound intellectual—an avowed Marxist who influenced not only members of the Zionist Socialist Party with which he associated himself but also left-inclined fellow students like Rusty Bernstein and Jock Isacowitz (who was to become, in turn, a Zionist Socialist, a Communist, a leader of the radical war veterans' organization, the Springbok Legion, and ultimately also a key figure in the short-lived Liberal Party).

The autobiographical work of Norma Kitson, born in Durban, similarly attributes nothing significant to the Jewishness of her family background, even though it was far more weighty than Rusty Bernstein's. Kitson's parents were second-generation South Africans possessed of average, conventional Jewish awareness. She describes her mother as an apolitical self-indulgent person from a wealthy family who "lived for parties, cards and coffee mornings."[116] But, in somewhat perfunctory manner her father, and his library of books to which he referred her, planted some seeds of political dissent in relation to South African society: "A progressive brand of history which was not to be found in our South African school text books." She writes that this made her "excitedly aware that there had always been people who resisted the system we lived under in South Africa." These seeds of dissent germinated during five teenage years as a boarder pupil at Redhill, an exclusive English-language private school in Johannesburg. "I became opposed to privilege for whites," she writes, "because I learned it led to brutality to black people."[117] After completing her schooling she sought work in Johannesburg and found lodging with a Jewish family. Her induction to political activism was through a fellow lodger, Helen Navid, who took her along to participate in an ANC Defiance Campaign event in June 1952. Intense radical involvement ensued, and she married David Kitson, a long-standing Communist Party member active mainly in the trade union field and later in the Umkhonto we Sizwe underground.[118] David was arrested in June 1964 and imprisoned for twenty years. After also suffering detention and harsh interrogation by the security police (one called her "bloody Jewish Red muck," she recounts), Norma went into exile in London, taking her two young children with her. There she became the founder in 1982 of the controversial City of London Anti-Apartheid group that conducted an ongoing picket—a relentless forty-eight-hour vigil outside the South African embassy demanding the release of Nelson Mandela and an end to apartheid.

In sum, the available autobiographical evidence, examples of which have been considered above, fails to bear out a "Judaic values" theory. It suggests an explanation for the phenomenon of Jewish radical opponents of apartheid in terms of a sociological factor—marginality or outsider status in relation to the established elites and interests of white South African society, compounded by alienation from the normative life of the Jewish community. It is also suggested here that one ancillary factor discernible in a considerable number of cases is awakening of social and political awareness through exposure to the Zionist youth movements even though they were integral to the organized life of the Jewish community. These factors may well be associated with "Jewishness," but this is not the same as saying they derive from Judaism in the sense of religion or a specifically Jewish ethos. Given the resultant predisposition to look critically at the conventional norms of society, it seems that the inspiring influence of certain role models was in many cases the decisive factor in the making of Jewish radicals. In the preapartheid years, these role models and the political ideas they communicated were mostly encountered in the antifascist arena. Later they were mostly met at the English-language universities in Cape Town and Johannesburg. In some cases they were preceded by influences experienced in school years. Some of these role models were themselves Jewish; others were bearers of liberal or radical traditions of British provenance (in some cases inspired by Christian religious values) that were the main inspiration and basis for the overall opposition to apartheid shown by whites in general. Yet the factors thus identified are no more than rough regularities or common denominators. In the final analysis—it must be acknowledged—one cannot conclude that these suffice to account fully for the making of Jewish radicals and the phenomenon of their disproportionate involvement in the radical opposition to the apartheid system. The individual differences between Jewish radicals are myriad. Levels of identifiable Jewish substance in their upbringing and awareness vary considerably, and no generalization can cover every single case.

Jewish Liberals and the Community

The discussion up to this point has focused on Jewish radicals. Turning now to autobiographical evidence that might account for the Jewish liberals, that is to say, those who conducted their opposition to apartheid more or less within the parameters of legality set by the white polity, one difference is noteworthy. Liberals (bar a few conspicuous exceptions) were less alienated from the Jewish community than radicals and in some cases even participated actively in its institutional life. Ellen Hellmann, whose important role in the Institute of Race Relations was discussed earlier in this chapter, is a good example. Indeed, she even sat for some ten years on the executive of the Jewish Board of Deputies in the critical period of the 1950s and 1960s and served on its important Public Relations Committee. Likewise, numerous Jewish liberals of lesser prominence who were active in the Liberal or Progressive political parties and in a variety of protest movements, such as the war veterans' Springbok Legion or the women's Black Sash, were at the same time active in the life of the Jewish community and the Zionist movement.

Helen Suzman, the most prominent of all liberal opponents of apartheid, never involved herself as closely as did Hellmann with Jewish communal life, but neither did she actively dissociate herself. Among the many awards that have been showered upon Helen Suzman in recognition of her distinguished career in the battle against racial discrimination and for democracy are also citations by Jewish bodies such as the World Council of Synagogues and the United Synagogue of America, which expressed appreciation of "the fact that she draws her sustenance for the wonderful work she is doing from Judaism."[119] This is very much what such Jewish organizations would like to believe. But the story of her life provides little real basis for this attribution of Suzman's liberal political convictions to inspiration derived from Judaism.

Suzman's parents, Samuel and Frieda Gavronsky, were immigrants from Lithuania. Of her father she recalls: "He had very little sympathy for the underdog, and very little sympathy for the blacks in this country." Her mother died shortly after her birth, and her father remarried when Helen was still a child. Helen's stepmother was from England and shaped a very English-acculturated home environment, capped by sending Helen to a private Christian school—the Parktown Convent. There is very little in her recollections that would indicate a home atmosphere marked by values of identifiably Jewish provenance. Helen herself has said, "I do not have a religious background at all. . . . I never joined any Jewish clubs, I never went to synagogue, there were no rabbis who ever had any influence in my life."[120]

It was only when Helen was well into her academic career as a lecturer in economic history at the University of the Witwatersrand and also began to take an interest in the work of the Institute of Race Relations that her political consciousness was seriously stirred. In the course of research on migrant labor and attendant conditions of urban Africans that she did for the Institute of Race Relations in 1947 she became acutely aware of the sufferings of the black population and the evils of South Africa's racial laws. Questioned on the genesis of her liberal political convictions, she has said: "It was the actual knowledge of what was going on which motivated me . . . it was a gradual development. The Institute [of Race Relations] was a great educational factor in my life."[121] In sum, as described by Helen Suzman herself, exposure from a somewhat academic perspective shocked her into identification and action. In that context she has identified the influence of certain personalities, including Ellen Hellmann and Julius Lewin, a colleague at the university and an expert on the labyrinth of oppressive laws that governed the lives of those who were not white in South Africa.

The famous novelist Nadine Gordimer, whose opposition to apartheid found poignant expression in her literary work, seems to have been influenced by a home environment remarkably similar to that of Helen Suzman. She too was sent to a convent school. Her social values were shaped in childhood primarily by her mother, whose parents had brought her with them from England when she was six years old, and whose attitudes to Jewishness were the product of several generations of middle-class Anglo-acculturation. Nadine's father, by contrast, came from a poor family in Latvia. When he was only eleven years old he left school to learn the skill of watch mending, which became the source of his livelihood, and he knew not a word of English when he arrived in South Africa at age thirteen. It was an unhappy marriage, and Nadine's mother dominated the home environment. Nadine has said that her father "wasn't allowed to have any Jewishness" and recollects: "My mother despised my father's background. We didn't ever go to synagogue; my father went on the High Holidays on his own. We didn't keep kosher—we ate bacon."[122] Nadine was brought up to pass as a South African of purely English cultural background dissociated not only from Judaism as religion but also from the prevalent social life of young Jews centered around Zionism: "From my mother I got the feeling that I was a South African, what has Israel got to do with me?" Nadine recalls that whereas even helping the German-Jewish victims of Nazism who came to South Africa did not particularly interest her mother, she was not without social conscience in regard to a liberal project such as starting a crèche for black children in the townships.[123] As for her father's attitude, Gordimer describes it as wholly compliant with white racist norms. Indeed she is shamed and saddened by his being an example of former victims of racism adopting the same racist attitude toward others.

One may therefore deduce from Nadine Gordimer's own description of her upbringing that it fostered a strong impulse to break out of the given marginality situation of Jews in relation to white society in order to be identified as a purely English-speaking South African, and that this was greatly compounded by alienation in relation to the Jewish community.[124] Given this background it is not surprising that Nadine Gordimer has repeatedly discounted Jewishness as a factor in shaping the liberal values that made her an opponent of apartheid. Interviewed by former Russian Jewish prisoner of conscience Natan Sharansky, she told him: "I don't think that my Jewishness is an influence, and I get rather annoyed when people say that my opposition to racism comes from being Jewish. It's a terrible deflection if you have self-interest in acting against racism."[125] "Judaic values" being clearly nonoperative in her own case, it would appear—quite typically—that the only sense in which Jewishness might be regarded as a factor is sociological. Yet even Gordimer finds it difficult to evade the conventional public perception that Jewishness commands liberal attitudes, for in the very same interview she herself averred to Sharansky: "I believe that as Jews, we must be especially sensitive to racism," a belief scarcely compatible with her previously expressed opinion that Jewishness ought not to be relevant in the first instance.

Far more obvious and acknowledged Jewish roots mark the personality of Leslie Rubin, one of the founders of the Liberal Party of South Africa and the first candidate of that party to be elected to South Africa's Senate. He was born in 1909 into an orthodox family. Indeed, his father was for twenty-five years minister of an orthodox Jewish congregation in Durban, and Leslie joined the Young Israel movement and served for a time as chairman of the Durban Zionist Association and as a member of the executive of the Council of Natal Jewry, an affiliate of the national Jewish Board of Deputies. His wife Pearl was also active in Jewish communal affairs both in the Zionist Bnoth Zion and as chairperson for a time of the Cape branch of the Union of Jewish Women.

Rubin studied at the Universities of the Witwatersrand and Natal, qualifying as a lawyer and later gaining a doctorate in law. He served in the armed forces during the Second World War, during which time he visited Palestine. It was as one of the "natives' representatives" that Rubin was elected to the Senate in 1954. Although he was of course wholly opposed to the entire edifice of apartheid, including this form of representation, which was a relic of preapartheid white supremacy, he used his seat in parliament to oppose apartheid vigorously from within the system, much as did the communist Sam Kahn, mentioned earlier in this chapter. He too was the object of antisemitic taunts.[126] But when the natives' representative seats were abolished by the apartheid regime in 1959, Rubin left South Africa to take up academic positions first in Ghana and thereafter in the United States, where he became a professor of government at Howard University in Washington, D.C.

It is difficult to know how many Jews seriously took up the cudgels in liberal-mode defiance of the apartheid system, notwithstanding their upbringing as privileged middle-class whites and their attendant conditioning to the "natural" social order of white superiority and domination. Probably they numbered in the hundreds over the four decades of apartheid rule. The names of some, like Helen Suzman, are inscribed alongside many more gentile names in the history of the opposition to apartheid, even if sometimes only grudgingly acknowledged by the radicals, whose role in the "liberation movement" is far more valorized in post-apartheid South Africa. However, most of the Jews who were numbered among apartheid's white liberal opponents have remained anonymous. Many chose to leave the country of their birth for reasons that, at the least, included their repugnance for the system and the sense that leaving the country was the only morally defensible alternative to active resistance at the risk of being banned, harassed, and incarcerated, or worse.

Behind and around Helen Suzman were many dedicated rank-and-file Jewish liberals who sincerely opposed apartheid but never fell foul of the security authorities in a measure sufficient to incur arrest and imprisonment. Not many of these have so far provided posterity with published autobiographical records or memoirs that cast light on their emotional and intellectual passage to a liberal critique of the system and to compassionate identification with its victims. One who has is Phyllis Lewsen, best known for her academic works on South African history. That the blurb on her autobiographical book, *Reverberations,* published in 1996, could state that "she describes herself unashamedly as part of the liberal tradition of South Africa" poignantly reflects the devalued status of the liberal in postapartheid South Africa, in contrast with the valorization of the radicals.

Phyllis Lewsen's parents were immigrants from eastern Europe who had come to South Africa in their teens. She grew up in the 1920s, long before the accretion to power of the Afrikaner nationalists, in a thoroughly Jewish family within the small Jewish-community milieu of rural Potchefstroom. Most of the descendants of her maternal grandfather, Chaim Sack, were very active in the life of the community, especially in Zionist activity. She experienced the marginal-outsider situation of Jews from an early age. "It was a mixed kind of upbringing," she writes, "but I always knew that as Jews we were different." She also notes that antisemitism "was inherent in our environment."[127] It is noteworthy that despite what amounts to a highly conscious Jewish upbringing (and her well-trained historian's sense for causality)[128] Phyllis Lewsen mentions nothing in the Jewish home environment that might explain her path to liberal values applied critically to South African society. But she does mention that in the girls' high school, which she attended after primary schooling in a Catholic convent, she encountered a history teacher (aptly, Miss Fair by name) who was a liberal. "She gave me my first, unforgettable lesson on the evils and stupidity of racism," writes Lewsen. "My views became liberal: a change that took place deep inside me."[129] In 1932 she began her academic career, studying for a B.A. in history and English at the University of the Witwatersrand. As described in her published memoir, her entry into modest political involvement was via membership in the Institute of Race Relations, in her words, "a liberal body, committed to the careful recording and analysis of facts as the only valid means of persuasion."[130] She felt a strong intellectual and moral affinity to the institute's leaders, who included fellow historian Leo Marquard, Edgar Brookes, and the writer Alan Paton, and became especially close to Ellen Hellmann. Phyllis Lewsen also was one of the first to enlist in the Black Sash women's organization that came into being in 1955, initially to resist the national government's abolition of the Cape colored vote. Together with her husband, Jack Lewsen, whose political activity was as a United Party member of the Johannesburg municipal council, in the early 1950s she was involved in efforts to create a liberal political association that ultimately issued in the formation of the Liberal Party.[131] Later she became a close supporter of Helen Suzman and the Progressive Party.

Phyllis Lewsen's story is that of a first-generation Jewish South African. Another autobiographical source is illuminating of the path of rank-and-file liberal activists who were second-generation Jews in South Africa. Its little-known author is Janet Levine, who with her husband and two young children chose to leave South Africa for the United States in 1984, after some two decades of involvement in liberal opposition to apartheid. Her activities began as a student and included journalistic work, membership in the Progressive Federal Party—particularly work in support of Helen Suzman's election campaigns—and election to the Johannesburg City Council, where her role as passionate liberal opponent of apartheid paralleled, in minor key, the larger role in parliament of her mentor, Helen Suzman.

Levine writes revealingly: "I have searched my memory to determine how and where my burgeoning sense of racial and social justice germinated in the backdrop of my family's bland, white, middle-class life style." She certainly does not find any seeds to have been planted by her South African–born parents, one generation removed from eastern Europe. "My family's stereotypical responses to blacks were based on their interactions with servants," she writes—"none of them had ever met a black person in any other circumstance."[132]

According to Levine's description of the influences in her early life, neither as religion nor as cultural identity did Judaism play any role. It would appear that her critical view of the moral deformities in the society around her was generated by stages largely through chance exposures to certain adult role models. One was the nursery school teacher Anna Marais, who was active in the Black Sash protest movement (and the wife of the Witwatersrand University historian J. S. Marais). Another was a schoolteacher, an Englishman, of whom she writes: "It was he who first opened my eyes to the injustice of apartheid." It is noteworthy that Levine's recollections too illustrate the sense of marginality and alienation that has been suggested earlier in this chapter as the underlying factor in the making of Jewish radicals. However, Levine depicts this as a characteristic of English speakers generally rather than something specific to Jews like herself. Thus she says that her school education, especially the study of history mediated by a skeptical teacher, engendered a sense of critical alienation from and irreverence for the blatantly racist, Afrikaner-centered narrative of South African history:

> It was "their" monument, to "their" battles and killings of black warriors from whom "they" took the land. We were interlopers. At all times the Afrikaner Nationalist version of history was seen to have little to do with us, the English-speaking white South Africans. If one of the ends of the creation of the Afrikaner political mythology was to inculcate a broad patriotism among whites, it failed lamentably to do so for us. In fact, it reinforced our feeling of alienation from the Afrikaner power bloc.[133]

Levine writes that after years of enthusiastic political activity she came to a realization that all liberal opposition had exhausted its efficacy and reached a dead end. Explaining the decision to leave South Africa, Levine writes candidly: "My way did not lie in a political prison, in banishment, under house arrest or under a banning order. . . . Like so many others before me, the way of self-exile—of self-banishment from the country I loved, from my people—beckoned in the darkness South Africa had become for me."[134]

Levine was one of numerous Jews who, far from being career politicians, made what may be described as temporary forays into the arena of legitimate politics out of purely moral antiapartheid convictions. Frustrated by the ultimate inefficacy of intrawhite politics, they often dropped out of this activity. Some chose to leave the country. An example of those who withdrew after a stint in politics but remained in South Africa is Dr. Selma Browde. Setting aside her medical profession, she entered the political arena in 1972 as a Progressive Party candidate, and after election to the Johannesburg City Council she concurrently served on the Transvaal Provincial

Council from 1974 to 1978. Much as Helen Suzman was doing in parliament, Browde fought the system at the local level with every available legal means and availed herself of every possible strategy to alleviate the plight of its victims. In 1982 she resigned from politics and returned to her career in medical research.

As is typical of so many other Jews who actively took a stand against apartheid, retracing Selma Browde's path to antiapartheid convictions provides little that can be identified as specifically "Judaic values."[135] She was born into a white South African–acculturated home of second-generation Jews. As a child, the selfless humanitarian dedication she witnessed in her father's medical practice left a deep impression. He died when she was still young, and a cousin, Monty Berman, became something of a father figure for her and an influential role model. He and his wife Myrtle were active communists at that time. Inspired by the Bermans, while still a schoolgirl Selma was already distributing the leftist paper *The Guardian.* When she became a medical student her outspokenness and fraternization with the sole black fellow student in her class already attracted the attention of the security police. Selma never went so far as to join the Communist Party, and her marriage to advocate Jules Browde exposed her to a pronounced Jewish social and intellectual milieu, since he had a strong Jewish awareness rooted in his first-generation immigrant home and in the Habonim Zionist youth movement. Indeed, for over two decades in the apartheid years, he served as the honorary head of Habonim in South Africa. Like most Jewish liberals who acted politically upon their antiapartheid convictions, Selma Browde emphatically held that it was a moral imperative for a Jew to oppose apartheid. Yet, in empirical terms one may question whether she—and many other like-minded and activated Jews—had become opponents of apartheid because of their awareness of "Jewish values." Is it not more likely that they retrospectively read putative Jewishness into the liberal ideas and values disseminated by role-model personalities to whom they were exposed by dint of their social situation as Jews in South Africa?

One important aspect of opposition throughout the apartheid era was the tenacious survival power of the free press. Notwithstanding the smothering of the radical press (mostly communist and minuscule in scale) and the severe restrictions and controls placed upon the English-language newspapers, criticism of apartheid and revelations of its cruel injustices could not be wholly suppressed. In this sphere of opposition too there were Jewish journalists of note. Benjamin Pogrund is one outstanding example. As a journalist for twenty-six years, from 1959 to 1985, on *The Rand Daily Mail,* which led the way as critic of the apartheid regime, Pogrund was at the forefront of the relentless effort to maintain press reportage of the politics of the liberation struggle and of the social carnage and human suffering wrought by apartheid. A survey of his career may serve to illustrate not only this aspect of the anti-apartheid struggle but as well to further illuminate what went into the making of Jewish liberals and how they interrelated with the life of the Jewish community.[136]

Pogrund's parents belonged to the Yiddish-speaking immigrant generation. In the manner characteristic of most South African Jews of their generation, they were moderately observant of Jewish religious precepts. They imparted to Benjamin no particular political or social awareness; nor did his schooling, which concluded with his matriculation at the South African College School (SACS) in Cape Town. If anything, it was only in the Zionist youth movement Habonim, during the late 1940s, that the adolescent Pogrund was first exposed to a measure of ideological and social awareness. By age sixteen, like many of his friends, he had formed the intention of settling in a kibbutz in Israel. However, as a student at the University of Cape Town in the early 1950s he was drawn into the antiapartheid campaigning of the National Union of South African Students (NUSAS), made his first friends across the color line, and immersed himself deeply in the activities of the Students' Representative Council. This involvement was in tune with many of his Jewish friends who, like him, had passed through the youth movement experience provided by Habonim and Hashomer Hatza'ir. Whereas some gravitated into the communist circle—Lionel Forman, who had been in Hashomer Hatza'ir, was an outstanding example—Pogrund's inclination was liberal from the outset, and in the course of the ideological rivalry that developed between communists and liberals in NUSAS, his repugnance for doctrinaire communism became acute.

After completion of his master's degree in psychology, Pogrund shifted his sphere of involvement to the Liberal Party. Moving to Johannesburg in 1957, he conducted the party's work in the black township of Sophiatown. In 1958 he was taken on as a journalist by *The Rand Daily Mail,* whose new editor, Laurence Gandar, was honing the paper into a sharp press instrument in the struggle against apartheid. Pogrund went on to become the paper's foremost reporter, much of it seminal investigative reportage, on everything concerned with the affairs of the "non-European" public—trade union activities, black politics, the deplorable jail conditions of black prisoners, police raids, conditions in the rural areas, and so forth. He became a single-handed pioneer of the genre of reporting that later came to be associated with what was known as the alternative press. From 1977 until the closure of *The Rand Daily Mail* in 1985, he was deputy editor. In the course of his work Pogrund developed a close friendship with the Pan-Africanist Congress leader Robert Sobukwe, a relationship he sustained also in the period of Sobukwe's imprisonment on Robben Island. Pogrund later authored a much acclaimed book on the life of Sobukwe.[137]

Antagonizing upholders of the apartheid system, at various times Pogrund was denied a passport, detained for refusing to disclose the identity of an informant, prosecuted for reports courageously exposing appalling jail conditions of blacks and political prisoners, and subjected to police searches in his home. Unlike Jewish communists, Pogrund was never beyond the pale of the Jewish community. He was after all only functioning, however audaciously, as a liberal with the legal license of press freedom, much as Helen Suzman was doing in parliament. Moreover, at no time did Pogrund detach himself from Jewish identification, although he was very critical of the official community's silence on apartheid. Indeed, in the mid-1960s he became a regular participant in religious services at Johannesburg's Oxford Road orthodox synagogue. After leaving South Africa in 1986 he associated himself with the social-concern activities of the Jewish Yakar Educational Foundation in London, and in 1997 he moved to Israel to assume directorship of

Yakar's new center for social concern in Jerusalem, whose projects included the daunting attempt to foster Jewish-Arab understanding.

In common with many other whites, Jews were to be found in a varied range of ideological orientations and forms of protest or opposition. Especially in the 1950s the lines between communist-oriented Congress of Democrats involvement and liberal forms of opposition and social action were sometimes blurred, and often enough ordinary antiapartheid foot soldiers, as it were, may not easily be categorized as radicals or liberals. Esther Levitan, who was born in Lithuania and came to South Africa as a child, has authored an autobiographical book that provides insights into the making of this variety of apartheid's lesser-known Jewish opponents. Her story too illustrates the nature of such forms of activism and the personal suffering that was the cost. Her vigorous activities, beginning in the early 1950s and sustained over a period of more than three decades, are a striking illustration of resistance to apartheid by a liberal who described herself as a fellow traveler of the communist left.

Also in Levitan's case one may hardly attribute her political disposition to any putative values inhering in Judaism or imbibed in the home. Indeed, she writes that her mother "was a staunch supporter of the Nationalist Party which she regarded as the only assurance of white/Jewish survival in South Africa," and this even years after her daughter had fallen foul of the authorities and suffered cruel detention.[138] Only in her late teens was Esther first exposed to any political ideas critical of the society into which she had been socialized, the result of a chance meeting with a young communist activist in Cape Town, whom she married but soon after divorced. Moving to Johannesburg, she went on to engage herself in an array of welfare and political organizations and activities associated one way or another with the "liberation movement." During this period she was married to Jack Levitan and raised a family. Her husband was one of the Jewish lawyers who selflessly lent their professional support to victims and opponents of the apartheid regime. Esther Levitan never joined the Communist Party, but she was nevertheless "named" by the government authorities in the late 1950s.

At the same time Levitan had sporadic associations with Jewish activities. As early as 1948, when she was in her early twenties, she was selected by a local Jewish organization to work for a year in the American Distribution Committee's relief program for Holocaust survivors in Europe. Although the Levitans were very secular, the Passover seder was celebrated in their home with many guests including black friends. She took part in the Union of Jewish Women's welfare work. At the Union's national conference in October 1977 she lobbied (unsuccessfully) for a resolution that formal protest be made against the new wave of arrests and banning connected with the emergency the government had declared.[139] Later, she accepted a job with the Women's Zionist Council, becoming its public relations officer. It was on the premises of the Women's Zionist Council offices in the building of the South African Zionist Federation that the security police arrested Esther in 1982. An illegal act a few years back—hiding an escaped political prisoner in her home for about ten days prior to his being successfully spirited out of the country—unexpectedly caught up with her after the police arrested and elicited a confession from the organizer of the escape. Levitan, now in her late fifties, had to endure months of imprisonment, interrogation, and solitary confinement before finally being released in the wake of illness and hospitalization. Of her coworkers in the Zionist Federation, she writes that, although not sharing her political views, they behaved toward her "with impeccable rectitude and fairness."[140]

Even after her release, Esther had to report periodically to the police, was denied a passport, and suffered intimidating harassment from politically motivated vandals. Like many others who had fought the apartheid system, she finally decided to leave the country she loved so dearly on an exit visa. The United Kingdom Home Office had granted her the right of permanent residence, but she chose to try living in Israel, not at all, as she candidly declared, for ideological reasons but simply because she found it difficult to cope with the cold climate of England. In Israel she was soon active in fostering an "Israelis Against Apartheid" organization as well as in far-left demonstrations advocating Palestinians' rights. Ultimately, after the dramatic transformation to nonracial democracy in South Africa, she returned to the land she regarded as her only true home.[141]

What can be said in conclusion of this survey of Jewish opponents of apartheid? It cannot be claimed that the various cases of radical and liberal Jews considered above are a scientifically representative sample. The basis for their selection as examples is simply the fact that they have published autobiographical works or been meaningfully interviewed concerning their Jewish background. Yet even these limited examples show that the pathways, whether radical or liberal, taken by Jewish South Africans against apartheid were multifarious. At most, a few regularities or common factors are inferable. Although what might be called Jewishness is a factor in a variety of ways and degrees, the evidence does not sustain an explanatory theory of "Judaic values." A more plausible hypothesis is that the characteristically "Jewish" social condition of marginal-outsider status is the underlying factor that predisposed Jews to imbibe liberal or radical values that challenged the apartheid system. Of course, this factor is by no means a self-sufficient predictor of radical or liberal behavior. The same marginal-outsider social situation obviously could engender in those who became acutely critical of the social order alternative patterns of political behavior. In not a few Jewish families, siblings embarked with equal conviction on divergent political courses.[142] As we have seen, the constrained liberal option of standing for election just left of center was about as far as most politically active Jews allowed themselves to go in opposing apartheid. There were also a few Jews whose response to marginal-outsider status was to seek acceptance into newly empowered Afrikaner circles by demonstrating their support of apartheid policy. Then there was the Zionist option, which, if taken seriously, meant choosing to leave rather than participate in an evil society in relation to which one was in any case a marginal outsider—an option whose ideological basis will be discussed in the next section of this chapter. Finally, there were others who simply chose to emigrate, heading for places that offered good material prospects, free of racial problems.

Nevertheless, identifying this outsider-marginal social condition goes at least some distance toward explaining the disproportionate role of Jews in the opposition, whether radical or liberal, to apartheid. For such Jews, values incompatible with apartheid appear to have been mediated mainly by role models generated within the intellectual ambience of South African English speakers in which most Jews were socialized and educated. These models drew upon British strains of humanitarian compassion and liberal ideas. Radical Marxist ideas were more likely to be radiated within immigrant families from eastern Europe. In some cases these influences converged with what can perhaps be described as specifically Jewish compassion and ideas; in other cases assumed Jewish values were retrospectively read into them. But a comprehensive and adequate answer to the question why some Jews imbibed these values and acted upon them whereas others did not remains elusive. Imponderables such as idiosyncratic personality traits and chance exposures to inspiring role models or to the warm embrace of supportive social groups enter the equation and perhaps are the ultimate differentiating factors. In this respect social-psychological studies have a contribution to make.[143] In the final analysis, one cannot entirely dismiss the frustrating thought—but one that the social scientist or historian is bound to resist, however Sisyphean the effort—that radicals and liberals are not made but simply born that way.

Discord over Communal Policy

Although the Jewish Board of Deputies' policy of noninvolvement in politics—and the compliance with it of almost all of the rabbinate—undoubtedly enjoyed a broad consensus of support among Jews, it did not go entirely unchallenged. By and large, it was the moderate and liberal type of Jewish activist rather than the communist radicals who cared to engage in public censure of the communal leadership for adopting this policy. The explanation for this may well be the far greater estrangement and detachment of communist radicals from anything Jewish. There were however some exceptions, notably Sam Kahn and Eli Weinberg, whose unusually substantial Jewish roots were discussed earlier in this chapter. Writing in *New Age* in late 1955, Kahn attacked the strongly Zionist Jewish leadership from a patently communist, radical perspective. He accused it of submitting to the nationalist government's blackmail for the sake of gaining support for Israel and assuring permission to transfer funds. The price to be paid was toeing the National Party line and eliminating opposition to apartheid and race persecution of the non-Europeans. "For centuries the Jews have cried out passionately for world sympathy and help against anti-Semitism and persecution," he wrote. "South African Jewry dare not remain deaf and indifferent to the equally passionate cry for emancipation which comes from the lips of the Non-Europeans."[144]

From time to time Eli Weinberg was similarly moved to vent his views in both the general and the Jewish press. "I notice that Rabbi Kossowsky, purporting to speak on behalf of ALL Jews, has pledged their undivided loyalty to the Republic," he once wrote in *The Rand Daily Mail.* "As one of the many Jews whose families were exterminated in the name of race superiority, I must refuse to subscribe to a pledge committing me to be loyal to a Republic blatantly based on racial domination."[145] In a second letter, this time to the *Jewish Times,* Weinberg attacked another correspondent, one Mr. Burgin, for demanding exclusion of all politics from the concern of the synagogue. It seems that his objections were directed particularly at the young rabbi Ben Isaacson. Responding to this, Weinberg quoted the teachings of the prophets, the Jewish injunction to "love thy neighbour," and other biblical passages adjuring Jews to heed their responsibilities toward the stranger in their midst. He deplored Burgin's view that Jews should show "due regard to the possible consequences" of any political statements they might make. This, he said, was to accept the definition of the social position of the Jews advocated by antisemites. He praised rabbi Ben Isaacson for daring to speak out. This was the true contribution of Judaism, Weinberg argued, and Africans would cherish Isaacson's expression of Jewish solidarity with another oppressed race.[146]

The files of the Jewish Board of Deputies contain a few direct appeals for support from radical organizations. In June 1950, the combined National Protest Committee of the African National Congress, Indian National Congress, and the Communist Party of South Africa invited the Board to participate in a National Protest Day. "Should the 'Suppression of Communism' Bill become law," they wrote, "we stand in danger of being deprived of the right to fight against the Pass Laws, Group and Ghetto Laws etc." In 1961 the Congress of Democrats sent a memorandum to the Board of Deputies expressing shock at what it interpreted as the Board's endorsement of South Africa's reproof of Israel for joining the United Nations' censure of Foreign Affairs Minister Eric Louw (an incident to which we have referred in the previous chapter). The hand of Ben Turok, at the time national secretary of the Congress of Democrats, is discernible in the memorandum's reasoning. It took the Board to task for making a statement of such obvious political import in contradiction to "its own constant protestations that it never interferes in matters of a political nature." The memo's author went on to say that since the Congress of Democrats had always found the Board's "self-imposed political censorship unrealistic and unhelpful," its objection in this instance was "not to the political involvement of the Board, but to its involvement on the wrong side, on the side of the advocates of apartheid." It also cautioned the Board "lest the people who will [inevitably] constitute the future non-racial Government should come to feel that the Board constitutes an antagonistic force."[147]

In consonance with its policy, the Board of Deputies did not respond to such approaches any more than to contrary approaches from progovernment political bodies.[148] These were not lacking. They included the John X. Merriman English-speaking branch of the National Party, which appealed for Jewish support, arguing disingenuously that "separate development" meant partition as in Israel's case, and "the only alternative to Dr. Verwoerd's policy of partition is a multi-racial State beyond which lurks the spectre of Communism." "If the Jewish people in South Africa consider what would have happened to Israel had a multi-racial instead of a partition policy been implemented," it submitted, "they will realise that it would now have been under the control of a strong Arab majority."[149]

The Board of Deputies tirelessly reiterated its disapproval of any political appeals to Jews as a group. This policy greatly aggravated the disaffected attitude already characteristic of most Jewish radicals and many active Jewish liberals. In turn, high-profile Jewish activists in the struggle against apartheid, especially if known to have or suspected of having communist affinities, were shunned by most Jews, ignored by Jewish organizations, and sidelined by the Jewish press, although not in the case of those who functioned legally.[150] To be sure, many radicals and liberals were sooner or later under banning orders that made it a punishable offense to meet with them or quote them. But this neither applied in every case nor at all times during the decades of apartheid rule. Fear certainly caused many Jews to distance themselves from such persons, but disapproval probably was no less a factor. Be that as it may, the experience of most radicals was of being treated as pariahs by the Jewish community and public. Typical is Baruch Hirson's bitter recounting of visits by the Jewish chaplain, the orthodox Rabbi Sydney Katz, to the Jewish political prisoners in the Pretoria local jail, where eight of the twenty-five were Jewish at that time:

> Our actions and beliefs hardly fitted with the Jewish community's idea of politics, but the frosty reception went beyond anything we had anticipated. We got a dressing-down as we stood on one side of the perspex window in the visiting room. We were a disgrace to Jewry; we were disreputable; we had acted disgracefully. . . . I came out of that session declaring that this was the end. I would not do it again. The man was narrow, bigoted, inhuman. . . . However, the others would not permit such defection. We needed the food.[151]

Pauline Podbrey, whose marriage to Indian radical leader H. A. Naidoo defied apartheid precepts, has described her experience when she tried to enroll their daughter in a Herzlia schools day nursery. Although the principal, Zalman Avin, welcomed her warmly, the school board chaired by Chief Rabbi Abrahams afterward countermanded this "with regret," fearing that acceptance of a colored child would jeopardize the school's government license. The parents of children at the school were divided into two opposing camps on the question. When a deputation of sympathetic parents went to Rabbi Abrahams arguing that the child was surely Jewish (since she had a Jewish mother), the most he could suggest was that they send the child to Israel with the financial help of the Cape Town Jewish community.[152] AnnMarie Wolpe relates a similar experience. When she was struggling to manage her family's life after the arrest and escape of her husband, Harold, the board of the King David Jewish school told her it was prepared to waive her daughters' nursery school fees until such time as she felt she was able to pay. But offensive, sanctimonious reproach on account of her husband's activities accompanied this message.[153] There were, however, exceptions. Rowley Arenstein, for example, related that the Jewish community in Durban "went out of its way to help us." It helped to look after his family and provided free tuition in the private Jewish schools.[154]

Several prominent activists in the struggle against apartheid penned cogent indictments of the Jewish community's stance. One of the sharpest critics was Ronald Segal, editor-publisher of the pungent, antigovernment journal *Africa South,* until both he and the magazine were banned in 1959 under the Suppression of Communism Act (although he was not by any means a member of the Communist Party). His passport having been withdrawn, Segal left the country illegally in 1960 during the state of emergency declared after the Sharpeville tragedy. He made his escape across the border to Bechuanaland together with ANC leader Oliver Tambo, Tambo dressed as his black chauffeur. From London he continued to play a major role in galvanizing world opinion against apartheid and pressing for economic sanctions against South Africa. Brought up in what he himself described as "a passionately Jewish home," both his parents having been prominent leaders of Cape Town's Jewish community, Segal was sharply critical of the political inaction of South African Jewry qua community. "South African Jews are forever conscious of injustice that they alone are made to suffer," he wrote. "How can this one-eyed morality be defended?" He was incensed by the contrast between their fervor for Israel's right to exist, on the one hand, and the complacency with which they watched "the innumerable daily manifestations of apartheid" and the denial of any rights whatsoever to the mass of South Africa's people, on the other.[155]

As exemplified by Ronald Segal's views, the critique formulated by the activist, liberal, or radical Jew may be reduced to three main premises. First, that it was an undeniable imperative of Jewishness to oppose the evils inhering in the South African societal system; an imperative emanating from either the ethics of Judaism or the historic experience of the Jews, or indeed both. As Segal declared: "I *do* believe that the Jews have a peculiar heritage and an especial character formed by that heritage. That heritage and that character give them a sharpened sense of the difference between right and wrong, between oppression and liberty and also a great capacity for sacrifice, yes, even for martyrdom." To the argument that the political alignment he demanded for the community might endanger its very security, Segal had a drastic response: "Is the idea that in certain circumstances an entire community should be composed of martyrs really so difficult to entertain?" he asked. "Is the whole history of medieval Jewry not proof sufficient of the possibility of such communal sacrifice?"

The second premise was that racial discrimination was indivisible and appeasement never paid. "If the injustice of the act counts for nothing, blatant self-interest alone should have dictated the community's protest," wrote Segal. "It may not always be only the non-whites who are mauled by the provisions of the Group Areas Act," he cautioned; "it needs only the addition of a word to the relevant clause—Jews, or Hebrews, have long constituted a separate racial group in government files and government thinking."[156]

The third premise common to the community's liberal critics was that by failing to act upon the imperative to oppose the South African racial system, Jewish leadership deserted its purpose and Judaism forfeited its relevance for the modern Jew. Segal cast doubt on the justification for a Jewish communal entity if it was false to Jewish values. "If the Jews are not a race like the Indians, nor a religious community like the Anglicans, what are they?" he asked. "If they are only just South Africans and nothing else, then the Jewish Board of Deputies has no business to exist."

An equally vehement critic of the community was Lithuanian-born Solly Sachs, the militant trade union leader whose career we have mentioned in an earlier chapter. Sachs left South Africa and settled in England after government harassment had paralyzed his trade union work. In 1958 he had a heated exchange of views with the Anglo-Jewish writer Joseph Leftwich, who had shown understanding for the policy adopted by South African Jewry's leadership. Asserting that the Board of Deputies' policy was both immoral and misguided, Sachs went so far as to invoke comparison with the Nazi Holocaust: "I wonder what the men, women and children who were asphyxiated at Treblinka . . . if they arose from their graves, would say to the Jews of Johannesburg and Cape Town today?" he asked.[157] Sachs too untiringly warned that the Afrikaner nationalists were still antisemitic and that discrimination was indivisible.

Both Segal and Sachs were by then criticizing from abroad. Within the South African Jewish community itself, bitter controversy flared up in 1964 over a statement made by Julius Lewin, professor of African law and administration at the University of the Witwatersrand and a long-standing liberal opponent of the apartheid regime. Lewin was not a high-profile personality. He neither associated with Jewish communal life nor went out of his way to criticize the community's leadership. But, invited to address a meeting of the local Yiddish Folkshul at a gathering to commemorate the Warsaw Ghetto uprising, he made some statements that caused quite a stir of controversy in the press. Lewin declared unequivocally: "The Jewish tradition is a liberal and progressive one, and it is wrong for the Jews of South Africa to deny or disguise this fact." He asserted, moreover, that the National Party was trying to intimidate the Jews. They had become the semiconscious victims of political blackmail. He too warned that appeasement would never pay:

> If men's minds were not clouded by fear they would realize that the prospects and positions of any minority group could only be as healthy as the society of which it was a part. South Africa is a sick society and the Jews cannot hope to enjoy permanent security while other non-conforming groups feel threatened in the atmosphere created by the ruling race.[158]

Leslie Rubin, one of the Liberal Party's foremost leaders, was another incisive critic of the Jewish communal leadership. As was mentioned earlier in this chapter, Rubin was the son of a rabbi and had been active in the Jewish community. There is thus no question that Rubin had substantial Jewish roots and knowledge. Rubin sharply censured the policy adopted by the Jewish Board of Deputies both before and after he left South Africa in the early 1960s and settled in the United States. "Quiescence becomes acquiescence," he charged; "passivity in the face of injustice becomes support for those who perpetrate it." "When the Sharpeville massacre of 1960 unleashed a flood of outraged protest throughout the world, the Board of Deputies had nothing to say," he complained. "On the other hand two Chief Rabbis delivered glowing eulogies when Prime Minister Verwoerd died." He argued further that:

> Viewed against the realities of the South African situation . . . the Board has failed in its attempts to find a compromise between outright opposition to the regime (thus exposing the community to the risk of retaliation) and unequivocal support for it (thus repudiating the basic principle of the Judaeo-Christian ethic). The policy it has adopted has been a double failure, satisfying neither those it designated to placate, nor those it is intended to protect.[159]

The critics cited thus far spoke as individuals who had to all intents and purposes dissociated themselves from participation in the life of the Jewish community. But similar criticism also issued from a small circle of grassroots Jews who represented the remnants of the leftist Yiddish groupings that had been active before 1948, such as the Yiddisher Arbeter Klub and the Geserd. Under the leadership of Michael Szur, in the 1950s they formed a small group called the Jewish Democratic Association. Through the medium (no longer in Yiddish) of a meager monthly newsletter styled *Jewish Opinion,* they carried on the diminutive legacy of now defunct leftist anti-Zionist groups in South African Jewry. Szur charged that the Board's policy emanated from the false Zionist view that Jews were really no more than temporary sojourners in the Diaspora. He said this policy was tantamount to a voluntary renunciation of the rights of South African citizenship and created a spiritual ghetto:

> The Jews dare not forget the days of oppression in Tsarist Russia and the days when the Hitler barbarians aimed to exterminate the Jewish people. We then complained justifiably that the people of the world did not rally to our defence. Now we witness the oppression of the majority of the people of South Africa. If justice was on our side when we demanded that the world should defend us, then as a community we cannot hide ourselves behind the false slogan of neutrality and keep silent when other peoples are in distress.

Like other critics of the communal leadership, the Jewish Democratic Association also advanced the argument of Jewish self-interest. It warned that "leaving morals and ethics aside . . . even from the point of view of Real Politik the Jewish community as a whole must, together with all the progressive forces and all those who are suffering under oppression, join the struggle and fight for freedom in South Africa."[160]

To be sure, throughout the apartheid years all the contentions of the liberal or radical critics had been thrashed out, with great pangs of conscience, in innumerable debates within the councils of the Jewish Board of Deputies itself. But neither there nor in the press did these contentions pass uncontradicted by other Jews speaking with equal conviction. Julius Lewin's brief foray into the community, for example, raised a furor of controversy in which the very premise that Judaism obligated a liberal approach was challenged. "On the contrary," responded an irate Jew in a typical letter to the general press, "Jews have always been traditional and conservative. . . . The more liberal a Jew gets the less Jewish he becomes, and the less he identifies with his traditional heritage, the more liberal he becomes."[161]

There is abundant evidence in the record of the Board's congress debates on public relations that, even assuming its elected leaders could unanimously accept the premises of critics like Segal or Rubin, they would never have passed at any plenum of the Board. Political opinion and personal party allegiance varied considerably, and, as we have seen, the consensus was repeatedly in favor of political noninvolvement as the only feasible policy for the community. If at least the first premise of the liberal critique, positing a moral imperative of Jewishness to oppose apartheid, matched the personal views of a number of the Board's leading figures, the same could hardly be said of the second premise, which posited that discrimination was indivisible and that Jews must inevitably also become its victims in South Africa. On the contrary, in the eyes of most Jews the logic of South African race relations pointed in quite the opposite direction. They held that if there were anything likely to precipitate antisemitism and discrimination against Jews, it was precisely the collective adoption of a liberal political position that flouted the government's policy.

If the contentions of the liberal or radical Jewish critic were thus doubted, even more were his motives mistrusted. Detached as he generally was from organized Jewish communal life, he was suspected of being concerned less with fulfilling the moral imperatives of Judaism than with using the Jews for political ends no matter how worthy. Hence, the credibility of critics like Segal, Sachs, Lewin, and Rubin was rather low in the eyes of most Jews actively involved in communal life, and this applied a fortiori to communists like Joe Slovo who were known to be anti-Zionists and worshipers of Stalin's Soviet Union. As for Szur and his associates, they remained a tiny minority voice of no significance in South African Jewry. Their reputation as "fellow travelers" of communism and their attendant hostility to the Zionist allegiance of South African Jewry relegated their views to the very fringes of the community's life. The Democratic Association petered out of existence by about mid-1962 when Szur himself left South Africa and settled in England.

Far more creditable and representative were those Jewish public figures who, upholding the policy of the Board of Deputies, combined firm Zionist and communal commitment with individual action in the liberal cause, thereby in effect invalidating the third premise of the Board's critics, namely, that Jewishness would forfeit all moral justification if the Jewish community failed to adopt a collective liberal view. They included important communal leaders and Zionists. An example was Dr. Ellen Hellmann of the Institute of Race Relations, who had been an active member of the Zionist Socialist Party in the 1940s and served on the Board of Deputies' executive council and Public Relations Committee for part of the period under review. Her sister, Inez Gordon, later Bernstein, was even more centrally involved in Jewish life, serving as one of the leaders of the Women's Zionist Council of South Africa prior to settling in Israel in 1963. Hellmann was of the opinion that the individual Jew had ample scope within universal frameworks for the expression of liberal imperatives derived from Judaism or Jewish historical experience. She found no contradiction between her primary commitment to liberal activism on the one hand and her association with the Jewish Board of Deputies and its policy of noninvolvement in politics on the other. She saw no cause to insist upon a collective Jewish standpoint in the circumstances.[162]

Hellmann's views were shared in all essentials by a host of other prominent Jewish personalities known to be political liberals. The example set by Israel Maisels, the celebrated legal champion of the accused in the epic Treason Trial, was very important, since he held at various times high office in both the Board of Deputies and the Zionist Federation. Although Maisels made a point of disagreeing with those who argued that Jews in general and rabbis in particular had best keep out of politics altogether, he added:

> I do not by any means wish what I am saying to be construed as propagating the view that Jewish organizations as such should throw themselves into the political questions of the country, save insofar as they affect the Jewish community as such. It would be wrong, if not fatal, for them to do so. As much as some may be tempted to bring the community as such into the struggle, this is, I think, to be avoided at all costs."[163]

Other Liberal role models who shared these views included, for example, Harold Hanson, for a time chairman of the Zionist Socialists, and Hettie Davidson, the Women's Zionist Council leader, as well as many political personalities who took no particular part in communal affairs but identified positively as Jews, the most famous of these being Helen Suzman. It is noteworthy that in regard to Jewishness and the Jewish community, Helen Suzman always maintained an unselfconscious and nonjudgmental attitude. She was quite unapologetic about Jews "looking after their own." Questioned in a postapartheid-era interview about the policy of the Jewish Board of Deputies, she was only moderately critical, recognizing in retrospect that the Board had been "just dead scared to bring the Jews under the beady eye of people like Dr. Verwoerd, who were outspokenly antisemitic, and they were not going to subject the small minority Jewish population to any strictures which the Nat government might have brought on them." She spoke appreciatively of her brother-in-law Arthur Suzman, who had played a foremost role in the Board of Deputies, for starting to speak out against apartheid, even if belatedly (in the mid-1970s, as we shall later see).[164] By dint of personal example, all these personalities vindicated the Board of Deputies' policy of distinguishing between the duty of political action as individual citizens and the prudence of noninvolvement as a collective Jewish communal entity.

A sensitive articulation of the view of Jews who, notwithstanding personal liberal convictions and abhorrence of apartheid, did not demand a collective Jewish stand was provided by the notable South African–born novelist Dan Jacobson, who had settled in England. In an exchange with Ronald Segal, conducted in the columns of the American journal *Commentary* in 1957, Jacobson commented that he wished he knew as confidently as Segal "what the Jewish tradition enjoins on Jews in a situation like that prevailing in South Africa." He challenged the relevance of the historical parallels that Segal had invoked in advocacy of Jewish self-sacrifice: "Does he really need to have it pointed out to him that the Jews in the

Middle Ages who sacrificed themselves did so for *their own* beliefs, *their own* way of life, that they sacrificed themselves for what they believed to be *their own* interests as Jews?" Jacobson doubted that authentic Jewish ethical and historical tradition demanded that Jews sacrifice themselves for the sake of the oppressed groups in South Africa. That Jews as individual citizens ought to adopt a liberal stand was one thing, but collective martyrdom was quite another. Although acknowledging that the Jewish community had "settled into what is admittedly an unheroic posture" and was first and foremost protecting its own interests, he disagreed with Segal's view that this was morally inexcusable and thus rendered the existence of the Jewish community morally unjustifiable.[165]

An executive that always had a high proportion of lawyers, some very eminent in the profession, guided the Jewish Board of Deputies. By and large this made for punctilious observance of the policy formula of political noninvolvement and careful scrutiny of, and resistance to, any attempt to draw Jews into a collective Jewish position, whether for or against government policy. Testimony to this may be found in the Board's rejection not only of the pretensions of National Party members such as Joseph Nossel but also in its attitude to quite another tangent of criticism—that which came from the pen of Henry Katzew, the prominent Jewish journalist to whose unique, if far-fetched, contribution to the dialogue with Afrikaners we have already referred. Katzew complained relentlessly that the Board of Deputies was derelict in its moral duty as a representative Jewish body by failing to bring the Jewish ethical and historical experience to bear upon the problems of South African society. He did not agree that moral issues were inseparable from party politics. But, as we have seen, his view was premised on empathy above all for the Afrikaner's survival struggle. Accordingly, it was Katzew's conviction that dialogue of a kind that he had conducted independently should properly have been promoted by the Board of Deputies. "I ask it to join the search for righteous (Afrikaner and White) survival as a body representing a South African group with special survival experience," he wrote. To this, another prominent Jewish journalist, Bernard Sachs (brother of famed trade unionist Solly Sachs), countered that members of the Board of Deputies were politically heterogeneous and included people who were averse to the Afrikaner cause insofar as it meant apartheid. Unlike Katzew, they held that "apartheid with justice was a contradiction in terms—a benign tumour as against a malignant one."[166]

In refusing to adopt Katzew's proposals the Board of Deputies was true to its declared policy. Yet it cannot be said that the Board always passed the test of consistency. Its attitude toward the Jewish Democratic Association is a case in point. The Board objected strongly to the Democratic Association on the grounds that it presented itself as a collective Jewish political voice. In late 1956 the latter planned a public meeting of Jews to protest against the government's Group Areas Act. It invited the Labor Party M.P. Leo Lovell, who was a Jew and a fervent opponent of apartheid, to address the meeting. Thereupon, the Board's general-secretary Gus Saron made a discreet phone call to Lovell, suggesting that he might consider withdrawing from his agreement to do so on the grounds that it would be harmful to the Jewish communal interest. Saron allowed himself to hint, moreover, at the implications of association with a group that had the reputation of being "fellow travelers" (of the communist left). This approach backfired badly. Lovell reacted with indignation. He wrote to the chairman of the Board of Deputies challenging its presumed "right to attempt (however courteously)" to influence him:

> Let me say that while I agree generally that there is no Jewish point of view, as such, in party politics, there is a basic and characteristic Jewish point of view (as I think there is a Christian point of view) concerning measures, even political measures which amount to the spoliation of groups solely on the grounds of race, like the recent Group Areas proclamation. I claim to be able to say this as a man and as a Jew by virtue of the suffering of our people in many lands throughout their history, solely on the grounds of religion or race. That Jewish point of view is to me as clear as the commandment "Thou shalt not steal."[167]

There can be no doubt that in this case the Board of Deputies' executive, carried away in all likelihood by its strong aversion to the Democratic Association's ideological texture, overstepped the propriety of its own principled position. In the strict terms of its avowed policy, the Board had no right to go beyond publicly dissociating itself, if it deemed this necessary, from any attempt by the gathering under question to speak collectively on behalf of all Jews.

The Jewish Board of Deputies' policy formula, framed by the astute legal minds who served on its executive, ostensibly encouraged Jews in general and rabbis in particular to express themselves on public moral issues and in politics in accord with their understanding of Jewish values. But the Achilles' heel of this formula was the rider that even the individual Jew should express himself with "a due sense of responsibility" for the safety and interests of the Jewish public. This caveat repeatedly entangled the Board in inconsistencies. There were no doubt occasions when rabbis felt themselves to be fettered by the apprehensions of the Jewish Board of Deputies. In the previous chapter we noted not only the extreme case of reform Rabbi Ungar, who disregarded the admonition of his senior, Rabbi Weiler, but also the discord between the Board and Chief Rabbi Rabinowitz, who balked at the restraint that he felt was being imposed on his freedom to speak out. There is anecdotal evidence of other instances when leaders in positions of communal responsibility, whether on the Board or in other organizations, tried to influence Jewish politicians to exercise restraint. Joe Slovo was fond of relating a story concerning Sam Kahn—perhaps apocryphal, but certainly reflecting Slovo's own view. The story went that on one occasion members of the Cape Town committee of the Jewish Board of Deputies, all wealthy businessmen, met with him and intimated that as a Jew he ought to conduct his political activity in a manner that would not cause harm to the Jewish community. To which Kahn responded: "I'll tell you what, gentlemen, as a gesture of concern for the Jews, let's enter into a bargain; you give up your business and I'll then give up politics."[168] Leslie Rubin claimed that "it is an open secret in South Africa that the Board does all it can to discourage individual Jews from opposing government policies." He attested that while in parliament he was told more than once: "My prominence as a critic of apartheid and a spokesman for the African people was an embarrassment to the Board of Deputies." But the Board's general-secretary, Gus Saron, vigorously denied this.[169]

The South African Jewish Board of Deputies was also subjected to scathing criticism from a wide range of Jewish individuals, newspapers, and journals in other countries, particularly Britain and the United States. Its files containing such statements became quite voluminous in the late 1950s and during the 1960s. Indeed, at times South African Jewry was condemned in terms no less vehement than those used by the critics of white South Africa as a whole. The most extreme example was a certain Fritz Flesch, a survivor of the Nazi concentration camps living in the United States, who conducted his own singular castigation of South African Jewry in a manner that can only be described as obsessive.[170] A particularly pungent example of another sort came from the pen of Professor Jacob Neusner in the United States, who satirically paraphrased the words of the prophets in censure of South African Jewry:

> Hear this word, Jews of Johannesburg:
> Thus says the Lord
> For three transgressions of Israel and for four
> I will not revoke the punishment
> Because they sell the black righteous for silver
> And the black needy for a pair of shoes—
> They trample the head of the black poor into the dust of the earth
> And turn aside the way of the black afflicted. . . .[171]

The thrust of these barbs of criticism from abroad was much the same as that posed by the internal liberal critics whom we have cited—that racial prejudice was abhorrent to Judaism, that it was a Jewish obligation to oppose apartheid, and that discrimination was indivisible and would ultimately be applied to the Jews as well. Whereas the criticism emanating from Britain was generally well informed of South African conditions, that emanating from the United States and Israel frequently bore the marks of simplistic and unctuous indignation from the safety of distance. At various international Jewish gatherings, the Board of Deputies' general-secretary, Gus Saron, and other representatives of South African Jewry found themselves having to defend and explain the Board's policy. In a number of memoranda drawn up for international Jewish organizations, Saron outlined the reasons why it was neither possible nor advisable for Jews collectively to endorse a specific solution to the country's racial problems: the diversity of political outlook that existed among Jews and made it impossible to formulate a stand; the inextricable interweaving of moral and political aspects of the policy of apartheid; the inadvisability of embroiling the Jewish community in the party-political arena. While pleading for understanding of the Jewish community's predicament, Saron steered carefully away from any statement that might be construed as apologetics for the South African government. To B'nai B'rith, for example, he submitted:

> We do not suggest that any overseas body should be deterred from doing what it conceives to be its clear duty, because of the possible repercussions upon the South African Jewish community. Nevertheless it is relevant to mention that when attacks upon South Africa have come from Jewish sources—and especially from the State of Israel at the United Nations—these have attracted a good deal of attention locally and there has sometimes been a tendency to identify the local Jewish community with these attacks.[172]

By and large the major world Jewish organizations, such as B'nai B'rith, the World Jewish Congress, and the World Zionist Organization, although deprecating apartheid, showed understanding for the policy of the Jewish leadership in South Africa. In contrast to the censure that frequently issued from Jewish individuals outside of South Africa, the political director of the World Jewish Congress, Alex Easterman, referred to the situation of South African Jewry in 1964 as one that was "complex and delicate and required restraint and prudence on the part of Jews everywhere." He considered that in the face of the dilemmas involved in the Board's situation, it was "an exemplary body which displayed a dignity and responsibility meriting admiration from world Jewry."[173]

A segment of the Jewish community affiliated to both the Board of Deputies and the Zionist Federation, but over which it had only limited control, was the Jewish student associations at the universities. This had serious implications for the communal policy of noninvolvement in politics, because it was among students of the English-speaking universities that the ideological tension over race relations in South Africa was at its most acute. Jewish student associations were subject to relentless pressure to align collectively with the opposition to the policy of apartheid. At the same time, advice of Jewish community leaders that such a course would be irresponsible from the communal point of view could not go unheeded. The leaders of Jewish campus associations found themselves caught between the impulse to align with antiapartheid actions on the one hand and a sense of responsibility to the Jewish community on the other. The pressure became well-nigh irresistible as protests rose against the government's interference with the right of the "liberal" universities to accept nonwhite students and as one after another of the leaders of the National Union of South African Students (NUSAS), including a conspicuously disproportionate number of Jews, was arrested or banned. Consequently Jewish students' periodicals such as *Hamatmid* and *Hashofar* acquired an increasingly liberal texture, and at the National Conference of Jewish Students held in July 1959, a resolution was adopted in "protest against all discriminatory legislation concerning colour, creed, race or religion."[174] Gus Saron, who was present as an observer from the Board of Deputies, could no more than urge that responsible consideration be given to the communal implications of their decisions.

As the aforementioned resolution's calculated avoidance of specific condemnation of the government's apartheid policy indicates, it cannot be said that the Jewish student associations went the whole way in aligning themselves with the forces of opposition to apartheid. Even their internal consensus was never unanimously liberal. At the 1959 conference, a handful of Jewish students from the Afrikaans-language University of Pretoria vigorously opposed the majority consensus, arguing that the policy of separate development was compatible with Judaism and Zionism. One of them was Aubrey Levin, a medical student and son of Mendel Levin, who, like Joseph Nossel in Cape Town, was an active member of the National Party. On balance, while student conferences continued to agonize over the moral dilemma attendant upon participation in an apartheid society, their declarations remained nearly as cautious as those of the Board of Deputies itself. Their moderation may be sensed in a resolution typical of a number passed at conferences in the 1960s:

> This conference whilst not associating itself with any particular party and having regard to the complexity of inter-racial group relations, but acting in accordance with its interpretation of the teachings and precepts of Judaism: reasserts its faith in the dignity and worth of the individual irrespective of race, colour and creed; expresses its conviction that each individual inhabitant of South Africa should have the opportunity to develop according to his potentialities; voices its opposition to racialism and discrimination in all its manifestations.[175]

Notwithstanding the concern reflected in such resolutions, the main focus of the student Jewish associations remained the promotion of Jewish and Zionist identification and knowledge of Judaism. All the same, the prominence of individual Jewish students in the leadership echelon of NUSAS, which vehemently opposed apartheid, was a perennial source of criticism from the Afrikaans press and even from the lips of government ministers. Thus in August 1968 Lourens Muller, Minister of Police and the Interior, publicly produced a list of students involved in recent protests against government policies to illustrate the disproportionate representation of students with Jewish names. He appealed to the Jewish community's leaders "to put their hand in their bosom and use their influence with their young people to respect authority and not to disrupt it." A storm of controversy burst out over this comment. The Jewish newspapers reacted with great resentment to "the minister's indiscretion," and the Board of Deputies responded that while it did not regard it as its function to express any opinion on the validity of the student protests, there were certain implications in the minister's statement that could not be allowed to pass unchallenged: "To fasten responsibility on the Jewish community for the actions of its individual members inevitably furthers anti-Semitism, albeit unwittingly. There can be no political regimentation."[176]

Students were a major factor in the life of a community whose members enjoyed a considerably higher level of educational attainment than the average for other whites.[177] However, it is important to note that from 1948 until the early 1980s, if not longer, the campus Jewish associations were not in fact the major setting for the specifically Jewish activity of students. Indeed, by far the larger and more committed segment of Jewish students found expression off-campus in the framework of the various Zionist youth movements, which continued to be the most important identity-forming asset of the Jewish community in South Africa.

At a conservative estimate, an average of about 30 percent of the age cohort from ten to eighteen were exposed to the youth movement experience throughout the 1950s and 1960s.[178] The leadership of the Zionist youth movements consisted almost entirely of university students. The only exception was Hashomer Hatza'ir, which encouraged members to learn trades suitable for kibbutz occupations. But its membership was small (only about 221 out of a total of 6,800 in all movements according to a census in 1966) and in constant decline from the mid-1950s until the movement dissolved itself in 1970.

The Zionist ideology fostered by the youth movements was suffused with values totally incompatible with racial discrimination and social injustice. Zionism was perceived as a personal revolution to free oneself from the faults inhering in the Jewish diasporic condition, *galut,* but equally to reject participation in a society based on racial discrimination and withholding of human and civic rights from the majority of the population. The avowedly Marxist Hashomer Hatza'ir movement, socialist-inclined Habonim, Zionist Socialist Youth-Dror (fused with Habonim in 1959), and even the nonsocialist Bnei Zion movement (fused with Habonim in 1961) all placed emphasis in their programs on living one's life in accordance with values of universal human dignity, equality, and self-labor. For example, from the youngest age group onward a critical attitude was fostered toward the exploitation of servants in the home and the indignities and discrimination suffered by all "non-whites."

These values were exemplified above all in the commune training farms, known as *hachshara,* whose members were preparing for a life of self-labor and equality in an Israeli kibbutz. The *hachshara* system was supported by the Zionist Federation and existed from 1943 until the early 1960s. The *hachshara* trainees, some of whom had gained university degrees but were willing to forgo practicing their professions, others of whom had waived the opportunity for university studies altogether, served as the most inspiring of all role models for Zionist youth. The primary interest of the Bnei Akiva (formerly Hashomer Hadati) movement was in promoting religious observance, but it too educated toward labor in a religious kibbutz. The ideology of the Betar movement was nonsocialist, but its primary emphasis on the principle of national liberation too was antithetical to the South African system of white minority domination and the oppression of the black majority.

Of course the youth movement leaders took great care to veil their antiapartheid attitude lest it call upon themselves the wrath of the government, embarrass the community, or even endanger the very existence of the movements. The Habonim movement had to be particularly discreet since it enjoyed official government recognition as the Jewish equivalent of the Boy Scouts movement and the Afrikaner Voortrekker youth. In 1959, when Habonim underwent a process of ideological clarification and reformulation, its new platform included the intentionally innocuous wording "Habonim believes in a democratic way of life, in social justice and the brotherhood of man," and the explanation accompanying this and translating it into educational terms stated that while these principles "would obviously have to be related to the South African scene," they represented "a fundamental set of values in relation to society," rather than alignment with any political forces in the country.[179] However, in practice the educational program for the senior age-group (known as the *shomrim*) purposively aimed at arousing sharply critical awareness of the evils of apartheid and fostering the conviction that it was unconscionable for a Jew to condone or be a beneficiary of such a depraved social order.

The Zionist Federation wholeheartedly supported the youth movements, and their activities, including scouting camps and study seminars, were integral to the life of the Jewish community. Children from the age of ten upward joined for social reasons, mostly encouraged by their parents, and could graduate to the status of counselors (*madrichim*) at the age of seventeen or eighteen, being the last year of secondary school or the first year at university. After high school matriculation, the most promising candidates for leadership roles were selected for a year of study at the World Zionist Organization's Institute for Youth leaders from Abroad in Israel, part of which time was spent experiencing life on a kibbutz.

The majority of the youth who passed through the youth movements remained in South Africa but retained strong Zionist sentiments. Indeed, not a few carried these sentiments with them even when choosing to emigrate to countries other than Israel. Only a small percentage carried out the highest youth movement goals by "going up" (*aliya*) to live in Israel, and even fewer settled for good in kibbutz communes. Their number fluctuated from year to year, but an annual average of a few dozen per annum from 1948 to the early 1980s would be a fair estimate. These might be termed "radical Zionists." Their ideological "going up" was in many ways at the same time a rather unnatural voluntary act of downward social mobility that involved uprooting themselves from the country of their birth and adapting to a much lower standard of living and a language, Hebrew, that was not their mother tongue. The explanation for this phenomenon lies at the deepest level in much the same social condition of outsider marginality experienced by Jews in South Africa's multisegmented society that underlay the alternative behavior of those who became radical opponents of that society's political and social norms. Also, the path to "radical Zionism" was no doubt influenced by exposure to role models, in this case within the youth movements, by generational transmission within families, and by idiosyncratic personality factors.

Most "radical Zionists" chose to opt out of South African society primarily for intrinsically Jewish reasons of the same order as applied to their counterparts in other communities of the Jewish Diaspora. But their reasons were not unrelated to the specific South African moral conundrum caused by apartheid. Indeed, that conundrum profoundly influenced the rationale for their Zionist convictions, imparting an ideological nuance that was unique to South African Zionism. This found its most articulate expression in the largest of the youth movements, Habonim. Sharing the same universe of discourse as Jewish liberal activists in the universities, the leadership of Habonim, itself in fact a body of students, found it increasingly necessary to enunciate the rationale for a Zionist resolution of the Jew's moral dilemma in South Africa.

The main thrust of this ideological rationale was the contention that the moral dilemmas plaguing the conscience of thinking Jews in South Africa constituted no more than a particular dimension of the general *galut* (exilic) condition of the Jews. Habonim accepted the premise of liberal critics of the Jewish community that both the Jewish religion and the historic experience of the Jewish people imposed an imperative upon South African Jews to oppose apartheid. However, it proceeded to argue that if the Jewish communal leadership was false to Jewishness because it evaded its universal imperatives, so too were the Jewish liberal activists because they ignored its national imperatives. On the one hand, out of concern for the community's safety and welfare, the communal leadership falsely denied that there was a collective Jewish imperative to oppose the evils of South African racial discrimination. Telling Jewish youth that if they felt they must oppose the evils of society they should do so not as Jews, but rather as individual citizens, was virtually a renunciation of the relevance of Jewish values to the actual lives of Jews; it dichotomized "the Jew" and "the man" and revealed the moral bankruptcy of Jewry in the peculiar South African variety of *galut.* On the other hand, the liberal activists thought nothing of jeopardizing the safety of the local Jewish community by advocating a communal stand on the volatile issues of South African race relations. They cared little for the vital Jewish concerns and aspirations manifested in Zionism and sought only to use the Jewish community for universalistic ends. Neither attitude could satisfy Zionist youth, who sought to embody a wholesome fusion of "the man" and "the Jew."

The Habonim thesis was, therefore, that the peculiar dilemma of Jews in an apartheid society should be recognized for what it was—evidence of the vulnerability and moral deficiency of the *galut* condition. Only in an autonomous Jewish society could Jews hope to harmonize the equally valid imperatives of prophetic Jewish particularism and universalism. Passive participation in the privileged white caste of South Africa was unconscionable. *Aliya* was the commanding answer, not a self-negating and futile attempt to change the character of a society in which Jews were ultimately marginal outsiders. Habonim therefore rejected involvement in the conflict over race relations in South Africa and offered the Zionist option "to revolutionize one's own life through *aliya.*" "The South African Jewish youth will find only in Zionism a possibility for the harmonious unity of the universal and the particular," it contended, "for with the consolidation of our own homeland we are establishing the first prerequisite upon which the Hebrew prophets' dream rests."[180]

CHAPTER 3

Adapting to Reformed Apartheid

Reformed Apartheid

Although the maintenance of white minority supremacy remained the irreducible basis of apartheid ideology and policy throughout some forty-six years of National Party rule, its racist implications underwent considerable modification over time. The sheer injustice, invasion of human dignity, and political repression inflicted on all who were not defined as whites, and also on all those whites who dared to defy the system, were evident to any person possessed of a moral conscience. Yet, one should not underestimate the capacity of ideological and rhetorical refinements to veil unconscionable realities and salve the conscience of ordinary people. An objective analysis of the behavior of Jews both as individuals and as a community therefore requires some consideration of the ideological refinement of apartheid and of modifications in its application over time.

Of course, apartheid's racist premises positing inherent intellectual and moral inferiority of nonwhite people had deep roots in white South African society and politics, and were shared normatively by English speakers—including Jews—no less than by Afrikaners. But by the time the National Party ascended to power in 1948, the horrors of war and the Holocaust wrought by Nazi racism had produced an atmosphere censorious of crass racism throughout the world. Hence, although still steeped in racist prejudices, almost from the outset the proponents of apartheid had pitched their case at least as much in terms of necessity and rational strategy for white survival in South Africa. Of course, the prerequisite for survival was deemed to be the preservation of "white civilization," and it was believed that this, in turn, could be assured only by white political supremacy under Afrikaner nationalist leadership. The policy of apartheid was advocated as the sole answer to the bogey of communism and to the danger of liberalism, portrayed as communism's unwitting handmaiden.

Within a decade of apartheid's installation as South Africa's regnant ideology, Afrikaner ideological discourse had not only subordinated its racist motifs to considerations of white survival as a morally defensible right, but had also begun to claim that apartheid embodied a progressive aspiration for the cultural and political self-expression of all the racial groups said to constitute South African society. It was presented not only as an existentially justifiable strategy for white survival but also as a form of multicultural idealism. Its proponents purported to prepare the nonwhites for the enjoyment of what was touted as "separate development" and cultural individuality; benefits that, so it was claimed, would be denied to them under an inevitably homogenizing, racially integrated, liberal system, not to speak of a communist regime.

These visionary idealistic pretensions of apartheid ideology were fed by economic, social, and intellectual changes within the now hegemonic Afrikaner public. The economy was growing exponentially hungrier for more permanent and better skilled and educated black labor, and the urban black population was outstripping all predicted growth. Signs of internal Afrikaner intellectual dissonance, lay and clerical, began to appear as increasing numbers of urbanized Afrikaners became upwardly mobile in business, finance, manufacturing, and professional occupations. Pragmatic considerations were eroding ideological dogmatism, and Afrikaner businessmen, no less than their English counterparts, began to balk at the dysfunctional aspects of apartheid in the economic sphere. They were also becoming increasingly sensitive to international censure, boycotts, and the pariah status of their country, not least of all affecting, particularly painfully, the area of sports.

Against this background, already in the late 1960s a division began to open between two main ideological factions that came to be loosely labeled as *verkramptes* (narrow-minded) and *verligtes* (enlightened). The *verkrampte* politicians were backed by some intellectuals and clerics but drew their support mainly from farmers and lower-level civil servants and white workers. They doggedly upheld rigid Afrikaner national exclusiveness and domination of the South African polity and uncompromisingly resisted modification of the apartheid system in deference to criticism from outside the country. *Verligtes* too were not about to forgo the National Party's control of the state. Nor did they contemplate dispensing with the fundamental division of the population into the four statutory groups, white, Bantu (African), colored, and Asian (Indian). However, they did tend to relinquish a measure of Afrikaner exclusivity for the sake of more white unity and to evince an open-minded attitude to modifications of apartheid that, while not substantially altering long-term goals of "separate development," would soften the hard image of apartheid.[1]

This bifurcation in Afrikaner nationalist thinking accompanied the progress of apartheid policy from the early 1970s onward. As our earlier survey of events showed, by the mid-1960s Hendrik Verwoerd's government, zealously deploying the full power of the state, had virtually crushed all political resistance, including that section of it which had gone underground and turned to acts of violence aimed at disrupting public order and white confidence in the apartheid state. This allowed the apartheid system another decade of relatively unhampered development. Under Balthazar John Vorster's premiership, which began in 1966, implementation of "grand" apartheid—vaunted as "separate development"—continued apace. Hundreds of thousands of blacks were forcibly "resettled" under appalling conditions in the designated "homelands" (labeled by critics as "Bantustans"), and the government legislated to attach the citizenship of all blacks to one or another homeland, irrespective of their place of birth or whether they had ever lived outside of white areas. Between 1960 and 1983 an estimated 3.5 million people were forcefully relocated. By the end of 1977 two homelands (Transkei and Bophuthatswana) had officially been declared politically independent, and another three were largely self-governing. All were creations of unilaterally decreed white policy, and none were genuinely viable. Parallel social engineering was applied to the colored people of the Cape, involving forced removals from areas designated for whites only, including the area in the heart of Cape Town known as District Six, which had been predominantly colored in population for many generations. The government also contrived a separate political system for the coloreds through the creation of a Coloureds' Representative Council but experienced considerable frustration at the hands of the nonpliant coloreds' Labor Party.

An ancillary requirement of the grand apartheid conception of "separate development" was the prohibition of all mixed-race organizations. This made it untenable for the Liberal Party to continue true to its principles. Consequently, it perforce dissolved itself in 1968. On the other hand, the advancement of grand apartheid facilitated a degree of pragmatic flexibility in regard to petty apartheid practices. For example, it became admissible to tolerate mixed-race sports events in certain circumstances and to allow black diplomats from abroad into certain hotels and restaurants. These modifications coincided with the Vorster government's growing foreign policy initiatives, aimed at finding a modus vivendi with newly independent neighboring states, as well as its military interventions to counter African National Congress and Pan-Africanist Congress guerrilla infiltration from outside South Africa.

Within the Afrikaner nationalist camp, the cumulative import of all these adjustments to the apartheid system increased the ire of apartheid hard-liners, who had already split from the National Party in September 1969 to form the rival Herstigte (Refounded) Nasionale Party (HNP) led by Dr. Albert Hertzog. From the other side, Vorster's regime confronted a burgeoning black consciousness movement, one of whose leaders was Steven Biko, who died at the brutal hands of the security police while in detention in 1977, a martyr to the liberation struggle of the blacks.

In mid-1976 popular mass resistance to the apartheid regime reached what proved to be an historic turning point. Triggered by resistance to the compulsory imposition of Afrikaans as a medium for instruction in black schools, a whole generation of school pupils in Soweto burst out into defiant rebellion. It was manifested also in destructive acts randomly directed against all white authority, including burning of schools and barbaric "necklacing" (burning of victims in petroleum-doused car tires) of fellow blacks suspected of complicity with the police. These Soweto riots set in motion a chain of disturbances and various forms of defiant resistance in other parts of the country that reerupted spasmodically throughout the remaining years of apartheid rule, reaching new peaks of intensity in the mid-1980s. The disturbance of public order in black townships proved to be uncontrollable despite enormous loss of life in the course of brutal suppression by the forces of the state, by now concentrated in an all-powerful Bureau of State Security directly under the prime minister. Draconian repression of all expressions of opposition was intensified in declared states of emergency over the apartheid years, subjecting thousands of persons, not excluding white opponents of the regime, to detention without trial, often involving torture, and to various terms of imprisonment.

Within the white population in general these developments only served to heighten fearful support for the government party, as was shown in the record-breaking victory scored by the National Party under Vorster in the white elections of 1977. But as fortune would have it, not long after, in September 1978, Vorster perforce had to resign as a result of the revelation of what was known as "the information scandal" involving the secret disposition of large government funds for such illegal purposes as the buying of controlled English-language press interests.

When Pieter Willem Botha replaced Vorster in 1978, he inherited a situation described as one of "total onslaught" on the (white) republic: a situation of barely controllable sporadic internal unrest, increasing guerrilla infiltration from ANC bases under the protection of neighboring African states, and escalating external pressure including international sanctions. But he also had at his disposal the powerful mechanisms of state security that were trained against all opposition. Having garnered experience as minister of defense in Vorster's cabinet, Botha intensified the expansion of military power during his premiership. He also focused on progress in cementing what was described as a "constellation" of southern African states. It was to include the "independent" homelands that continued to underpin the design of grand apartheid. Two more homelands took up independent status, Venda in 1979 and Ciskei in 1981, but KwaZulu, headed by Mangosuthu Gatsha Buthelezi, leader of the Inkatha Freedom Party, held out against independence.

At the same time, Botha's government sought continuously to refine the rhetoric of apartheid policy and its public face in a *verligte* vein. Moreover, the government also made what proved to be far-reaching modifications in labor and industrial relations when it began to allow blacks to form their own trade unions in 1979 and even went on to permit mixed-race membership of unions in 1981. The ire of *verkramptes* was aggravated by such measures. In 1982 the remaining hard-liners who hankered after pristine Verwoerdian apartheid were driven out of the party. Under their leader, Dr. Treurnicht, they created the Conservative Party, which succeeded in becoming the official opposition party in the all-white parliament when it gained more seats than the Progressive Federal Party in the 1987 elections.

Although still unswervingly white supremacist and unrelentingly repressive of all resistance, Botha's government was transforming the rhetoric of apartheid almost beyond recognition. This rhetoric was not without influence on the

English-speaking white public, including the Jews. It raised hopes, or wish-fulfilling illusions, that the crude racist elements of apartheid were being repressed by the governing National Party, paving the way for substantive structural reforms of the system and a much longed-for softening of world censure of South Africa.

The new mantra propagated by Botha's government was "healthy power sharing" between the four separately developing racial groups. Although the country's common affairs were to remain controlled by the whites, internal "own affairs" were to be left to each separate racial group. The linchpin of the new model of reformed apartheid was the institution of a tricameral parliamentary system to replace the Westminster-modeled parliament that had been in existence since the creation of the Union of South Africa in 1910. Submitted to the white electorate in 1983, the new constitution gained the approval of a majority of whites against the opposition of the conservatives on the right and the progressives on the left, and was unilaterally imposed on all racial groups. By its terms, P. W. Botha, who had served as prime minister since 1978, now became state president with executive powers; separate parliamentary chambers were created for the coloreds and the Indians; and an advisory President's Council including appointed persons from all racial groups was added. This ostensible step toward political power sharing was fundamentally flawed, however, not alone by the calculated supremacy of the white chamber but, even more importantly, by the total exclusion of the black African majority of South Africa's population. The channel for black political expression was still relegated to the various "homelands," four of which had by then accepted independence, while others were described as self-governing. As for South Africa's vast and still growing population of urban blacks, no more was held out to them than local urban councils with authority limited to what the lexicon of reformed apartheid referred to as "own affairs."

In sum, this reformed apartheid strategy manifestly aimed at preservation of white supremacy by means of co-opting the Indian and colored racial groups while permanently excluding the African majority from the parliamentary center. Largely in reaction to this government strategy, a new alignment of opposition movements sprang into existence in August 1983—the United Democratic Front (UDF). Emanating initially from the World Alliance of Reformed Churches headed by Dr. Allan Boesak, the UDF soon reached a multiracial following estimated at some two million people in a wide variety of trade unions, civic and students' organizations, sports clubs, religious groups, and the like. It appealed for a democratic nonracial society in the spirit of the Congress movement's "Freedom Charter" of 1955 and called for boycotting the all-white referendum on the proposed new constitution as well as the ensuing elections to the Indian and colored chambers.

A groundswell of black popular resistance exploded once more in 1985, expressed again in boycotts of schools, trade boycotts, workers' strikes, and communal riots. The government responded in July 1985 with a renewed state of emergency that facilitated massive repression of opposition, including the deployment of army troops in the townships, and showed no signs of ending. In August 1985, expectations that President Botha would make a major "crossing of the Rubicon" announcement of new concessions to blacks in a scheduled address to a National Party congress were disappointed. Botha drew back at the last moment and, instead, reaffirmed basic apartheid policy. This precipitated the imposition of debilitating international sanctions and led to a flight of capital from South Africa.

As a highly decentralized umbrella organization, the UDF was better able to evade total governmental suppression than had its predecessors in the liberation struggle, such as the Congress movement of the 1950s. But many of its leaders were harassed, detained, and arrested, and a more comprehensive clampdown was inflicted on it in February 1988. After suffering a stroke, President Botha was pressured by his party into resigning in 1989. By that time there could be little doubt that the viability of the apartheid regime, reformed or not, was in a grave state of crisis, embattled from within the country and bombarded by international condemnations and sanctions from without.

Shifts in Jewish Political Behavior

If, as we have noted, in the 1950s and early 1960s very few Jews had supported the National Party, and the handful who demonstratively joined that party had done so at the cost of evoking an embarrassed if not disdainful response from fellow Jews, by the early 1970s there were signs of a change. The split in the National Party in September 1979 and the *verkrampte* nationalists' creation of the Herstigte Nasionale Party (HNP) under Albert Hertzog meant that the National Party had rid itself of its most racist elements and was no longer on the extreme right of the political spectrum. In Jewish eyes this was bound to be a positive development. Apprehensions were now diverted from the mainstream nationalists to the new HNP, which declared that it stood squarely on "Christian principles" reminiscent of the antisemitic tendencies of Afrikaner nationalists before 1948. One of its candidates, J. Jooste, was reported to have said that since the party was based on the Bible, not only atheists but also Catholics and Jews were unwelcome! However, the poor showing of the HNP in the 1970 elections—it gained only 3.5 percent of the (white) vote—and in subsequent polls allayed Jewish fears that it might one day displace the National Party.

In early 1970 Mendel Levin and his son Aubrey, both National Party members already hardened against the scorn they had to face within the Jewish community, made claims that "hundreds of well-known Jewish businessmen, industrialists and professional men," had joined the National Party.[2] Yet, as has already been mentioned in a previous chapter, the 1970 elections still showed that the overwhelming majority of Jews continued to support the United Party.[3] However, in 1975 the United Party began to disintegrate. Harry Schwarz, a rising political star who had already attained prominence within the Transvaal's provincial council, broke ranks to form the Reform Party in early 1975. Those who joined him included a number of other Jewish members of both the provincial and the Johannesburg city councils.[4] When the Progressive and Reform Parties combined in July 1975 to form the Progressive Reform Party, soon to become the Progressive Federal Party, it immediately attracted noticeable Jewish support. Indeed, one Afrikaans newspaper labeled it a "Jewish-English Party," an expression that uncomfortably evoked old antisemitic images.[5]

Concurrently, a body of Jewish support for the National Party government was growing. Allie Dubb's sociological study of Johannesburg Jewry, to which we have referred in another context, showed that by the late 1960s 28 percent favored the United Party (6 percent as members and 22 percent as supporters); 15 percent favored the National Party (2 percent as members of the party and another 13 percent as supporters); and 17 percent favored the Progressive Party (6 percent as members and 11 percent as supporters).[6] An opinion poll conducted in 1974 by Lawrence Schlemmer for the 1820 Settlers National Monument Foundation showed that as much as 21.3 percent of the Jews polled supported the National Party, compared with 34.5 percent for opposition parties (18.9 percent for the United Party and 16.6 percent for the Progressive Party). This was part of a general process of change in the white electorate shown by polls in the 1970s, which indicated that English-speaking whites were shifting from the disintegrated United Party to the order of 70 percent for the National Party and 30 percent for the Progressives.[7]

In a more penetrating analysis of Jewish voting behavior, the sociologist Henry Lever focused on the period of the 1977 election. On the basis of a series of three electoral surveys conducted by the *Rapport* newspaper, the percentage of Jews who said they supported the National Party rose progressively from 24.3 to 27.1 to 31.3 percent. Asked if and how they had voted in the 1974 general election, a little more than half said they had voted and in the following proportions: National Party 12.5 percent, United Party 35.7 percent, and Progressive Party 51.8 percent. Lever inferred that Jews had been progressively abandoning the United Party since 1966. This was a process that applied to all English speakers, but it seemed that Jews had begun earlier than gentile English speakers. By 1977 it was clearly the Progressive Federal Party that commanded the largest body of Jewish support, rising from 50 percent to 59.3 and 59.4 percent in the three surveys. Lever concluded: "The available evidence does not indicate a distinctive Jewish vote"; socioeconomic status, primarily education and secondarily income and age, were more important determinants than Jewishness.[8]

Sensing the signs of a new Jewish receptivity to the reform-apartheid policies of the government, in the 1977 general election the National Party sponsored the candidacy of a Jew, Abe Hoppenstein, in a Johannesburg constituency (Bezuidenhout) known to have a considerable Jewish population. Hoppenstein, a lawyer by profession, was a National Party member of some twenty years standing and, at the same time, an identifying Jew associated particularly with the Revisionist Party of Zionism. In 1974 he was appointed South Africa's trade commissioner in Israel and shortly after that became political counselor in South Africa's Washington embassy. Fresh from that post he entered the electoral lists to challenge an Afrikaner candidate of the Progressive Federal Party, Japie Basson, who had undergone a leftward odyssey in politics after expulsion from the National Party. Hoppenstein declared: "Voting for the National Party is the best way to provide for our survival in the face of pressure from abroad. We are the only party that can and will bring about effective, meaningful change."[9] In the outcome, although Basson was elected, he gained a mere 50 votes more than Hoppenstein, and it was evident that a considerable number of the estimated 3,000 Jewish votes in the constituency had been cast for the latter. Although Hoppenstein's defeat meant that there was still no Jew on the National Party benches in parliament—whereas five Jewish candidates for the Progressives took their seats in the parliament of 1977—his candidacy and close miss were a sign that supporting the National Party was no longer out of the question for the average Jew.

To be sure, Hoppenstein's candidacy and his election campaign stirred quite a controversy within the Jewish community. Members of the South African Union of Jewish Students (SAUJS) declared that support of National Party policies was a travesty of Jewish ethics and deprecated what they termed Hoppenstein's "contorted rationalizations" in justifying his actions. True to its policy, the Jewish Board of Deputies deplored the injection of what was described as a "Jewish angle" with appeals for a collective Jewish vote.[10]

Although more Jews were thus veering toward support of the government, there is little doubt that the Progressive Party attracted the majority of Jewish voters into the 1980s. This was again shown in a municipal election in March 1984, when the National Party ventured to challenge the Progressives in the heavily Jewish ward of Houghton, Johannesburg. The National Party fielded a Jew, Israel Pinshaw, as a candidate. He was not without some Jewish support, but the Progressives won the election decisively, with 1,310 votes against Pinshaw's 573.[11] Still, the signs of previously unheard-of support for the government that were first illuminated by the Hoppenstein electoral experience continued to be evident in subsequent contests, especially at the municipal level.

There had always been a remarkable prominence of Jews in the municipal councils of major cities, particularly Johannesburg and Cape Town, reflected also in the disproportionate number of Jewish mayors.[12] The predominance of Jews among the Progressive Party's candidates was demonstrated by the fact that they accounted for as many as nineteen of the thirty-eight Progressive candidates in the country's municipal elections of March 1977.[13] By 1986, sixteen of the Progressives' representatives on the Johannesburg City Council, as well as the mayor himself, were Jews. But in a municipal by-election in the Bellevue–Judiths Paarl Ward of Johannesburg in February 1986, a Jewish National Party candidate, Sam Bloomberg, challenged this record in a particularly bitter contest against the Progressive Party's Jewish candidate, the promising twenty-nine-year-old Tony Leon. Bloomberg was much the senior person. He was well known as a public-minded businessman who had made a name for himself as a pioneer of suicide prevention activities and founder of Suicides Anonymous. He was also a colonel in the South African Reserves. Although Bloomberg was defeated, it was by a very narrow margin—39 votes. Since it was reliably estimated that some 35 percent of the eligible voters were Jews, there can be little doubt that many of them had voted for the National Party candidate. During the contest emotions had run high in the Jewish community—on the one hand, National Party posters were defaced; on the other, ultraorthodox Jewish residents in the area, mostly elderly persons, were conspicuous in support of the National Party's candidate.[14]

It is not difficult to account for the fact that a percentage, however minor, of the Jewish electorate was voting for the National Party. In part, the reason was, no doubt, the by now well-proven record of the National Party government in jettisoning antisemitism, entering into close cooperation with the State of Israel, and facilitating Jewish material support for Israel. Over time, this record redeemed the National Party in the eyes of not a few Jews. Moreover, now that *verligte* ideological rhetoric had replaced the crude racism of apartheid ideology and dogmatic apartheid faith seemed to be giving way to pragmatic considerations of business interest and economic reality, the government party was becoming a palatable, even attractive, political option for Jews.

The transformation of the government's ideological rhetoric, and the delicate balance between change and continuity that it veiled, may be illustrated by the National Party's electoral campaign in mid-1987. The party declared that it would continue the policy of reforms, but only by its own lights and not in surrender to sanctions and threats. It upheld "individual freedom without race discrimination," but predicated this on preserving "the group character" of South African society. Moreover, the National Party affirmed that "separate residential areas and voters' rolls for the various groups" remained official policy. It promised political "power sharing" but qualified this as "own decision making on own affairs and joint decision making in matters of common concern, without the domination of any group by another." The party contrasted this formula for power sharing with the policy of the Progressives, which, it declared, "amounts to a handing over of power."[15]

To the right of the National Party on the political spectrum, the Conservative Party, spawned in 1982 by the right-wing reaction of Afrikaners to Botha's reformist policy, rejected "power sharing" out of hand. It called for the retention of all apartheid laws, including those that forbade miscegenation and mixed marriages, demanded "the restoration of separate development in practice, especially with regard to white residential areas and public amenities," and raised the notion of a partition solution. The Conservatives, furthermore, affirmed what they called "Christian white civilization," although at the same time claiming to "respect freedom of conscience and worship for others."

In 1987 the Progressive Federal Party, for its part, advocated ultimate universal suffrage in "an open society, free from statutory apartheid," federal arrangements, and a bill of rights, all to be shaped by a national convention comprising the acknowledged leaders of all sections of the population. This implied the inclusion of African National Congress leader Nelson Mandela, who would have to be released from prison.

The grave moral faults of apartheid even in its reformed phase were obvious to any thinking person. However, the government party's ostensible renunciation of racist premises and softening of petty apartheid measures, together with its pitching of the reformed apartheid case on the basis of the right of the whites to ensure their own survival against the assumed danger of black majority rule, struck a responsive chord among many Jews, along with other English speakers. This was perhaps best illustrated in the views of Israel Pinshaw, an active member of the National Party who was rewarded for his contribution by being appointed to the State President's Council in 1985. It is a telling testimony to the transformation of National Party political discourse that Pinshaw, as identifying a Jew as any in the Jewish community, could depict his role in the party's ranks as that of a Jew inspired by Jewish values. This meant being solicitous of human rights irrespective of color or creed, but at the same time favoring ethnic-cultural particularism (for this, read "own affairs") as a legitimate structural basis for society. Pinshaw claimed that, as a Jew, he was urging the National Party leadership to move faster and more convincingly toward reforms. In the Jewish press he was reported as stating:

> I sincerely believe that the philosophy of the National Party has completely changed over the years. . . . As a Jew I find bigotry and discrimination repulsive and I believe that through the efforts of the National Party accommodation can be achieved amongst our various race groups . . . and as a Jew I will endeavour to see that the decisions to which I am a party will be so designed that they are equitable, just and fair.[16]

In the general election of May 1987 to the white chamber of parliament it was clearly the Progressive Federal Party that fielded the majority of Jewish candidates—five out of seven—and gained most of the votes of Jews in districts known to have large Jewish concentrations.[17] Two Jewish Progressive Party candidates were reelected, Helen Suzman and Harry Schwarz. However Sam Bloomberg, once more standing as a National Party candidate, at last succeeded. This time he had faced a Progressive Party candidate who was not Jewish and defeated him comfortably (in the Bezuidenhout constituency). Bloomberg now became the first Jew ever to be seated in parliament as a duly elected representative of the National Party.[18] His fellow party candidate in the Cape, Esmé Chait, was defeated in her constituency, but also entered parliament as a member nominated, under the terms of the constitution, by the National Party. The total number of Jewish members of the white chamber thus remained at four, the same as at the close of the previous parliamentary session. But the fact that this number was now equally divided between the government party and the Progressive opposition was surely indicative of the transformed image of the National Party in the eyes of Jews.

Israel Pinshaw's apologia notwithstanding, within the Jewish community a stigma remained attached to those who chose to represent the National Party. They were a source of moral embarrassment to the progressive-minded majority of Jews, and it is likely that many of the Jews who voted for the National Party in the 1970s and 1980s kept this to themselves. Indeed, much to the chagrin of the few Jewish candidates put up by the National Party, in June 1987 a resolution condemning them was passed by several hundred participants in a meeting of a new organization called "Jews for Social Justice," whose formation will be discussed in the next chapter. Sam Bloomberg complained bitterly to the Jewish Board of Deputies, which responded with a denial of any involvement in the issue.[19] National Party supporters were still hard put to defend their position. They argued that there was nothing un-Jewish in their political preferences. In the run-up to the

1988 local government elections an active National Party member, Stan Treisman, declared that it was "a gross insult and in itself un-Jewish to imply that Jews who support the NP no longer have a sense of Jewish values." He claimed that Jews were turning to the National Party in greater numbers for "Jewishly" sound reasons such as the government's genuine movement toward reforms, its prompt and effective action against antisemitism, its generous assistance to various Jewish institutions, and the fact—so he averred—that the South African Defense Force was the only army outside Israel that supplied kosher food for Jewish servicemen! Treisman's Progressive Federal Party opponent in the Yeoville-Bellevue constituency, Martin Sweet, and the Yeoville-Berea Progressive candidate, C. F. Garrun (both Jewish), jointly replied that no real reform had taken place in South Africa. "As South African Jews, we may be privileged and free," they wrote, "but what of the millions of our fellow South Africans?"[20]

Public debate over Jewish voting had crested toward the end of the year 1988 as the date drew near for the first local government elections held concurrently for all racial groups. In Johannesburg as many as twenty-six Jewish candidates vied with each other in no less than seven wards—fifteen Progressives, six Independents, and five Nationalists.[21] The perceived threat of the Conservative Party on the right of the political spectrum was perhaps one consideration that influenced some Jews to vote for the National Party. At any rate the National Party, in appealing to Jews, referred to this threat. For example, at a dinner that a Johannesburg businessman hosted for the purpose of recruiting Jewish support for the National Party, the guest of honor, Frederik Willem de Klerk (destined soon to become the country's president), conceded that Jews had traditionally voted against the party but now urged them to rally to it so as to block the Conservative Party.[22]

Against this backdrop, a perceptive analysis in the *Weekly Mail* posed the question "Does the Jewish Nat betray his roots?"[23] Noting that the "Jewish vote" had become an issue in imminent municipal elections, the author, Fran Buntman, wrote that various "rabbis, Jewish leaders, educationalists and politicians do not deny the general Jewish swing to the Nats." Many Jews had come to hold a genuine belief in the sincerity of the government's much vaunted reforms. Buntman quoted National Party candidate Stan Treisman: "I am very, very strong on human rights, both as a Jew and a jurist. Jews in South Africa are turning to the National Party in greater numbers because it abandoned . . . apartheid many years ago." Buntman found that many Jews harbored fears of black antisemitism under the guise of anti-Zionism, fed by the links between the African National Congress and the Palestinian Liberation Organization. They contended that the lessons of history showed a recurrent pattern: betrayal of Jews involved in "alien causes." Invoking the precedents of Stalinist purging of Jewish revolutionaries and the upsurge of antisemitism among American blacks that had supervened Jewish involvement in the civil rights movement, they pointed to certain Muslim groups that were calling for the exclusion of Jews from the antiapartheid struggle. Buntman noted, on the other hand, that progressive-minded Jews were outraged and embarrassed by this shift. In their view, any support of apartheid, no matter how ostensibly reformed, was "a betrayal of [Jewish] history, culture and religion."

In the wake of these municipal elections of 1988, the question whether Jews had swung toward the National Party was debated in the Jewish Board of Deputies, in itself an indication of changes in the policy of the Board, a subject to which we shall return. The impression of several well-informed Jewish leaders was that the party had indeed gained considerable Jewish support. Chief Rabbi Cyril Harris expressed the view (with implied displeasure) that there had indeed been such a swing, but speaking from his experience in the political thicket, Harry Schwarz opined that even in the recent municipal elections there had only been a slight swing to the right. He said divergence from the progressive voting pattern of Jews was not nearly as extensive as some people believed. Although the Board's chairman found it prudent to repeat the refrain that there was no such thing as "a Jewish vote," in his estimation Jews still tended to vote "to the left of the National Party."[24]

Be that as it may, the number of Jews who sought election to the whites' parliament as National Party candidates reached a peak in the general elections of September 1989. Five Jews stood as National Party candidates, all in constituencies known to have a considerable Jewish electorate. By contrast, there were only four candidates for election on the ticket of the newly formed Democratic Party, which had superseded the Progressive Party. It is, however, more significant that none of the National Party aspirants were successful, whereas three of the Jewish Democratic Party members did gain election. One was Harry Schwarz, reelected unopposed in the heavily Jewish Yeoville constituency. Another was Lester Fuchs, a young commercial practice lawyer who had been elected to the Johannesburg City Council a year earlier and now defeated the National Party's young Jewish candidate, Tony Wasserman, in the Hillbrow constituency. Overall, the National Party had certainly been gaining a growing segment of the Jewish vote, but many more Jews still cast a progressive, Democratic Party vote. The persistent National Party candidate, Sam Bloomberg, failed to retain his seat. He lost to another Jewish candidate, G. C. Engel of the Democratic Party. In the Houghton constituency, in which a predominantly Jewish electorate had repeatedly returned Helen Suzman until her retirement prior to the 1989 elections, the young rising star Tony Leon replaced her, despite Suzman's outspoken preference for another candidate (Irene Menell, also Jewish). Leon went on to defeat decisively the National Party's Jewish challenger, Dr. Shlomo Peer, a sixty-five-year-old businessman who had immigrated to South Africa from Israel in 1966. Peer had promoted a branch of the government party in Houghton and was a member of the National Party's executive in the Transvaal.[25]

In these elections even the Conservative Party made efforts, however futile, to win Jewish votes, particularly in the Hillbrow constituency. A flyer distributed by its candidate, T. J. Ferreira, was at pains to deny what it described as the lie that the Conservative Party was antisemitic or in any sense racist: "The Conservative Party," it claimed, "simply rejects the NP and DP policy of having the Blacks rule the Whites." It was for self-determination of each group in its own geographical area. "This policy is known as PARTITION. And if you know your history, this is exactly how the State of Israel came about!" Given the anti-Israel posture of the

ANC, the author of the flyer purported to know that "there is not a single responsible South African Jew who believes that he or she will be better off under a black government."[26] This was a line followed also by Dr. Andries Treurnicht, the Conservative Party leader. In a speech at the Johannesburg City Hall in March 1990, he declared that the Conservative Party caucus had in the past year gone to Israel and met with the leaders of all the political parties. "We asked them whether they would be willing to have power sharing with the Palestinians. All the party leaders told us 'never.' The CP is a white Christian Party but it is not against other people. . . . We are in favour of Whites."[27]

Even if the government's reformed apartheid policy had gained a measure of support by the end of the 1980s, there can be no doubt that it was still the Progressive Party's Helen Suzman who personified the public image of the Jews in the politics of South Africa both inside and outside of South Africa. As we have noted in a previous chapter, for decades Helen Suzman had been the very symbol of parliamentary opposition—at times solitary—to the apartheid system. However, it is perhaps her fellow Progressive Harry Schwarz who came closer to epitomizing the normative political orientation of South African Jews. For whereas Suzman had never taken particular interest in Jewish communal life, Schwarz had been actively involved and, indeed, could be regarded as one of the community's foremost leaders. Born in Cologne, Germany, in 1924, Schwarz came to South Africa in 1934 during the brief influx of German-Jewish immigration that was soon to be blocked by the 1937 Aliens Act. During the Second World War he served as an officer in the South African Air Force. Afterward he practiced law and engaged in business and merchant banking. After entering parliament in 1974 as a representative of the United Party, Schwarz broke away to found the Reform Party, which joined the Progressives, and went on to form the Progressive Federal Party in 1977. Although he was very progressive on social and economic policies, Schwarz was generally identified with the conservative wing of the Progressive Federal Party, mainly due to his favoring strong military defense and his insistence that change must take place without disruption of law and order. Much as Suzman was consistently returned to parliament by the Houghton electorate, so Schwarz was successful in the Yeoville constituency of Johannesburg, which also had a considerable Jewish population.

Beginning in the mid-1970s, Schwarz played an increasingly important role on the Jewish Board of Deputies, serving as chairman of its committee on international relations and often acting as spokesman for the Board to Jewish agencies abroad. He argued that violent change could ultimately lead to a nondemocratic regime, compatible neither with Jewish ethics nor with the legitimate interests of the Jewish community:

> To be against apartheid is one thing, but what do we want in its place? What will the post-apartheid regime be like? Will it be a free world type democracy in which human rights are respected and minorities protected? Will it be a regime under which South African Jews will, like other citizens, have religious freedom and under which our communal institutions can be maintained and our love for Zion expressed?[28]

When President de Klerk at last released Nelson Mandela in 1990 and embarked on negotiations for a postapartheid South Africa, Harry Schwarz was his choice as ambassador to the United States, a post he occupied in the transition period from 1991 to 1994. His known record of opposition to apartheid, tempered by some of the relatively conservative positions he had adopted within the Progressive Party, made him an admirable representative of the government's new course. Apart from this, given the assumed role of Jews in American liberal circles, Schwarz's being a Jew was surely not considered a disadvantage.

Shifts in Communal Policy

The transformation of apartheid's ideological rhetoric and the introduction of reforms in its implementation may not have redeemed the cause of white supremacists, but they certainly had the effect of extending the boundaries of public moral criticism permitted by the white consensus. This is the key to understanding the changes in the policy of the Jewish community's representative body—the Jewish Board of Deputies. In the 1970s it became possible for the Board to vent views that would have been regarded only ten years earlier as disloyal, if not treacherous. Accordingly, the Board continued to uphold its traditional policy of noninvolvement in politics but formulated statements that, while obviously antiapartheid in connotation, were sufficiently equivocal or euphemistic to be compatible with the discourse of *verligte* Afrikaners and hence with the trend of government policy. A typical resolution in this vein called for "the promotion of understanding, goodwill and cooperation between the various races, peoples and groups in South Africa and toward the achievement of a peaceful and secure future for all inhabitants of the country, based on the principles of justice and dignity of the individual."[29] The intention of those who passed this resolution was certainly not to support apartheid, but its wording was hardly at odds with government policy, at any rate not as it was being publicly articulated and justified at that time.

At the Board of Deputies' twenty-sixth congress in mid-1970, the chairman of its Public Relations Committee, Arthur Suzman, surveyed the period since 1967. He was able to say that he could not recall any time freer of tension and incident for the Jewish community during the eighteen years of his membership on the Board's executive council. Suzman attributed this to a number of factors apart from the "buoyant economic climate." One was the "vastly improved relationship and understanding" between South Africa and Israel. Another was the moderating tendency of government policy and the recent resounding electoral defeat of the HNP *verkrampte* Afrikaner nationalists.[30]

In the same address, Suzman offered a perceptive analysis of current opinions within the Jewish community and their reflection in the Board of Deputies. There were the "neutralists," who contended that neither Jews as individuals nor as a group ought to regard themselves, by dint of their Judaism, as bearing responsibility either greater or lesser than that of other citizens. There were the "pragmatists," who went further and contended that Jews should remain inconspicuous, keeping well away from unpopular causes. Their reasoning was that history has repeatedly shown Jews ending up as victims of the very groups whose causes they had altruistically espoused—witness the aftermath of the civil rights movement in the United States. Finally, there were the "idealists," who believed that precisely because of the historical experience of the Jews, not to speak of Judaism's values of social justice, Jews should be at the forefront of the battle against all forms of racial discrimination.

Suzman himself reaffirmed the Board's policy as the only responsible and balanced answer to the dilemma, namely, involvement in the political arena was a matter of duty or choice by individual Jewish citizens but never by the Jews as a collective. He added, however, an appeal from the heart for Jewish leadership not to evade moral issues, and to focus attention on what should be done within the Jewish community. He called this approach "pragmatic idealism." "Our task must be to arouse an awareness among our own community," he stressed, "and to create a consensus that race relations are not exclusively a matter of politics, but concern human values." What this meant in practice was that Jews should of their own moral volition set themselves standards of liberal, just, and compassionate behavior in all their domestic, business, and other interrelations with the underprivileged people of the country. Arguably, Suzman's exposition was more in the nature of a salving of moral conscience than a program of action in any way commensurate with the harsh realities of injustice and suffering inflicted by the apartheid system.

In his address to the Board of Deputies' twenty-seventh national congress in May 1972, Suzman began to take note of the widening scope for legitimate expressions of liberal sentiment allowed by the new discourse of reformed apartheid:

> Perhaps the most significant feature of our changing political scene is that members of the dominant ruling group—members of the "establishment" and particularly intellectuals and academicians—are themselves, in increasing numbers, openly questioning the validity of long-held basic beliefs, and this without any longer incurring the taint or odium of heresy. Furthermore, the magic word "dialogue" is heard on all sides.[31]

He reiterated that if collective action was to be ruled out, as it seemed it must, this did not mean "the individual must remain silent and stand aside." At an interprovincial consultation of the Board of Deputies in June 1973, Suzman summed up the new policy precept thus: "In other words, we conceive that the proper role of the Board is to address itself to the members of our own community rather than to the world at large."[32] At that consultation it was decided that the Board itself would set an example in regard to fair wage and job opportunities for black employees in Jewish institutions and in Jewish-owned businesses and industrial enterprises. These included, "wherever possible," not discriminating on the basis of race or color in respect of the wages paid for any particular post and again, "wherever possible," arranging for medical aid membership and for retirement pension schemes.[33] The caveat "wherever possible" implied wherever such measures were not in breach of the law, although in fact it could scarcely be said even of the apartheid laws that they prevented the voluntary implementation of such measures by employers. Of course, the Board had no legal authority to monitor the responsiveness of Jewish organizations and businessmen to these high-minded exhortations, not to speak of power to enforce them.

As chairman of the Board's Public Relations Committee, Arthur Suzman repeatedly had to deflect barbs of criticism aimed at its policy, which at this time emanated most stridently from the Students Jewish Association at the University of Cape Town. Its magazine, *Strike,* was calling for a Jewish stand on the fateful moral issues at stake in the country. "It has been argued that although the Board cannot speak with one *political* voice, it can and should speak with one *moral* voice," responded Suzman. "The difficulty, of course, is to determine where morality ends and politics begins . . . for the Board to enter the political arena on every issue which has moral overtones would, we believe, be self-defeating and counterproductive."[34] "It is not a question of sacrificing principle for expediency," Suzman averred. He said that the Board was bound to object not only to any political appeal to Jews as a group, from whatever source, but also to political appeals *by* Jewish groups, such as the students' associations. At the same time the Board had always encouraged every Jew as an individual citizen to act in accord with the teachings of Judaism and was exhorting all Jews to work for a moral and just society in their personal attitudes and dealings.

Of course, implicitly—and ofttimes explicitly—excluded from such exhortations were any acts of an "illegal" nature in terms of South Africa's legislation relating to the implementation of apartheid and repression of its opponents. Therein lay an unredeemable (some might argue, also unavoidable) failing of the Board of Deputies' position. Given the government's delegitimation and draconian suppression of almost all forms of opposition that in principle rejected white privilege and domination, the Board's much vaunted exhortation that Jews act on their Jewish convictions, but only in their capacity as citizens, was hollow. It excluded acknowledgment, not to speak of endorsement, of any Jew who took up the really consequential forms of resistance to the apartheid regime—those forms that were branded "illegal" and exacted the sacrificial price of arrest and imprisonment or exile. At any rate, in the eyes of all Jewish radicals and many Jewish liberals the Board's policy remained shamefully expedient if not hypocritical. In retrospective mitigation, however, the record allows one to say objectively that, notwithstanding continuous pressure not only from the Afrikaans press but also from numerous members of the Jewish public, the Board's executive was careful never ever to make a statement censuring by name any person involved in the radical antiapartheid struggle.

It is unlikely that a person of Suzman's liberal persuasion was unaware of this inescapable defect in the Board's self-justification. After all, at the Board's twenty-ninth national congress in May 1976, Suzman himself exercised the prerogative of a distinguished lawyer to devote much of his address to a sharply critical analysis of the erosion of the rule of law in South Africa.[35] That Suzman could even allow himself to utter such criticism publicly was indicative of the broadening parameters of consensually permissible self-criticism within white South Africa. Incrementally more outspoken, yet venturing only ever so slightly beyond the norm of the government's own *verligte* rhetoric, resolutions of the Board's congresses into the 1970s called for the elimination of "unjust discrimination so that all, regardless of race, creed or colour, be permitted and encouraged to achieve the full potential of their capabilities and live in dignity and harmony."[36] A turning point was reached in 1976 when Prime Minister Vorster returned from a visit to Israel, where relations between the two countries were cemented with a series of trade agreements. These included military weaponry agreements of unprecedented scale and mutual importance, but the Jewish community leaders did not yet know the details. In the congenial atmosphere of Afrikaner-Jewish relations that attended Vorster's visit to Israel, the Board of Deputies honored the prime minister with a banquet. On this occasion the Board's chairman, David Mann, allowed himself to make a statement that could not have been ventured a decade earlier. He said:

> I believe that there is a wide consensus today that attitudes and practices, the heritage of the past, bearing upon the relations between our various racial groups are no longer acceptable. I believe that there is a new sense of urgency abroad in our land, a realisation that we must move away as quickly and effectively as is practicable from discrimination based on race or colour, and that we must accord to every man and woman respect and human dignity and the opportunity to develop to their fullest potential. Our task is to translate into concrete patterns of living, and of relationships between man and man and group and group, the great injunction of the Bible, "Justice, justice shalt thou pursue, that thou may live and inherit the land which the Lord thy God gave thee."[37]

In the context of the Board's long-standing policy Mann's statement was unprecedented. Yet it remained an implied rather than an explicit criticism of apartheid. Moreover, the fact that it evoked no noticeable displeasure on the part of Vorster was indicative of the ideological shift that was in process within the Afrikaner regime itself.

As the trend toward reform of Verwoerdian apartheid gained momentum under Vorster's successor President Botha in the early 1980s, the Jewish Board of Deputies became incrementally less consistent and at times even self-contradictory in regard to its official policy of political noninvolvement. On the one hand, it scrupulously refrained from taking any position on the 1983 whites' referendum for the tricameral parliamentary constitution (signifying the new reformed apartheid strategy for preserving white dominance). "As a matter of policy," it reiterated, "the Board has never tried to influence members of the Jewish community in political matters and never issued any directive on how to vote." On the other hand, the cumulative significance of a series of unprecedented interventions in politically related matters undeniably amounted to a change of course. The first such initiatives were taken by the Board of Deputies council in Cape Town, which then exerted growing pressure on the national leadership in Johannesburg to follow suit. Indeed, already during 1977 and 1978 the Cape council became sharply critical of the national executive. A number of its members urged a conscious change of policy—expansion of the Board's conception of its legitimate concerns to go beyond matters directly affecting the Jewish community by including all issues of human rights and racial discrimination.[38] The national executive in Johannesburg at first hesitated but soon followed suit. The old guard, which had grown to maturity in the intimidating pre-1948 period of Afrikaner antisemitism, was being replaced by a younger generation of leaders. These included the young and dynamic executive director of the Board, Denis Diamond, and the brilliant young lawyer Michael Katz, who succeeded Suzman as head of the Public Relations Committee and became national chairman of the Board in the early 1980s. A growing body of executive opinion was advocating that the Board of Deputies should cease conceiving of itself purely as a Jewish defense body and passive reflector of the Jewish public. They felt it should assume the role of interpreting the Jewish conscience of the community, and of leading and shaping Jewish opinion.

The Board's public relations work began to be punctuated with sporadic statements and interventions of a kind that had earlier been deemed patently political and therefore taboo. In 1981 it made appeals against specific evictions of blacks and pass-law arrests and, in 1982, criticized detention without trial. Moreover, in unacknowledged contrast to the Board's silence on innumerable specific acts of apartheid policy a decade earlier, it began to invoke Jewish values and historical experience in support of such interventions. Thus in 1983 and 1984 the Cape council of the Board took a clear stand in objecting to the ongoing saga of what it called the authorities' "inhuman practice" of destroying shelters at the Crossroads squatter settlement near Cape Town. It sent a delegation to the responsible government minister with a memorandum stating that the Jewish community urges cessation of such actions "on humanitarian grounds, and on the grounds of its [the Jews'] own history of suffering." In like vein, the Board's national executive appealed to the government in 1983 to withdraw a bill limiting, by means of a new quota, admission of blacks to white universities.[39]

Although the record of the Board's statements and some of its actions thus show unmistakably that it was actually on a new course of policy, it clung almost atavistically to its traditionally cautious formula, officially reaffirming that its terms of reference excluded any political involvement. Only in rather muted fashion did the official reports of the executive to the Board's congresses allude to change. For example, the report to the biennial congress of 1978 noted that if the Board's previous attitude had "reflected an introspective concern with its own requirements," now, in response to the demands of the time, it was "realising, to an ever increasing degree, the need to be involved with issues of broader social concern." Without acknowledging that it was stepping into the political arena, it claimed to be issuing statements purely "on moral issues expressing views in conformity with the ethical ideals of Judaism."[40] To the congress held in 1980, the chairman, Dr. Israel Abramowitz, merely commented: "With significant and far-reaching changes taking place in South Africa, the leadership of the Board of Deputies has begun to direct attention to issues beyond those which are of specific concern to the Jewish community."[41]

In the late 1970s and into the 1980s the executive directors of the Board of Deputies, Denis Diamond and Aleck Goldberg, who took over after Diamond left to settle in Israel in late 1979, made increasing efforts to reach out for some form of contact and dialogue with black leaders. However, their connections were limited mainly to persons still functioning within the framework of the apartheid system, not major leaders of the black resistance and liberation movement. Thus the Council of Border Jewry in East London held a function in honor of Lennox Sebe, chief minister of the Ciskei, while in Johannesburg Dr. C. N. Phatudi, chief minister of Lebowa, was hosted.[42] Club 44, which was the young leadership training group of the Board, hosted Dr. Nthatho Motlana, chairman of the Soweto Council of Ten.

A major step in the direction of the government's *verligte* reforms was the parliamentary appointment in 1983 of a Select Committee to consider amending what were probably the most notoriously racist pieces of apartheid legislation ever promulgated—the prohibition of mixed marriages and Section 16 of the "Immorality Act" of 1957. When this racist legislation had first been passed, the Board of Deputies had been silent, but now, in March 1984, it made representations to the ongoing parliamentary committee. Claiming that it had consistently pleaded "for the amelioration and ultimate removal of all unjust and discriminatory laws based on race, creed or colour," it called for repeal of these racist provisions.[43] The culmination of this new—but hesitatingly admitted—course of policy was reached in 1985 at the Board's thirty-third national congress with the unanimous passing of a resolution that, for the first time, used the term "apartheid" and explicitly rejected it: "Congress records its support and commitment to justice, equal opportunity and the removal of all provisions in the laws of South Africa which discriminate on grounds of colour and race, and rejects apartheid." This resolution was reiterated and elaborated at the Board's April 1987 congress in a series of unequivocal resolutions, including the following:

> Congress resolves that there is an urgent need for enhanced and accelerated dialogue, negotiation and meaningful reform in South Africa, and records its dismay at the lack of meaningful progress in this direction, whilst acknowledging the steps already taken by the Government to repeal certain laws and abolish certain discriminatory practices. . . . Congress recognizes that apartheid is the principal cause of political violence in South Africa and that continued oppression under that policy exacerbates the climate of political unrest and believes that apartheid and racial prejudice are in complete contradiction to the teachings of Judaism.[44]

This turning toward increasing political involvement also found expression in the highly charged question of international sanctions against South Africa, which reached a crescendo in the mid-1980s. On no issue with political implications had the Board ever taken so clear-cut a position—it resolutely opposed sanctions and took active steps to make this known to other Jewish communities. In so doing the Board was of course wholly within the progovernment consensus as well as safely in the company of many important white opponents of apartheid, including major Jewish political progressives such as Helen Suzman and Harry Schwarz. On the other hand, the Board had to confront the fact that the State of Israel, under pressure from the United States, was one of the countries currently considering sanctions. At stake was the flourishing cooperative relationship between South Africa and Israel, with all the benefits it bestowed on the activities of South African Jewish organizations. Yet, in contrast to the equivocations that had characterized the Jewish leadership's treatment of Israel's participation in the international anti-apartheid chorus of the early 1960s, both the Board of Deputies and the Zionist Federation now resolutely expressed opposition to sanctions.[45] Indeed, both bodies even became proactive on the matter, seeking to influence both the State of Israel and Jewish organizations in the United States. "Whilst reaffirming its rejection of apartheid," declared the Board's national executive council in February 1987, "it was of the view that disinvestment and the imposition of sanctions (by whomsoever) is not conducive to the creation of conditions and circumstances which promote reforms resulting in a just society in which all sections of the population can attain their legitimate rights and opportunities."[46]

Concurrent changes in the same spirit were taking place throughout these years in the Board of Deputies' important affiliate, the Union of Jewish Women. Indeed, the women leaders' outspokenness exceeded that of the Board. In her presidential address to the Union's conference in 1976, Leah Rosettenstein recommended that the women should become more vociferous in their protests: "Freedom is indivisible and the Union of Jewish Women should take a stand on issues that affect the human rights of others. Unless we do so, we will directly contribute to their continuation." In an unprecedented outpouring of Jewish self-criticism, the Union's national organizer, Marian Nell, asked: "Where are we, as South Africans, when people are detained without trial, when hundreds are transported to resettlement areas, and thousands deprived of their homes by Government decree? Have we no opinion whatsoever when people are deprived of their homes or when families are forcibly separated?" She concluded that the time had come for the Union of Jewish Women to take the initiative and make its own commitment for change in South Africa.[47]

Under the presidency of Rose Norwich, which coincided with the wave of rebellion in Soweto, the change continued to be perceptible. At the Union's 1979 conference she declared that "history has shown us that it is not possible for one section of the population forever to dominate another," and the national organizer, Anna Morris, called for an end to the Jewish "ostrich syndrome." "Of course we are not a political organization," she said, "but there is a slender line between politics and morality, and if our Judaism teaches us anything it teaches us what is right and what is wrong. I believe strongly that it is time that the Union [of Jewish Women] stopped being an ostrich."[48]

Concurrently with these changes in the community's collective stance in regard to political issues, the Board of Deputies continued to concern itself with its original and primary function of monitoring antisemitic manifestations and taking action against them where necessary. Although such manifestations had by then ceased to be a serious problem, they never entirely disappeared.[49] Resurgent antisemitism emanated from a reactionary right-wing group founded in 1981 under the name the Afrikaner Weerstandsbeweging (Resistance Organization) and led by Eugene Terre'Blanche. This was a racist, neo-Nazi organization, which harked back to the various Greyshirt movements that had mushroomed in the 1930s as purveyors of Nazi and antisemitic views. However, it was gratifying to know that President Botha had condemned the views and activities of the Weerstandsbeweging on a number of occasions. In late 1982 it was reported that the police had uncovered arms caches belonging to the group and that a number of arrests had been made.

The Rabbis and Reformed Apartheid

There was a consensus in the Jewish community that the rabbinate ought to enjoy greater latitude than the lay leadership in expressing a Jewish voice on moral matters of race relations and social justice. As was noted in an earlier chapter, however, the Board of Deputies' oft repeated caveat—"with due sense of communal responsibility"—was an effective constraint. Not that this left more than a handful of rabbis champing at the bit. By and large, a distinct predisposition favoring a social order that fostered ethnic-religious particularism inhered in the orthodox rabbinate, which served over 80 percent of synagogue-affiliated Jews. Given this predisposition, as apartheid ideology ostensibly shook off its racist trammels and projected a purified rhetoric that stressed the right to white ethnic-cultural survival and solicitousness for the "own affairs" of every ethnic group, this was bound to strike a chord of sympathy. The record shows that most rabbis, particularly the ultraorthodox newcomers whose numbers increased in the 1980s (a subject to which we shall return in a later chapter), gave but scant attention to the issue of apartheid over the years, some even speaking out in support of government policy.[50] Their outlook was insular. They tended to compartmentalize Jewish concerns and to detach themselves from any sense of responsibility for society as a whole. By their lights, apartheid and its attendant evils were the doing and affair of the gentile majority of white society. Besides, they usually held that Jewish involvement—and the actions of rabbis inevitably would be interpreted as such—would only invite hostility to the Jews and divisiveness in the Jewish community. To be sure, in 1986 an independent group of modern orthodox scholars in Jerusalem who made an attempt to analyze the implications of apartheid theory for the *halakha* (Jewish religious law) arrived at the unequivocal conclusion that apartheid was "absolutely opposed to the heritage of the Oral tradition and to the Jewish world-view." They even drew the extreme inference that "as far as the Jews of South Africa are concerned . . . it turns out that there is a special obligation of *kiddush ha-Shem* (martyrdom) to devote themselves, even to the point of danger, to the repair of these injustices."[51] But this *halakhic* exercise was no more than a curiosity; it carried no authority and received neither recognition nor any particular attention in South Africa.

The majority of the orthodox rabbinate followed the lead of Bernard Casper, who succeeded Louis Rabinowitz in 1963 as chief rabbi of the United Hebrew Congregations of Johannesburg and the Federation of Synagogues. This body became the countrywide Union of Orthodox Synagogues when it incorporated also its Cape counterpart in 1986. Rabbi Casper was born in London in 1917 and had settled in Israel prior to accepting the call to South Africa. He differed greatly from his predecessor in temperament if not in basic policy regarding the primacy of communal responsibility. From the outset of his incumbency as chief rabbi, he perceived his task to be limited to nurturing the religious life of the Jewish community; it did not, by his lights, extend to carving out a Jewish role in the reformation of the societal order as a whole. To be sure, Rabbi Casper too sporadically expressed Judaism's revulsion against racism. On occasion, he also joined Christian clerics in peaceful demonstrations of protest against extraordinarily acute travesties of justice.[52] However, he was at all times judiciously careful to avoid provoking government censure, and unlike Rabinowitz he never complained about the implied constraints of the Board of Deputies' policy. He outspokenly opposed international sanctions against South Africa and appealed to colleagues overseas to adopt a stand against them: "Sanctions can only mean hunger and frustration and riots and chaos. I think that is a moral stance that all of us should be emboldened to pursue." During the mid-1980s antiapartheid campaign to end compulsory military conscription—often involving participation in suppression of rebellious blacks in ghettolike locations such as Soweto—Casper made it known that the *halakha* could not sanction refusal to do military service. "People may have very strong reasons for not wanting to go into the army," he said, "but I haven't got a religious basis for it. It would be wrong for me to pretend that we have a halachic basis for it."[53]

To the youth of the community, grappling with the incompatibility between "Jewish values" and the realities of South African society, Rabbi Casper held out a Zionist message: "Go home to the land which belongs to our people, where your views will be welcomed in the society we believe in." Taking leave of the community on the eve of his return to Israel in March 1987, after twenty-four years in South Africa, Rabbi Casper cautioned the Jewish community to adopt a low profile: "In South Africa we are a small identifiable foreign body and we fool ourselves if we think otherwise, and we as a Jewish community should be careful not to act in such a way as to convey the impression that we can influence the course of events."[54]

Most orthodox rabbis shared Casper's view that, in the final analysis, Jews ought to recognize that they were really no more than "guests" in the lands of *galut* (the exile). For instance, Rabbi Zalman Kossofsky, who grew up in South Africa, both his grandfather and father having served locally as prominent rabbis before him, once explained that his purpose in life was not to be a hero in the local political struggle but simply to make sure that South Africa's Jews were safe and preserved their Jewish identity. He said that Jews were in a very difficult situation as "guests of an establishment that is being immoral to a segment of the population . . . [but] so far in Jewish history, not once have the downtrodden been grateful for our efforts and our blood."[55]

In contrast to Chief Rabbi Casper's example, a handful of rabbis, both orthodox and reform, not only were outspoken against apartheid from the pulpit but also took an active part in public protests. In almost every case the most active of these rabbis decided sooner or later to leave South Africa, motivated at least in part by the conviction that it was unconscionable to continue participating in such a society. They included the South African–born orthodox rabbi Abner Weiss, a protégé of Louis Rabinowitz, who was the chief minister of the orthodox congregations in Durban from late 1969 until late 1976. Concurrently Weiss was also a professor in Hebrew and Jewish studies at the University of Natal, as Chief Rabbis Rabinowitz and Abrahams had been in Johannesburg and Cape Town respectively. Although Weiss made a point of using his pulpit for sharp criticism of the social evils and injustice of the South African political system, it was primarily through his university association that he had been drawn into antiapartheid activity in the early 1970s on a scale far beyond that which had been practiced by his mentor, Rabbi Rabinowitz. Indeed his passionate and eloquent speeches drawing upon Jewish references soon made him much in demand at protest demonstrations on and off the campus in the company of such prominent figures as Alan Paton, Catholic Archbishop Denis Hurley, and the Indian leader Fatima Meer.[56] These activities called upon him the threatening attention of the state security police, but Weiss was undeterred. He was highly motivated to fill the badly felt need for an emphatically Jewish role model in the opposition to apartheid and felt rewarded by the positive response of many young Jews. Moreover, he enjoyed the approbation and respect of his congregants in Durban. Nor did the Council of Natal Jewry (the local affiliate of the South African Jewish Board of Deputies) ever subject him to restraints.[57] Disillusionment came, however, from another quarter. At the outbreak of the Yom Kippur War in late 1973, Weiss was appalled by the hostile attitude toward Israel evinced by many of the antiapartheid activists with whom he had stood shoulder to shoulder at so many demonstrations, particularly, but not only, Fatima Meer. Mixed feelings concerning the Jewish moral conundrum in South Africa and the personal safety of his family made him amenable to attractive offers of a rabbinical position abroad. In late 1976 he left his pulpit in Durban for the United States, where he went on to become one of modern orthodoxy's most distinguished rabbis, serving first in New York and later in Los Angeles.

Another orthodox minister of religion who stood out as an inspiring Judaic role model for liberal-minded South African Jews was the young rabbi David Rosen, a son of the famous Anglo-Jewish rabbi and educator Kopul Rosen. David was born and educated in Britain but had settled in Israel when he was invited to serve a stint as adviser for the Jewish student associations at South African universities. Soon after, he accepted a call to the pulpit of the Cape Town congregation of Sea Point, numerically the largest in the country. Rosen served as rabbi of the congregation from 1975 to 1979, during which time he became increasingly outspoken on political issues. Typically, the local press reported him declaring at an Institute of Citizenship protest meeting held in St. George's Cathedral Hall: "Religious leaders, particularly Jewish religious leaders who separate politics from religion fail in their duty." When the Board of Deputies and Zionist Federation hon-

Fig. 1. Advocate Israel Maisels carried by jubilant supporters at the successful conclusion of the Treason Trial, March 1961. (By permission of UWC-Robben Island Museum Mayibuye Archives.)

Fig. 2. Visit of President Nelson Mandela to the Green and Sea Point Hebrew Congregation, May 1994. *Left to right:* the congregation's rabbi, E. J. Steinhorn; Israeli Ambassador A. Liel; Chief Rabbi C. K. Harris; President Nelson Mandela; Board of Deputies national chairman M. Smith. (By permission of S.A. Jewish Board of Deputies Archives.)

Fig. 3. Opening session of the S.A. Board of Deputies Congress, August 1962. (By permission of the Gitlin Library, Cape Town.)

Fig. 4. Protest demonstration in Cape Town against the United Nations anti-Zionist resolution, 1975. (By permission of the Gitlin Library, Cape Town.)

Fig. 5. Arthur Suzman addressing the S.A. Jewish Board of Deputies Congress, 1983. (By permission of the S.A. Jewish Board of Deputies Archives.)

Fig. 6. Mendel Kaplan speaking at a meeting in Cape Town, 1991. (By permission of Mendel Kaplan.)

Fig. 7. Helen Suzman addressing a meeting of the Jewish Board of Deputies, August 1987, flanked by communal leaders Gerald Leissner *(left)* and Hanns Saenger *(right)*. (By permission of S.A. Jewish Board of Deputies Archives.)

Fig. 8. Pupils at the gateway to the Herzlia middle school, Cape Town. (By permission of the Gitlin Library, Cape Town.)

Fig. 9. The Ohr Somayach study hall, Johannesburg. (By permission of the S.A. Jewish Board of Deputies Archives.)

ored Prime Minister Vorster on his return from a visit to Israel in 1976, Rosen refused to attend and said so outspokenly from his pulpit, to the applause of the Cape Town University Students Jewish Association. The Jewish press reported Rabbi Rosen's candid view that "the only way to remain in this society as a Jew is to stand up for principle and stand against injustice and iniquity."[58]

Not surprisingly, Rabbi Rosen soon began to receive anonymous death threats believed to be sent by white right-wing extremists, and he became aware that the security police were tapping his phone. Criticism was also forthcoming from some members of his congregation and other Jewish individuals in the community. After the Afrikaans daily *Die Burger* reacted critically to what it called Rabbi Rosen's "politieke preek" (political preaching), letters of bitter complaint at Rosen's behavior reached the Cape office of the Board of Deputies.[59] But these were ignored. Rosen felt he had the backing of the vast majority of his congregants and also the discreet support of Rabbi Dushinsky, who headed the *Beth Din* (rabbinical court). He enjoyed nothing but sympathy and even encouragement from the Board of Deputies' national executive director, Denis Diamond, and his executive council.[60] That he was not exactly persona grata in the eyes of the security police was evident in the authorities' refusal to renew Rabbi Rosen's work permit in 1979, but he had all the same never intended to stay much longer in South Africa. After returning to Israel, Rosen went on to become a foremost international promoter of interfaith relations, a sphere into which he had first been introduced in the context of the struggle against apartheid in Cape Town.

Another orthodox rabbi who engaged actively in antiapartheid activities was South African–born Selwyn Franklin, who succeeded Rabbi Abner Weiss in Durban. Reports in the general press quoted him declaring that South African society was "iniquitous," and that "detention without trial, influx control and forced eviction of people were anathema to the Jewish faith."[61] Rabbi Franklin intensified his antiapartheid outspokenness in the 1980s when he moved to the Sea Point congregation that had formerly been served by Rabbi Rosen. He gave vent to explicitly political appeals in his sermons and joined multiracial Christian and Muslim leaders in a series of interfaith services dedicated to peace and justice in South Africa. "Together with other leaders of major religious denominations," he declared, "I call for consultation and negotiation with the legitimate leaders of the black community so that peace, tranquility and justice will prevail."[62] Franklin also formed a Jewish Relief Committee, which actively assisted the victims of vicious intercommunal fighting that erupted in the Crossroads squatter camp near Cape Town while the police stood aside. He also took a leading role in the formation in 1985 of a Jewish social action group called Jews for Justice, a transforming development in the Jewish community to which we shall have cause to return in the next chapter.

On the question of conscientious objection to serving in the military, which was advocated by part of the antiapartheid coalition in which Jews for Justice participated, Franklin took issue, behind the scenes, with Chief Rabbi Casper's ruling that this was not sanctioned by *halakha*. Franklin formulated an alternative interpretation. He contended that the apposite principle of *dina de'malkhuta dina* (the law of the land is the law) did not necessarily apply in the case of a fundamentally unjust political system. Like Casper and most of his rabbinical colleagues, Franklin was stoutly Zionist and advocated *aliya* ("going up" to Israel) as the best and most rewardingly Jewish option in the face of the Jews' apartheid dilemma. But he did not hold back from outspoken criticism of the rising levels of cooperation between Israel and the South African government in the 1980s. He deplored the military support Israel was giving, warning that it was antagonizing the blacks and in the long run would not serve the best interests of either Israel or the local Jewish community.[63] In contrast to the experience of Rabbi Rosen, Franklin's activities met with a mixed response in the Cape Town community. On the one hand, many liberal-minded Jews welcomed them as a redeeming corrective to the poor record of orthodox Judaism in regard to apartheid. He also faced no opposition whatsoever from the Cape council of the Board of Deputies. On the other hand, some politically conservative members of his congregation's board of directors held that he was excessively preoccupied with politics and agitated against renewal of his contract. In 1988 Franklin decided to leave and settle in Israel. He later took up a pulpit in Sydney, Australia.

Another rabbi who chose to leave was Richard Lampert, also South African–born, of Johannesburg's progressive Temple Emmanuel. Lampert frequently was outspoken in his sermons but was otherwise not demonstratively active in public antiapartheid activities. On the eve of the Yom Kippur fast day in November 1976, he led his congregation in reciting an improvised adaptation of the solemn Kol Nidre prayer. Copies of the additional version were distributed to the congregation on printed sheets. It referred to "the sin we have committed by forgetting we were oppressed . . . the sin we have committed by disrupting family lives for our personal convenience . . . the sin we have committed by keeping silent in the face of injustice."[64] Lampert later discovered that the police had been tipped off that he had "subversive pamphlets" in his home and was left with a strong suspicion that the source was from a person or persons within his own congregation.[65] The rabbi found himself the object of a demeaning security police house search. Not long after, he decided to leave South Africa and take up a pulpit in Sydney, Australia.

Other rabbis who were similarly outspoken against the moral depravities of apartheid rule stayed the course. Foremost of these was Ben Isaacson, the charismatic, maverick rabbi who had been an outspoken antagonist of apartheid from the start of his career in 1958. As has been sketched in an earlier chapter of this book, the course of Ben Isaacson's checkered career included *aliya* to Israel in 1965, where he took up work in education. However, the narrow-minded mode and coercive tendency of the orthodox religious establishment in Israel was not to his liking, and he began to take an interest in progressive Judaism. This led to his being invited back to South Africa in 1974 to serve as a progressive (reform) rabbi. These were the stormy years of the first school pupils' rebellion in Soweto and renewed government repression. It did not take long before Isaacson began to identify himself vigorously with the liberation struggle on a scale unheard of since the ill-fated brief foray of Rabbi Ungar in the mid-1950s. Controversy revolving around not only his fervent political activity but also his personal marital life precipitated another fallout with part of his congregation.

Disillusioned with what he had come to feel was the shallowness of reform Judaism in South Africa, Isaacson at first considered founding, with those of his congregants who remained loyal to him, a new movement of conservative Judaism. However, heeding the pleas of some former orthodox rabbinical colleagues, he settled instead on formation of a single independent congregation named Har-El in 1982. In his personal observance, Isaacson was reverting to orthodoxy, but the synagogue was conducted on lines close to those of American conservative Judaism, particularly in regard to equal participation of women and mixed seating at religious services.

From his base in the new Har-El congregation, Isaacson intensified his opposition to the apartheid regime, explicitly in the name of Jewish religious values. He took part in a variety of protest activities such as the Release Mandela Committee and the End Conscription Campaign. He also worked closely with the Reverend Beyers Naudé, the "renegade" Afrikaner cleric who had become general-secretary of the South African Council of Churches, and the fervid Bishop Desmond Tutu, who was calling for international sanctions against South Africa—not a popular cause even in otherwise antiapartheid Jewish circles. Isaacson tongue-lashed the Jewish communal leadership for failing in their moral duty as Jews to oppose racial discrimination and social injustice, and he castigated Jews at large for tacitly enjoying the evil fruits of the apartheid system. A typically abrasive Isaacson statement that reverberated in the general press was: "It is a blatant lie that Jews in South Africa have supported the cause of blacks. One day they will have to answer for it. Racism is seen as kosher as long as it does not apply to Jews."[66] He also accused Jewish leaders of distorting Bishop Tutu's statements and willfully spreading the false notion that antisemitism was rampant among blacks. Balking at the consensus of the communal leadership, lay and clerical, he persistently advocated international sanctions against South Africa and opposed compulsory military conscription, on the grounds that it was directed against those who had just grievances and thus did not meet Judaism's criteria for a just war.[67] To Jewish youth entering military service, Isaacson did not shrink from advising that they respectfully request the authorities to refrain from using them to suppress blacks in the townships! Characteristic of the acerbic tenor of his sermons as reported in the general press was this comment:

> The Jewish establishment, taking its cue from the ruling political party, has slowly begun to jump onto the bandwagon of reform and now at least makes the right sounds—albeit spluttering and gurgling sounds. . . . As Jews we should have known better. We should have instinctively recoiled from perpetrating on others the injustices that we, more than any other people, have suffered.[68]

Isaacson went on to deplore the flight of Jews from South Africa because of the wave of unrest that was sweeping the country and the uncertain future of white domination. He did not question the motives of those going to Israel, but of others he declared bitingly: "Refrain from the hypocrisy of claiming to emigrate because of a sudden overnight aversion to apartheid." In explicitly political terms he called upon all Jews to act: "We must encourage the hesitant President Botha to stop hesitating, to stop looking over his shoulder, to stop talking about reform. . . . One cannot reform an unjust system, one must abolish it. Apartheid cannot be refined. It must be dismantled, not overnight but expeditiously."

Most other rabbis and Jewish communal leaders frowned upon Rabbi Isaacson's tempestuous style of protest and his abrasive castigation of the community. Even rabbis who had themselves consistently, if cautiously, made it known to their congregants that apartheid was in no way justifiable in terms of Judaism demurred at his sweeping censure of the community. Orthodox Rabbi Bernhard more than once took issue with Isaacson for giving the community "an undeserved bad name." He contended that with few exceptions Jews "abhor the iniquities and injustices of apartheid, and have always felt uncomfortable about being even a passive part of such a society." As for those who chose to leave the country, although Bernhard—following the advice of his mentor, the Lubavitcher rebbe in America—never encouraged this, he nevertheless noted that over the years many "outraged and frustrated" South African Jews had turned their backs on luxury and privilege, friends and family. They had preferred to uproot themselves and venture to foreign lands rather than stay and enjoy the fruits of apartheid. He also contended that if less support than might be expected was forthcoming for those individual Jews who actively fought the system, "It was not through lack of sympathy for the cause but because these people were frequently self-declared atheists and communists."[69]

Isaacson's unrestrained political interventions and scathing criticism of the Jewish community ultimately alienated many of his own Har-El congregants. This was compounded, as in the past, by some criticism of his personal life as a twice-divorced person. By his own retrospective admission, his behavior was as if driven by a reckless "self-destructive impulse."[70] Finally, in mid-1987, after Isaacson made a fiery antiapartheid lecture tour in the United States together with a black clergyman, the Reverend Zachariah Mokgoebo of Soweto, in the course of which Isaacson was reported to have disparaged his own congregants along with South African Jews in general,[71] the lay leaders of Har-El served him notice and disbanded the congregation.

At a time of great personal difficulty caused by another marital failure, Isaacson found himself isolated, abandoned, and unacceptable to any Jewish congregation in the Republic of South Africa. He was eventually given a pulpit in Zimbabwe, first in Harare and afterward in Bulawayo. There Isaacson was able to animate the religious life of this much diminished Jewish community and at the same time join the exiled African National Congress—a first for a rabbi—and freely associate qua Jewish minister of religion with leaders of the liberation struggle. But he felt that he had virtually become ostracized by his home Jewish community. Indeed, in the annals of clerical resistance to apartheid, few ministers of religion suffered as much damage to their personal career at the hands of their coreligionists as did this irrepressible, prophetlike rabbi. In this respect, Ben Isaacson was largely his own worst enemy. Yet even after account is taken of his combative personality, abrasive style, and problems related to his personal life, it is arguable that his experience is not incomparable with that of some Afrikaner clerics, such as Beyers Naudé and Albert Geyser, who rebelled against the theological and policy norms of their own Dutch Reformed Churches.

Rabbi Norman Bernhard, who had served the important orthodox Oxford synagogue in Johannesburg since 1963, practiced a contrasting approach to societal issues, cautious and temperate. In 1980 he established an "Oxford Synagogue Social Action Committee (OSSAC)." It launched a social action program aimed at improving the quality of life of black domestic workers living and working in that area. Social and recreational facilities, adult education, and insurance plans were provided. The congregants formed various subcommittees. One, headed by a prominent Supreme Court judge, called together a number of legal men in the congregation to form a legal advice bureau; another conducted a survey of accommodation and amenities needs. It was found that the project most desired by black people in the area was classes for self-improvement in literary skills and academic subjects. In late 1985 Bernhard also lent his support to the founding of the clearly antiapartheid social action group Jews for Social Justice in Johannesburg.

Distinctive of Rabbi Bernhard's stance was his repeated insistence on an optimistic prognosis for the future of South Africa. His inspiration for this derived from the Lubavitcher rebbe, Menachem Schneerson, whom Bernhard revered as one endowed with *ruah ha-kodesh,* the gift of divinely revealed insight and foresight. To his coterie of followers in South Africa, the rebbe had repeatedly urged that Jews not leave and expressed optimism that South Africa would ultimately provide a bright and prosperous future for all its peoples. Echoing the famous rebbe, Bernhard pointed approvingly to the reforms implemented by the South African government and averred that there still was a great reservoir of residual goodwill between all the races in the country. He said that "despite its blunders and heavy-handedness, the government has, in fact, taken many major—and until recently, previously unimaginable—practical steps in dismantling the legislative foundations of apartheid." Bernhard appealed to fellow Jews to be calm and confident despite the disturbances that were rocking the country at the time: "The only justifiable alternative is a *positively* motivated aliyah to Israel. As I am fond of telling you: To go from one Galut [exile] to another is no *chochmah* [wisdom]. Either go *home,* or stay home!"[72]

Rabbis of progressive (reform) Judaism, whose congregants in the 1970s accounted for some 18 percent of synagogue-affiliated Jews, followed a somewhat more uniform approach on matters relating to society at large than did the much larger group of orthodox rabbis. Rabbi Saul Super, whose relatively less restrained views and frequent participation in the protests of Christian clerics were discussed in a previous chapter, set the tone until his return to Israel in 1975. As well, mention has already been made of Rabbi Lampert, not to speak of Rabbi Isaacson's stormy period in progressive Judaism. Also in Cape Town various rabbis spoke out and joined Christian clerics in demonstrations, notably the veteran rabbi David Sherman.[73]

Progressive Judaism in Johannesburg, which had been ailing on account of internal dissension, gained a new lease on life with the arrival in 1985 of Ady

Assabi, a charismatic thirty-eight-year-old widower who came with his two young sons. Assabi was born and educated in Israel and ordained in 1971 at Leo Baeck College in London. He had served congregations in London and in Germany, and prior to coming to South Africa he worked for some eight years as executive director in Israel of the progressive movement of Judaism. His tenure coincided with the reimposition of severe emergency laws to deal with widespread black rebelliousness throughout the country. From the outset he was outspoken in his deprecation of the situation and took part in acts of protest, including on one occasion a prayer meeting for political detainees held in St. Mary's Cathedral. Moreover, by dint of his appealing personality, he enjoyed considerable exposure in the general press—not something that endeared him to all Jews. He was very critical of the way the apartheid system had "rubbed off on the Jewish community." "I cannot understand the limited Jews in our communities who suggest there can be a distinction between religion and politics," he told one admiring reporter. "Judaism deals with life, and politics is an integral part."[74] He was reported as saying that the authentic values of Judaism could not allow South African Jews to simply sit on the fence in regard to the struggle against apartheid. There were only two authentic options—to remain and be totally involved in the struggle or to pack and go![75]

Much as orthodox Rabbi Bernhard had done some years earlier, Assabi urged his congregants to give expression in the first instance to Jewish values of social justice close to home. To that end, he issued a pamphlet stipulating detailed minimum requirements regarding wages and other working conditions for domestic employees. He aroused a storm of controversy within the community when he took the initiative in inviting Nelson Mandela to speak at his synagogue a few months after his release from prison in 1990. Not long before, Mandela's much publicized embrace of Yasser Arafat had set off alarms of anxiety in this strongly Zionist Jewish community. So intense was the reaction that unidentified extremist elements within the community hurled crass insults at Assabi and even tried to deter him with death threats.[76]

In sum, throughout the period of reformed apartheid, moral objections to the system in general (and to specific iniquities in particular) reverberated within the walls of several major synagogues. These were often reported in a positive vein by the English-language press and in the Jewish newspapers. Moreover, the mainstream Afrikaans press no longer was punctuated by explicit or veiled threats of retaliation, as had been the case in the first two decades of National Party rule. As we have seen, the experience of those rabbis who had become outspoken varied considerably. Much seems to have depended on the style of protest adopted by the individual rabbi. Rabbis still had to contend with some opposition from congregants, but the strong constraints of the 1950s and early 1960s had greatly receded. For many a Jew, the young in particular, the outspokenness and actions of at least a few rabbis went some way toward redeeming the bad conscience of Judaism in the troubled South African scene. At the same time, even in this transition period leading to the abandonment of apartheid—the second half of the 1980s—the overall record of the rabbinate was far from satisfying the expectations of already alienated Jewish radicals or liberals still in exile, not to speak of others deeply immersed in the liberation struggle spearheaded by the United Democratic Front's various affiliates. The bitter criticism of such critics of Judaism's representatives in South Africa began to be allayed only in 1988 after the arrival from England of Rabbi Cyril Harris to assume the pivotal position of Chief Rabbi of the orthodox Union of Hebrew Congregations—a subject to which we shall have to return in the concluding chapter of this book.

The Voice of Foreign Jewish Organizations

Throughout the apartheid era, the leadership, both lay and religious, of South African Jewry was hard put to explain and justify itself to a variety of foreign Jewish organizations concerned with the fight against racism, discrimination, and denial of civic rights. South African apartheid was bound to evoke their severe condemnation. Moreover the international legitimacy of so-called interference in the internal affairs of any country practicing racial discrimination was an important matter of self-interest for any Jewish organization concerned with protection of fellow Jews in all countries. The list of such organizations was long; it included the World Jewish Congress, the American Jewish Committee, B'nai B'rith's Anti-Defamation League, and the National Jewish Community Relations Advisory Council (NJCRAC) in the United States.

Troubled by their conscience as privileged participants in apartheid society and anxious not to be ostracized, South African communal leaders were very sensitive to criticism from such organizations. It was therefore gratifying for them to know that the delicacy of their situation was by and large well appreciated. After attending international Jewish conferences, Board of Deputies chairmen repeatedly reported that "South African Jewry ranks high in the estimate of other countries," and that their explanations of the community's moral predicament and the Board's policy were received "with great understanding and appreciation."[77] In late 1966 the Board's general-secretary, Gus Saron, made an extensive lecture tour of the United States, delivering some forty addresses and meeting the leaders of major Jewish organizations, including the National Jewish Community Relations Advisory Council, the American Jewish Committee, and the Conference of Presidents of Major Jewish Organizations. He returned gratified by the universally sympathetic reception given to his explications of the South African community's situation and the Board's policy.[78]

A major difficulty in explaining the community's position abroad arose from the tendency of Jewish organizations and newspapers abroad to depict the Jews of South Africa as victims of rampant antisemitism. The South African Jewish leadership was ambivalent about such overseas perceptions of their situation. On the one hand, justification of the Jewish Board of Deputies' policy of political non-involvement implicitly required an appreciation of the community's vulnerability against the background of the past record of Afrikaner nationalist antisemitism. On the other hand, exaggerated reports of current antisemitism, implying that it was the natural ancillary of apartheid racism, were worrying. Not only were such reports in fact groundless; they also were likely to provoke a justifiably indignant reaction from Afrikaner and progovernment quarters. Yet, in repudiating these overseas perceptions, the Board of Deputies had to tread carefully lest it sound like it was making excuses for the apartheid regime.[79]

An impassioned exposition of South African Jewry's dilemma of conscience was made by the Board of Deputies' executive director, Denis Diamond, to a plenary assembly of the World Jewish Congress in February 1975. Diamond did not deny that South African Jews were shamefully privileged participants in an inexcusably racist society. "It is indefensible and repugnant to any Jew to find himself participating, however peripherally, in the politics of oppression and discrimination," he submitted. What is more, he assured the gathering that "no Jew would be chosen to any position of leadership in South Africa if he did not feel that way." But by the same token he expected other Jewish leaders in the world to appreciate that no Jewish public would tolerate anyone who used his position of communal leadership to commit the whole community to a unified stand against the government of the state. Whereas the Jewish individual could and should decide for himself whether and how to oppose the apartheid system, responsible communal leadership was duty-bound to avoid exposing the whole community to danger. Stressing the vulnerability of his community as "a minority within a minority," Diamond explained that the South African government was determined in its course and "would simply put down any attempt by the Jewish community to impede its onward march."[80]

As world concern with South Africa reached new peaks in the wake of the Soweto uprising of 1976, the strain of explaining and justifying Jewish communal policy increased. After representing the Board of Deputies at the World Jewish Congress conference held in Geneva in November 1976, Board chairman David Mann reported back that the former understanding attitude "was changing." He claimed that only after he was able to show that the Board of Deputies was beginning to express a collective point of view calling for real change in South Africa had he sensed a perceptible renewal of support. He said he had been able to make his point by citing his own relatively forthright address delivered in the presence of Prime Minister Vorster at the reception honoring Vorster's 1975 visit to Israel.[81] As we have noted earlier, Mann's speech on that occasion, although still cautiously restrained, indeed marked a turning point in the Board of Deputies' policy.

If the record shows that South African Jewry enjoyed a consistently sympathetic hearing from both global and American Jewish organizations, the same cannot be said about British Jewry, at any rate not as far as its leading newspaper, the *Jewish Chronicle*, was concerned. Just about the only harsh criticism of the Board's policy that seriously perturbed its executive emanated periodically from correspondence columns of this reputable Jewish organ. In part the *Jewish Chronicle* acted periodically as host for searing criticism penned by radical Jewish activists who were now exiles in Britain. An example is veteran trade unionist Solly Sachs's sharp assault, which was discussed in a previous chapter of this book. A different kind of critic was the popular author and newspaper columnist Chaim Bermant. Upon returning from a visit to South Africa in 1979, Bermant, himself of Litvak extraction, was unstinting in his praise of what he recognized as the warmth and intensity of Jewish life in this most remarkably Litvak of communities. On the other hand, he found the community's apparent complicity in the apartheid system insufferable and said as much in his *Jewish Chronicle* column, much to the chagrin of the communal leaders who had so warmly hosted him in South Africa.[82] However, voices more authoritative than that of Bermant showed empathetic understanding. Chief Rabbi Immanuel Jacobowitz, for one, was of the opinion that "the realities in South Africa are far too foreboding for Jews and whites generally to justify outbursts of righteous indignation against a remote community trapped in the vice of an insoluble moral dilemma."[83]

American Jewish visitors to South Africa generally were less critical than the British, and their endorsement grew perceptively after 1975, as they perceived that the Board of Deputies was making statements calling for political change in South Africa. Typically, Sidney Vincent, the highly regarded executive director emeritus of the Cleveland Jewish community's federation, returned home after a guest visit in 1978 with a most favorable and empathetic impression. "I found no Jew who defended apartheid," he reported. Vincent described his visit as "an inspiring and at times heartbreaking experience." He praised the "extraordinarily high level of Jewish commitment," noting that "devotion to Israel is a passion," and "the Zionist organizations are easily the most powerful Jewish groups there."[84] Most important for South African Jewry was the consistently supportive attitude of the World Jewish Congress. Indeed, its president, Edgar Bronfman, having come as guest of the Board of Deputies' congress in 1983, offered what some of the Board's own members might have regarded as an inordinately enthusiastic endorsement of its policy. "I can tell you that the Jewish world as a whole salutes and supports the South African Board of Deputies," he declared, "for its determination to apply the highest Jewish moral values to issues that are so socially and politically sensitive."[85]

As South Africa's pariah status and international isolation became critical in the wake of the enormous eruption of unrest and its harsh suppression of the mid-1980s, it became all the more important for the Jewish community to maintain its links with global and American Jewish organizations. In 1985 the Board of Deputies formed a new committee to promote its Jewish international relations. Harry Schwarz, the highly experienced politician and Progressive Party M.P. who, propitiously, had begun to take an active interest in the work of the Board, was appointed chairman of the new committee. Schwarz himself traveled abroad to attend a number of major Jewish gatherings. He addressed a session at the General Assembly of the Council of Jewish Federations, and met with the American Jewish Committee and the National Jewish Community Relations Advisory Council. Schwarz's record as a prominent parliamentarian and political opponent of apartheid made him a highly credible and persuasive advocate of the South African Jewish community's stance. Indeed, although none could at the time have expected this, within a few years Schwarz was to be appointed by President de Klerk to the important diplomatic post of South African ambassador to the United States.

With characteristic political sophistication, Schwarz analyzed the interests and anxieties that motivated certain American Jewish organizations to be vocal and assertive not only in opposing apartheid but also in joining the growing chorus of pressure for stepping up disinvestment and economic sanctions against South Africa.[86] In his view, such activity was regarded by American Jewish agencies as a helpful no-cost measure for demonstrating to African-Americans the Jewish desire to heal the serious breach that had developed between them and Jews after the halcyon days of the 1960s civil rights struggle. Taking an assertive stand in favor of sanctions and the international isolation of South Africa represented a far more serviceable "trade-off" than other domestic issues could provide. Schwarz advised that in the light of this situation it was all the more important for the Board of Deputies to maintain close liaison with American Jewish organizations in order to keep them apprised of the authentic concerns of South African Jewry.

Of all overseas Jewish organizations, it was the American Jewish Committee that, out of empathetic concern for the South African Jewish community, made the greatest efforts to learn about the situation on the spot. In October 1985 it made the first of a number of study visits to South Africa. At its conclusion, the visiting delegation told the Board of Deputies that what its members had learned moved them to "identify with the anguish felt by the Jewish community, whom they found to be extremely hospitable." Indeed, they felt that South African Jews bore "an unnecessary desire to flagellate themselves for past attitudes to apartheid." In their view, the Jewish stance had been one of which the Jewish community could be proud. It is noteworthy that they also gained the impression that "the Afrikaner community is certainly not the monolithic monster which they had been led to believe it is." The delegation admitted to having become disenchanted with the idea of radical disinvestment and sanctions, but felt that given the current American climate they might not be in a position "to come right out and support an anti-disinvestment campaign."[87]

In the second half of the 1980s international sanctions against South Africa became a major concern of the Jewish Board of Deputies, as the issue rose to the fore of public attention in the United States and, by extension, also shook up Israeli foreign policy. As has already been shown, on this issue the Board did a complete volte-face in relation to its traditional policy on local political affairs. It took a decisive and resolute stand against sanctions and even campaigned actively vis-à-vis Israel as well as overseas Jewish organizations. In the United States the National Jewish Community Relations Advisory Council, motivated by its domestic concern with relations between blacks and Jews, was at the forefront of sanctions advocacy. Since the mid-1960s it had taken a special interest in the South African issue. In 1986 it vigorously supported the U.S. Congress's enactment of the Anti-Apartheid Act over a presidential veto. Even after President de Klerk's dramatic release of Nelson Mandela and the onset of negotiations with the African National Congress, NJCRAC took a position against what it regarded as premature lifting of American sanctions. NJCRAC persisted with this policy even after one of the Board of Deputies' leaders, Hanns Saenger, attended the plenum of the organization's conference in April 1991 to urge moderation.[88] Even the Union of Jewish Women of South Africa was "appalled and dismayed" at the continuing support for sanctions given by its sister organization in America, without the courtesy of consultation.[89]

Another initiative in pressing for radical disinvestment and sanctions came from Rabbi David Saperstein, director of the Religious Actions Center of reform Judaism's lay and rabbinical organizations in the United States. This encountered bitter resentment from reform Judaism's own South African counterpart, the Union for Progressive Judaism, especially since the Americans had not bothered to consult it at all. "We feel let down by the American Jewish Reform movement," it complained.[90] The South African progressive movement deplored the "high-handed" position adopted by Rabbi Saperstein on behalf of American reform Jewry. Claiming that the credentials of South African progressive Judaism in opposing apartheid were "impeccable" and that it therefore was speaking "with a clear conscience and conviction," it rejected sanctions and disinvestment as a misguided policy that would only harm the people it purported to help.[91]

In contrast to the American reform movement, the Union of Orthodox Jewish Congregations of America, also a participating agency in NJCRAC, went almost to the opposite extreme in identifying with the feelings of South African Jewry. It took a dissenting position within NJCRAC and in rather hyperbolic terms claimed that its long-standing condemnation of apartheid had always been "in close consultation with the courageous Jewish community of South Africa, which has played a significant role in ongoing efforts to alleviate the suffering of black South Africans."[92]

In sum, barring the intense dissonance occasioned by the debate over sanctions in the late 1980s and early 1990s, the record shows that, by and large, the policy of the South African Jewish Board of Deputies, and indeed also the behavioral record of South Africa's Jews in general, was sympathetically understood, if not endorsed, by the major organizations concerned with intergroup relations and transnational Jewish affairs.

CHAPTER 4

Dissonance and Change

Reversion of Israel–South Africa Relations

As we have seen in an earlier chapter of this book, the Six Day War of 1967 proved to be the turning point in restoring good relations between Israel and South Africa. Especially in Afrikaner eyes the Six Day War demonstrated that Israel was a power hindering the advance of Soviet influence into Africa. Typically, *Die Burger* commented: "Israel and South Africa have a common lot. . . . The anti-western powers have driven Israel into a community of interests which had better be utilized than denied."[1] When David Ben-Gurion, the eminent founding father of Israel, by then retired, accepted the invitation of the South African Zionist Federation to visit South Africa in 1969, *Die Vaderland* made an editorial statement that expressed the underlying trend of Afrikaner thinking about Israel after the Six Day War:

> Nothing would please us more than a sound growing spirit of mutual understanding and goodwill between Israel and the Republic, for our sakes as Afrikaners who, spiritually aligned with the old nation of Israel, have frequently in the past been distressed by the new state's attitudes towards us in the council chambers of the world, but above all, for the sake of our Jewish fellow-citizens who were thereby cruelly torn in their loyalty to South Africa. . . . When we, from our side, look realistically at the world situation, we know that Israel's continued existence in the Middle East is also an essential element in our own security. . . . If our Jewish citizens were to rally to the call of our distinguished visitor—to help build up Israel—their contribution would in essence be a contribution to South African security.[2]

Clearly, the South African government's fundamental geopolitical interest in Israel's defeat of communist Russia's Arab protégés on the northern tip of Africa overrode all cumulative resentment at Israel's diplomatic alliance with African states against white South Africa. It showed this by responding positively to some minor military needs of Israel during the war,[3] and by lifting the ban on transfers of funds to the Jewish Agency in Israel. These judicious actions did not fail, in turn, to spur a renewal of cooperation between the two governments. At this stage it remained limited to trade relations. In January 1968 two Israeli right-wing political personalities of note, Shmuel Tamir and Eliezer Shostak, took the initiative in forming an Israel–South African Friendship League, which dedicated itself to the principle that disapproval of South Africa's internal affairs ought not to prevent normal bilateral relations. Whereas in 1967 the volume of mutual trade stood at only about $7 million, by 1973 it had risen to $39.5 million.[4]

Putting aside its pique at Israel's continued antiapartheid votes at the United Nations, the South African government began to seek normalization and upgrading of diplomatic relations with Israel. (It should be recalled that South Africa had never fully reciprocated Israel's diplomatic mission.) In June 1970 South Africa's foreign minister, Hilgard Muller, raised the question at a meeting with his Israeli counterpart, Cape Town–born Abba Eban. Muller listed several mutual advantages that might accrue. These were their common interest in nuclear research as well as in resisting communist influence in Africa. Muller stressed South Africa's importance as a supplier of uranium. He also mentioned South African Jewry's contribution of funds to Israel.[5] But Eban was evasive. He was not ready to risk possible damage to Israel's still thriving relations with a large number of African states.

Not only did Israel continue to vote against South Africa in the international forum, but in an endeavor to counter signs of increasing Arab influence within the Organization of African Unity (OAU), in April 1971 it offered to make a small financial contribution to that body's African Liberation Committee. Instantly interpreted by the South African communications media as a direct gesture of identification with terrorist attacks on South Africa, this incensed not only whites who were progovernment but also many who were not supporters of apartheid. The government went so far as once again to suspend fund transfers, pending "clarification" from Israel. "I certainly do not understand how Israel, which itself has a terrorist problem, can justify contributions to other terrorists," commented the annoyed Prime Minister Vorster, while the Afrikaans press accused Israel of ingratitude and hypocrisy.

Astonished and pained by these developments and finding the implications of support for terrorism wholly inexcusable, the Jewish Board of Deputies and the Zionist Federation issued a joint statement condemning "support for terrorism from whatever source." They declared that the "South African Jewish community has great difficulty in accepting the report that a contribution, albeit of a contemptuous amount, has been made by the Government of Israel to the OAU for the purpose of furthering so-called freedom movements."[6] It was only after a flurry of behind-the-scenes diplomacy that the damage to Israel–South Africa relations was repaired, Israel first explaining that the proposed gift was intended not as aid to terrorists but for purely humanitarian purposes such as provision of food and medicines, and afterward redirecting its offer of aid to the education fund administered by the United Nations Commission on Refugees. If this awkward solution proved satisfactory, it was because the South African government was certainly not interested in a breach. It promptly withdrew the ban on fund transfers.[7]

That the South African government's earlier gesture of sympathy with Israel in its time of need made a positive impression on public opinion in Israel was evident in Israeli press criticism of the embarrassingly bungled affair of the OAU contribution.[8] Nor were objections raised in 1972 when South Africa at last took up its option to reciprocate Israel's long-standing unilateral representation, thereby opening a consulate general in Israel and at the same time assuring Foreign Minister Eban that it would "respect Israel's wish that we keep a low profile."[9]

Meanwhile, apart from a breach with one country, Guinea, Israel's bilateral diplomatic relations with African states were still expanding, reaching thirty-two missions by 1972, as were its various technical-assistance programs and trade ventures. But ominous rumblings of an imminent avalanche were beginning to be sensed. Between March 1972 and May 1973 seven African states broke off relations with Israel. On the eve of the Yom Kippur War in October 1973, two more followed. Finally, the Yom Kippur War precipitated the collapse, with nine more African states severing relations before the fighting was over, and another ten soon after. By 1974, Israel was left with diplomatic relations with only four African states: Mauritius, Lesotho, Malawi, and Swaziland. At a more symbolic level, the ultimate blow, which crippled all Israel's endeavors and aspirations in regard to amity and cooperation with the states of Africa, came in November 1975 when they voted overwhelmingly in favor of the United Nations resolution insidiously equating Zionism with racism. This was a great victory for Arab-cum-Soviet propaganda.

Israel's disastrous failure in Africa had little to do with its relationship with South Africa. A combination of factors was involved.[10] These included the leftist radicalization of various African regimes, the political activation of Islam in Africa, and the powerful economic pressure of the oil-rich Arab countries. As President Senghor of Senegal bluntly stated, "The Arabs have the numbers, space and oil. In the third world they outweigh Israel."[11] Once the avalanche of diplomatic ruptures with Israel was in motion, even OAU member states that were reluctant to forfeit cooperation with Israel—and in many cases actually managed to preserve its benefits unofficially and discreetly—found it unavoidably expedient to follow suit in breaking off diplomatic relations.

After the enormous efforts that Israel's governments had invested in relations with Africa, the wholesale desertion by the African states was a searing disappointment and virtually drove Israel into the all-too-willing arms of South Africa. Particularly forthcoming was Defense Minister P. W. Botha. In a speech delivered soon after the outbreak of the Yom Kippur War, he described Israel and South Africa as two vital "gateways between East and West" guarding against communism. He said that the people of South Africa felt a deep sympathy with Israel in its life-and-death struggle against communist-supported forces. Botha did not fail to include a gesture to the Jewish community: "I want to convey to the South African Jewish community our deepest sympathy and assure them that we as a small nation feel their plight. What is happening to them today may happen to us tomorrow. I have no doubt we shall find ways and means to prove our goodwill to Israel."[12]

In the aftermath of the Yom Kippur War, Foreign Affairs Minister Golda Meir, who for over a decade had enthusiastically prioritized and mothered Israel's now discredited African policy, was out of power. Israel's post–Yom Kippur War government, which took office in 1974 under Prime Minister Yitzhak Rabin and Minister of Defense Shimon Peres, reacted sharply to the country's abandonment by the African states. It embarked resolutely on a course of pragmatic and expedient self-interest in regard to South Africa. Exports from Israel to South Africa rose rapidly from $12 million in 1973 to $34.7 million in 1975.[13] Moreover, former restraint over formal upgrading of diplomatic relations fell away, and in 1974 and 1975 Israel and South Africa at last raised their mutual diplomatic representation to ambassadorial level. Finally, Israel agreed to receive an official visit by Prime Minister Vorster in April 1976, the first by a South African prime minister since Dr. Malan's private visit in 1953. Vorster was received with full honors and signed a number of wide-ranging trade and technical cooperation agreements. It was also announced that a ministerial committee representing both countries would meet annually to review their progress. Thenceforward the two governments were set on a path that resolutely fostered bilateral relations on all levels of mutual interest including military-related trade and cooperation. At the same time Israel's first ambassador, Yitzhak Unna, continued frankly to express disapproval of apartheid—at times more demonstratively than any other ambassador to South Africa.[14] But in the context of the gratifying expansion of cooperation with Israel, the South African government tolerated this kind of criticism as no more than a minor irritant.

A series of reciprocal visits by government ministers and senior officials followed the agreements made with Vorster. These included two visits by South Africa's minister of the interior Connie Mulder in 1975 and 1976. In 1978 Israel's minister of finance, Simha Ehrlich, visited South Africa, and in 1980 his South African counterpart, Horwood, reciprocated. One outcome was authorization of business investments in Israel, initially limited to about $41million but afterward raised to $60 million, with transactions allowed in commercial rands, which were considerably higher than the financial rand that applied for the world rate.[15] Economic cooperation reached new levels with the creation of joint Israeli–South African companies, notably Iskoor, which combined the resources of the Israel labor movement's large Koor company with that of the giant South African Iron and Steel Corporation (ISCOR). Some aspects of economic cooperation enabled the reexport of certain goods partly produced in South Africa, thereby facilitating the circumvention of European and American sanctions against South Africa. At the same time Israel and South Africa had a strong mutual interest in keeping their relations on as low a profile as possible. It is indicative of the importance South Africa still attached to its ongoing trade links with Arab countries, particularly in regard to oil imports, that its ambassador, Charles Fincham, was instructed to request the Israelis "to refrain from using the example of South Africa's trading relations with other countries in order to justify their relations with South Africa."[16]

Although Israel was careful never officially to recognize the "Bantustans"—Bophuthatswana, Ciskei, Transkei, and Venda—it had difficulty curbing the enthusiasm of some Israeli industrialists to invest in these official homelands. The Israeli Foreign Ministry did manage to see to official rejection of invitations to attend the ceremony marking the independence of the Transkei,[17] but could not prevent dozens of Israeli entrepreneurs from investing and undertaking various enterprises, especially in the Ciskei. Private Israelis also got involved in providing military training and arms for the Ciskei. Nor did the Foreign Ministry prevent President Lucas Mangope of Bophuthatswana from visiting Israel in 1980 and 1983, and President Patrick Mphephu of Venda in 1980. Ciskei's president Lennox Sebe made several visits in 1983, and Chief George Matanzima of the Transkei came in 1984.

In 1977 Menachem Begin came to power in Israel at the head of a right-wing government. The South African government welcomed this development especially since it coincided with growing pressure against South Africa at the United Nations, which culminated in the UN Security Council decision of November 1977 to impose an arms embargo on South Africa. Although officially Israel's new foreign affairs minister, Moshe Dayan, declared that Israel would comply with this ban, there can be no doubt that Israel sought to evade it and in fact continued to expand the sale of military equipment to South Africa. South Africa's ambassador in Tel Aviv reported back that Foreign Minister Dayan and Defense Minister Weizmann were both "highly sympathetic." Summing up the "very close military cooperation between Israel and South Africa," he said: "It mainly covers the supply of weaponry but also includes other important aspects such as the supply of specific 'know-how' and specialized training." He noted that while the figures for the increasing pace of trade indicated a favorable trade balance for South Africa, they did not include amounts for "classified" exports, that is to say, military equipment, which, if included, would certainly indicate a trade balance in Israel's favor.[18] The relationship was further enhanced during the tenure in South Africa from 1981 to 1985 of Begin's appointee as ambassador, Eliahu Lankin.

Given the increased pressure of the United Nations, the South Africans had all the more cause to ask Israel not to resort to publicizing South Africa's continued trade relations with other countries in order to excuse its own policy. Raising the matter with Israel's Foreign Ministry in October 1979, the South African ambassador mentioned that South Africa was carrying on an intensive trade with some forty-eight African states to the tune of about $800 million per annum, but for obvious reasons did not publish this.[19] Indeed, the conventional trade relationship between Israel and South Africa, although greatly increased, remained small compared with both countries' trade with the rest of the world. Even at its peak it still accounted for only between 1 and 2 percent of the total (declared) foreign trade of both countries.[20] However, the diamond trade was never included in this reckoning, since it was conducted through the international commodity market, and it must have been considerable, since it is known that Israel cut about half of all gem diamonds sold through De Beer's central selling agency. Moreover, the declared figures did not include the closely guarded secret trade relating to military matériel. This was the subject of oft extravagant journalistic conjecture, on the one hand, and consistently stubborn denial by the two governments, on the other.

The precise nature of the military-related trade and its full scale will become known only if and when the defense and security archives of either country become available. However, there can be no doubt that already by 1977 both governments attached enormous importance to their military-related trade and cooperation. According to a memorandum submitted by the South African Defense Forces to the government's Trade Relations Committee in the wake of the United Nations sanctions resolution of 4 November 1977, the South African Defense Forces were confident that Israel had a strong interest in continuing to cooperate even if it would now have to be careful not to include identifiably American parts and expertise. The South Africans thought that for the foreseeable future South Africa would continue to remain "Israel's best single client for weapons purchases," and that "Israel would do all its in power to carry out its obligations and look for ways and means of evading the UN-imposed sanctions." The memorandum went on to report that as of 31 December 1977 weapons sales obligations to Israel amounted to approximately $740 million, of which $439 million was still outstanding, to be spread over the years 1978 to 1981.[21] While the full facts of Israel's military exports to South Africa remain elusive, when American pressure to stop them eventually became compelling, the public debate within Israel made it evident that this trade had become a truly major factor in Israel's economy.[22]

From the vantage point of this book's concern with the effect of Israel–South Africa relations on the Jewish community, one might usefully make a distinction between military-related aspects that remain unverifiable, on the one hand, and others that became common knowledge more or less verified by firsthand observance or reports in the press of both countries, on the other. The unverifiable category includes speculation concerning such matters as joint development of a fighter plane and long-range guided missiles, supposed Israeli training of South Africans in anti-insurgency methods, and even direct involvement of Israeli advisers in the war in Angola. But most of all it relates to alleged cooperation in the development of nuclear weaponry. That there was scientific cooperation in the nuclear sphere is evident.[23] However, the exact nature of this cooperation remains unknown. There has been much conjecture about the exchange of South African uranium for Israeli technical expertise in the joint development of a nuclear military capability, especially in connection with a much publicized "flash" in the South Atlantic Ocean off the coast of South Africa said to be detected by a United States reconnaissance satellite in September 1979. But this was never conclusively proved to have been the testing of a nuclear explosion.[24]

As for the verified category of Israel–South Africa military relations, it was well known that as early as the 1960s South Africa started producing the Israeli Uzi submachine gun under license from a company in Belgium. It also became common knowledge that Israel was making direct sales of some of its advanced weaponry, beginning in the early 1970s with a number of naval vessels equipped with missile systems. Numbers of South African citizens doing their military service could not but become aware that Israel was supplying sophisticated electronic systems such as radar, electronic fences, and night vision equipment. The visits of scores of Israeli military technology and scientific experts made it obvious that there was considerable cooperation and joint ventures in these fields even if the details remained closely guarded secrets.

All of these known facts were sufficient to make the average Jew aware that a significant level of military-related trade was in progress between the two countries. However, the South African Jew's perception of these matters was clouded, not only by the shroud of secrecy surrounding them and the reiterated categorical denials issued by both governments, but also by deeply ingrained mistrust of the accusations voiced by sources known to be hostile to Israel a priori. These selected Israel alone for obloquy out of all the countries in the world that had relations with South Africa and made it out to be motivated by an inherent racist affinity to the apartheid regime. The very extravagance of such prejudiced anti-Israel charges undermined their credibility in the eyes of the average Jew, irrespective of whether he was for or against the South African government's policies.

At the same time there can be little doubt that, after the discomfiting tensions of the 1960s, for the Jews as a community it was gratifying that the country's government now had a very cordial relationship with Israel. This certainly influenced the perceptions and opinions of most of the leaders of the main Jewish institutions—the Board of Deputies, the rabbinate, and above all the Zionist Federation, whose very raison d'être made it dependent on the goodwill of the South African government toward Jewish links with Israel. Nevertheless, on the whole the communal leadership accepted at face value the justifications and refutations provided by Israel's spokesmen. As in all matters concerning "politics," the Jewish leadership did not wish to rock the boat. It asked no probing questions, perhaps preferring not to know too much. It seems that uncovering the full extent of Israel's military cooperation with the forces upholding white supremacy under apartheid would have created intolerable cognitive dissonance. Yet, as has been noted earlier in this book, many communally active and Zionist Jews were supporters of the Progressive Party's opposition to the government's apartheid policies, and as we shall have occasion to note anon, outbursts of vocal criticism issued periodically from students in the Zionist youth movements who were acutely ashamed of the military connection. What Israel was doing ran contrary to their conception of Zionism and their idealized image of Israel.

Much the same might be said of the South African Jews who had settled in Israel over the years. Only a small number took to acts of protest or even voiced dissent concerning Israel's military relations with the white minority government of South Africa. Given the Zionist youth movement background of many, there can be no doubt that they found the apartheid system repugnant. Yet their basic identification remained with the Jewish community they had left behind and perhaps even more with the needs and interests of the State of Israel. Insofar as they had some form of organized or institutional expression, this was an office known as "Telfed," run by a voluntary committee and some paid officials. Telfed was a subordinate branch of the South African Zionist Federation and neither could nor wished to adopt an independent attitude toward the internal affairs of South Africa. Indeed, South Africa's ambassadors to Israel generally were highly appreciative of their relations with Telfed and of the fondness former South Africans still had for the land of their birth. Ambassador Charles Fincham reported on this to his superiors in 1978: "I feel that we should be very aware of the kind of goodwill which ex–South African Jews assist in building up for us here."[25]

As has been shown, the progenitor of Israel's post–Yom Kippur War policy of cooperation with the South African government in military-related supplies and technical knowledge had been the labor-led coalition under Yitzhak Rabin, which succeeded that of Golda Meir. Yet in the early 1980s dissatisfaction rankled within the Labor Party in an innovative circle, which formed the intention to bring about a change in policy toward South Africa. The key actors involved were two political science academics active in politics, Dr. Yossi Beilin and Dr. Shimshon Zelniker. Beilin was an up-and-coming leader in the Labor Party closely associated with Shimon Peres. He had developed a keen interest in Israel's policy toward South Africa ever since, as a young journalist, he interviewed Arthur Goldreich after his escape from detention in South Africa and arrival in Israel in 1964.[26] Zelniker was at the time on the academic faculty of Bet Berl Teachers Training College in Israel and a lecturer at the University of California in Los Angeles. Their plan was to initiate nongovernmental contact with up-and-coming persons in the black community and labor organizations within South Africa with a view to offering the kind of cooperation and training programs (mainly in community and labor organizing and governance skills) that Israeli agencies had so successfully provided to many African states in the past.

Quite independently of these developments an ongoing academic critique of Israel's policy toward South Africa was sustained by some Israeli academics. Foremost was a Hebrew University specialist on Africa, Naomi Chazan, who later entered politics as a member of the Knesset for the liberal-left Meretz Party. Already in 1983 she had published an acerbic attack on the "fallacies" underlying Israel's policies. Chazan contended with great conviction that "Israel's South African connection is morally, Jewishly and instrumentally indefensible."[27]

In 1983 Shimshon Zelniker undertook the daunting task of secretively seeking out contacts in South Africa in order to open an alternative channel in Israel–South Africa relations. With single-minded determination and extraordinary resourcefulness, Zelniker fulfilled his clandestine task against all odds.[28] Indeed, he went on to conceptualize and bring to realization a program of cooperation, entirely devoid of governmental involvement, that went well beyond the expectations of its initiators. Funding for the program was made possible by a fortuitous convergence of initiatives. One was the idea of an American-mediated initiative to improve relations between South African black leaders and Israel mooted by Clive Menell. He was a South African industrialist and concerned Jew who had extensive contacts with black leaders in South Africa and also with American political personalities, one of whom was California state assemblyman Tom Hayden. Another convergence was with a concerned political group in Los Angeles styled the Center for Foreign Policy Options.[29]

Initially, implementation of the training programs in Israel was entrusted to the Afro-Asian Institute established by the Histadrut, the Israel labor movement's powerful general trade union organization. The first group of South African blacks, numbering some twenty participants, came in the spring of 1986. Zelniker went on to develop the entire project along even more self-dependent and imaginative lines through a new organization, The Israeli Center for International Cooperation (ICIC). Arthur Goldreich served on ICIC's board of directors. By the time the ICIC celebrated its tenth anniversary in 1997, some four years after the political reconstitution of South Africa, it had some 1,200 alumni in South Africa.[30]

Zelniker's work in South Africa was accomplished almost single-handedly and entirely without the involvement, or even the knowledge, of local Jewish community organizations. He did at one point confide in the heads of the Zionist Federation and the Board of Deputies, at the time respectively Morris (Mockie) Friedman and Michael Katz, but only as a prudent courtesy. He found them to be sympathetic, and in due course helpful, insofar as it became necessary discreetly to allay the suspicions of the authorities that his work was dangerously subversive. Invaluable practical assistance in establishing contact with grassroots black community leaders was forthcoming from a few Jewish individuals who had such contacts by virtue of their political and social activities in the opposition to apartheid. One was Clive Menell, as mentioned earlier one of the originators of the project, who was a liberal in the Progressive Party mold. His wife Irene was a close political associate of Helen Suzman. Help also was given by Dr. Selma Browde, whose energetic political and civic work in Johannesburg as a Progressive Party councillor had won the confidence of many black community leaders. From the Israel side, Zelniker had not only the wholehearted political backing of Beilin but also the professional support of Hanan Bar-On in the Foreign Ministry and the confidence of Israel's ambassador in South Africa, David Ariel.

Of course, almost from the outset Zelniker's activities could hardly escape the searching eyes of the South African security police. He soon encountered visa difficulties, and became aware that he was under police surveillance and that some of his black contacts were being interrogated. But his project was not blocked. According to Ariel, "We could only have conjectures as to the behavior of the authorities."[31] It seems obvious, however, that a calculated decision lay behind their allowing Zelniker to pursue his purposes. Presumably they did not judge the nature of the training programs in Israel to be sufficiently dangerous to warrant any action that might impair the smooth progress of invaluable Israel–South Africa cooperation at the governmental level. Certainly, had they thought otherwise they would not have hesitated to arrest and deport Zelniker or prevent his repeated coming and going.

Zelniker's activities were at a grassroots level and had no bearing on intergovernmental relations. The Israel Defense Ministry looked askance at them, if not worse, and even the Foreign Ministry kept officially aloof. But in 1986 Yossi Beilin at last was in a position to influence official policy when he assumed the position of political director of the Foreign Ministry under Shimon Peres as foreign minister. This took place when Yitzhak Shamir switched positions with Shimon Peres in the rotation phase of Israel's unity government. Beilin brought in a kindred spirit, Alon Liel, as a political aide and adviser and placed the ministry's South African desk under his care. (Six years later Liel was appointed Israel's ambassador to

South Africa.) Both Beilin and Liel considered Israel's policy toward South Africa to be a moral blight on their country and damaging to Israel's long-term interests. They were determined to bring about a change. Part of their strategy was the dispatch of an energetic diplomat with a special assignment. He was to work alongside the incumbent ambassador, David Ariel, concentrating intensely but discreetly on efforts to create a relationship with elements of the resistance struggle in South Africa such as the United Democratic Front and the trade union movement. The person chosen for this assignment in spring 1987 was Shlomo Gur, a young diplomat who identified wholeheartedly with the task at hand.

The impetus that at last precipitated a decisive reassessment of policy toward South Africa was an imminent U.S. State Department report on other nations' arms trade with South Africa, which carried with it a threat to cut U.S. military assistance to countries engaged in such trade. The process of reassessment in late 1986 and early 1987 temporarily thrust the question of Israel–South Africa relations to the forefront of Israeli public attention. Not since David Ben-Gurion defended his government's alignment with African states against South Africa in the early 1960s had the subject commanded such attention in the Knesset.[32] Also the press debate on the subject was of unprecedented intensity.[33]

The Israeli cabinet's timely decision in favor of a reassessment of its relations with South Africa, on 18 March 1987, a month before the release of the American report, helped to avert the anticipated harm to American relations with Israel. Of course, the very act of reassessment and the ensuing decisions ostensibly to phase out what had never been acknowledged to exist served to confirm that covert military-related trade on a formidable scale had been going on between the two countries. The Israeli announcement reiterated condemnation of the policy of apartheid, and went on to state that it had been decided "to continue to curtail Israel's relations with South Africa," and "to refrain from new undertakings between Israel and South Africa in the realm of defense." In September 1987 Israel's inner cabinet duly approved a series of sanctions conforming to those adopted by the European Common Market countries. These covered a range of industrial, commercial, scientific, and cultural activities.[34]

The change in Israel's policy evoked predictable disappointment and resentment from the South African government and press, but not out of proportion to their reaction to other countries that had preceded Israel in adopting similar sanctions. The contrast with the hostile atmosphere created by Verwoerd in the 1960s is striking. President P. W. Botha set the tone during an election rally in March 1987, when he said that he sympathized with Israel's position, as it had been "bullied" by the United States and intimidated by the prospect of losing billions of dollars in American aid. One newspaper, *The Star,* provided the following vivid metaphor: "Israel has been handed a knife and told to stab a friend—or be stabbed instead."[35]

Israel's reassessment of policy toward South Africa alleviated but little the dilemmas of concerned Jews in South Africa. On the one hand, the real core of the problem—existing arms-related contracts—remained a source of moral embarrassment for liberal-minded Jews. On the other hand, as has been mentioned in the previous chapter, both the Jewish Board of Deputies and the Zionist Federation for their part had decisively declared themselves opposed to the application of international sanctions against South Africa. Moreover, between the announcement of reassessment in March 1987 and the adoption of specific measures in September, they made persistent representation to the government of Israel urging it not to embark upon a course of sanctions. The *Zionist Record* reported the chairman of the Zionist Federation, Julius Weinstein, as saying: "We abhor apartheid—it is un-Jewish, inhuman and we do not accept it as Jews, but we will not participate in any threats or blackmail or sanctions that the western world or any other countries wish to impose against this country."[36]

In these circumstances Israel's sanctions decision of 1987 neither undermined Israel–South Africa relations nor injured the Jewish community's standing in the eyes of President Botha's government. Nearly five more years were to pass before the Israel Foreign Ministry made a decisive effort to reorient its official diplomatic focus in anticipation of black majority empowerment in South Africa. In 1992 Alon Liel was appointed ambassador to South Africa. Previously, Liel had twice visited South Africa during the period when Israel was deliberating on its sanctions package. There he had gained a small measure of encouragement and assistance from some important black activists in the liberation struggle, a few of whom also agreed to make low-profile visits to Israel in the course of 1988. Noteworthy among these were Dr. Nthatho Motlana, head of the Committee of Ten of Soweto, Franklyn Sonn of the Cape Town Technikon, and Frank Chikane, successor to Desmond Tutu at the head of the Council of Churches. The prominent women's leader Albertina Sisulu was particularly helpful, as also was Sali Motlana of the League of Domestic Workers. On the whole, however, Israel's image remained extremely negative on account not only of its known record of cooperation with the apartheid regime but also because black activists in the liberation struggle identified almost instinctively with the Palestinian cause against Israel. Moreover, the tenure from 1989 until 1992 of Zvi Gov-Ari, as ambassador appointed by the right-wing Likud Party government, had amounted to a serious setback for the new course of policy set by Beilin and Liel. Gov-Ari was very wary of the ANC's fraternal relationship with the Palestinian Liberation Organization and alliance with the communists. He placed a premium on cultivating the willing friendship of KwaZulu's Mangosuthu Buthelezi rather than persons who were identified with the United Democratic Front and the ANC. Liel dedicated himself to the by now highly daunting task of wholly unraveling and transforming Israel's role and image in South Africa. Ironically, he was now the appointee of a government whose head, Rabin, had earlier launched the policy of cooperation with the white South African regime.

Nothing better illustrates the role that local Jewish liberal opponents of apartheid now began spontaneously to play in encouraging the new course in Israel's policy represented by Liel than his own description of the unexpected circumstances that enabled him to meet Nelson Mandela for a frank and encouraging discussion within a few days of his arrival. Given the understandable anti-Israel sentiment prevalent in the ANC, Liel had thought it would require a year or more of effort and persuasion until Mandela might give him a hearing. As it happened, participating within a day of his arrival at a reception that happened to be held by the Friends of the Israel Museum, he met Jules and Selma Browde and confided in them his diplomatic apprehensions and aspirations. To his surprise and delight, two days later he received a telephone call. Selma Browde was on the line, telling him that she was in the company of Nelson Mandela. "He wishes to speak with you," she said.[37] From that moment on Liel was on a successful course toward at least partial repair of Israel's damaged relationship with the leadership of the black majority that was soon to take over the reins of government in the new South African democracy.

Black Perceptions of the Jewish Community

It is characteristic of the immersion of Jews within the dominating white segment of South Africa's caste-like society that interest in their own public image remained limited to the attitudes of other whites. Indeed, the only reasonably scientific data ever to come to light on the attitudes of blacks toward Jews derived from a 1971 survey of secondary school matriculation pupils resident in the black township of Soweto, adjacent to Johannesburg. The survey examined the pupils' attitudes toward various categories of whites. Its author was Melville L. Edelstein, at the time chief welfare officer in the townships. His findings showed that the sense of "social distance" experienced in relation to Jews was greater than toward English speakers in general and was exceeded only by that felt toward Afrikaners.[38] Edelstein himself, no less than the Jewish community's leaders, thought this a most unexpected and disturbing finding. How to account for it did not, scientifically speaking, fall within the scope of Edelstein's research, but, noting that his respondents had only the barest actual contact with Jews, and that there appeared to be some correlation between antipathy to Jews and membership in white-oriented churches, he suggested that the explanation possibly lay in New Testament teaching and the cultural transmission of anti-Jewish stereotypes. With tragic irony, Edelstein, who had selflessly devoted himself to welfare work in Soweto, lost his life as an innocent victim of random violence in the midst of the 1976 Soweto riots.

Similar indications of negative stereotyping of Jews by blacks and coloreds can be culled from incidental references in other works of research. An example is a study of social groups and racial attitudes in a small South African town called Port Nolloth. Although there were very few Jews in the town, it was found that insofar as colored people distinguished between Jews and other whites, Jews were considered more tolerant. However, there was also "a stereotype of them as being avaricious and cunning."[39] Henry Lever, the Witwatersrand University sociologist, who published a study of South African society largely based on attitude surveys in the 1970s, noted that the lack of data on attitudes and opinions of blacks was "a serious gap in the knowledge of the social scientist." He found that Jews were not often commented on spontaneously in the life histories of blacks or in unstructured interviews. One of the surveys had suggested that the Jews' attainment of economic affluence could result in a hostile attitude of "have nots" toward "haves."[40]

The way in which attitudes toward the Jews are manifested and expressed in South African English fiction has been sensitively examined by Marcia Leveson, a professor of literature at the University of the Witwatersrand.[41] Her study shows mixed or ambivalent stereotyping in the few works of black writers in which the Jew features. He is most often a shopkeeper or landlord and sometimes a lawyer, teacher, journalist, or social worker. On the one hand, the Jew is depicted as somewhat more compassionate and liberal in relation to blacks, a trait often explicitly attributed to the historical experience of Jews as a persecuted minority. On the other hand, the same negative stereotyping inherited from European models abounds, such as the correlation of ugly physical features with debased moral attributes—Shylock-like moneygrubbing and guile. Leveson notes that the only Indian writer who dealt with the subject of the Jews of South Africa was Ahmed Essop. Writing in the 1970s, he critically projected a divided loyalty image of the Jew. In one of his stories the character Harry Levine has identified himself with the blacks, but this admirable stance is tarnished by the moral incompatibility of his Zionist sentiments, which move him to fight for Israel against Arab victims. As we shall see, this imagery faithfully mirrors the general trend of Muslim animosity toward the Jews in South Africa.

In publicist writing by black journalists and political personalities throughout the apartheid years there is a paucity of reference to Jews. This, no doubt, reflects the fact that black perceptions did not generally distinguish between Jews and other English-speaking whites. Whatever specific reference to Jews is to be found in published sources has had to be solicited by Jewish journals or organizations. These references generally are critical of the Jews for not siding en bloc with the blacks in their struggle, but not devoid of understanding for the Jewish community's sense of vulnerability and consequent dilemma of conscience. They are also appreciative of the conspicuous role of individual Jews in the opposition to wrongs of the South African system. For example, the writer Bloke Modisane, asked by the *Jewish Quarterly* (published in London) to contribute his reflections, wrote that the African does not expect the Jew to fight his battles for him, but he does expect him to speak out in condemnation of the government's racial policies on religious and moral grounds. At the same time he felt that "there exists a bond, a kind of affection for the Jews on the part of the Africans." He thought that prejudice had bound them together and noted that "Africans in South Africa would rather work for Jews—they are less mean than the English, less brutal than the Afrikaners; and even though they may exploit African labour like the rest, there is a quality about them which has earned them this preference." Displaying a measure of empathy that some Jewish critics might consider undeserved, Modisane thought that "the presence of the Jew in South Africa is a tragedy, either way his values are not sure. If he remains silent, then in the eyes of the Africans he is included among the enemies of their cause. If he speaks denunciations against apartheid, then by this very act he might arouse the dormant wave of anti-Semitism."[42]

When one does come across an instance of spontaneously generated comment relating to Jews as a distinctive category of whites it usually matches Modisane's solicited views. The well-known expatriate writer Lewis Nkosi, for example, wrote appreciatively: "If one was foolhardy enough to have girl friends across the colour line, they were likely to be Jewish; if one had white friends of any sort they were most likely Jewish; almost eighty percent of white South Africans who belonged to left-wing and liberal organizations were Jewish; whatever cultural vitality Johannesburg enjoyed was contributed by the Jewish community."[43]

In the mid-1980s an illuminating source of information on attitudes and views of black political personalities was provided on the initiative of two young scholars, Alan Fischer and Tzippi Hoffman, who conducted extensive interviews with leading personalities across a broad spectrum of political and ethnic groups in South Africa.[44] Not all of them were aware that the interviewers were Jews. The candid answers elicited by the interviewers' probing questions cast new light on the attitudes prevailing at that time among major political activists outside of the white group.

Although some appreciation for the prominence of Jewish individuals in liberal and radical opposition to apartheid was evident in these interviews, this sentiment was overshadowed by a generalized hostility toward the Jewish community. The declared object of this hostility was "Zionism," but anti-Jewish undertones were conspicuous. These were rooted in stereotyping engendered by vaguely Christian perceptions of Judaism as well as by images of Jews as exploitative businesspeople. Thus "Zionism" was interpreted wholly in negative terms as an expression of the Jews' belief in their being a "chosen people," an ethos that signified arrant exclusivity and racism. Typical was the view of Dan Habedi, a leader of the black consciousness Azanian People's Organization (AZAPO). He brusquely denied the legitimacy of the State of Israel and blandly equated Zionism with Afrikaner Calvinism: "They believe that they are the Chosen People, like those who colonized this land believe they are the Chosen People."

Although ostensibly directed against the State of Israel, this hostility attached itself to the local Jewish community, whose intimate affinity with Israel was all too evident. The community was perceived as having chosen to side with the oppressors of blacks in South Africa just as with the oppressors of the Palestinians in the Middle East. Another AZAPO leader, Saths Cooper, explained that in addition to the tendency of blacks to equate the Zionism of Jews with the Calvinist racism of the Afrikaners, "the Jewish community, rightly or wrongly, has been seen to be based in capitalism, and capitalism has meant propping up apartheid." Aubrey Mokoena, at the time on the national executive of the United Democratic Front and the national secretary of the Release Mandela Campaign, was more blunt. He said that the Jews not only "fail to stand up and be counted" in the struggle against apartheid, but "they screw our people in their shops, and they criticise through their liberal press the policies of the government, while they secretly pray for the restoration [*sic*] of the Afrikaners in power because they give them their security." Mokoena said that Israel's cooperation with South Africa had "bedevilled relations between blacks and Jews," and judged that Zionism meant racism and apartheid. He justified this verdict with obtuse reasoning: "Because Zionism really says we close our ranks on an ethnic basis. If you are Jewish it's okay, if you are not Jewish, *out.*"[45]

This distinctly negative perception of Zionism was shared even by Desmond Tutu, archbishop of the Anglican Church in South Africa, who was recognized throughout the world as an inspiring emblem of the struggle against apartheid. Although he harbored no ill will toward Jews or Israel, as might be expected he called upon the Jews of South Africa to oppose apartheid, and censured Israel on account of its ties with South Africa. Lecturing at the Yakar Jewish Center in London in March 1987, he said: "Israel's integrity and existence must be guaranteed. But I cannot understand how a people with your history would have a state that would collaborate in military matters with South Africa and carry out policies that are a mirror image of some of the things from which our people suffered."[46] Yet Tutu too went further and credulously adopted much the same anti-Zionist mantra as was recited by other black activists. He told Hoffman and Fischer that Zionism "looks like it has very many parallels with racism" because Israel "excludes people on ethnic or other grounds over which they have no control and treats them as lesser humans."[47]

Some of Archbishop Tutu's comments made in South Africa as well as abroad, including a visit to Israel in late 1989, aroused resentment in Jewish quarters. Rumors that he was antisemitic were so rife that the Jewish Board of Deputies found it necessary to refute them publicly. Still, Jewish sensitivities continued to be pricked by Tutu's impulsive tendency to draw rhetorical parallels between apartheid and the Holocaust perpetrated by the Nazis. Some Jews took exception, arguing that the evils of apartheid had never extended to systematic annihilation of the blacks. They pointed out that no rabbi in Nazi Germany had been allowed the freedom to criticize the regime that Archbishop Tutu enjoyed. His response was to describe this "as a kind of Jewish arrogance." "Jews seem to think that they have cornered the market on suffering," he complained to his interviewers.[48] During a television debate in November 1989, an awkward remark by Tutu that "the nations of the world went to war over the death of six million Jews" caused so much offense that two reform rabbis in Cape Town took him to task in a public letter.[49]

Mangosuthu Buthelezi, president of the Inkatha Freedom movement and chief minister of the KwaZulu semiautonomous territory, was a striking exception to the general rule of animosity toward Zionism and Israel. Although undoubtedly an important figure in the South African political constellation, Buthelezi was something of an outcast from the mainstream of the black liberation movement. His commitment to an ethnic Zulu constituency was considered dangerously divisive, and he refused to toe the African National Congress line on a range of matters, including advocacy of sanctions by outside countries. Buthelezi refrained from aiming selective criticism at Israel compared with other countries in the world. Moreover, defying the prevalent black taboo on Israel, Buthelezi accepted an invitation to visit there in 1985. In a revealing comment to the interviewers, Fischer and Hoffman, he explained that the ANC had Arafat, Hanoi, and Cuba as their friends; he too needed friends.[50]

In the mid-1980s apprehensions were widespread in the Jewish community concerning the attitude of the ANC in exile toward South African Jewry and Israel. After all, government propaganda had long fed the white public with alarming descriptions of the ANC as a communist-controlled terrorist organization allied to the Palestinian Liberation Organization and other sworn enemies of Israel such as Qaddafi's Libya. Nor could any comfort be found in the experience of newly independent Zimbabwe, which had welcomed PLO representation with outstretched arms and imposed restrictions on the Zionist activity of its small Jewish community. Leaders of the National Union of South African Students (NUSAS), who included some Jewish students, elicited the first explicit statement of ANC views in relation to the Jewish community in early 1986. Defying anti-ANC public opinion of whites in their own country, they met with ANC leaders outside of South Africa, in Harare, Zimbabwe, to ascertain their views on a variety of subjects. One of the questions raised concerned Zionism and the PLO. The students reported that "the ANC distinguishes between the religious manifestation, with which it has no problems, and the political manifestations of Zionism, which they argue, has denied the fundamental rights of the Palestinian people to independence." At the same time, the ANC said it was opposed to antisemitism and was not antagonistic to the Jewish community in South Africa, which "had offered up many white democrats who actively opposed apartheid."[51]

Amplification of this attitude was provided in Hoffman and Fischer's interview with Neo Mnumzama, the ANC's chief spokesperson stationed at the United Nations.[52] Recognizing the "different political colours" of South African Jews, he said that the ANC regarded "in a positive light" those Jews who belonged to the broad struggle against apartheid. However, it disapproved of those members of the community who had Zionist affiliations. Arguing that there was a distinction between antisemitism and anti-Zionism, Mnumzama averred that "a major obstacle to Jewish participation in the struggle against apartheid has by and large been Zionism," and that "Zionism as an ally of apartheid is certainly an accomplice in the perpetration of the crimes that Pretoria commits against the South African people." Asked to define Zionism as perceived by the ANC, Mnumzama answered that Zionism was "an exclusive organization to which only Jews can belong," "a segregationist movement" on religious and ethnic lines that carried a strong reminder "of the reality of apartheid under which we have to live." He said that Israel, like South Africa, was based on the uprooting and dispossession of the indigenous majority population. Hence, he averred: "You cannot struggle against apartheid and still adhere to Zionist positions." Mnumzama also criticized Jews for willfully refraining from translation of their "dominant role in the South African economy" into political power against apartheid. Moreover, he scoffed somewhat at recent statements of the Jewish Board of Deputies calling for the abolition of apartheid. He said that the situation was too far gone for mere statements of condemnation: "People must translate verbal denunciations into active struggle." Asked what was in store for South Africa's Jews after the attainment of the ANC's objectives, and whether Jews would one day be punished, Mnumzama considered that while a free South Africa would "not tolerate a Zionist presence in our country," Jews, like all people, would "have a choice to either abandon segregation as practice and join with the rest . . . in building a free, united, non-racial and democratic South Africa or, to exercise their freedom to leave the country."

In light of these inimical black perceptions of Israel and the closely related record of Israel–South Africa relations discussed earlier, it was hardly surprising that neither Israel itself nor the organized Jewish community of South Africa had meaningful communication with black leaders. The conspicuous exception was Buthelezi, himself in an ambiguous situation within the politics of black liberation. Beginning in 1980, the Jewish Board of Deputies' executives in the various provinces of South Africa initiated some "outreach" forums and invited various black leaders to address them.[53] These included, for example, Dr. Nthato Motlana, a prominent civic leader in Soweto, persons in the trade union and labor relations field, and Archbishop Desmond Tutu, who addressed a committee meeting of the Board in June 1986. Given the gravity of the situation in South Africa and the issues at stake, these activities appeared rather perfunctory and futile. Indeed, the Jewish Board of Deputies' invitations to some black bodies met with blunt refusals, and the Progressive Party M.P. and Jewish community leader Harry Schwarz candidly commented that addresses by those who agreed to speak "have been masochistic experiences for the audiences and have probably achieved very little."[54]

Relations with the Muslim minority of the black population were an even greater cause of Jewish apprehension. The worst manifestations of hostility toward Jews, equaled only by the antisemitism of the Afrikaner right-wingers, emanated from sections of the Muslim community. According to the census of 1996 Muslims in South Africa numbered 553,584 (1.4 percent of the population).[55] They were mainly the descendants of two population groups. The first derived from seventeenth-century Indonesians who were brought to the Cape as slaves, political exiles, or convicts banished from the eastern possessions of the Dutch East India Company. After generations of considerable miscegenation and accretions from other ethnic groups, white as well as black, the descendants of these early Muslims were part and parcel of the racial group designated in apartheid legislation as "coloreds" and remained concentrated mainly in the Cape. The second population group was ethnically Indian and came to South Africa in the second half of the nineteenth century, mainly as indentured laborers assigned to work in the Natal sugar plantations. At the end of their term of indentured labor (a contract for five years, renewable for another five), they were entitled to free passage back to India or could opt for release from indenture and remain in Natal. Most chose not to return and turned to other occupations—becoming hawkers, shopkeepers, artisans, and the like—and some made their way to more promising economic pastures in the Transvaal. In addition to the indentured laborers, Indian immigrants known as "passenger" Indians (since they paid their own passage) also came to Natal. These were mostly Muslims, some of whom became quite prosperous traders and merchants over the years. By 1991 the official census figures for all persons designated "Indian" was 864,000, over 80 percent of whom were still living in Natal. Some 57 percent were Hindu, 24 percent Muslim, and 18 percent Christian. In all, they constituted a little under 3 percent of South Africa's total population.[56]

Against this background it is not surprising that South African Muslims were far from constituting a particularly cohesive minority community. They were divided by many ethnic, linguistic, and intrareligious differences, all generated by their diverse origins no less than by regional variations in their socioeconomic situation within South Africa. Their status under South Africa's long-established system of white domination was determined by their "non-European" race classification rather than by their religion. Both Muslims whom apartheid classification designated as coloreds and Muslims who were designated as Asiatics or alternatively as Indians were subject to social, political, and civic forms of discrimination long before these were rigidly entrenched and manipulated by the apartheid regime's legislation. Some of the disabilities were directly injurious even to the religious freedom of Muslims, for example, denial of the right to own mosque properties.

The leadership of Islam in South Africa was embodied in the various *ulama* theological leadership councils in different provinces of the country,[57] in mosque leaders, the various imam worship leaders, *shaykh* leaders and teachers who had studied in one or other Arab country, and *mawlana* religious scholars who had graduated from Indian or Pakistani Islamic seminaries. Notwithstanding the grave disabilities, discrimination, and indignities to which they were subjected as "non-Europeans," this traditional Muslim religious leadership on the whole adopted an accommodative if not compliant posture.[58] Rather than defying the authorities, the traditional *ulama* councils and mosque leaders concentrated over the years and well into the apartheid period on enhancing the orthopraxis of internal religious life. They looked after the interests of their flock mainly by negotiating for concessions and favors and taking advantage of loopholes in the restrictive laws.

Jews, being beneficiaries of exclusively white status and privilege, evinced no special relationship with Muslims that might be characterized as qualitatively different from their relations with Hindu or Christian members of the Indian or colored racial groups. At most it might be surmised that there was greater socioeconomic distance between Jews and Africans than between Jews and Muslim Indians because the latter were more likely to be employed in semiskilled and managerial positions within merchant and trading businesses belonging to Jews. At the same time, a degree of economic competition existed because a growing number of Muslim Indians themselves became middle-class traders and merchants. But neither Jewish communal records nor the Jewish press over the years provide evidence of particular Jewish concern for the position of Indians in South Africa. The episode of Jewish involvement in Gandhi's satyagraha struggle for the advancement of Indians' rights in the early twentieth century was a noteworthy exception. Gandhi himself was a Hindu, but his struggle was on behalf of all Indians whatever their religion. As has been mentioned earlier in this book, several Jews became intimately associated with Gandhi's work. The most noteworthy of them, Henry Polak and Herman Kallenbach, continued their dedicated support for the cause of South Africa's Indians for many years after Gandhi returned to India in 1914. We also noted earlier that throughout the years individual Jewish politicians, notably the eminent member of parliament Morris Alexander, as well as Jews in the Communist Party of South Africa and the left wing of the Labor Party and trade union movement were sympathetic to the plight of Indians no less than to that of other "non-Europeans." Moreover, active communists and trade union leaders had a comradely relationship with ideologically kindred Indian personalities. Also, some Jewish members of the teaching profession chose to serve in Indian education both in Johannesburg and Natal. A noteworthy example was Alex Levine, a prominent leader of the Jewish community, who served as principal of a training college for Indian teachers in Natal before settling in Israel in 1970. But on the whole, the organized Jewish community avoided involvement with the plight of the underprivileged Indian population.

It was not until the late 1930s that expressions of sympathy and support specifically for the cause of the Indians issued from the Jewish Board of Deputies. This was a facet of the Board's growing conviction that its defense against antisemitism called for an alliance with all liberal forces in the country. In the 1940s and especially after the Second World War, sympathy with the Indians' plight and opposition to new discriminatory legislation was allowed expression in Jewish newspapers such as the *Zionist Record* and in the Board of Deputies' journal, *Jewish Affairs*. Particularly at issue was the Smuts government's Asiatic Land Tenure and Indian Representation Act of 1946, whose main objective was to stem Indian "penetration" into white areas by further confining to certain areas the rights of Indians to own or occupy property. In reaction, the government of India lodged strong objections, and the Natal Indian Congress launched a passive resistance campaign. Articles in *Jewish Affairs* argued that this legislation had a special claim on Jewish concern and sympathy because it was "a ghetto measure," and because Judaism enjoined the fearless demand for social justice and "social justice means justice for Indians too."[59] These views were aired before the National Party came into power in 1948. They were not repeated when apartheid legislation such as the Group Areas Act descended callously on the Indian as well as African and colored racial groups. As we have seen, the Jewish Board of Deputies' adoption of its policy of political noninvolvement proscribed any collective Jewish intervention or advocacy in such matters.

Overall, it may be said that neither Indian-Jewish relations in general nor Muslim-Jewish relations in particular were ever seriously on the agenda of the organized Jewish community. But this began to change after about 1967 and by the 1980s had become a major concern. Two contemporaneous and ultimately convergent factors were the cause. One was the rising political activation of a section of the Muslim population, in turn an outcome of a general Islamic resurgence. The other was the expanding cooperation between the Israeli and South African governments, which triggered strong Muslim identification with Palestinians as members of the universal Muslim *ummah* (peoplehood) and, in turn, produced a potentially toxic potion comprising pent-up socioeconomic resentments toward Jews together with Muslim theological antagonism toward Judaism.

The progenitors of Islamic resurgence in South Africa were members of the younger generation who had been able to complement their traditional Muslim education with exposure to the few modern educational institutions that became available to them. In the first two decades of apartheid rule there were already some manifestations of "progressive" Islamic resurgence and attendant political assertiveness, notably the activity of imam Abdullah Haron in the Cape during the 1960s. On visits to Mecca and Cairo he also gave publicity to the struggle against apartheid. After keeping him under surveillance the security police arrested him and kept him in custody. In September 1969 it was reported that he was "found dead" in his cell. A sense of shame and betrayal at the failure of traditional Muslim leadership to raise the banner of protest even at this cruel travesty of justice has been noted as one of the stimulants for the emergence of the Muslim Youth Movement in 1970, followed by the Muslim Students Association in 1974. These groups marked the inception of a process of Islamic resurgence that sought social and political relevance not only in the modern worldly sense but also in the local context of the struggle for liberation from apartheid and white supremacy.

In June 1984 The Call of Islam, an offshoot of the Muslim Youth Movement and the Muslim Students Association, was founded by Farid Esack and a group of students in Cape Town. Esack was a *mawlana,* a religious scholar who had graduated from a Pakistani seminary, and stood at the forefront of progressive Islamic thought in South Africa. He has described The Call of Islam's way as a "search for a South African qur'anic hermeneutic of pluralism for liberation."[60] He justified solidarity with the "Other," that is working alongside people of other faiths in the struggle against apartheid. Accordingly, in response to the government's attempt to perpetuate white supremacy in the guise of the new tricameral constitution, The Call of Islam participated in the formation of the United Democratic Front.

A politically more extreme organization had emerged in 1980—the Qibla movement, founded by Achmat Cassiem and a group of students in Cape Town. Notwithstanding the almost wholly Sunni adherence of South African Muslims, Qibla drew its inspiration from the Shiite Iranian revolution, avidly copied its anti-American and anti-Zionist mantra, and went so far as to tout the slogan "Islamic revolution in South Africa." It had an affinity with the Pan-Africanist Congress, which shunned the idea of a shared white-black struggle and had therefore split from the African National Congress in 1959. Not only Qibla but also the Muslim Youth Movement held that the Muslim struggle involved both a specifically Islamic form of justice and a uniquely Islamic methodology.[61]

Throughout the 1980s there was tension between the traditional leadership's accommodationist approach and the liberation theology of these "progressive" Islamic groups. The conservatives were apprehensive of communist presence in the antiapartheid movement, feared the *fitnah* (disorder) that might result from the breakdown of lawful authority, and disapproved of the intermingling of sexes during antiapartheid rallies. Above all, they sought to preserve religious exclusivity and were suspicious of interfaith solidarity, fearing that it would dilute Islamic faith and observance.

These developments in the Muslim community, at a time when the Arab-Israel conflict frequently occupied the international news headlines and the State of Israel was known to be deepening its cooperation with the South African government, were to have far-reaching implications for South African Jewry. They resulted in an upsurge of Muslim hostility toward Jews that rivaled, and soon replaced, white right-wing antisemitism as the primary threat as perceived by the Jewish community.[62]

In one of the above-mentioned interviews conducted by Hoffman and Fischer in the mid-1980s, Farid Esack, the foremost intellect of The Call of Islam, regretfully characterized the relationship between the Jewish and Muslim communities as "one of seething antagonism."[63] With blunt candor, he provided a most enlightening insider's analysis of this situation, which left no doubt that deep-seated anti-Jewish prejudices were at the root of Muslim antagonism. On the one hand, Esack explained that the Arab-Israel conflict greatly influenced Muslim attitudes and generated vehement "anti-Zionism." He said that there was an intense identification with Palestine that stemmed from the Muslim "sense of togetherness" as part of the universal Muslim *ummah.* Thus Muslims in South Africa identified with the Palestinians against Israel just as they would identify, for example, with Libya against American "imperialism." Yet, on the other hand, Esack submitted that "if one is honest about the question, then the Muslims of South Africa are not anti-Zionist. They are anti-Semitic." He confided to his interviewers that they would not find any other Muslim theologian who would venture to admit this, because "these things are kept within our own ranks." Esack enumerated a range of stereotypes and prejudices prevalent among Muslims—"that Jews are misers, the long-nosed ones . . . that you can't trust Jews," and the like. He said that conspiracy theory was rife—the Jews were believed to be out to destroy Islam in South Africa. He attributed these beliefs and phobias largely to the nature of the socioeconomic contact with Jews experienced by "our mothers and fathers"—the Jew was the debt collector or the moneylender.[64] Hence, he observed, whereas blacks in general were hardly aware of the distinction between Jews and whites as a whole, "the Muslim mind discriminates very definitely between Christians and Jews." According to Esack, the association between Jews and Zionism was so complete in Muslim minds that only the more intellectually sophisticated Muslim, like himself, would make a distinction between Zionism and Judaism and say that he was not anti-Jew but only anti-Zionist. Asked the question, "For any Jewish body to be accepted by the Muslim community, will it have to renounce all recognition and support of Israel?" Esack replied, "Nothing that the Jews do will be enough for Muslims," so deeply rooted were their prejudices and hostility. Esack himself, while unreservedly justifying that which he termed anti-Zionism, dissociated himself from blanket antisemitism or anti-Judaism.

The validity of Esack's pessimistic description of the normative Muslim view was borne out by Hoffman and Fischer's interviews. Thus Sheikh Nazeem Mohammed, president of the Muslim Judicial Council, not only condemned Zionism and criticized the Jews for having "thrown in their lot with the Afrikaners," but also asserted that the white press and universities of South Africa, no less than the country's finances, were wholly controlled by Jews. He said that it was inherent to the doctrine of Zionists that Jews gain control of the media and the educational and financial institutions of the country—of its "brain structure." Asked whether in his view this was a Zionist or a Jewish aspiration, Nazeem Mohammed answered: "Well, I wonder. I can't even distinguish between the two anymore."[65] Ebrahim Rasool, the Western Cape secretary of the United Democratic Front, and also a member of The Call of Islam, corroborated the fact that anti-Jewish stereotypes abounded in the Muslim community and added that its religious disdain of the Jews drew from the Q'uran itself.[66] Also the national president of the Muslim Youth Movement, Abdurrashid Omar, confirmed Esack's characterization of Muslim attitudes: "We as young people distinguish between Jews and Zionists, although the elders in the community don't see any distinction. They just look at Jews and Zionists as the same." Hence the Muslim Youth Movement would cooperate with Jews unless it was discovered that they were Zionists.[67] Also interviewed by Hoffman and Fischer was Dr. Taj Hargey, a Muslim academic at the University of Cape Town. He explained that the traditional Muslim clergy was uneducated and hence unable to deal with Zionism on an intellectual and rational basis. Consequently it responded by "sheer emotive anti-Semitism"—Shylock imagery and the scurrilous "Protocols of the Elders of Zion." As for himself, he said: "I am fervently anti-Zionist, but not anti-Semitic. Many Jews are good friends of mine. Those Jews who are anti-Zionist." In his view to be antiapartheid and pro-Zionist was a contradiction in terms.[68]

The rhetoric of crude antisemitism in its purportedly "anti-Zionist" form was all too evident in leaflets, posters, and slogans brandished at public demonstrations in support of the Palestinian cause. One leaflet distributed anonymously in 1985 listed the names of major business companies, some owned by Jews and others mistakenly attributed to Jewish ownership. "If you have any policies or accounts with these companies," it exhorted blacks, "please cancel them and take out with other companies. These companies are Zionist and send 80 percent of their profits to Israel . . . who buy arms to murder our Arab brothers. . . . By exploiting our black workers these companies are keeping alive the illegal regime of Israel as well as South Africa."[69] The front lines of Muslim-Jewish confrontation were on the university campus. From a Jewish point of view, it was ironic that the reentry of growing numbers of blacks, coloreds, and Indians into the English-speaking universities—a modification of the apartheid system that was favored by most Jews—cleared the way for anti-Israel agitation on the campus.

The first serious clash took place at the University of the Witwatersrand in June 1982, when Israel invaded Lebanese territory in an attempt to root out the Palestinian Liberation Organization's bases there. In the course of the fighting that ensued, Lebanese Christian militiamen allied to Israel's forces perpetrated a massacre of Palestinians in the refugee camps of Sabra and Shatila. On the campus of the University of the Witwatersrand a "war of posters" broke out, the Muslim Students Association supported by the Black [African] Students Association plastering the walls with inflammatory posters equating Zionism with racism, and the South African Union of Jewish Students responding with posters condemning the PLO as a terrorist organization. Indicative of the indivisibility of anti-Israel and anti-Jewish rhetoric was the following statement included in a flyer: "South African Israelists [*sic*] are amongst the most zealous agents of anti-Arab imperialism. Once in Israel their primitive racist mentality makes them the natural leaders of Begin's death squads. They are amongst the most brutal, sadistic and vicious proponents of the anti-Palestinian extermination policy of Israel."[70] At that time Jewish students still outnumbered Muslim students at the university, and in the face of anti-Jewish provocation some of them became aggressive. Hundreds of Jewish students gathered outside the hall in which a Muslim meeting was being held, and when someone emerged from the meeting and shouted, "I hate Hitler; you know why, because he didn't kill enough of you," punches began to be thrown. The clash was so serious that the university's vice-chancellor had to intervene with the help of security officers. A number of Jewish students were afterward suspended from studies. The Union of Jewish Students turned to the Zionist Federation for help in obtaining a pardon or legal assistance for the suspended students on the grounds that they were responding to severe provocation. At the Zionist Federation, the prevailing sentiment was that although the Jewish students "had not acted correctly," it was "heartening that so many young people had gone along to protest just because they felt Jewish."[71]

Throughout the 1980s and into the 1990s there were fluctuating levels of tension between Muslim and Jewish students at the University of the Witwatersrand, University of Cape Town, and to a lesser extent also at the University of Natal. Clashes were nearly always triggered by Muslim demonstrations on what was called the annual Al Quds day. The Muslim Students Association and The Call of Islam deliberately kept the Arab-Israel conflict on the campus agenda as well as on that of the United Democratic Front, harnessing the issue to serve the local liberation struggle.[72]

On Al Quds day in 1987, a rally of the Muslim students at the University of Cape Town brandished banners calling for "Death to Zionist Imperialists." Another typical slogan declared that "the Crimes by Begin and Gang Make Hitler Look Like an Amateur." Mawlana Ebrahim Moosa, regional coordinator of the Muslim Youth Movement, stated: "We will not tolerate Zionism's attempts to infiltrate the liberation movements in South Africa. . . . If Arafat is a terrorist, then so are Mandela and Tambo."[73] A Muslim Students Association pamphlet warned, typically, that the presence of certain Jews was "a disturbing feature in our struggle." It stated: "The oppressed in South Africa can never be liberated if we collaborate with Zionism and imperialism in any of its guises. . . . We welcome Jews who participate in the struggle on the basis of their religious convictions. But as long as they continue to maintain relations with, and legitimize the Zionist and racist State of Israel in occupied Palestine, their role will remain suspect and hypocritical."[74] The physical clashes that ensued required the active intervention of the vice-chancellor, Dr. Stuart Saunders. In May 1988 the response from the Jewish side was particularly aggressive. A group of young Jews, who were not themselves university students, attacked some Muslim students outside a Muslim prayer room. The culprits were apparently members of the Jewish Defence League that had come into existence in emulation of the militant organization that had earlier been formed by Rabbi Meir Kahane in the United States.[75]

A particularly vulgar genre of invective directed against Judaism no less than against Israel issued from an organization in Durban that styled itself the Islamic

Propagation Centre International (IPCI). Its founder and leader was a Muslim Indian, Ahmed Deedat, a one-time employee in the enormous business of the Jewish Beare family, Beare Brothers. Challenging both Christianity and Hinduism, Deedat conducted a demagogic proselytizing drive for Islam among blacks, in the course of which he lectured, held debates, and disseminated flyers and pamphlets. So demagogic and offensive was his manner that it embarrassed most Muslim leaders in the country and aroused considerable opposition. Voicing the majority opinion, one Muslim periodical asked in 1986: "Can this community continue to remain silent in the face of emerging threats through Deedat's aggressive and provocative method of propagating Islam?"[76] Deedat's hate-mongering invective turned increasingly against Jewry, ostensibly on account of its Zionism and support of Israel. A typical example was a booklet titled *Arabs and Israel: Conflict or Conciliation?* which was widely distributed in the late 1980s and again in somewhat revised form into the 1990s. It was a patchwork of incoherent text and fabricated illustrations calculated to instill hatred of Israel and all those who supported it. Typically, its cover featured a manipulative photograph purportedly showing an Arab woman snatching her child from the cruel clutches of Israeli soldiers. Readers were invited to caption the photograph for cash prizes.[77] This type of propaganda was in itself too infantile and degenerate to be credulous in the eyes of any reasonable person, but Deedat aroused the concern of the Jewish community, especially in Natal Province. He was believed to be the recipient of huge financial grants from Saudi Arabia. In 1986 he had been awarded the King Faisal International Award for service to Islam. The Jewish Board of Deputies and the Zionist Federation found it necessary to circulate a joint statement unmasking the distortions disseminated by Deedat. They considered taking legal action but decided against this in order not to further raise his public profile.[78] When some Muslim clerics launched a "Campaign for Religious Tolerance" in 1995, the Jewish community welcomed this. But manifestations of Muslim hostility remained a major problem for the Jews of South Africa.

It should be noted that the developments that have been traced above all fall into the category of intergroup relations characteristic of South Africa's highly segmented, ethnically plural society. The unique nature of Judaism as an ethnic religion, or religious ethnicity, precluded the kind of symbiosis that enabled the incorporation of any variety of self-affirming ethnic groups, white or black, into Christian denominations or Islam. There was one contingency, however, that posed, at least theoretically, the potentiality for some such symbiosis with Judaism in South Africa. It arose from the claims of a particular black ethnic group known as the Lemba.

Over the years various black groups have claimed to be Jewish or of Jewish descent. But these claims have never been even remotely credible from the point of view of the South African Jewish community. In terms of the Jewish religious code of law, the *halakha,* they were unquestionably inadmissible, and the rabbinical authorities, whether orthodox or reform, scrupulously avoided any proselytizing or outreach whatsoever. Not only was proselytizing activity proscribed in contemporary Judaism, but in the case of South African blacks there was an additional deterrent—it would inevitably embroil the Jewish community in contravention of the apartheid system. An example of the phenomenon of groups staking outlandish claims to be Jews was one that appeared in Soweto, mainly in its "middle-class" section, Dube. It was led by Vayisile Joshua Msitshana, a Xhosa born in 1917 in Queenstown, Cape Province, raised as a Methodist, and employed for a time in the South African police. In 1961 he founded in Bloemfontein a religious group named by him the Black Philadelphia Church. In 1966, after an unsubstantiated claim that he had been converted to Judaism, he moved to Soweto. Leading a following that numbered about one thousand, he repeatedly knocked at the doors of various Jewish communal bodies, orthodox, reform, and Zionist, seeking embrace by the Jewish community and financial assistance. These approaches were politely but firmly dismissed. Since leaving the Methodist Church, Msitshana had claimed to become successively a member of a variety of Christian denominations, ranging from Roman Catholicism to Jehovah's Witnesses. Mindful of this, even Rabbi Arthur Saul Super, chief minister of progressive Judaism and not the least liberal of the community's rabbis, said he saw no reason to respond to what could only be regarded as Msitshana's current fad. In 1974 Super told a journalist, who was sympathetically investigating the black group's activities in Soweto, that the phenomenon of self-styled "Jewish" sects that practiced some Judaic-like rites was not uncommon, and in this case there was no more basis than in others for considering the sect's adherents Jewish. He therefore saw no reason why the Jewish community should become involved.[79]

The most persistent and potentially serious case of a black sect's claim to be Jewish by virtue of ancestry and intent was and remains that of the Lemba, a Bantu-speaking people whose hallowed oral tradition holds that its forefathers were led out of ancient Judea and on to southern Africa by a man named Buba. Although many of the Lemba had become members of Christian churches or Muslims, most had long been known to practice several Judaic-like rites. These included circumcision of males (but between twelve and fifteen years of age rather than in infancy as Judaism prescribes), avoidance of eating pork, separation of meat from milk, and ritual slaughter of animals for food in a manner similar to the Jewish laws of *shehita*.[80]

Estimates of the numbers of the Lemba in southern Africa range widely from twenty-five thousand to forty thousand, mostly living among the Venda people in the Northern Province of South Africa (formerly the northern Transvaal), but latterly spreading to other places, especially urban Soweto. The name "Lemba" may have been derived from the Swahili *chilemba,* meaning the turban headgear of East African Arabs, or from *lembi,* a word in many African languages meaning "non-African" or "respected foreigner." In the mid–nineteenth century the Boers appeared to regard the Lemba as Islamized Africans, calling them "slamzie." But during the period of Paul Kruger's presidency of the South African Republic (1883 to 1900), they began to call them "Kruger's Jews." Jews in South Africa were neither particularly aware nor entirely oblivious of the existence of the Lemba, but they were never regarded as more than an intriguing curiosity.

In 1947 the Lemba Cultural Association was formed. It sought to foster the

Lemba's separate and distinctive cultural identity. Its founder was Mutenda Bulengwa, a teacher who also had worked for a time in the household of a Jewish family in the town of Louis Trichardt. There he had had the opportunity of observing the similarity of Jewish dietary and other rituals to those of his own Lemba customs. It is likely that this stimulated his initiative in promoting and fostering the identification of the Lemba tradition with Judaism. As the association's logo he chose an elephant inside a Star of David.

The Lemba have been the subject of considerable anthropological and other academic research. Professor Gina Buijs of the Department of Anthropology at the University of Venda has offered an explanation for the Lemba Cultural Association's fostering of identification with a non-African past, in the form of Jewish ancestry, and its related efforts to appropriate a present Jewish identity. She suggests that the underlying motivation was to advance the material welfare of the Lemba ethnic group within the context of what seemed to be the irreversible South African reality of white domination together with the apartheid system's encouragement of black ethnic differentiation.[81] However, this explanation does not preclude the possibility that there is some veracity in the Lemba myth of Jewish ancestry. Indeed, recent genetic studies have tended rather dramatically (yet not conclusively) to confirm its credibility.

In the late 1980s Professor Trefor Jenkins and his associates at the University of the Witwatersrand conducted a genetic study on a small sample of the Lemba women and men. The genetic variations on the Y chromosome, which is inherited by male offspring from their fathers, indicated that the Lemba are indeed largely descended from Semitic male ancestors. But Jenkins notes that the paucity of comparable data on Arab populations makes it impossible to know whether these were Jews or Arabs.[82] Concurrently the anthropologist Tudor Parfitt of the School of Oriental and African Studies in London has also seriously considered the hypothesis that the origins of the Lemba are retraceable to South Arabian Semitic antecedents.[83] This hypothesis gained some credibility, although certainly not definitively so, from separate studies by an Oxford University geneticist David Goldstein and others on the genetic markers that were found to characterize *cohanim* (that is, Jews of the priestly caste). It was then found that this genetic marker was also significantly present among the Lemba.[84]

The compound effect of these genetic and anthropological studies in the late 1990s raised the credibility of traditional Lemba beliefs in their Jewish ancestry, even if they were still far from establishing Jewish rather than Arab ancestry. This has been grist to the mill of the Lemba Cultural Association's main leader and spokesman, Professor M. E. R. Mathivha (formerly a vice-principal of the University of Venda), who has not only persistently propagated the Lemba tradition of Jewish ancestry but also adopted additional Jewish customs such as the wearing of a yarmulke and tallith (prayer shawl) and sought to establish synagogues. Over the years the case of the Lemba has been taken up by several maverick or self-styled rabbis and Jewish individuals or associations. These are driven by a compulsion to locate and return to the Jewish fold the mythical "lost tribes of Israel" or later generations of Jews who had been coerced into conversion to other religions.[85]

Encouraged by such initiatives, in the late 1990s Mathivha regenerated Lemba efforts to appropriate recognized status as black Jews. In 1997 the Lemba Cultural Association made more assertive approaches to Jewish communal agencies, such as the Shalom television programs and the Jewish Board of Deputies. It even threatened that should the Jews of southern Africa choose to continue ignoring the appeals of their needy Lemba brothers and sisters, they would have to conclude that "we like many other non-European Jewish communities are simply the victims of racism at the hands of the European Jewish establishment world-wide." They would then have no choice but to begin a "public campaign to protest and ultimately destroy Jewish Apartheid."[86]

However, Mathivha has not resorted to such confrontational measures even though neither the rabbinate in South Africa nor any of the lay community institutions have been inclined to contemplate any symbiotic engagement with the Lemba. In terms of the *halakha,* the Lemba are not at all comparable to the Falasha Jews of Ethiopia. As a group they have no conceivable status within Judaism. As Rabbi Bernhard explained in a radio talk-show discussion with Professor Mathivha conducted by Jon Qwelane, DNA does not in itself establish the putative Jewish identity of the Lemba people. Nor does the observance of some rites derived from, or bearing a resemblance to, those of Judaism carry weight in *halakha.* Bernhard clarified that there was only one way that a member of the Lemba group could be recognized as a Jew—conversion to Judaism by formal *halakhic* process. "Anybody who wants to do that would be welcomed with open arms," he said.[87]

The reality of contemporary Jewry simply invalidates Mathivha's implicit comprehension of Judaism as a pluralistic, ethnically neutral, religious framework, which could encompass the Lemba as one of its constituent modes alongside Sephardi and Ashkenazi Jews. Nor is it likely that the Lemba population would be desirous of wholly exchanging its own ethnic-cultural identity for the rigors of full religious conversion and absorption into the exclusive ethnoreligious identity of contemporary Jewry.[88]

Jewish Student Discontent

As has been shown above, the university campus was the front line of encounters and even physical clashes revolving around attempts to vilify Israel and to stamp Zionism with the stigma of "racism." Just how many Jewish students there were in South African universities remained obscure throughout this period. No more than rough estimates were ascertainable. Marcus Arkin, director general of the South African Zionist Federation and a former professor of economic history at Rhodes University, investigated the situation in late 1974. He reported that the community's ignorance was most pronounced in regard to the University of the Witwatersrand campus in Johannesburg, where estimates varied from just over 3,000 to as many as 4,500. The University of Cape Town had an estimated 1,300 to 2,000. The total was roughly estimated at 6,000 Jewish students.[89] In 1976 the countrywide framework had changed its name from South African Federation of

Students Jewish Associations (SAFSJA) to South African Union of Jewish Students (SAUJS). Throughout the years its core of enrolled membership encompassed only a fraction of the total number of students, between 400 and 500 in Johannesburg and about 300 in Cape Town. Some campus activities, however, could attract 1,000 or more.

Turning our attention inward to the activities and dilemmas of conscience of Jewish students, it should also be recalled that there was considerable overlap between the active core of the Jewish student associations at the various campuses and the senior age-group of the Zionist youth movements. Most of the active students were either former members of the movements or simultaneously involved in both spheres. In either case, the more serious and active among them were chronically torn between strong Zionist identification with Israel and the attendant imperative of *aliya* (that is, the act of "going up" to settle in Israel), on the one side, and the impulse to join the antiapartheid struggle, on the other. Was it conscionable to get really involved in the local struggle if one intended to leave the country for good?

This dilemma was recurrently aired in student newsletters and periodicals and at conferences and seminars. For some, the Zionist youth movement imperatives leading to *aliya* were too exclusively demanding and "a denial of the very real responsibilities a South African white has to the society into which he was born."[90] The Jewish students and Zionist youth movement leaders faced constant intellectual pressure from liberal student leaders of the National Union of South African Students (NUSAS), Jewish and gentile, who questioned the compatibility of Zionism's ethnic particularism with the universal struggle for a new, nonracial South African identity that would purportedly supersede all ethnic differences.[91] At Rhodes University, Grahamstown, one Jewish student wrote: "There is no easy way to reconcile the irrationalities involved in living in a racialist society while detesting the very foundations upon which such a society is based. The dilemma is redefined and restated every day as the liberal takes his or her position as a privileged, though perhaps unwilling racialist in a morally unbalanced social environment." This particular student posed four alternatives: avoid getting "mixed up in politics" and enjoy the privileges while they last; remain a split personality attempting to reconcile one's liberal beliefs with one's role as a participant in a racist society; turn to resistance and suffer the punitive consequences; or, finally, emigrate. "A distressing choice," he submitted in conclusion.[92]

The publications of the various Jewish student associations thus reflected the poignant ideological dilemma of politically aware segments of South African Jewry in general. Indeed, some of the debates call to mind, if on a minor scale, the classical ideological conflict that characterized the Jewish experience in European countries from the beginning of the period of Jewish emancipation until recent times. According to one student critic of the Jewish student associations' concern for Israel or Jewish "refuseniks" in Russia, "a twisted morality is produced when Jewish youth are taught to concern themselves with moral issues thousands of miles away from their own reality." "The real moral challenge," he averred, "is to fight to end apartheid and build a new South Africa."[93] By contrast to these views, the distinctively South African ideological matrix of Zionism was reflected in the following account of one Jewish student leader's intellectual odyssey until settling in Israel:

> I had always thought that I was a South African and my contribution should be there: to work toward the abolition of the apartheid system and all the iniquities arising out of it. My degree in social anthropology and African culture was, I felt, further testimony to my commitment to the African struggle. . . . My decision to get involved in the South African Union of Jewish Students, and later in the formation of "Jews against Apartheid" was based on the premise that the South African reality had to be taken cognizance of from a Jewish perspective. . . . The turning point came, ironically enough, as a result of my participation in a seminar on the Holocaust at Yad Vashem [Jerusalem] in July 1985 . . . "Thou shalt not be a perpetrator; thou shalt not be a victim; and thou shalt never, ever be a bystander." The awful clarity hit me then; by returning to South Africa, I would be guilty of violating all three, whether or not I wanted to. . . . In the ultimate analysis, the bitter truth for me was that the South African Diaspora had been unable to accommodate both my Jewish and African identities and, however difficult, I had to confront reality and be brutally honest with myself and finally make a choice.[94]

Criticism of the policy of the Jewish Board of Deputies, emanating sporadically from the Jewish students' associations, especially in Cape Town and Johannesburg, was a frequent source of concern and dissonance within the Jewish community. At the national congress of the Jewish Board of Deputies in May 1972, the students' delegation staged a walkout when its resolution calling on the conference outspokenly to condemn all forms of "racial discrimination" in South Africa was shelved, although even this resolution did not mention the word apartheid explicitly. Instead, the conference passed the standard innocuous resolution calling piously for "stable and peaceful relationships between all races," and for acknowledgment of "the right of all to live in dignity and security, to maintain their group identity and distinctive culture and to exercise the opportunity to advance in all spheres."[95] The students at the University of Cape Town were particularly assertive. A few months later, in October 1972, they made another attempt to introduce a resolution at the Board's Cape conference, this time phrased as a call for expressions of Jewish concern on moral issues arising from specific injustices and acts that caused human suffering. They posed the familiar question—how could Jews condemn the indifference of others to past and present discrimination and persecution suffered by Jews if the struggles of other peoples to secure human rights were betrayed by the Jewish community? Although in the course of the emotive debate that ensued many delegates, besides the students themselves, favored the resolution, the Cape Board's chairman, Hymie Wolffe, persuaded the majority to settle for a reaffirmation of the cautiously worded resolution that had been adopted at the national conference in May. This precipitated the resolve of a group of Cape Town university students to take an independent line of their own, however intemperate in the eyes of their elders. "Our community of 120,000 is fully part of a white-controlled exploiting machine. We must come to terms with our own racism," they declared. "In this task we can expect no help from the Board."[96]

At about the same time a group of twenty-three students at the University of the Witwatersrand published in both the Jewish and general press an open letter of protest addressed to Chief Rabbi Casper. They were ostensibly responding to a conventional Jewish New Year's message issued by Rabbi Casper that had appeared in one of the Sunday newspapers, expressing the sentiment that South African Jews were grateful for the freedom and welfare they enjoyed in South Africa. "As Jewish students, we would like to say that we are not grateful to live in a country in which millions of our fellow men are persecuted because they are black," protested the students indignantly. "We are ashamed," they said, "that members and spiritual leaders of a religion two of whose central tenets were 'justice, justice shalt thou follow,' and 'thou shall love thy neighbour as thyself,' could stand by while around them they saw a total absence of justice or brotherly love."[97]

Although recognizing "the sincerity of his young critics' motives," Rabbi Casper stoutly defended his statement. He compared the freedom and understanding enjoyed by Jews in South Africa to the Jews' past experience in Europe as well as the contemporary condition of the Jews in Russia and the Arab world. "Gratitude itself is a virtue not unconnected with moral uprightness and honesty," he noted. While agreeing that it was "the right and perhaps the duty" of the students as citizens to involve themselves with the problems of South African society, he did not think they had the right "to speak as though this is the special burden and responsibility of the Jewish community and its leaders." But the students continued to balk at Rabbi Casper's stance. The leaders of the association at the University of Cape Town avowed in their newspaper, *Strike,* that while they identified fully as Jews, they too shared the feelings of estrangement from the Jewish community felt by the Johannesburg group that had written the open letter to Casper. "All we are trying to do is to apply Jewish ethic and historical experience to our situation in South Africa. We are asking our representative communal organizations to take a stand on moral issues in South Africa." They reasoned that this would not necessarily entail an official political stand against the government. It merely meant taking a moral stand against absolutely indefensible injustices such as the cruel exploitation of migratory labor, below subsistence wages resulting from racial wage discrimination, the evils of the so-called Immorality Act, and detention without trial. Of course, in the eyes of the more politically seasoned and responsible lay leadership of the Jewish community no less than in those of Rabbi Casper, the view had long been firmly established that no distinction could be sustained between full political embroilment and this proposed targeting of specific evils. They were, after all, the very elements constitutive of government ideology and policy.

In the first half of 1973 a group of students who harbored particularly militant antiapartheid convictions took the lead in the Students Jewish Association of Cape Town. They launched a campaign unprecedented in the stridency of its criticism of the Jewish community. In his response to the protest letter of the twenty-three students, Chief Rabbi Casper had asserted that far from the Jewish record being shameful, Jews were more motivated by moral concerns than most other people. The Cape Town student activists now set out to challenge this claim. Homing in on recent headlines concerning a wave of black worker strikes in Natal, the students targeted the disreputable role imputed to a Jewish textile industrialist, Phillip Frame. His vast network of mills in Natal was at the center of the wave of strikes, thousands of grossly underpaid workers having left their machines and brought production to a halt in his mills. A lengthy article in *Strike* expressed shame at Phillip Frame's role, noting that he was a prominent leader of the Jewish community. He had served for many years on the Council of Natal Jewry, the Board of Deputies' wing in Natal. "Despite the argument by Jewish communal leaders that Jews are more motivated than most other white groups to work for social change," charged the article, "these leaders do not seem to realize that it is members of their very own community that cause the conditions that motivated Jews are trying to change." The students asserted that "Jews form a large segment of the white upper crust, enjoying the fruits of privilege which are a result of the total disregard of their workers' welfare."[98]

In the course of 1973, this group of Jewish students at the University of Cape Town turned *Strike* into an organ so outspokenly antiapartheid as to bear comparison with banned newspapers of the 1950s Congress of Democrats period. One article, for example, derided the University of Cape Town itself as a "reactionary campus." Setting out to show that its much vaunted liberalism was a myth, it denounced the university's vice-chancellor, the financial magnate Harry Oppenheimer (widely regarded as a political progressive) as the "epitome of a racist capitalism exemplified by a promised R60 average monthly black wage in a gold mining industry whose net profits exceeded R200 million last year."[99] Another article heaped reproach on the Jewish Board of Deputies, the Zionist Federation, Chief Rabbi Casper, and the Jewish press for the words, both of grief and praise, all had seen cause to express after Dr. Verwoerd's assassination back in 1966. The writer compiled a scathing account of Verwoerd's antisemitic agitation in the 1930s. He charged that "representative Jewish organizations, not content with affirming their loyalty [to the country and its people as a whole] went on to a spineless and naive fear of giving offence," thereby committing moral suicide for which all South African Jews shared culpability.[100]

The provocative accusations of *Strike* raised alarm bells in the Jewish community. The *Jewish Times* published an editorial insinuating that the libels of the Cape Town students' paper against the Jewish community were grist for the mill of antisemites.[101] To this the students responded by mobilizing a petition with 250 signatories demanding that the *Jewish Times* editor retract and apologize. The Cape Committee of the Jewish Board of Deputies debated whether to continue financially supporting the Students Jewish Association and *Strike*, and the national executive of the Board of Deputies in Johannesburg decided that the seriousness of the matter warranted convening of a special meeting with the Cape Town students.[102] General-Secretary Gus Saron wrote to his Cape Town counterpart:

> The feeling here is that "Strike," by its various articles, has involved itself completely in the major controversial political and ideological issues in South Africa. In so doing, it has departed from the official policy of the Board and of the community, namely, to disapprove when Jews seek to enter, under a Jewish banner or Jewish auspices, into the general political issues of the country. When other organizations in the past were tempted to follow such a line, the Board expressed its unequivocal opposition to this.[103]

Saron pointed out that the criticism the Board was directing against *Strike* was based on principle—that is to say, to uphold the Board's policy—and would apply even if the student associations and *Strike* itself were not subsidized from communal funds. "The fact, however, that they are so subsidized," he wrote, "is relevant because to that extent, the Board and the Zionist Federation are implicated in the policies being pursued by the paper." But he considered it important first to ascertain how far in fact the Students Jewish Association as a whole supported *Strike*'s apparently new line. Irked particularly by the inclusion of what was deemed an anti-Israel article that had appeared in *Strike,* also the executive of the Zionist Federation deliberated on the issue. Some were of the opinion that a clique that was not really representative of Jewish students had appropriated the students' association. Others, including not only the youth movement representatives on the executive but also the Zionist Federation's director, Lionel Hodes, and veteran Revisionist Zionist leader Joe Daleski, evinced regard and understanding for the students. It was pointed out that there was no evidence of outside influences and that the main students involved, Brian Walt and Alan Horwitz, were former youth movement leaders and head prefects of the Jewish high school Herzlia.[104]

A meeting duly took place with the participation of Students Jewish Association representatives, honorary officers of both the Board of Deputies and the Zionist Federation in the Cape, and Gus Saron and Lionel Hodes from the national offices. The Cape Board's chairman, Hymie Wolffe, who presided over the meeting, insisted that for reasons of propriety all should agree to keep the discussion "private and confidential." However, some of the students were not prepared to give this undertaking and insisted on recording everything said and reporting the discussion, whereupon the chairman determined that there was no point in carrying on, and the meeting was declared closed.[105] Much to the chagrin of the communal leadership, and notwithstanding a decision by the Cape Board of Deputies to withhold financial support dedicated to publication of *Strike,* the militant group of students continued to publish a number of other issues in the same vehemently antiapartheid vein during 1973.

It was in the nature of student activism that it fluctuated in intensity owing to the short span of time that students spent within the university's walls. As it happened, the acute spate of antiapartheid rhetoric and criticism of the students' own Jewish community described above abated after 1973. Indeed, even the actions of the 1973 militants were far from reflecting an overwhelming consensus among all Jews who were students at the time. The majority were in fact indifferent to political issues, and even such outbursts as the open letter of the twenty-three students to Rabbi Casper had met with repudiation from some other students. These took issue with what they called their "holier than thou" tone and censured them for saying they were ashamed of the Jewish community's leadership.[106]

Notwithstanding this unresolved tension, which passed once this unusually rebellious generation of students ended its stint in office, there was one sphere in which the Cape Town Jewish students managed successfully to influence policy decisions within the Board of Deputies. It related to the wages of black employees in Jewish communal organizations. An initiative of the Students' Representative Council and some faculty members of the University of Cape Town had set up a series of commissions inquiring into wages of blacks in Cape Town. As part of this initiative, the Jewish students undertook their own inquiry into Jewish communal organizations in Cape Town. After a resourceful and thorough inquiry they issued a very critical report debunking the notion that the record of the Jewish community was any better than the norm, and making strong and specific recommendations for wage increases in the various organizations.[107] This issue was in due course taken up by the Cape Board of Deputies and thereafter at the national level too, after determined prompting from the Jewish students and a young mathematics lecturer, Manfred Green, who had himself been chairman of the South African Federation of Students Jewish Associations in the mid-1960s. He later settled in Israel.

In retrospect, it seems that the *Strike* controversy of 1973 marked the peak of tension between Jewish students and the community's leadership. Thereafter relations improved because, as has been noted in an earlier chapter, the year 1975 saw the beginning of a change in the Board of Deputies' policy, signified by chairman Mann's statement at the banquet honoring Prime Minister Vorster on his return from a visit to Israel. Not that the act of celebrating Vorster's visit passed without sharp criticism by some students. Writing in *Strike,* Dennis Davis, at the time one of the most articulate of the students (later, in the new South Africa, he was appointed to the bench), reminded the community that Vorster was "the leader of a political party whose politics, based so firmly on race, are the antithesis of the very body and soul of Jewish ethics." "We surely cannot honour and pay homage to the leading proponent of such policies," he objected, "even if he has pulled off a diplomatic coup with Israel."[108]

All the same, from the mid-1970s the Board of Deputies' veering, however cautiously, toward a position more consonant with the antiapartheid sentiments prevalent on the university campus took some wind out of the sails of the more assertive students. The focus of dissonance now moved to criticism of the swelling cooperation between Israel and the South African government and also to Israel's policies in regard to the Palestinians. This aroused the special concern of the Zionist Federation. As we have seen earlier in this chapter, the notorious United Nations resolution of October 1975 equating Zionism with racism resonated strongly in South Africa. Intellectual—and at times even physical—defense against Muslim students' anti-Israel propaganda and demonstrations became the major concern of the Jewish student associations, especially since the Muslims drew in considerable support from blacks who were not Muslims. As has been mentioned earlier, hostility on the campuses was fanned to a point of hysteria during Israel's 1982 war in Lebanon. The Black Students Association condemned what it called "the Israeli massacres." Jewish students rallied to the defense of Israel but did so by echoing the critical voice of the Zionist left in Israel. The South African Union of Jewish Students (SAUJS) released a statement condemning the massacre of Palestinian civilians and demanding the immediate appointment of an impartial committee of inquiry but at the same time reaffirming its "unequivocal support for the State of Israel and the Zionist movement."[109]

Throughout the 1970s and 1980s, the major student leaders were members or ex-members of Habonim, which as a movement identified strongly with the Zionist left in Israel. They were increasingly embarrassed and disconcerted by Israel's military-related trade with South Africa as well as by Israeli government policies directed at establishing settlements in areas under its military occupation with a view to ultimate incorporation of those areas in the Israeli state. By the same token, students who were members, present or past, of the Betar and Bnei Akiva youth movements tended to identify unreservedly with those right-wing Israeli policies. But the latter category of students was not the tone setter. At one point the newspaper of the South African Union of Jewish Students at the University of the Witwatersrand in Johannesburg went so far as to feature a cover depicting an unfortunate marriage à la mode between groom "Afrikaner Nationalism" and bride "Zionism."[110]

Thus, disenchantment of liberal-minded young Jews with Israel's policies, and by extension with Zionism, was the price paid for Israel–South Africa cooperation. "Of all the western countries, including Mrs. Thatcher's Britain, Israel has been the least convincing in its support for a democratic non-racial South Africa," wrote the former avidly Zionist student leader Dennis Davis in 1987 (by then he was an associate professor of law at the University of Cape Town). "It is sad in the extreme," he added regretfully, "that Israel, born of such universal ideals of national liberation and peace for all, should have less moral qualms than any other western country about dealing with a country which stands for the very antithesis. In itself this should be enough to motivate a comprehensive reexamination of Zionist ideals."[111]

However, the excesses of Muslim "anti-Zionism" on the campus more than counterbalanced this internal Zionist dissonance. These baneful excesses had the effect of galvanizing Jewish students in defense of Israel and drawing in even more campus involvement by those students whose priority commitment had been to work off-campus in the Zionist youth movements. A core of students who identified themselves as "progressive Zionist students" were, at one and the same time, critical of Israel's growing cooperation with the South African government and defensive in principle of Israel's basic positions in relation to the Arab world. They argued that precisely because they were firmly rooted in a "Zionist ethic," they were obliged to "voice their concern" at the flagrant disregard for the principles of social justice that the Israeli government was showing in its policy of cooperation with the South African government and with homeland heads such as Lennox Sebe of the Ciskei.[112]

As we have noted, Muslim influence was strong in the United Democratic Front that emerged in the early 1980s as a wide-spectrum alliance in resistance to the apartheid regime. Propagating the libel that Zionism was nothing but Jewish racism, the Muslim students tried to disqualify any Jew who supported Zionism from participation in the antiapartheid struggle. The question whether one could simultaneously be a Zionist and a legitimate participant in the South African liberation movement was highlighted in the pages of *Wits Student,* the organ of the Students' Representative Council at the University of the Witwatersrand. It featured "a Leftist non-Zionist" who wrote: "The whole of Zionist history is bound up with racism, exploitation, territorial expansion and aggression. No you cannot be a Leftist Zionist." The paper did, however, allow another viewpoint penned by a student and leader of Habonim, Johnny Broomberg. He presented the perspective of the Zionist left in Israel—that this was a tragic conflict between two nationalisms and that the key to a solution was mutual recognition of the national aspirations of both the Jews and the Palestinian Arabs. Broomberg argued that the real obstacle to peace was the PLO's uncompromising stand based on the false assertion "that the Jews are nothing more than a religious group and that only the Palestinians have legitimate national aspirations, as stated in article 20 of the PLO Covenant, 'Judaism in its character as a religion is not a nationality with an independent existence.'"[113]

On balance, anti-Zionist campaigns on the campus resulted in invigoration of the South African Union of Jewish Students, both in its activities and in its Zionist resolve. At its national conference in 1987, SAUJS unanimously passed a resolution defying attempts to exclude Zionists from the freedom struggle and reaffirming the belief that "Zionism is the spiritual aspiration and the national liberation movement of the Jewish people." The resolution averred that "Zionists can identify with the struggle for freedom in South Africa; A Zionist who fails to voice his/her opposition to apartheid, does so at the expense of his/her Zionist philosophies."[114] At the same time, for those Jewish students whose primary commitment was to the Zionist youth movements, the provocative calls of the Muslim students for exorcising Zionists from the struggle against apartheid simply served to vindicate the Zionist contention that Jews could be fully at home only in their own national state, Israel. Either way, this challenge to the legitimacy of Jewish identification with Zionism and Israel dominated the concerns of the Jewish students' associations and youth movements into the 1990s, as South Africa moved, by fits and starts, out of the cycle of popular resistance and state suppression and into a negotiated settlement.

Yet, in retrospect it seems that the increasingly controversial image of Israel did have the long-term effect of eroding its function as the primary anchor for the Jewish identification of students. Secular Zionism was gradually being displaced by a turn to religiosity. Already in the mid-1970s one contributor to a students' magazine noted perceptively that a change was becoming discernible. The gist of his observation was: whereas the tendency of Jewish youth to express their identity purely on an ethnic level underlay the unparalleled success of the Zionist youth movements, this purely secular "ethnic nationalism" was now giving way to a desire on the part of young Jews "to fill the religious void created in their Jewishly bankrupt homes." He argued that their nationalist-Zionist identification now remained consequential "only when born out of religious motivation."[115] This change was most evident in Johannesburg, where, as we shall see in the next chapter of this book, an innovative *kollel* (yeshiva study group) germinated around the formerly isolationist Adath Jeshurun congregation, and this was followed by the introduction to South Africa of Lubavitcher Hasidism. These strictly orthodox groups now began gratuitously to provide campus rabbis who conducted religious teaching sessions (*shiurim*) that proved to be increasingly attractive to students.

Budding Jewish Social Action

The suppression of the radical opposition to the apartheid regime in the 1960s left almost all white persons (many Jews included, as we have seen) who had been involved in one or other branch of that opposition in exile, in prison, or under severe banning orders. Still, many Jewish individuals were to be found among the whites in a variety of forms of social action and liberal opposition functioning, however precariously, within the bounds of South African legality. The English-speaking universities were one arena for ongoing opposition. Of course, the overwhelming majority of Jewish students went about their studies and university life in complete conformity to the norms of complicity with the political and social status quo. But, alongside the segment of students who were involved in the activities of specifically Jewish associations that we have discussed, other Jewish individuals continued to be prominent in the antiapartheid agitation of the various Students' Representative Councils and the National Union of South African Students.

Jews were also conspicuous in a variety of civic spheres of activity that alleviated the iniquities of apartheid or militated against the system. The legal sphere was the foremost of these.[116] As in the early years of apartheid, individual Jews continued to be very prominent in legal defense of persons of all races who fell foul of the system. Liberal antiapartheid proclivities often found expression in the course of the routine work of lawyers and judges, through attempts to deploy whatever legal means could be manipulated in order to protect human rights and ease suffering caused by the laws that constituted the apartheid system. This may be illustrated from the legal career of Richard Goldstone, described on one occasion by colleagues as "an outstanding commercial lawyer who had shrewdly and inventively applied the law to secure justice in politically controversial and human rights cases."[117] After practicing law in this spirit throughout the 1960s and 1970s peak apartheid years, in 1980 Goldstone was appointed a judge in the Transvaal. In a crucially important case that frustrated a good deal of the government's "group areas" segregation prosecutions, Goldstone set aside an order to evict a certain individual from her home in a white area by ruling that a person convicted under the Group Areas Act could be evicted only if alternative accommodation was available. He also heard one of the first cases that resulted in a court ordering the release of a political detainee. In the transition period that followed the release of

Nelson Mandela in 1990, President de Klerk appointed Goldstone to head the important Standing Commission of Inquiry into Violence and Intimidation, and in 1994 he was appointed to the new Constitutional Court.

Several Jewish lawyers joined a group called Lawyers for Human Rights formed in 1979 under the chairmanship of Johan Kriegler. He was succeeded as chairman in 1985 by advocate Jules Browde, a Jew who had for many years been the honorary titular head of the Habonim youth movement. Lawyers for Human Rights acted as an advocacy agency for protection and enhancement of human rights. It set up a mobile law clinic and tried to inform members of the underprivileged and victimized public throughout the country how they could have recourse to whatever legal rights remained available under the constitution. A major operation undertaken in the mid-1980s, for example, came to the aid of grossly exploited black farm laborers in the northern Cape area of Colesberg.

The most important activity aimed at alleviating and countering the iniquities of the system was the Legal Resources Centre, established in 1979. The center provided desperately needed legal services for thousands of victims of the day-to-day operation of the apartheid system. It offered employment to selected law graduates in a fellowship program, ran training programs for young black law graduates and equipped paralegal personnel with the elementary legal skills needed to contend with the maze of apartheid laws that governed the lives of blacks. The moving spirit of this remarkable legal aid enterprise was Arthur Chaskalson, who selflessly left a brilliant private practice at the Johannesburg bar in order to dedicate himself to this work.[118] Chaskalson had never been a political activist. But together with several colleagues at the bar he had placed his formidable legal ability at the disposal of victims of the repressive political system in a series of trials in the 1960s—among them the Rivonia Trial, the trials of Bram Fischer and of African Resistance Movement members, and the *Rand Daily Mail*'s trial concerning the prison conditions revelations made by journalist Benjamin Pogrund. The Legal Resources Centre, which Chaskalson founded together with Geoff Budlender and Felicia Kentridge, was the pinnacle of his work. Several more Jews served on its staff or were among its trustees, including Basil Wunsh, who was concurrently also active in Jewish organizations. The Legal Resources Centre gained the financial support of some major American Foundations, and by 1990 it had more than a hundred full-time employees operating throughout the country, mostly paralegal assistants and administrators, and also some forty fully qualified lawyers.

The work of Arthur Chaskalson demonstrated a form of activity that, probably even more than direct political involvement, characterized the endeavors of Jewish individuals in numbers quite disproportionate to the size of the Jewish population. It was the activity of persons born into the privileged status of whites but whose moral conscience drove them to dedicate themselves resolutely and inventively, within the parameters of what remained legally possible, to alleviating the indignities, deprivations, and repression inflicted by the apartheid system. At the same time, their efforts formed part of the broader struggle to obstruct, resist, and ultimately abolish that system. Chaskalson's work was accorded high recognition by the political leadership of postapartheid South Africa. In the transition to democracy of the 1990s he played an important role in the drafting of the new constitutional order, and in June 1994 President Mandela appointed him the first president of South Africa's newly established Constitutional Court.

Arthur Chaskalson is perhaps the most outstanding example of a category of Jews whose moral conscience and liberal outlook, analogous to that of a much larger number of gentile white colleagues of kindred spirit, defies explanation purely or even primarily in terms of identifiable Jewish influences. Yet, unlike some of the intensely radical political opponents of apartheid, the type exemplified by Chaskalson never evinced bitter attitudes of Jewish self-reproach. "I have always had the sense that I am Jewish. I have never had any doubts about that being a factor in my own life and upbringing," Chaskalson characteristically told an interviewer, adding, "I don't, however, regard it as an important factor. I regard it more just as a fact."[119] Although his mother, Mary Adler, was very active in Jewish communal life, most prominently in the Women's Zionist Council and on the executive of the Zionist Federation, Arthur had never been exposed to either a compelling Jewish religious environment or even a Zionist youth movement experience. He was only five years old when his father died, and his formal education was in elite, English-language, private schools. He completed his secondary schooling in Hilton College, Natal. As in the case of several other Jews (discussed here in a previous chapter) who took a stand against apartheid, whether as radicals or liberals, it is difficult to attribute the sources of his outlook to specifically definable Jewish factors or to distinguish them from the South African English-speaking cultural environment in which he grew up.

A different exemplar of such nonpolitical, but in other ways equally effectual, modes of resistance to apartheid was Franz Auerbach, whose major sphere of operation was education. Auerbach taught for many years in white high schools in Johannesburg and played a role in teacher association affairs. Concurrently he was very active in night-school education for blacks. In 1960 he authored a study on history textbooks and syllabi that showed how race prejudice was being inculcated by the educational system. It was published in 1965 under the title *The Powers of Prejudice in South African Education,* by which time Auerbach had been elected president of the Transvaal Teachers' Association. Predictably, the authorities never allowed him promotion within the state education system. There followed some twenty years of intense activity in the development of Teacher-in-Service-Education, which by the mid-1970s began to incorporate also black teachers in its programs. From the mid-1980s he also ran the Funda [a Xhosa word meaning learning] Centre in Soweto, which provided black teachers with supplementary training. Auerbach also served from 1981 to 1983 as president of the South African Institute of Race Relations, one of the great pillars of liberal values in South African society.

In contrast to most of the Jewish individuals who threw themselves into radical political opposition to apartheid, Franz Auerbach's liberal convictions are unmistakably traceable to his Jewish background. Born in Germany, he fled with his family from the Nazis in 1937 when he was fourteen years old. By his own account, his experience as a Jew engendered an intuitive repugnance for the institutionalized racial discrimination prevalent in South Africa. Concurrently with his tireless activities in the broader societal arena, he maintained his association with the Etz Chayim orthodox congregation in Johannesburg and took a lead in the South African Yad Vashem Foundation. In about 1982 he became active on the Jewish Board of Deputies, and in 1991 he undertook part-time professional work for the Board. When an initiative called Jews for Social Justice (to which we shall return) was formed in 1985 Franz joined it, and in June 1989 he was elected to serve a term as its chairman.

Franz Auerbach exemplified a consciously Jewish liberal humanism, which resisted apartheid less in terms of politics than as, in his words, "an objection ultimately to a morally evil system."[120] He has described his personal credo as a "Jewish humanism," rooted in a harmonious integration of self-affirming multiple identities. This meant a refugee's sense of gratitude to the country that had saved him, but equally a commitment to all of the peoples that constituted its society, not only to the whites who governed it, and certainly not to so unjust a system of governance. At the same time, he also embraced his Jewish identity and his German cultural inheritance. "Some people feel a passionate loyalty to a single cause, and look upon themselves as belonging to a single human group to the exclusion of all others. I am not one of those," he explained in a personal exposition of his credo.[121]

Auerbach did not shrink from drawing parallels between Nazi Germany's treatment of its Jews and apartheid. He argued that there was a key parallel in "the organization of a society in which the most important attribute of human beings is their race, as assigned by the state." In defense of similar comparisons made by Archbishop Tutu, Auerbach said that forced removal of black people to so-called homelands where there was little food and work was an inhuman practice, even if in the South African case there was no intention of killing people. "The persistence of legally enforced race discrimination," Auerbach opined, "makes a comparison between apartheid and Nazism a perfectly valid analogy. In fact I have always held that the experience of the Holocaust obliged me to oppose racial discrimination, especially where it is enforced by law."[122] Typical of Franz Auerbach's mode of moral protest was a declaration he made public in 1988 to the effect that he was not willing to be classified as a white. This was a demonstration of his repugnance for apartheid racial classification that sought to embarrass and confound the government's Department of Home Affairs.[123]

Neither Chaskalson nor Auerbach suffered arrest and imprisonment during the waves of repression that swept the country in the 1970s and again in the 1980s. But Jews were plentiful among those whites who did fall foul of the regime as suppressed radical resistance resurfaced in new forms within the United Democratic Front (UDF), established in 1983. Its "liberation struggle" rhetoric, calling for the creation of a nonracial, democratic South Africa, implicitly echoed the language of the 1950s Congress of the People and the voice of the exiled ANC.[124]

In 1986 a "Call to Whites" campaign initiated by the UDF appealed to white South Africans to join in the building of a nonracial, democratic South Africa. The UDF's affiliates included the End Conscription Campaign (ECC), the Institute for Democratic Alternatives, the Johannesburg Democratic Action Committee

(JODAC), and its Cape counterpart, the Cape Democrats (CD), launched in April 1988. Concerned Citizens was formed to protest the declaration of a state of emergency, and the Five Freedoms Forum was formed in March 1987, serving in effect as a subsidiary umbrella organization of the UDF to coordinate the efforts of antiapartheid organizations in the white community. Belonging to it were organizations as diverse as JODAC, the Progressive Federal Party, Young Christian Students, Lawyers for Human Rights, and Women for Peace. Another organization led by whites was the Detainees' Parents Support Committee. Some whites also found a place in trade unions and other labor-related organizations.

Once again, the names of Jews were conspicuous in these burgeoning manifestations of resistance—the family of Max and Audrey Coleman, for example. In the countrywide security police sweep of 1981 their twenty-one-year-old son, Keith, who was active in student antiapartheid circles, was arrested and detained for five months. When he was released, banning orders restricted his freedom. In the emergency sweep of 1985 his brother Neil, who had been involved in various antiapartheid activities over the past decade, underwent similar detention followed by banning orders. A liberal antiapartheid atmosphere had always pervaded the Coleman home. Max and Audrey had some affinity with the Congress of Democrats in the 1950s, and Audrey had joined the Black Sash organization. Now, after the arrest of Keith, Max and Audrey joined in the founding of a Detainees' Parents Support Committee. Solitary confinement and reports of torture made this a particularly distressing time also for the families of detainees. In February 1982 the cruel treatment inflicted on a white detainee, Neil Agget, apparently drove him to suicide while in detention. The Detainees' Parents Support Committee protested, raised funds, agitated in defense of the thousands of detainees of all races, and challenged the whole system of detention without trial.

Interviewed in 1995 on the question whether there was anything in Judaism's ethical teachings that might have inspired them, the responses of the Colemans, both parents and sons, showed rather bitter Jewish self-reproach and certainly did not provide credence for theories that postulate the influence of Jewish religious values in the making of Jewish liberals. Keith Coleman said: "Do you really want me to answer that? Let me tell you that the very first time I read the Old Testament was in jail—because it was the only book I had for a long time—it and the New Testament. I was rather shocked at its contents. It seemed to promote dissension and violence—like the idea that the Jews were obliged to kill off the Philistines." The father, Max, said that religious ethics were not really a subject discussed in their home and from quite an early age his sons were critical of the Jewish community, as were he and his wife Audrey. Neil thought that if Jewish culture had any effect on him it was only insofar as it incorporated a lot of *ubuntu* (an African term denoting humanism and a sense of human brotherhood), a comment hardly complimentary to Judaism itself. The Coleman family had felt shunned and isolated by the Jewish community because of their antiapartheid activities. "For me, the Jewish community became more of an albatross than something to be proud of," explained Neil.[125] That they could harbor so strong a sense of alienation from the institutional Jewish community even through the 1980s when, as we have seen, the

Jewish Board of Deputies had begun to speak out against apartheid, attests to the great gap that still existed between the expectations of Jewish antiapartheid activists, on the one hand, and the cautious change in the Board's policy, on the other.

Individual Jews were also to be found in major humanitarian projects that developed alongside UDF resistance to the apartheid system in this period. An example was the major relief organization Operation Hunger. Its extensive feeding programs, conducted on the principle of cultivating community self-help, reached a peak of an estimated two million people. From 1980 to 1993 Ina Perlman led it. Her long record of voluntary social work went back as early as 1949, to the African Feeding Scheme founded by Father Trevor Huddleston in Sophiatown. She was active also in the Black Sash and in the Institute of Race Relations as well as in a variety of community projects and women's groups. Ina Perlman's parents had come to South Africa from Germany. "I regard myself as Jewish and I believe deeply in God. Obviously my whole moral code is Jewish," she told an interviewer. However, she felt more comfortable with reform Judaism than orthodoxy and was critical of what she perceived as the tendency of South African Jews to make Zionism a substitute for religious faith and an evasion of involvement in the situation in South Africa.[126]

Another major impetus to modification and ultimately to dismantling of apartheid came from white business circles in the 1980s. Here the role of Jews was inherently ambiguous. Heavy concentration in entrepreneurial, business, and manufacturing occupations was an historical characteristic of their economic activity in South Africa.[127] They were therefore long-established beneficiaries of the economic exploitation promoted by white domination. Jews had long been particularly prominent in production and distribution of a host of consumer goods such as garment textiles, blankets, furniture, processed foods, and other department store products. The accretion of German-Jewish refugees in the 1930s had added new categories in spheres such as the diamond trade, ceramics, and fashion ware. The huge insurance company Liberty Life, developed by Donald Gordon, was another example of big business ventures by Jews. They were less salient in heavy industries with the notable exception of some branches of steel production, such as those developed by the companies of Eric Samson and Mendel Kaplan.

Whether big business was a factor either in buttressing apartheid or undermining it has long been a moot point among academic analysts as well as political activists.[128] Be that as it may, in the period of reformed apartheid some Jews were in the forefront of those businessmen who, out of enlightened economic self-interest as well as social concern, advocated the incremental dismantling of apartheid restrictions. At the same time, they vigorously called upon foreign corporations not to disinvest and boycott South Africa but rather to remain "constructively engaged" and add their weight to the strategy aimed at attaining change via the economy. Tony Bloom, head of the mammoth Premier Milling Group, reputedly among the five largest companies in the country, stood out in this regard. Bloom personified the avowedly capitalist but liberal advocacy of freedom for labor unionization, "gentle affirmative action" favoring advancement of blacks into management positions, and social responsibility programs for employees.

Throughout the 1980s Bloom was prominent in initiatives aimed at freeing the business sector from the fetters of apartheid policies. Speaking avowedly as "a South African white businessman with a vested interest in the survival of the free enterprise system," he called for abolition of all statutory racial discrimination, the unbanning of black political organizations, the release of Nelson Mandela, and negotiations for a postapartheid society and economy. In 1983 Bloom took a leading role in forming a delegation of business leaders to meet with exiled African National Congress leaders, much to the chagrin of the government. The exchange of views that took place in Lusaka, since it raised confidence that negotiations could lead to a new dispensation, and one in tune with Western democracy and capitalist free enterprise rather than with Marxist models, was a milestone on the path to the negotiated settlement that was ultimately to transform South Africa. In 1985 Bloom again took the lead in drawing up a manifesto, signed by ninety-two of the country's top businessmen, calling for an end to apartheid and for government negotiations with black leaders, not excluding those in detention. At the same time, together with other business magnates, Bloom vigorously opposed economic sanctions against South Africa, arguing that they would not persuade the government to accept change and would "intensify the paranoid siege mentality which ripples below our national psyche."[129] Bloom was an identifying Jew but took little interest in Jewish communal affairs, except for a short-lived entry into the work of the Jewish Board of Deputies in mid-1983 when he was elected to that body's Transvaal council. This raised an embarrassing protest from orthodox circles on account of his having married out of the faith. "The tacit approval of intermarriage, implied by his election," complained the Federation of Synagogues' organ, "is surely nothing less than a vote for those forces contributing to the assimilation of the South African Jew."[130]

Yet Tony Bloom's progressive advocacy was the exception rather than the rule in the business world, as much of whites in general as of Jews in particular. On the whole, much as was true of the behavior of Jews in the political system of the country, those in business and industry conformed to the apartheid system and thrived on the prodigious economic benefits of cheap labor that it conferred. Earlier in this chapter mention was made of Jewish student denunciation in the early 1970s of Phillip Frame, the industrial magnate in Natal, when he became the focus of labor strikes against severely exploitative wages. The Jewish Board of Deputies was rather hard-pressed to find and hold up for praise the all too few Jewish business people who took a lead in regard to raising the universally low wage levels of black labor.[131] Vaunted examples were Chambers of Commerce leaders such as E. P. Bradlow and Harry Goldberg, the latter instrumental already in the heyday of apartheid in establishing the Bantu Wages and Productivity Association for the purpose of examining and improving the nonwhite wage structure. Other exemplars were Raymond Ackerman and Helmut Hirsch, heads respectively of a mammoth chain of supermarkets and a large photographic and fancy goods company, who saw to improvements in the wage and labor conditions and managerial opportunities of their employees.

Among those business magnates who took a lead in Jewish communal affairs there were some who also stood out as progressives in the conduct of their economic enterprises. Steel industrialist Mendel Kaplan is an example. His company, Cape Gate, provided black employees with a range of services and aid programs, including a crèche to care for children of employees during working hours, interest-free loans for purchase of their own homes, and scholarships for tertiary education of employees' children, 962 of which were granted between 1979 and 1997. Cape Gate also contributed toward community development projects in the Boipatong Township, an area from which it drew part of its labor force.[132]

The example set by Mendel Kaplan was all the more significant because, within a decade of beginning his dedicated communal involvement in the mid-1970s, he had become, arguably, South African Jewry's most dynamic and influential communal leader. He was the foremost leader in the major fund-raising organs of the community, first the United Communal Fund and thereafter the United Israel Appeal, and was himself a generous benefactor of a variety of philanthropic causes and innovative educational and cultural projects. Among these were the establishment of the country's only viable academic center for Jewish Studies, the Isaac and Jessie Kaplan Centre at the University of Cape Town, and later also the South African Jewish Museum in Cape Town. Furthermore, Kaplan attained unprecedented stature in international Jewish affairs. In June 1987 he was elected chairman of the Board of Governors of the Jewish Agency for Israel, the only non-American Jewish leader ever to be elected to this paramount position in international Jewish organizational life. In 1986 Kaplan authored a book on the historical role of the Jews in the South African economy, in which he averred that the solution to South African society's problems "will be dependent on the acceptance of every South African by his fellow South African with equality, irrespective of race or religion." Kaplan concluded his study with the statement that "if Jewish businessmen, in particular, fail to give leadership in the movement to abolish all discriminatory practices, they will be betraying their heritage in the country which gave the Jewish people their freedom and opportunities."[133]

Measured against the record of the organized Jewish community in the past, the most innovative development in regard to Jewish social action was the emergence in late 1985 of groups of Jews specifically dedicated to collective Jewish expression of opposition to the apartheid system. In Cape Town one such group initially called itself Jews against Apartheid but, with a view to adopting a more positive and less provocative posture, soon changed its name to Jews for Justice. At about the same time a group of similar composition was founded in Johannesburg under the name Jews for Social Justice. Among the participants were Jewish individuals associated with various groups active in resistance to government policies, such as NUSAS, the Johannesburg Democratic Action Committee (JODAC), and area committees of the United Democratic Front. Also students and members of the Zionist youth movements joined. Moreover, several rabbis participated, notably Rabbi Selwyn Franklin in Cape Town and, for a time, Rabbi Norman Bernhard in Johannesburg. The combined enrolled membership of these groups was small, only a few hundred, but their public meetings were able to attract hundreds more.

What made this group distinctively different in the South African Jewish experience was its attempted synthesis of two purposes—bold public protest against the apartheid system, and at the same time self-affirming Jewish identification. This purported representation of a collective Jewish voice in an unmistakably political sphere clearly flouted the official policy of the Board of Deputies. To be sure, the attempt to organize a collective Jewish voice in opposition to apartheid was not entirely without precedent. In an earlier chapter, mention was made of a small and short-lived leftist group called the Jewish Democratic Association, which had been formed by Michael Szur in the 1950s. Unlike the contemporary Jews for Justice, however, many of whose members considered Zionism and support of Israel to be intrinsic to their Jewishness, the Jewish Democratic Association had upheld the communally deviant legacy of leftist anti-Zionism.

In a newsletter appealing to Jews to join its ranks, Jews for Social Justice declared that it was intended to fill the need for a "united Jewish response" to the South African situation:

> Our history of persecution imposes a special duty on us to protest any form of discrimination against any people. Judaism is a religion of faith expressed in action; therefore its teachings about human dignity and social justice make it unacceptable for us to be guilty of the complicity of silence in an oppressive society. . . . A vast proportion of the Jewish population does desire a just society and wishes to stake its claim to a future in a democratic South Africa. It is therefore essential for a united Jewish voice to be heard in the struggle for justice.[134]

Jews for Social Justice and Jews for Justice joined several major demonstrations of protest. In Johannesburg, for example, their members took part in a public demonstration against detention without trial, alongside the Black Sash, JODAC, and the End Conscription Campaign.[135] In their own activities emphasis was placed on celebrating Jewish holidays in a spirit relevant to the struggle in South Africa. Accordingly, in April 1987 Cape Town's group held a "freedom seder" during Passover. It was addressed by Archbishop Desmond Tutu—his first to a public meeting under Jewish auspices. Despite a bomb threat, a thousand people came to hear him say, inter alia, that although Jews had been in the forefront of the antiapartheid struggle from the outset, South Africa's blacks currently felt a sense of disappointment with the Jewish community because of Israel's close ties with the white regime. In March 1987 Johannesburg's Jews for Social Justice participated in the founding of the Five Freedoms Forum. Similarly, Cape Town's Jews for Justice, while declaring that "the major source for change in South Africa is to be found in the extra-Parliamentary struggle," formulated an appeal "for those who wished to oppose apartheid by voting in the 1987 election" to support only those candidates who "oppose a social system based on statutory racial classification; oppose a legal system in which detention without trial forms an integral part; support a political system in which all South Africans will enjoy the same rights irrespective of colour and in which all will be able to be represented by persons of their own choice."[136]

The onset of conscientious objection to military service in the late 1980s placed the Jews for Justice groups in a dilemma because there were deeply rooted restraints in the Jewish community, bolstered by rabbinical opinion, concerning this demonstrative form of dissociation from the duties of citizenship. Nevertheless, they came out strongly in solidarity with two trend-setting Jewish objectors, Dave Bruce and Saul Batzofin, who were sentenced to imprisonment during 1988. Emphatically Jewish motivations were dramatically highlighted in the case of Bruce, who in July 1988 was sentenced to six years in prison (he gained release after nineteen months). Moving testimony was heard from his blind sixty-year old mother who, at age eleven, had escaped from Nazi clutches when her mother managed to flee with her to South Africa in 1939. Bruce told the court that in his view the role of the South African Defence Force was to uphold and defend racism. He said that his awareness, from childhood, of the Nazi Holocaust and the suffering endured by his mother and her family made service in such a military force unconscionable for him. Nor was he prepared to flee the country. "My mother is a refugee from racism. I am not prepared to be another one," he declared.[137]

The line adopted by Jews for Justice became: "Jews for Justice supports Jewish conscientious objectors but will not promote them."[138] In October 1989 the Jews for Justice newsletter reported that there were 31 Jews among the 771 men who were currently on record as refusing to do military service. Most of the young Jews involved were graduates of Jewish day schools and former or present leaders in the various Zionist youth movements.[139] They had formed an organization called Jewish Conscientious Objectors, which declared that they were acting "as Jews, members of a people who possess a religious tradition of social justice and who have endured a history of oppression." It was their explicit contention that refusal to serve in the military was an expression of their Jewish heritage and an act of loyalty to the majority of South Africans, but they declared willingness to do nonpunitive, alternative community service.

In late June 1989 Jews for Social Justice representatives participated in a large delegation of the Five Freedoms group that visited Lusaka to meet with leaders of the ANC in exile. During the sessions a Jewish delegation held a special meeting with representatives of the ANC to discuss frankly its attitude toward the Jewish community. In a document titled "Four Days in Lusaka," Jews for Social Justice chairman Franz Auerbach reported what had transpired in an optimistic vein. The delegation had explained that as a minority group the Jewish community was apprehensive about its future in a South Africa in which a black majority would control the government. It sought reassurance on several points. The ANC replied that "anti-Semitism is totally alien to the ethos of the ANC," and supported freedom of conscience, including freedom of religious observance. It gave an assurance that it would not discriminate against the Jewish community in South Africa and that there was no problem in the Jewish community continuing to run its own day schools. It was not opposed to private schools, "provided they did not practice racial exclusivity."

Rather more ambiguous and less reassuring for Jews was the discussion on South Africa–Israel relations. Auerbach had explained that for Jews the world over support for Israel was a fundamental tenet. Although this did not necessarily mean support for each and every action of an Israeli government, it did mean that care for the safety and welfare of Israel was a deep concern of the Jewish community in South Africa as of communities throughout the Jewish Diaspora. The ANC's reply was that it "regarded Palestinians as an oppressed people" and adhered to the policies of the Organization of African Unity, which was very critical of Israel and supportive of the PLO. The ANC was particularly averse to the way Israel was "handling the intifada." To this the Jews for Social Justice representatives responded that they themselves had issued statements expressing concern over this issue. They explained, however, that the disinclination of South African Jews to express public criticism from outside Israel was not dissimilar to the reluctance of blacks to express public criticism of the policies and shortcomings of particular governments in Africa, even when they disapproved of such policies and actions. On the positive side, the ANC representatives reassured these Jewish interlocutors that an ANC-led government would maintain friendly relations with all nations, not excluding Israel, and that South African Jews would be free to support the State of Israel. But they added the caveat that "this would only become a problem in the highly unlikely event of an ANC-led government breaking off relations with Israel."[140]

The prevailing hostility to Israel not only in the exiled ANC but even more ominously within the United Democratic Front, spurred by its Muslim affiliates, constituted the Jews for Justice members' most difficult ideological and emotional dilemma. They had to cope not only with Muslim objections but also with their own acute embarrassment at Israel's known cooperation with the very same military force that was being negated by Jewish conscientious objectors. Notwithstanding the agitation to disqualify participation in the UDF of any Jew who identified himself also as a Zionist, the leaders of both Jews for Social Justice in Johannesburg and Jews for Justice in Cape Town sustained their principled identification with Zionism and Israel, while reluctantly "feeling compelled," as they phrased it, to condemn Israel's actions in the West Bank territories, "having condemned similar behaviour in South Africa." "We urge our fellow Jews in Israel," they added, "not to proceed along the path which led South Africa into its vicious cycle of civil violence."[141]

In the final analysis, Jews for Social Justice and Jews for Justice were more significant as an expression of change in the image of the Jewish community and as an outlet for positively identifying young Jews who were embarrassed and frustrated by the record of the Jewish community, than as a force within the freedom struggle.[142] It cannot be said that they enjoyed enthusiastic support from the Jewish community at large. Indeed they encountered some active opposition and even threats of violence from a small right-wing section of the community. Its adherents adopted extremist, nationalist-religious views akin to those of the notorious Rabbi Meir Kahane, founder of the Jewish Defense League in the United States and the Kach Party in Israel, which had duly been debarred from the Israeli parliament on the grounds of its being racist.

On the other hand, despite the Jews for Justice and Social Justice groups' flouting of official Board of Deputies policy, the Board's leaders soon come round to an appreciation of their value as an outlet for actions that the Board could not hazard to take upon itself. Nothing better indicates the change that the Board had by now undergone. Moreover, the groups enjoyed the wholehearted support of Rabbi Cyril Harris, who had replaced the far more conservative and restrained Rabbi Casper in 1988.[143] As for the response to the Jews for Justice phenomenon on the part of the South African authorities, it seems that they did not regard it as really dangerous. This was indicated when they spared it in the harsh clampdown of the late 1980s on most of the antiapartheid forces with which it had aligned itself. Of the twenty-two political, religious, and communal groups with which Cape Town's Jews for Justice was associated at the outset of its involvement in assisting the destitute black inhabitants of the Crossroads squatter camp, all but Jews for Justice itself and the women's Black Sash were muzzled.

A number of individuals associated with Jews for Justice were arrested and held in detention for long periods, but this was obviously on account of their primary involvement in major organizations within the United Democratic Front alliance. Lisa Seftel, who was an organizing secretary of JODAC, was one. Another was Maxine Hart, who was detained for the second time in 1986 and held in solitary confinement for two and a half months. A social worker by profession, she had formed a group called Concerned Social Workers and had also joined JODAC when it was launched in 1983. In Cape Town, Amy Thornton was arrested in October 1988, held incommunicado for seventeen days, and even after release still subjected to severe restrictions.[144] The foremost antiapartheid activist who also made the gesture of associating himself with Jews for Justice was Raymond Suttner, a university lecturer in law, who was on the executive of the United Democratic Front. After serving a seven-and-a-half-year jail sentence from 1975 to 1983, he was again detained without trial during the 1986 state of emergency. Jews for Justice took part in protests against his cruel treatment by the authorities.[145]

CHAPTER 5

A Transformed Community

Changing Fortunes of Zionism

As we have seen, the Six Day War of 1967 marked the end of the South African government's punitive response to Israel's alignment with the international assault on South Africa. Permission was again granted for the local Zionists to transfer the accumulated funds they had raised for the Jewish Agency, and the confidence of the Zionist movement in South Africa was restored. The Ministry of Finance approved transfer of R 18 million over six years.[1] Despite the preceding six crisis years, the South African Zionist Federation had maintained its record as what its leaders liked to call an "umbrella" under which was conducted every aspect of activity relating to Jewish identification with Israel and world Jewry's concern for Israel. Moreover, relative to the rapidly declining Zionist organization worldwide, it continued to be an impressive organization in the following years. As late as 1986, the director of the World Zionist Organization's treasury department, Moshe Haskel, described the South African Zionist Federation as "a model for the WZO," and said that his visit to South Africa was "the most inspiring trip" he had made in twenty-five years of work in the Jewish Agency for Israel.[2]

Zionist fund-raising served as the major practical expression of Jewish identification with Israel and was an impressive index of the continued valence of Zionist sentiment among South Africa's Jews. It was conducted through the campaigns of Israel United Appeal (IUA), which represented the Keren Hayesod (Foundation Fund) of the World Zionist Organization–Jewish Agency (WZO-JA). The Keren Hayesod provided the Jewish Agency's income from all countries outside of the massive Jewish community of the United States, which was, of course, by far the major source but channeled its contribution independently through its United Jewish Appeal (UJA). South African Zionism's extraordinary record—second only to the United States in absolute figures prior to 1948—had declined relative to the various Keren Hayesod appeals in other countries since the establishment of Israel. Yet in the first decade of Israel's existence, South African Zionists remained in the lead as per capita contributors, and came close to equaling in absolute figures the funds raised in the much larger Jewish communities of Britain and Canada.[3] As we have noted earlier, from 1961 to 1967 the South African government withheld permission to transfer funds. When the ban was removed in the wake of the Six Day War, South African Jewry resumed its importance as a fund-raising source for the Jewish Agency. Although no longer contributing at quite the same extraordinary level as it had attained in earlier years, South African Jewry still held a per capita record until at least the end of the 1980s.[4] Moreover, the South African record remained impressive in respect of the number of contributors that it tapped. In 1972, Zionist Federation chairman Julius Weinstein reported that out of an estimated 30,000 potential male contributors nearly 20,000 were being reached.[5] This attests to the tremendous identification of South African Jews with the Zionist movement and Israel. No other cause could command so high a level of support in the Jewish community.

Fund-raising was not of course the only function of Zionism in South African Jewry. Its influence on the life of South African Jews was reflected no less in the remarkable strength of the Zionist youth movements, all of which were affiliates of the Zionist Federation. A census conducted in 1966 showed a total of 6,800 registered members in the Zionist youth movements, of which 952 were over the age of sixteen. The largest of the movements was Habonim (later Habonim-Dror) with 3,618 members, followed by Betar with 1,483, Bnei Akiva with 1,478, and Hashomer Hatza'ir with 221.[6] The youth movements continued to grow. In 1969 the total membership rose to 8,535, of which Habonim numbered 4,566. It may be estimated that this represented almost 42 percent of the Jewish youth in South Africa aged ten to eighteen.[7] Throughout the 1970s and 1980s the youth movements maintained their important role as a formative influence in the lives of Jewish youth in South Africa. The highest goal of these movements was *aliya,* meaning the decision to live in Israel, with strong emphasis placed by the major movement, Habonim, on settlement in a kibbutz. Youth leaders were expected to set a personal example for such *aliya,* but many failed to live up to this expectation. However, of those who remained in South Africa not a few became community leaders. By the early 1980s the lay and professional leadership of almost all the Jewish community's institutions and organizations was constituted by former members of one or other youth movement. Indicative of the remarkably extensive exposure of Jewish adolescents to these youth movements is one of the findings of a national survey of South African Jews completed in 1999 by the London-based Institute of Jewish Policy Research. It showed that no less than 71 percent of the adult respondents had been members of these movements when in their teens.[8]

From the outset the Women's Zionist Organization provided the broadest membership base of the adult Zionist movement in South Africa, and the relative role of women in the actual everyday work of Zionists increased progressively after the creation of the State of Israel. The objectives of the women's organization were "to organize Jewish women in South Africa and to stimulate their Zionist consciousness," meaning education toward an appreciation of Israel's centrality in Jewish life, material support of the Jewish Agency for Israel and of specific humanitarian projects in Israel, and also encouragement of *aliya.*[9] It was an affiliate of the vast Women's International Zionist Organization (WIZO), which initiated and supported hundreds of philanthropic, humanitarian projects in Israel.

Aside from the youth movements, the women's organization engaged in more intense educational programming than any other segment of the Zionist movement. It conducted numerous seminars and lectures as well as energetic fund-raising through novel functions and campaigns, mostly launched by visiting emissaries of note from abroad. The beneficiaries were mainly projects related to the integration of immigrants into Israel. By 1975 membership of the Women's Zionist Organization of South Africa peaked at about 18,000 in sixty-six women's societies, but it declined to 14,500 nearly a decade later. The main cause of this decline was demographic—the emptying out of small-town communities owing to the drift to the large cities, mainly Johannesburg, and also emigration from South Africa. Whereas membership had always been very high in the small country towns, formerly active members mostly failed to join the women's societies in their new places of residence in the cities.[10] Despite efforts to create a reservoir of future leaders in the younger generation, such as the creation of a program of intensive seminars, by 1988 registered membership had fallen to 12,500.[11] Nevertheless, relative to the general decline in membership of Zionist parties and associations beginning in the early 1970s, the women Zionists remained the mainstay of the adult Zionist movement.

In contrast to the thriving fund-raising, youth movement, and women's Zionist aspects of Zionist activity in South Africa, the constitutional structure of the Zionist Federation, based since the late 1940s on representation of the various Zionist political parties at its biennial conferences and the election of its executive on a party key, was becoming increasingly dysfunctional. It was a source of perennial controversy throughout these years, a major body of opinion favoring reversion to a nonparty system of representation.[12] In theory, the Zionist Federation was the most democratically structured body in the Jewish community, but in practice, no Zionist election had been held since 1952. In that election nearly 30,000 cast their votes out of a total membership of 41,740 (that is, men and women over eighteen years of age who purchased the shekel membership card) in a community numbering about 108,500. The General Zionist Party gained the most votes, followed by the Zionist Socialists, the Revisionist Zionists, the Association of South African Zionists (which was opposed to the party system), and the Mizrahi orthodox-religious Zionists. That election's results continued to determine the key for representation at succeeding conferences.

In the mid-1960s the World Zionist Organization initiated a global commission on reorganization. A South African section of the commission under the chairmanship of Israel Maisels proposed that the South African Zionist Federation conference should be reconstituted so as to fit it to serve as an electoral college optimally representative of all Jewish organizations that subscribed to Zionism's aims. However, the major parties vigorously resisted such reorganization, sensing that it must inevitably lead to the eclipse of the party system, which they considered to be the prerequisite for ideologically viable Zionist endeavor. The Maisels commission's proposals were shelved, and in their place the parties and the opponents of the party system agreed to negotiate a compromise formula for reconstituting Zionist conferences.[13] The outcome was a cumbersome system, which, while permitting delegates to opt either for parties or for status as independents, regulated the conference's composition in such a way as to ensure that no more than 15 percent of the participants in the conference were independents.[14]

This system still prevailed in 1971 when, pressured by decisions of the World Zionist Organization and encouraged by the return to normalcy in relations between Israel and South Africa, South African Zionists held democratic elections for the first time in nineteen years. The results of these elections reflected a drastic decline in the public's interest in intra-Zionist politics. Although 30,000 purchased shekel membership cards, only 16,763 voted. The Revisionist Zionist Organization emerged as the largest single party with 6,032 votes (35.99 percent of the total) followed by the nonparty United Zionist Association with 4,222 votes (25.18 percent). A striking result of the election was the extraordinary success of one of the Zionist youth movements, Habonim, which, having ventured to contest a Zionist election for the first time, obtained 2,628 votes (15.68 percent), entitling it to larger representation than either the Socialist Zionist Party with 1,842 votes (10.99 percent) or the religious Zionists, Mizrahi–Bnei Akiva, with 2,039 (12.16 percent).[15]

The deeply ingrained Zionist sentiments of most South African Jews remained constant, but the growing incongruity between the Zionist Federation's formal structure based upon the Zionist political parties, on the one hand, and the lack of public interest in these effete organizational units, on the other, was a major debilitating factor. Several Zionist membership drives failed dismally.[16] Unwillingness to risk display of diminishing party membership and to face accusations of wasting Jewish public funds (raised after all mainly by nonparty IUA contributors) made for a consensus against elections. This was bolstered by the intuition that intense Jewish preoccupation with Zionist elections would be inappropriate at a time of tremendous public unrest and emergency rule set off by the 1976 Soweto uprising.[17] The latter consideration continued to carry weight into the 1980s as the country underwent further eruptions of rebellious unrest and governmental suppression. This consensus was disturbed, however, by the periodic emergence of new groups, prompted or encouraged by party leaders in the World Zionist Organization, seeking a share in the executive of the Zionist Federation. These groups then held the existing parties to ransom by demanding that an election be held unless they were granted representation by mutual agreement. This situation sporadically precipitated crises that preoccupied the Zionist Federation's leadership.[18] Numerous proposals for enlarged representation of the Zionist public on a "best-man" basis (as the pre–politically correct phraseology had it) were aired at conferences. However, the Federation proved unable to rise above its ossifying political structure except by the palliative measure of co-opting certain individuals as independents.[19] Not until the forty-third conference, held in July 1994 shortly after the first democratic elections of the new postapartheid South Africa, was the atrophying party-based constitution of the Zionist Federation at last changed. The new constitution put an end to the Federation's outmoded party-political key and made it an open-membership organization.[20]

However, this constitutional change came too late to stem the dwindling of the institutional Zionist structure in South Africa.[21] For in the intervening years attrition of the World Zionist Organization had had far-reaching local repercussions. In 1971 the Jewish Agency for Israel had been reconstituted as a partnership between the veteran WZO structure and the major fund-raising organs (primarily in the United States), which provided the Jewish Agency with its financial resources. Representation on the governing bodies of the reconstituted Jewish Agency was fixed at 30 percent for the United Israel Appeal of America, 20 percent for the Keren Hayesod fund-raising agencies (one of which was the South African IUA) in other Diaspora communities, and 50 percent for the World Zionist Organization.[22] It so happened that the major architect of this reconstituted Jewish Agency was the former South African Aryeh (Louis) Pincus, who held the important position of chairman of the WZO-JA from 1966 until his death in 1973. (Prior to settling in Israel in 1948, Pincus had been the leader of the Zionist Socialist Party in South Africa.) Pincus's partner on the "non-Zionist" or fund-raiser side was the eminent American Jewish leader Max Fisher.

From this time onward the fund-raising segment preponderantly represented in the board of governors of the Jewish Agency became increasingly involved in the disposition of funds within Israel and the administration of the Jewish Agency's affairs. Although the reconstitution agreement assigned the elected chairmanship of the new Jewish Agency's executive to candidates presented by the Zionist political parties (which in practice meant the Israeli party that gained the most Knesset seats), the fund-raising members of the board of governors incrementally exerted their power of the purse. First, they exercised the right of "advise and consent" in regard to appointment of the chairman and heads of major Jewish Agency departments. Then they appropriated control over particular projects, notably "Project Renewal" (urban renewal of disadvantaged towns and suburbs whose residents were largely immigrants). Thereafter they took under their wing a unified Education Authority that encompassed most of the educational services formerly controlled by the WZO alone. Finally, in the 1990s, they radically restricted the remaining budget and functions of the WZO.

Initially, the South African Zionist Federation's functioning was barely affected by the reconstitution of the Jewish Agency, because the IUA fund-raising organ in South Africa was fully under the authority of the Zionist Federation itself and not a separate body, as was the United Israel Appeal in the United States. However, the South African Zionist framework too eventually succumbed to the global transformation of power relations between the political-party Zionists and the non-party fund-raisers. The local process of change may be traced back to the late 1970s, when Mendel Kaplan became the chairman of the IUA in Johannesburg.

At the time, Kaplan was a brilliant young industrialist raised in a deeply and generously committed Jewish family of typically Litvak origin. As an adolescent in the early 1950s he had also been a member of one of the Zionist youth movements. He was destined to become a foremost leader at the level of global Jewish organizations, as treasurer of the World Jewish Congress in 1981, chairman of the Board of Trustees of world Keren Hayesod in1983, and ultimately, in 1987, chairman of the board of governors of the Jewish Agency. Kaplan's involvement in communal leadership had begun in 1972 when some talent-scouting elders of the

Jewish Board of Deputies persuaded him to agree to co-option onto the Board's executive. Within two years he was chosen to lead the United Communal Fund's campaign, which, together with another outstanding young leader, Ivan Greenstein, he raised to unprecedented levels of income. Soon after, he was chosen to head the Israel United Appeal, first in Johannesburg and then nationally.

Kaplan entered into a fund-raising framework already marked by a dysfunctional disparity between the IUA leadership and that of the Zionist Federation. The link between the Federation and the fund-raisers was tenuously maintained, mainly by Israel Maisels, who had been the Federation's chairman from 1967 to 1970—but was himself strongly opposed to the party system—and Julius Weinstein, Federation chairman from 1972 to 1978, who was a party man of the Revisionist Zionist Organization. Both served as heads of the IUA while maintaining their important roles in the Federation. The IUA, although in a real sense the very lifeblood of Zionist work, had long been sustained by dedicated lay leaders who set an inspiring example of generous giving, but were quite outside the party political units that dominated the Zionist Federation. The most outstanding among them was the legendary fund-raiser Fritz Frank, a wealthy merchant belonging to the small, highly enterprising wave of German-Jewish immigrants that had reached South Africa in the 1930s.

Already at the thirty-first South African Zionist Conference in 1978 Mendel Kaplan, then chairman of the Johannesburg IUA, became the spokesman for those who sought to redress the glaring imbalance between the dominant role of the largely defunct political parties and the subordinate status of the vital IUA fund-raisers as mere departmental components of the Zionist Federation. Addressing the conference, Kaplan said that IUA fund-raisers should have status at least equal to that of party members. "I believe we should think in terms of restructuring the mechanisms whereby the present Federation relates to our community," he declared. "I believe I am entitled to be a full member of this Federation without being a political ideologist."[23] In 1982 he turned from the platform to the conference's guest of honor, WZO chairman Aryeh Dulzin, and said: "You have no right to impose on our communities a political structure based on the electoral requirements of Israel." He appealed to Dulzin "once and for all to remove politics from the Diaspora and the Diaspora from politics."[24]

From the end of 1983 until July 1984 the Zionist Federation deliberated and anguished over the demand that the IUA "cease to be a department and become a full partner in the Federation." Some of the party leaders warned that this was "the beginning of a take-over or dissolution of the Federation."[25] Alternative proposals were made simply to grant more representation to the IUA leaders within the existing Federation structure. But this did not satisfy the IUA. It would settle for nothing less than being recognized as an equal constituent body of the Zionist Federation. By mid-1984 these demands were met, and amendments were accordingly made to the Federation's constitution. Another major step that elevated the status of the fund-raisers and weakened the Zionist Federation was taken soon thereafter, in 1986, when, as a cost-saving measure the IUA's administration merged with that of the United Communal Fund, which supported local communal needs. The South African fund-raising system now approximated to that of American Jewry—a highly significant change from the former strict separation and autonomy of IUA under the authority of the Zionist Federation. The first joint IUA-UCF campaign took place the following year. It followed a practice similar to that of the American Jewish communities, although still allowing the donor much greater discretion in stipulating the exact designation of his contribution. A few years later, in 1990, the independence of the combined IUA-UCF was symbolically underlined by its decision to remove its administrative offices from Zion Centre, the building of the Zionist Federation. Not long after, in 1992, it moved to new premises, which also housed the Jewish Board of Deputies. Some of the Federation's leaders felt that this rather ironic move from the orbit of the Zionist Federation to that of the Board of Deputies was a slap in the face. Relations with the Zionist Federation were further embittered when the IUA-UCF launched a lively new Jewish monthly in March 1990, the *Jewish Voice*. In the Zionist Federation this was perceived as an affront. It hastened the demise, in December 1993, of the Federation's eighty-five-year-old weekly newspaper the *Zionist Record*, which had for some years been floundering in financial difficulties.[26]

By the 1990s budgetary and administrative attrition of the WZO was profoundly affecting the South African Zionist Federation, resulting in drastic reduction of its budget, personnel, scope of activities, and status in the communal structure. It might be regarded as ironic that much as South African Jewry's Louis Pincus, in his capacity as chairman of the WZO, had been a major player in the reconstitution of the Jewish Agency, so too South Africa's own Mendel Kaplan, as chairman of the Jewish Agency's board of governors, was a key person at its helm when it was responsible, even if indirectly, for imposing the most seriously crippling budgetary restrictions on the South African Zionist Federation.

Whereas the atrophying party-political system and the status of the Israel United Appeal were major points of contention for South African Zionists, the promotion of personal settlement in Israel as a major task of the Zionist movement was never in dispute. More than in most other Jewish communities of the western Diaspora, Jews in South Africa acknowledged *aliya* as the highest expression of Zionist conviction. The record of the leaders of the Zionist Federation in setting a personal example was also far better than that of Zionist organizations in most Western countries. Of twelve chairpersons of the Federation who served from 1947 to 1998, seven had settled in Israel by the year 2000. Likewise, many rabbis and active leaders, lay and professional, through the entire range of communal institutions settled in Israel. Orthodox Chief Rabbis Rabinowitz, Abrahams, and Casper, as well as progressive Rabbis Weiler and Super, all settled in Israel or, having come from Israel, returned there.

Precise statistics of the number who fulfilled this Zionist ideal have never been ascertainable. But estimates were made from time to time by the Zionist Federation's Tel Aviv office on the basis of its own records, however imperfect, and also by professional demographers on the basis of government statistics. Thus in mid-1981 the Tel Aviv office estimated that the number of South African Jews who had come to Israel with the intention of settling permanently was 13,802: from 1952 to 1959, 1,099; 1960 to 1969, 4,480; 1970 to 1975, 3,380; and 1976 to 1979, 4,843.[27] It was considered that as many as one-third of these had left Israel over the years, some returning to South Africa and others moving on to other Diaspora countries. Inclusive of children of South Africans born in Israel, it was estimated that in 1981 there were some 12,000 Jews of South African origin living in Israel. If theoretically regarded as a subcommunity of South African Jewish origin, it might be said that this constituted a daughter community about 10 percent the size of the mother community in South Africa. (There were an estimated 118,000 Jews in South Africa in 1980.) This was a proportion well in excess of that achieved by other comparable Jewish communities of the English-speaking Diaspora such as those in the United States and Canada.

According to a sociodemographic survey conducted by Professor Allie Dubb under the auspices of the Kaplan Centre for Jewish Studies and Research at the University of Cape Town, an estimated 21,000 Jews emigrated from South Africa between 1970 and 1979. About 38 percent (7,980 persons) went to Israel, almost 25 percent to the United States, and smaller proportions to Britain, Australia, and Canada in descending order. But between 1980 and 1991, when a further 18,000 left, the pattern changed: 23 percent each emigrated to Israel and Australia and another 27 percent to the United States. As might be expected, Dubb's sociodemographic survey showed that peaks in the graphs of emigration largely correlated with major upsurges of political unrest in South Africa, after 1976 and again after 1985. This correlation was most marked in regard to choice of Israel, the reason being, Dubb suggested, that Israel was the only country open to South African Jews without any preconditions. Those who chose destinations other than Israel had perforce to time their emigration according to the requirements and conditions stipulated by those countries' immigration policies, and this often meant that they had to sit out periods of political crisis in South Africa and delay their departure.[28]

By the late 1980s it was evident to all concerned that greatly increased white emigration was one of the by-products of the massive transformation of South Africa from white supremacist apartheid society to genuine democracy with an overwhelming black majority. Within the Jewish community authoritative demographic surveys were hardly needed to show that contemplation of emigration was on the agenda of large numbers of South African Jews, particularly young people. It seemed that if ever there was a time when the influence of Zionist ideology and sentiment might be put to the test it was then. Hence, it was highly frustrating that in fact the number of emigrants who chose Israel dropped progressively relative to those who opted for other destinations. By the 1990s those going to Israel averaged less than half the average of the previous decade.[29] The trend proved irreversible notwithstanding an intense program of *aliya* promotion and facilitation developed by the Zionist Federation, prompted and assisted by its Tel Aviv office. Nor was there a lack of resolutions repeatedly proposed by youth movement delegates and sometimes actually passed at South African Zionist conferences declaring personal *aliya* to be the supreme goal of Zionism. Some even called upon all executive members of the Zionist Federation to commit themselves to making *aliya* part of their scheme of life or resign.[30]

By the 1990s it began to seem that concentrations of former South Africans in favored places such as Perth in Australia or Toronto in Canada exercised a magnetic attraction in excess of Israel, partly propagated by earlier immigrants to these places. Ironically—from a Zionist point of view—the attractiveness of these Diaspora alternatives to Israel did not exclude considerations of a rewarding Jewish communal life and education. As it became apparent that the much vaunted Zionism of South African Jewry was failing the test of the times, a pervasive demoralization set in at the Zionist Federation itself. This compounded earlier damage to Zionist morale inflicted by the immigration of non–South African–born Israelis to South Africa. In Zionist ideological parlance they were known judgmentally as *yordim* (literally, those who descend from the Holy Land). This was a process that extended back over the past decades. As early as 1970, rumor had it that there were no less than 20,000 such *yordim*. As is wont to happen with wholly unsubstantiated rumor, the same figure was still current more than two decades later! But Professor Dubb's research led him to a maximum estimate of 9,634 Israelis legally resident in South Africa in 1991.[31]

Whatever the exact number, the palpable fact that so many Israelis chose to leave Israel for South Africa, in effect offsetting South African Zionism's *aliya* contribution to Israel, had long taken its toll of Zionist morale in South Africa. But the exponential failure of *aliya* at a time in which emigration was surging had an ever more demoralizing effect. Disappointment was felt particularly among veteran settlers in Israel active in the wide-ranging activities of the Zionist Federation's Tel Aviv office and anxious to help in the promotion of *aliya*. They now tended to criticize their Zionist colleagues in South Africa. The record of discussions in the executive councils of the Zionist Federation throughout this period reflects the increasingly demoralizing sense that the South African movement was being "bad mouthed" in the corridors of the World Zionist Organization in Jerusalem, in the Israeli press, and even by former South Africans in Israel. Coming at a time when the Zionist Federation's functioning was being subjected to severe budgetary constraints imposed by the WZO—itself hard-pressed by the Jewish Agency fund-raisers for reasons discussed earlier—the South African body felt it was being treated in a disrespectful and cavalier fashion. Another process that attenuated the status and functioning of the Zionist Federation was an indirect consequence of the turn to religiosity, which will be discussed later in this chapter. As the expanding ambience of religiosity filled the vacuum created by the decline of the Zionist parties, the orthodox Mizrahi party alone was able to retain viability.[32] Since Mizrahi in South Africa followed not only the orthodox religiosity of the National-Religious Party in Israel but also the latter's right-wing political line, this ideological amalgam increasingly colored the public image of the residual Zionist organization in South Africa.

It will be noticed that the concerns of South African Zionists detailed in the preceding discussion were almost entirely isolated from South African politics and societal issues. Zionism was, for the Jews of South Africa, both an integral expression of the Jewish religion and a normative mode of highly positive ethnic identification. Few South African Jews were as intellectually qualified to articulate Zionism's ideological meaning for South African Jews as was Professor Marcus Arkin, a noted economic historian and former head of the department of economics at Rhodes University, Grahamstown, who served as director-general of the South African Zionist Federation from 1973 to 1985. In a paper delivered at the Zionist Federation's 1980 conference, he defined the meaning of Zionism as "a conception of the Jewish people as constituting one nation whose centre is in Israel and whose future depends on the survival and prosperity of that state." "In other words," he explained, "Zionism is that aspect of Judaism which emphasizes the centrality of Israel in the individual and collective outlook, commitment and behaviour of the Jewish people."[33]

Zionist convictions thus understood transcended the particular circumstances in which Jews found themselves in any particular Diaspora setting. Hence, Zionist activity had to be compartmentalized as a sphere of Jewish commitment wholly unrelated to the politics of South African society. This view of things was in full accord with the policy of the Jewish Board of Deputies, whose leadership, as a matter of fact, largely overlapped that of the Zionist Federation. Moreover, it had long become an accepted axiom in the governance of South African Jewry as a community that all matters relating to the status and welfare of Jews in South African society and politics were the province solely of the Jewish Board of Deputies. The Zionist Federation was to be involved in such matters only if and insofar as they were perceived to affect the pursuit of Zionist activity itself. This included anything that had a bearing on the connections of Jews with Israel and their ability to participate in the multifaceted concern for Israel felt by all of world Jewry.

The quality and tenor of the Israel–South Africa relationship was thus a crucial affair of the Zionist Federation. It valued and indeed took pride in whatever role it could play in fostering good relations between Israel and South Africa.[34] It is therefore not surprising that the Zionist Federation enthusiastically welcomed Prime Minister Vorster's auspicious visit to Israel in April 1976. It offered the services of its Israel branch, Telfed, and it was the Federation's chairman, Julius Weinstein, who proposed that on Vorster's return a dinner should be held in his honor and asked the Board of Deputies to join in its sponsorship.[35] Harry Hurwitz, the Revisionist Zionist leader, said that notwithstanding a small protest demonstration, Vorster's reception in Israel and the agreement between the two countries "could be regarded as the most positive development in years."[36]

The growing sympathy of the South African government also expressed itself in the granting of permission by the Treasury for certain categories of investment in Israel. Moreover this was permitted in commercial rands, which had a more advantageous exchange rate than financial rands. But such investment was closely controlled, and the income generated had to be remitted to South Africa. Addressing a Zionist Federation conference in 1978, one of the exemplars of South African investment in Israel, Ivan Greenstein, made a strong appeal for South African Jews possessed of the appropriate means to follow his example. He had set up an industry in Israel that at the time was employing eighty-five people, mostly Jews who had emigrated from Morocco, in which the top managerial positions were manned by former South African Jews.[37] To be sure, at the World Zionist Congress of 1978 Simha Ehrlich had come under fire from some delegates for what they considered the excessively warm cooperation he was conducting with the South African government. But the chairman of the South African Zionist Federation, Julius Weinstein, stoutly defended Ehrlich. He said that the Zionist Federation had implored Ehrlich to make his visit to South Africa and claimed that it had been extremely beneficial to South African Jewry, not least of all for the promotion of *aliya*, and for Zionist fund-raising. Israel was, in his view, fully justified in promoting economic relations with any and every country irrespective of its internal regime.[38]

In sum, from the point of view of the Zionist Federation, good relations between the South African and Israeli governments were a necessary precondition for the fulfillment of its tasks. It thus consistently welcomed and promoted, in whatever way it could, friendly relations and trade between the two countries. The extent to which that trade had come to include military material was not considered the legitimate concern of the Zionist Federation. That it existed could not be hidden. Rumors were rife among Jews. Those enlisted in military service knew they were sometimes using weapons made in or licensed from Israel. Visits by ranking military experts from Israel, no matter how secretive, did not entirely evade the eyes of ordinary members of the Jewish community, not to speak of its communal leadership. However, substantiated knowledge of the exact nature and extent of the military-related cooperation between the two countries was extremely elusive. Indeed, the precise details of this cooperation were so exclusively conducted and closely guarded by the military establishments of the two governments that even their foreign affairs personnel, including Israel's serving diplomats in South Africa, were probably kept in the dark.[39] Be that as it may, in consistently welcoming improved relations between Israel and South Africa, the leadership of the Zionist Federation—or for that matter of the Board of Deputies and all other communal institutions—had no interest in making a distinction between commercial and military relations.

Since it is known that the Jewish communal leadership included many individuals who were genuinely opposed to the whole apartheid system—some of them politically active—it may well be suggested that sheer cognitive dissonance placed them in a state of denial in this regard. At the same time, the alarmingly antisemitic overtones of vitriolic anti-Israel propaganda, increasingly disseminated by Muslim groups and resonating in the black liberation movement, had the effect of galvanizing all Jewish opinion in unqualified defense of Israel. This rallying Jewish response went back to what was perceived by all Jews as the notorious calumny equating Zionism with racism that the Arab states and their Soviet supporters maneuvered through the United Nations General Assembly in 1975. At that time, the Zionist Federation jointly with the Jewish Board of Deputies vigorously launched a series of protest rallies. The Federation issued this media statement:

This unbelievable resolution has further degraded the United Nations Organization by introducing a distinct element of anti-Semitism into the deliberations of the world body. . . . This resolution is not only a slur against Israel, but against the whole Jewish people which has suffered more than any other from racial discrimination. The Jewish community of South Africa, in whose name we speak, is overwhelmingly Zionist in its sentiments and outlook and will take a steadfast stand against this vicious onslaught on the ideals of the world body.[40]

The Zionist Federation's information department had its hands full coping with anti-Israel manifestations that marked off Israel from all the countries that had relations with South Africa and insidiously depicted Israel as a kindred racist spirit and the arch-ally of apartheid South Africa. Such accusations were vigorously refuted as calumnies, which cynically hid the truth that Arab states such as Saudi Arabia and Kuwait were crucial suppliers of oil to South Africa, whereas Israel–South Africa trade accounted for less than 1 percent of either country's imports and European powers such as France provided South Africa with important military resources. Israel's cordial and cooperative relationship with South Africa was defended as a legitimate expression of its vital national interests when one after another of the African states, with whom Israel had cultivated the most friendly and helpful relations, turned their backs on Israel in compliance with Arab pressure. Stress was placed on the fact that "successive Israeli governments and their ambassadors in Pretoria have made it abundantly clear that this relationship is a matter of national self-interest which in no way implies endorsement of South Africa's internal policies."[41]

Precisely because denunciation of Israel's relations with South Africa was suffused with patently antisemitic motifs, Zionist counterpropaganda went a long way toward satisfying the almost existential need felt by Jews to justify these relations. But as we have noted in the previous chapter, they scarcely made a dent in the receptivity of Muslim and allied elements within the black public to the Arab-inspired and Soviet-backed propaganda war against Zionism and Israel. This had a deep and lasting influence on both the African National Congress in exile and its liberation movement counterparts struggling inside South Africa. Although perturbed by this, the Zionist Federation was unable to muster the will, nerve, and enterprise to launch a concerted endeavor aimed at influencing black opinion against such overwhelming odds. With its sights focused solely on its inherent purposes relating to Israel, it was dependent first and foremost on the continued goodwill of the white government. To all intents and purposes, it was locked into the white-dominated South African system.

It followed that the Zionist Federation was alarmed when Israel, responding to heavy American pressure, began seriously to reconsider its relations with South Africa in 1986. It undertook endeavors to dissuade Israel's government from falling in line with the imposition of severe international sanctions on South Africa. Of course, the fact that leading liberals, notably Helen Suzman, took a stand against sanctions on the grounds that they would do more to harm the victims of apartheid than to defeat apartheid facilitated intervention of the Zionist Federation.

Never before had it taken so unequivocal and energetic a stand on a political issue. Its actions stood in striking contrast to Jewish self-restraint shown in the 1960s despite the palpable harm that Israel's active role in international opposition to apartheid caused to the community at that time.

In July 1986 Zionist Federation chairman Morris Friedman went directly to Israel's Foreign Ministry, appealing against the impending application of sanctions. He argued not only that many opponents of apartheid were against sanctions but also that Israel's actions would have an effect greatly detrimental to the Zionist organization's most important work in South Africa—fostering the live connection of Jews with Israel and facilitating *aliya*.[42] In September 1987 Israel duly fell in line with the international imposition of sanctions but tempered its actions by declaring that it could not break existing contracts; it would only undertake not to renew them. In an effort to avert punitive suspension of permission for monetary transfers to Israel, representatives of the Federation and the Board, respectively Julius Weinstein and Gerald Leissner, met with South Africa's minister for foreign affairs, Pik Botha, to discuss the subject. The minister showed sympathetic understanding and said he would advise the Treasury that transfer of funds should not be suspended.[43]

Once again the Jewish community had to weather an extreme oscillation in Israel's relations with South Africa. It carried on uninterruptedly with the fundraising work for the Jewish Agency of Israel that it had maintained ever since permission to transfer funds had been renewed in 1967. But acquiescence in, or paralytic disregard of, burgeoning Israel–South African cooperation in military-related spheres took its toll within Zionist ranks. As has already been related in the previous chapter, throughout the 1970s and 1980s there were periodic eruptions of internal discord emanating from the leadership of the Zionist youth movements and university students' Jewish associations.[44]

At successive conferences of the Zionist Federation the youth movement and student delegates gave vent to deep feelings of disapproval and embarrassment at what they perceived as the complacent satisfaction of the Zionist Federation with the close military relationship that had developed between the Israeli and South African governments. The national chairman of the South African Union of Jewish Students (SAUJS), Neville Eisenberg, told a conference in 1982 that the students were hard put to defend the case of Zionism as the national liberation movement they sincerely believed it to be. They had to bear the brunt of increasingly vicious attacks launched at rallies of solidarity with the Palestinians when the attackers were able to draw upon the spectacle of close Israeli military collaboration with the apartheid government. "What other section of the South African Jewish community is so openly and aggressively confronted with blatant anti-Israeli propaganda by their colleagues and peers?" he asked. "Our very right to exist as Jews and Zionists is contested almost on a daily basis." He said that Jewish students could not allow themselves the luxury of detachment from the realities of South African society. They were under constant pressure to take a stand in terms of their own Jewish heritage. In support of this view, the current leader of Habonim and chairman of the Zionist Youth Council, Johnny Broomberg, declared with much passion:

> It is not easy for us as young Zionists because of world trends which seem to link Zionism with racism and . . . seek to portray South Africa and Israel as partners in a racialist, imperialist nexus. . . . For us, as young people, who abhor apartheid and everything that it stands for, it is not easy to stand by and watch the ideals and values which we hold so dear linked with a value system which we hate so much.[45]

Such passionate outbursts by the Zionist youth prodded the conscience of many a senior Zionist in the community, but could scarcely counter the Zionist Federation's fundamental interest in promoting good South Africa–Israel relations and the communal policy to which it adhered of avoiding any involvement in South African politics.

By the same token, throughout the apartheid era the Zionist Federation managed to keep scrupulously clear of any political trouble with the governmental authorities. Only two inconsequential brushes with the government's security police are worthy of mention. One concerned the Hashomer Hatza'ir youth movement, which was an integral part of the South African Zionist Youth Council within the Federation structure. Having over the years interrogated several radicals who had at some time been members of Hashomer Hatza'ir, the South African security police had cause to be suspicious of this particular youth movement. It is very likely that the movement was under police surveillance. In 1956 one of the Israeli Hashomer Hatza'ir emissaries (*shlichim*) to the local movement, Heinie Bornstein, was called in for police questioning on the movement's suspected Marxist ideology and activities.[46] But the authorities appear to have been satisfied that there was no cause for preventative or punitive action, notwithstanding Hashomer Hatza'ir's socialist ideology, because the movement was clearly focused on the ideal of settlement in Israeli kibbutz communes. Within the Jewish community, however, Hashomer Hatza'ir's reputation as a nursery for radical socialist ideas that could lead to local political embroilment deterred many parents from allowing their children to join the movement. This was a major factor in the drastic decline of the movement's membership. Another was the movement's dogmatic insistence that its seniors had no place in its ranks unless they committed themselves to settlement on a kibbutz, forgoing university study in favor of trades or agricultural training. Even so, until the late 1950s Hashomer Hatza'ir, although by then a mere shadow of its former self, was still shedding, so to speak, a few recruits for the radical opposition to the apartheid regime. Mostly they were rank-and-file operatives in the radical resistance whose names have remained in obscurity. One example was Leslie Stein, who while serving as the organizing secretary of the movement in the late 1950s was attracted into the Trotskyist circle headed by former Hashomer Hatza'ir activist Baruch Hirson. Stein left Hashomer Hatza'ir and undertook trade union work, becoming full-time organizer of the white Union of Distributive Workers and unofficial part-time organizer of the African hospital orderlies. However, after experiencing a number of scary visits by the security police, Stein decided to leave the country. In 1960 he went to England and later settled in Australia.[47]

As late as 1970, by which time Hashomer Hatza'ir was reduced to only a few tens of members, the security police questioned an emissary serving in the movement. He was Baruch Reitstein, a South African–born graduate of the movement who had settled in kibbutz Barka'i in Israel. It was in all likelihood no coincidence that the officer assigned to the task of questioning him was also a Jew (a rarity in the police service), Maurice Edelstein. The fact that Reitstein's sister, Amy Thornton, was a known radical opponent of apartheid who had been detained by the police no doubt heightened police suspicions concerning Reitstein's work in Hashomer Hatza'ir. However, by all known accounts Edelstein appears to have been satisfied that the diminutive movement was by now truly innocuous. Not long after, following consultation with the Hashomer Hatzai'r world movement's headquarters in Israel, a decision was taken in the Zionist Federation to close its South African branch. The proximity of this decision to the security police questioning of the movement's emissary was conducive to a myth that the police had intimidated the Zionist Federation.[48] However, the records of the Zionist Federation's honorary officers' deliberations do not bear this out. Rather, the closure of Hashomer Hatza'ir was motivated primarily by the inordinate cost of maintaining a movement so tiny in membership.[49]

Another marginal brush that the Zionist Federation had with the authorities was occasioned by the arrest and detention of one of its employees, Esther Levitan. As has been mentioned in an earlier chapter of this book, Levitan was for a time a paid worker in the offices of the Women's Zionist Organization, which was in turn a constituent part of the Zionist Federation. In January 1982 she was arrested in a sudden security police swoop on the offices of the women's organization. As it happened, the police evinced no suspicion that her Zionist work was related to her antiapartheid activities. The incident of her arrest did, however, cause nervous concern on the part of the Zionist leadership. The Federation's honorary officers now discussed adding a question on its staff application form to ascertain whether the prospective employee was connected to any proscribed political activity.[50] On the other hand, the Federation's chairman, Isaac Kalmanowitz, and executive director, Herbie Rosenberg, in their capacity as her employers, also decided to do everything possible to be of help to her. When Esther Levitan was at last released after a number of months of detention, the honorary officers, after consultation with the Jewish Board of Deputies, unanimously decided that she should be fully reinstated as a member of the Zionist Federation's staff.[51]

Expansion of Jewish Education

The declining fortune of Zionism within the community's institutional structure—but, it should be emphasized, not in respect of the identity mode of most Jews—was only one aspect of the transformation the Jewish community was undergoing. Another aspect was, of course, demographic. We have already referred to Professor Allie Dubb's estimate that 21,000 Jews emigrated from South Africa between 1970 and 1979, and a further 18,000 between 1980 and 1991.[52] This emigration, mainly of young people, placed the community in a condition of chronic demographic decline. Dubb estimated that whereas in 1980 there were an estimated 117,963 Jews, by 1991 there were between 91,925 and 105,711. This constituted only some 0.3 percent of all South Africans and between 1.8 and 2.1 percent of whites. The contrast with the Jewish population's historical peak of 4.5 percent of all whites in 1936 or even 4.4 percent in 1946 is telling.

Yet, it might be said that this quantitative erosion of the Jewish community was balanced by two compensatory qualitative gains. One was the phenomenal expansion of Jewish education, the other the remarkable turn to religiosity. The outcome was a perceptively shrinking community, but one whose core was becoming more intensely Jewish. At the same time, as we shall see, the swelling cost of Jewish day schools strained the coffers of the Jewish community to the breaking point. Consequently, gaining state support for Jewish education became a necessity, making the community's interrelationship with the state's educational authorities a matter of critical importance.

Until the creation of day schools in the 1950s Jewish education had been a rather neglected aspect of Jewish life in South Africa. In the small towns, the teaching of children was left to the Jewish congregational minister, and in the large cities, such as Johannesburg and Cape Town, it was provided in a form of afternoon classes popularly called *cheder* (literally, room, that is, the room in the teacher's home, as had been common in traditionalist eastern Europe) but more properly named Talmud Torah (literally Bible study) schools.[53] Only the rudiments of Hebrew, prayers, Bible, and basic observances were taught, generally not beyond the age of thirteen, when these studies were capped and concluded by the bar mitzvah ceremony conducted in a synagogue. Initially the Talmud Torah schools were the responsibility of independent congregations, and tuition was mostly in the hands of professionally unqualified teachers belonging to the Litvak immigrant generation. Local training of teachers only began as late as 1944, when the Rabbi Zlotnik-Avida Hebrew Teachers' Training College was established in Johannesburg.

Not until the late 1920s were the first steps taken to coordinate these disparate afternoon schools. In 1928, on the initiative of Chief Rabbi Landau, the Zionist Federation and the Jewish Board of Deputies convened the first effectual conference on Jewish education. It issued in the creation of a special South African Board of Jewish Education. In 1932 a separate Cape Board of Jewish Education was established as the administrative and supervisory body for the Cape Town area.

The ideological foundation of Jewish education was a subject of sometimes heated controversy. There was a consensus on its essentially Zionist orientation, but not on the degree of orthodox religious compliance required of teachers and tuition. The religious Zionist party, Mizrahi, headed by Rabbi Isaac Kossowsky, not only opposed inclusion of progressive Judaism's schools but also disapproved of what it considered the lax approach to orthodox observance, and the superficial religious content, of the afternoon schools. Rabbi Kossowsky insisted that the Board should "guide, direct and control" Jewish education along orthodox lines, and demanded that "whatever the degree of Jewishness in the South African community, its teachers and educationalists must be religious men." His demands met with opposition from leaders of the other Zionist parties.[54]

Finally, at the seventh conference of the South African Board of Jewish Education in March 1945, the ideological question was thrashed out in a major debate. A compromise formula was at last reached for incorporation into the Board's constitution: "Jewish education based on broadly national-traditional lines, it being understood, however, that the Board will render educational service to any institution which requires and applies for such service."[55] This was a compromise formula authentically mirroring the South African Jew's normative code of identity. Thus, the "traditional" facet of the formula aimed to expose the pupil to a modicum of observance and knowledge of basic texts, concepts, rituals, and values of orthodox Judaism, while the "national" facet aimed to foster identification with the Jewish national revival epitomized by the Zionist movement and Israel. The formula's adoption signified a tolerant and noncoercive disposition in the matter of actual observance, thereby reflecting recognition of the rather lax mode of observance in most pupils' homes. This compromise formula fell far short of the aspirations of the leaders of Mizrahi, who had unsuccessfully fought for the wording to be "*strict* national-traditional lines." But they had succeeded at least insofar as progressive Judaism was implicitly denied any formal status on the Board of Education or in the formulation of its curriculum.

Building on the "national traditional" ideological foundation, the idea of a Jewish day school had a prolonged germination within the two Boards of Jewish Education in the 1940s. In Cape Town, an amalgamated "United Hebrew School" had evolved by 1940 into a small elementary-level day school whose classrooms were used as an afternoon school for older age-groups. Out of this nucleus several day schools developed in suburbs of Cape Town, crowned by the founding of Herzlia high school in 1956. In Johannesburg, the Board of Jewish Education founded its first day school at elementary level in January 1948, out of which grew the impressive King David schools network, whose first high school was founded in 1955. By 1967 there were fourteen such schools, encompassing 5,500 primary and secondary schoolchildren or about 30 percent of the Jewish population of school age. Research conducted in the 1970s showed that in 1974 about 40 percent of the five to seventeen age-group were in Jewish day schools.[56] By the 1980s the percentage estimated to be in all of South Africa's Jewish day schools had reached 60 percent, and by the year 2000 it exceeded 80 percent.[57]

How is one to account for this phenomenal expansion of Jewish education manifested mainly in the growth of the day schools? The founding of these schools coincided with the ascent to power of the Afrikaner nationalists, but as the preceding survey indicates, the ideological-educational basis of day school education was laid well before 1948. No doubt part of the explanation lies in the tremendous stimulation for Hebrew study provided by the creation of the State of Israel, which in turn spurred the dedicated efforts of a nucleus of professional educators, notably Rabbi Isaac Goss, director of the Board of Jewish Education since 1949, together with lay leaders such as the Board's early chairmen Solly Yellin, Louis Sachs, and Ivan Greenstein. By dint of ardent conviction and dedication, they were able to mobilize public support and promote the ideological rationale for day schools as the preferred mode of modern Jewish education. As in other communities of the Jewish Diaspora, they had to dispel the apprehension that it meant "segregation" of Jewish children from their peers in the majority society (in this case, white society). It was argued that this would accentuate differences and thus render Jewish children less capable of mixing freely with their fellow citizens in later life.

Rabbi Kopul Rosen, a pioneer of Jewish day school education in Britain and an inspiring public speaker, was invited to help in presenting the case of day school advocates. He argued that the best education was one that produced a well-balanced and harmonious person, and a Jewish child was more likely to develop into such a person in a school where he could experience a complete sense of belonging, had no minority inhibitions, and imbibed a positive and knowledgeable Jewish identity.[58] The graduate of the Jewish day school, it was argued, would be all the better equipped as a self-respecting and confident citizen and member of society. Rabbi Isaac Goss reasoned that only the day school could provide a wholesome synthesis of Jewish studies and Jewish living. "Let us not be frightened by those who like raising the bugaboo of 'segregation,'" he declared; they were merely echoing the views of non-Zionists who raised the bugaboo of dual loyalty. "Why," he asked, "is 'segregation' something that applies only to the Jewish day school and why does it not stand in the way of Jews congregating in sports clubs?"[59]

Eloquent as the proponents of the day schools might have been, their rationale would not have resonated as well as it did within the Jewish public if not for the deeply rooted ethnic identification that characterized the Jews of South Africa. Whatever weakening of ethnic bonds had come to pass through acculturation of the second generation after immigration had been much repaired and bolstered by the experience of antisemitism throughout the two decades preceding the accession of the Afrikaner nationalist government in 1948. Concurrently Jewish ethnic solidarity had been greatly reinforced by the upsurge of Zionist identification that accompanied the creation of Israel. Moreover, Jews were complete outsiders to the assertive Afrikaner political and cultural hegemony that the elections of 1948 inaugurated, and they feared its implications for their own future. Against this background, one may understand the appeal that a protective day school ambience had for many Jewish parents. It would spare their children exposure to the type of inhospitable school environment they had themselves experienced or now anticipated.

Above and beyond these considerations there was another facet of the cultural and educational policies attendant upon Afrikaner nationalist hegemony that may well have influenced the inward turn of Jews to an educational shell of their own. Much as we have noted that the dualism of the society fostered and legitimized an ethnic mode of Jewish identity, so it is plausible to suggest that the insistence of the politically ascendant Afrikaner segment on its own school system rooted in "Christian National Education" (CNE) tended to legitimize the development of Jewish "national-traditional" day schools. After all, "Christian National" meant not only the particular principle that a Christian education for Afrikaners had to be "based on the Holy Scripture and expressed in the Articles of Faith of our three Afrikaans churches," but also the general principle that "instruction and education of the children of European parents must be carried out on the basis of their parents' attitudes to life and to the world."[60]

Afrikaner observers sometimes regarded Jewish educational policy as a legitimate counterpart of their own CNE credo. As a columnist in *Die Transvaler* once put it: "The national-traditional policy is aimed at inculcating Jewish nationalism and the Jewish faith in Jewish children. This is the equivalent of South African Christian National Education."[61] However, there is no evidence that the Jewish formula was consciously copied from the Afrikaner example. Indeed, while CNE was systematically being formulated in the 1940s, the relationship between Jews and nationalist Afrikaners was at its nadir, and Jews tended to view CNE as yet another reactionary, and therefore potentially anti-Jewish, expression of Afrikaner nationalism.[62] As we have noted earlier, the Jewish policy emerged in the purely internal context of compromise between proponents of strict traditional-national (meaning orthodox-Zionist) education on the one hand, and of a laxer and more secularized national (Zionist) outlook on the other. The "national-traditional" formula was thus in its very essence different in intent from that of CNE. It is rather in a purely phenomenological sense that the Jewish community's concept of Jewish education had points of similarity with that of CNE, insofar as it too rested on the premise that the education of Jewish children ought to be conducted in the Jewish community's own schools and firmly rooted in their own religious-ethnic identity. Therefore, it was not explicitly in composing the "national-traditional" formula for Jewish education that CNE had influence but rather in regard to its implicit retrospective legitimization.

Furthermore, although CNE, as officially expounded, remained the preserve of the Afrikaans schools, which were attended by very few Jewish pupils, the vague specter of it being imposed also upon English-language schools aroused the apprehensions of Jews. After all, compulsory religious instruction applied also to the English-language schools, and the syllabus prescribed was explicitly Christian in spirit. Indeed, concern in the Jewish community was heightened after the enactment of a National Education Policy Act in 1967, which required in more general terms that all education in state schools have a "Christian character." The Jewish Board of Deputies, sensing that the trend was toward stricter compliance with this principle, took the matter up in a protracted series of representations to the Ministry of Education. In 1973, the Board resolutely adopted the view that Jewish children should not be exposed to Christian-centric instruction. Although the ministry remained firm in its policy, it treated Jewish concerns with understanding and made allowance for the right to withdraw pupils from the compulsory religious instruction classes.[63] Chief Rabbi Casper, who had from the outset taken a lead in dealing with this problem, undertook to shape an alternative system of Jewish religious instruction for withdrawal classes. In cooperation with the Pedagogic Center of the Board of Jewish Education and with partial funding from the United Communal Fund, a curriculum based on a series of readings and written assignments was devised. Within a year, some three thousand Jewish pupils in various high schools throughout the country were encompassed by this scheme. Although the issue was thus satisfactorily settled, the solution was of course far from providing an adequate Jewish education and manifestly demonstrated the great advantages of the Jewish day school.

It is perhaps ironic that, on the one hand, a state whose social and political structure was so conducive to the development of segmented ethnic or private schooling was, on the other hand, loath to provide any subsidization for such schooling. In South Africa, responsibility for education was vested in the provinces, which, except for Natal, chose not to provide state support for private schools. In the comparative perspective of other pluralistic or dualistic societies, the Jews of South Africa were thus at a great disadvantage in developing Jewish day schools. For example, in Canada's province of Quebec, which had dual French and English streams of education in many respects paralleling the duality of white South Africa, Jewish day schools were able to obtain substantial state support for the secular hours of study they provided. By contrast, the Jewish day schools of South Africa remained almost wholly dependent on the voluntary resources of the Jewish community for over three decades.

The phenomenal growth of the Jewish day schools placed an enormous financial burden on the Jewish community. Although South African Jews were well accustomed to philanthropy for overseas relief in Europe and even more so in Israel, the scale of fund-raising now required for local Jewish education was unprecedented. In these circumstances it was soon clear that the Board of Jewish Education's funding needs had hopelessly outstripped its income from endowments, fees, and its share of the United Communal Fund operated by the Board of Deputies. By 1952 the Board of Education was in the throes of escalating financial difficulties and began to appeal for aid to the Zionist Federation as the premier communal institution and one of its parent founding bodies. This appeal precipitated a grave dilemma and ongoing controversy within the community in general and the Zionist Federation in particular. The question was, Is it justified to use funds specifically raised to serve the dire human needs of Jewish immigration and welfare in Israel for the local purposes of a basically comfortable, if not opulent, Jewish public? Yet it was no less on the basis of explicit Zionist assumptions that the Board of Education's lay leaders, themselves mostly active Zionists, appealed for help. In the continuing debate that dominated Zionist conferences throughout the 1950s and 1960s, the proponents of using Israel United Appeal (IUA) funds either as grants or loans to help Jewish education out of its difficulties contended that the promotion of Jewish "national-traditional" education was a fundamental Zionist duty. Indeed, they were able to invoke repeated resolutions of the World Zionist Organization affirming that "Zionism considers the Hebrew education of the young generation a fundamental task of our people and every Zionist is duty-bound to extend his fullest assistance in the fulfilment of this task."[64]

The controversy reached a crescendo at the 1959 conference of the Zionist Federation when Solly Yellin, the current chairman of the Board of Jewish Education, presented with great emotion the case for the Zionist obligation of the Federation to allocate a portion of IUA funds to Jewish schools. "The Board of Education feels that it is entitled to use Zionist funds for Jewish education because Jewish education means Zionism," declared Yellin. Yet, the inhibitions of the majority at the conference were so great that Yellin's plea was rejected. The view prevailed that separate funds must be raised for the Board of Education. "I believe that the Jews in this country want Hebrew education and will pay for it," stated Zionist leader Simon Kuper. "At a Zionist Conference let us not talk about taking money which we raise for Israel for the local needs of our community."[65]

Investigations into the financing of Jewish education conducted by two separate commissions, one headed by Judge Simon Kuper in Johannesburg and the other by Judge Joseph Herbstein in Cape Town, failed to produce agreement on the legitimacy of using IUA funds for local Jewish educational needs. Not until 1974 did the Zionist Federation at last reach a decision to seek permission from the Jewish Agency in Jerusalem to allocate financial aid for the Board of Jewish Education. The grants ultimately permitted commenced with R 1 million over a three-year period, R 333,000 annually.[66] This rose considerably after renegotiation in the late 1970s, reaching an annual peak of R 1 million but then declining to R 500,000 in 1982.

Nevertheless, in the absence of state funding, the escalating expense incurred by the phenomenal expansion of day schools was bound to reach crisis proportions. By the late 1970s it seemed that only the Herzlia schools in Cape Town were managing to keep their heads above water thanks largely to effective participation of pupils' parents in the United Communal Fund's campaign. Cape Town also managed to create a local endowment fund that was able to subsidize the fees for almost one-fifth of the pupils.[67] But overall, the national Board of Jewish Education was in desperate straits. In 1974 it relinquished its own inadequate fund-raising effort and committed itself instead to participating actively in the United Communal Fund's (UCF) campaign of which it was a major beneficiary. But targets set failed to be met, and the Board in fact suffered further drops in its income. Moreover, as a fundamental principle of mutual community responsibility, the Jewish schools were committed to subsidization of any pupil whose parents could not afford the full fees. An average of some 20 percent of the income from fees was needed for this purpose. Only by continuously obtaining aid from the IUA, despite strong objections from part of the Jewish community, and by risking dangerous levels of debt, did the school system maintain itself.[68]

It was in an atmosphere of crisis that the Board of Education's Golden Jubilee Conference met in August 1978. Chairman Ivan Greenstein reported an anticipated deficit for the year 1978 of R 1.3 million, nearly half being interest on total liabilities of R 5.5 million. "The prognosis is so critical," said Greenstein, "that, unless a considerable injection of money is forthcoming immediately, I have grave doubts whether we will be able to continue with Jewish education."[69] The conclusion was becoming inescapable that only a measure of state aid could save the day.

If the Jewish leadership now could muster the confidence to broach the matter with the authorities, it was thanks to the more comfortable rapport with the government that accrued from its markedly improved relations with the State of Israel. In addition, the Jewish leaders could anticipate that what appeared to be the government's veering toward "reform" of the apartheid system might signify less rigidity in general. The Jewish Board of Deputies' campaign for state aid had formidable allies in the long-established networks of Catholic and Anglican private schools. Alongside them it was able to argue that parents had a universally recognized right to send their children to whatever school they wished and as taxpaying citizens they could expect the government to fulfill its obligation to help educate them. The state, it was claimed, should be paying the same for children in the private schools as it would if they were in public schools, including capital expenditure. Only expenses over and above that should be at the cost of the parents. Hopes were raised in 1979 when an Education Amendment Ordinance of the Transvaal Province's Education Department indicated that schools in financial difficulty might apply for assistance. However, after a delay of two years, nothing came of this, as the department concluded that it did not have the necessary budget.[70]

Notwithstanding all endeavors made within the Jewish community, the education crisis loomed ever larger. By 1985 the Board of Jewish Education's chairman warned that unless a target of R 20 million was reached within a few months, the five day schools under its wing would face closure or, at the very least, a radical reduction in pupils and staff members.[71] At this critical juncture the community leaders launched an imaginative and daring rescue campaign that at last pulled the Jewish educational system back from the edge of the precipice. It came to be known as the "debenture campaign." Energetically led by two very successful company executives, Gerald Leissner, managing director of Anglo-American Property Services, who was chairman of Yeshiva College, and Monty Hilkowitz, managing director of the immense Liberty Life insurance company, the campaign raised emergency funds through either outright donations or pledges that provided interest-free loans over a ten-year period in return for debentures underwritten by the Standard Bank of South Africa. By dint of Leissner's and Hilkowitz's ability to gain the trust of the bank and to mobilize across-the-board support of the Jewish public, the debenture scheme succeeded in wiping out a significant part of the Board's debt. To be sure, only a little over half of the target of R 20 million was reached, but many of the contributors in the end voluntarily wrote off the money owed to them. For the time being, collapse of the Board's educational edifice was averted.

Meanwhile, under pressure from the mainly Christian private schools, the provincial education authorities were at last coming round to recognition of claims to state aid. However, whereas by 1982 the Cape and Natal Provinces were providing subsidies, the Transvaal, which contained the overwhelming majority of Jewish day school pupils, failed to follow suit.[72] Hopes were again raised in the mid-1980s when F. W. de Klerk, at the time minister of national education, moved toward a new dispensation for the registration and financing of private schools as a responsibility of the national government. He announced that the government was ready to enter into negotiations with the representatives of private schools with a view to granting subsidies. The Board of Jewish Education's leaders formed the impression that the volte-face had come about because the government, foreseeing the end of apartheid, had in mind the possible future interests of Afrikaans private schools in a postapartheid society.[73] Be that as it may, negotiations were entered into in concert with other private schools. Jeffrey Bortz, who led the Jewish representations, succeeded in bringing them to a satisfactory conclusion by mid-1986. Most of the issues of concern to the Jewish community were resolved. Foremost were formal curricular approval of Hebrew and Jewish studies and recognition of teachers for these subjects who did not necessarily have official South African qualifications.

Another issue of concern in the King David schools was policy toward acceptance of gentile pupils, although there were in fact not many applications of this sort. The resolute policy of the modern orthodox Yeshiva College as well as the smaller ultraorthodox religious schools in Johannesburg (whose growth we have yet to survey) was from the outset that they only admitted Jewish pupils. But the mainstream King David and Herzlia schools initially were open to gentile applicants, subject to the requirement of compliance with the Hebrew studies and other Judaic aspects of the schools and noneligibility for fee subsidies. Nor was there, in principle, to be exclusion of "non-white" Gentiles in the unlikely case of such applicants appearing.

In Cape Town the United Herzlia schools consistently followed what was termed an "open and flexible" policy, making no distinction between the statutory racial groups as defined by apartheid legislation. All the same the number of gentile pupils never exceeded about 100 in any given year. As late as 1999, five years after the end of the apartheid regime, there were only 95 registered gentile pupils, almost all whites. In 1987, for example, there were only 24 "non-white" pupils in all of the Herzlia schools, which encompassed a total of 1,955 pupils and accounted for an estimated 70 percent of all Jewish school-age children in the Cape peninsula.[74]

In the Transvaal, the Board of Jewish Education deliberated rather less decisively over the question of accepting "non-white" students. Special permission from the Transvaal Education Department was required before blacks could be accepted in the first place. Board of Education director Morris (Meish) Zimerman reported that in 1985 there had been ten applications by black pupils in the Transvaal. In compliance with regulations, the Board had applied for permission from the provincial Education Department. The request was rejected outright. Zimerman called for a policy decision on this sensitive matter. There was much soul-searching, but the Board did not find its way to a clear stand. The Catholic private schools had for some years followed the practice of admitting black pupils even without permission. This defiant precedent prompted several Board of Jewish Education members to urge, unsuccessfully, that the King David schools have the courage to do likewise.[75] On the one hand, the Board's executive was not prepared to defy the authorities, but, on the other hand, it shrank from the very thought of adopting a policy of exclusion or quotas for black pupils. It was, however, a relief to know that in practice very few blacks looked to the Jewish schools for their education of choice. As well as the prohibitively high private fees, the specifically Jewish religious nature of the schools was an obvious deterrent for even the few black parents who could contemplate sending their children to privileged white schools.

The more immediate concern was the possible increase in the number of white Gentiles who, seeking a private school alternative for the declining standards of the government schools, might be attracted to the King David schools.

In early 1986 there were indications that the education authorities might grant the Jewish schools some measure of much needed financial subsidization, but only on condition that they comply with its regulations debarring blacks or at least allowing only a fixed quota. After earnest discussion of this prospect, the Board of Jewish Education took the view that in principle neither exclusion of blacks nor any quota system could be countenanced. If the authorities were to insist on such conditions for the granting of subsidies, then the Board would have no choice but to decline all subsidies no matter how badly needed.[76] To the relief of the Board, its main negotiator with the authorities, Jeffrey Bortz, was able to report in May 1986 that they had withdrawn stipulations demanding that a quota be applied to black pupils.[77] No doubt this was a reflection of growing "reformed" apartheid flexibility. In 1987 ten black pupils were admitted to the King David schools. The following year it was decided that the final decision on all non-Jewish enrollment should be left to the discretion of the Board of Jewish Education's chairman and director. Implicit unofficial policy was that while the children of non-Jewish employees of the schools and the siblings of non-Jewish children already in the system would be viewed sympathetically, all other non-Jewish enrollment would be discouraged.[78] It was feared that the Jewish character of the schools would be unacceptably compromised and might even eventually be effaced by an exponential growth of gentile enrollment.

In May 1990 the Board concluded that the practice of leaving decisions to the discretion of its chairman and director was unsatisfactory and finally decided that in future no gentile pupils would be accepted; only those already in the schools would remain unaffected.[79] This decision signified the resolution of the Board of Jewish Education to preserve the exclusively Jewish composition of the King David schools. It was predicated on the conviction that the right of any religious community to educate its children in its own private schools, and also to obtain a measure of financial support from the state, was fully compatible with the democratic and culturally pluralistic principles of the anticipated new South Africa.

Meanwhile the struggle to receive state financial support for private schools continued. It was only in February 1987 that the first government grant was finally received by the King David schools, and even then the amount was disappointing. According to the Board of Education's reading of the official criteria for subsidies, it received less than a third of what it had expected. It was left with no choice other than to increase day school fees and redouble its fund-raising efforts.[80] By 1990 the financial situation of the Jewish educational system had been stabilized. Chairman Russell Gaddin was able to inform the Board of Education conference that for the first time in many years financial crisis was not the watchword of all deliberations. He reported that in the previous year R 25 million had been collected in fees, the United Communal Fund (combined with the Israeli United Appeal since 1986) and the government had each contributed R 5 million, and other fund-raising had added another R 5 million.[81]

Jewish education was thus fortunate to find itself in a relatively stable financial situation at a time when South Africa was reaching the critical point of transition from white supremacy to nonracial democracy. The increase in emigration that accompanied the transformation meant that the schools continued to lose pupils and therefore also income, especially since the families who had the means to emigrate were mostly the ones who had paid full fees rather than those who needed subsidization. This loss was partly offset by a dramatic exodus of Jewish pupils, as of other whites, from the government schools, motivated by perceptions of a drop in standards after schools were opened to the formerly underprivileged mass of students. As a result, enrollment in all private schools rose dramatically, and private profit-making schools sprang into existence. One of these, Crawford College, attracted a fair number of Jewish pupils. By 1997 the demographic diminution of the Jewish communities in Durban and in Pretoria resulted in an agreement whereby the Jewish day schools were taken over by Crawford College. However, it made some allowance for instruction in Hebrew and Jewish studies and religious observances. In Port Elizabeth, which suffered even greater demographic decline, the school remained in the community's hands but could maintain viability only by taking in gentile pupils, who soon became the majority.

By 1998 it was estimated that, countrywide, three out of four Jewish children (75.5 percent) in the age-groups from nursery school to high school matriculation were encompassed by the Jewish day schools (a total of 7,443 out of an estimated 9,850). The financial base of the system rested on three major sources: fees provided some R 57 million annually; the government subsidy amounted to R 5 million; and the UCF allocation to R 3.5 million. The last allocation was designated primarily for subsidization of needy parents, who constituted as much as 18 percent of the total in 1997. Because of the high rate of divorce in the community, a growing proportion of the needy were single mothers. Although still lower than most private schools, fees were beyond the means of many parents. To cope with the subsidies shortfall that remained after use of the UCF allocation, a special King David Schools Foundation was created at the end of 1996. These cumulative efforts were able to sustain the basic Jewish communal principle that all Jewish children should have access to a Jewish education. No more than a handful of needy families were lost to the system owing to lack of subsidy funds.[82]

Government aid had made a major contribution to the viability of the Jewish day school system, but it proved to be short-lived. The legacy of apartheid left the new ANC government the mammoth task of uplifting the masses of educationally underprivileged blacks. It was not likely to be in sympathy with the claims of long-privileged white private education. The obvious priorities of ANC policy were well appreciated by the Jewish community's leaders, but they also noted with gratification that the ANC promised recognition of the rights of linguistic, cultural, and religious association. In a "Policy Framework for Education and Training" that the ANC issued in January 1994 and opened to public discussion, approval was accorded to schools that promoted cultural or religious identity so long as they did not practice discrimination. Responding to this policy document, the Board of Jewish Education emphasized that its schools, although in the category of private schools, were more in the nature of "community schools" whose purpose was to promote the essential and legitimate religious and cultural needs of South African Jews. In urging the continuation of subsidies for private or community schools, the Board contended thus:

> Whatever might be the cost to the State of subsidizing these schools, this is relatively insignificant in comparison with the cost which would be incurred by the State in educating the pupils at private/community schools were they to be absorbed into the general education system. The parents and associates of private/community schools, through the fees they pay and contributions they make to such schools, in effect save the State the expenditure, which the State would otherwise need to incur in educating the pupils at these schools.[83]

But this argument failed to carry weight with the new ANC government, and after incrementally reducing the scale of the government subsidy, in 1998 it devised a new formula whereby any school whose fees were "higher than 2.5 times the provincial average public cost per learner in ordinary public schools" would not be eligible for a subsidy.[84] Since the estimated cost of Jewish day school education was far in excess of this, it meant the end of the short-lived era of state aid. Thus, at the turn of the century the now fast-diminishing Jewish community had again to cope, by drawing entirely on its own voluntary resources, with what had developed into a ramified network of day schools whose demographic comprehensiveness was among the highest in all the communities of the Jewish Diaspora.

Turning toward Religiosity

By the 1990s the problem of funding the day schools was more than vying with Israel-directed Zionist work as the central axis around which Jewish communal activity turned and on which its leaders interacted with governmental authorities. This in itself marked a transformation of the community's character. But even more transforming in effect was the leadership's grappling with the ideological question, What are the goals of Jewish education? For the expansion of Jewish schooling, however welcomed, did not in itself resolve the controversy over the desirable quotient of religious content—a divisive issue that had preceded the creation of the day schools. The "broadly national-traditional" formula was a compromise that merely mirrored the norms of mainstream Jewish identity in the community.

These norms have been aptly described as "non-observant Orthodoxy."[85] Broadly speaking, they amounted to a mode of Jewishness characterized by deeply ingrained ethnic consciousness as well as recognition of, and respect for, the orthodox rabbinate and synagogue as *the* authentic expression of Judaism. Attendant upon this mode of Jewish identity were strong inhibitions concerning mixed marriage and also broad acceptance of orthodox auspices for basic rites of passage such as male circumcision, bar mitzvah, marriage, and burial. It meant, further, a relatively high level of formal affiliation to synagogue congregations and observance of selected elements of ritual observance, mainly those relating to kashrut (dietary laws), the Yom Kippur fast day, the Passover seder (festive meal), and the sanctification of the family Sabbath eve meal with candles and the kiddush (benediction over wine). At the same time, this mode of Jewishness involved little in the way of compliance with fundamental orthodox theological beliefs concerning God, His covenant (*brit*) with the Children of Israel, and divine revelation of the Holy Torah. Moreover, it did not mean high levels of synagogue attendance, not even on the all-important Sabbath day. Indeed, one striking peculiarity of the norms of Sabbath observance in South African Jewry had long been considerably higher attendance at Friday evening than Sabbath morning services, but even then arrival and departure by motor vehicle.

This generalized description is borne out by several social research surveys. Thus a mid-1970s survey showed that only 5.3 percent of Jews had no connection with any kind of synagogue, 77.1 percent supported orthodox synagogues, and only 16.6 percent reform (progressive) temples. Yom Kippur was observed by 88.9 percent of households (although not necessarily by fasting fully) and the Passover seder by 94 percent. Only 9.2 percent fully observed the Sabbath as a strict day of rest, but Sabbath eve lighting of candles was observed by 83.9 percent and kiddush by 67.6 percent. Kashrut was strictly observed by only 27.5 percent.[86]

The educational ethos of the King David and Herzlia day schools network, whose development was traced above, mirrored these characteristically South African norms of Jewishness. It was an educational ethos described by Professor Bernard Steinberg, a specialist in history of education, as "a compromise that attempts to comply with the outlook of the average South African Jew who cannot be described as thoroughly orthodox and yet for whom continued Jewish existence and group identity are vital considerations."[87] Only against this background can one appreciate the profound influence on the community's religious life exerted by the further ramification of Jewish schooling, which is now to be described. For, from the outset, rabbis who aspired to a deepening of religious observance in the community were critical of what was regarded as the new day schools' superficial religious content. Particularly dissatisfied were the rabbis of the Mizrahi national-religious party of Zionism, led by Rabbi Michael Kossowsky, the son of Isaac Kossowsky who, in the 1940s, had fought within the Jewish Board of Education for "strict" national-traditional education. Having lost that battle, these rabbis sought to develop an alternative educational stream. The turn to greater religiosity within the community was largely an outgrowth of their efforts. One may trace its beginnings to the creation in 1951 of the first homegrown nucleus of a yeshiva (religious study academy) type of school by the youth section of the Mizrahi movement, known as Hashomer Hadati (the Religious Guard) and after 1952 as Bnei Akiva (the Sons of Akiva). Initially it provided only afternoon classes, but in 1954 it began to provide full-day instruction for about fifty part-time pupils,[88] and in 1957 it was transformed into a fully fledged day school functioning parallel to the King David and Herzlia type of day schools of the Boards of Jewish Education. Now named Yeshiva College, it combined as thorough a secular curriculum as the other schools together with enhanced religious (Torah) study and also Hebrew in the modern idiom. It developed into a complex of schools in the Glenhazel suburb of Johannesburg, which was fast becoming a major Jewish population center. In 1963 Rabbi Avraham Tanzer, an American-educated rabbi, became Rosh Yeshiva (principal) of the Yeshiva College complex. Concurrently, he was the founding rabbi of the flourishing Glenhazel Hebrew congregation, in turn largely generated and nurtured by the Yeshiva College complex.

Although the original core of pupils in the Yeshiva College complex was from fully orthodox observant homes, it also accepted pupils from homes with a lax mode of observance. It soon became evident that in many cases the pupils were becoming more observant than their parents. Yeshiva College was becoming an important factor in the process that turned part of the Jewish community toward greater religiosity. By 1968 over 400 pupils were enrolled in the Yeshiva College complex, which now included two primary schools (opened in 1966 and 1967). A high school for girls opened in 1969. The total number of pupils rose to 770 by 1985.[89] Not only did some graduates spend a year or more at overseas yeshivas, mostly in Israel, but the Yeshiva College educational complex itself also streamed some graduate pupils into an advanced yeshiva framework—the Solomon L. Bronner Rabbinical Academy—which in turn gave rise to an independent full-scale Yeshiva-Gedola (Higher Yeshiva) established in 1979. Headed by Rabbi Azriel Goldfein, a graduate of the Telshe Yeshiva of Cleveland in the United States, it declared itself committed to "the long-term needs of the South African Jewish community—not encouraging its students to emigrate, nor undertaking the caring of distant vineyards at the cost of neglecting one's own vineyard."[90] It graduated rabbis, educators, and *shohtim* (ritual slaughterers). A number of its graduates went on to further yeshiva studies overseas and returned to become rabbis in the South African Jewish community. One notable example was Rabbi Lewis Furman, who later applied his charisma as a religious instructor to the outreach programs of Ohr Somayach.

It was thus out of a segment of the hegemonic Zionist core of the Jewish community—the Mizrahi party—that the seeds of an exponentially more strictly religious educational system emanated. That this should be so is somewhat ironic in light of the eventual weakening of the Zionist organizational structure described earlier in this chapter. For, as will later be shown, the intensified religiosity generated by the new strictly religious schools appears to have filled the void left by the contraction and attrition of Zionism itself.

Concurrently, but quite independently of these initiatives of the religious-Zionist Mizrahi party, in 1957 Chief Rabbi Louis Rabinowitz established his own training program for Jewish ministers. Its earliest graduates included three South African–born rabbis who were to make a significant mark on the religious and educational development of the community. One was Ben Isaacson, whose extraordinary record of public protest against apartheid has been discussed in an earlier part of this book, as has also that of Rabinowitz's second protégé, Abner Weiss. The third was Gerald Mazabow, who became a foremost educator.

The existence of the Yeshiva College network, providing a Jewish education in the spirit long advocated by the orthodox rabbinate, did not mean that the rabbis ceased taking an interest in the mainline day school system, which still catered to the overwhelming majority of Jewish children in the community. From time to time the rabbis exerted pressure. Thus in 1966 and 1967 a "Kulturkampf" controversy erupted over rabbinical demands, spearheaded by Chief Rabbi Casper and by Rabbi Norman Bernhard, for more religious instruction and observance in the King David schools. The *South African Jewish Observer,* monthly of the Mizrahi Zionist party, charged that the product of these schools was neither truly Zionist nor religious, and suggested that the reason was that Jewish studies was being taught by nonreligious teachers.[91] This criticism was rebuffed at the Board of Education's conference in 1967. Some delegates objected vigorously to what they described as the coercion into religious observance of both teachers and pupils.[92]

Whereas the initial impetus for intensified religious education and the attendant turn toward greater religiosity were thus generated, quite predictably, by the well-established religious-Zionist rabbis and lay leaders, the more sweeping enticement of nonobservant orthodox and even totally unobservant secularized young Jews emanated, surprisingly, from quite another source. This was a very small and hitherto isolationist congregation established in 1936 in the Yeoville suburb of Johannesburg by some Jewish immigrants from Germany. Known as Adath Jeshurun, its founders were a tiny segment of the few thousand German Jews who escaped from Nazi Germany and found refuge in South Africa in the period 1933 to 1937. They were adherents of the neo-orthodox tradition founded by Rabbi Samson Raphael Hirsch in mid-nineteenth-century Frankfurt. This tradition upheld the principle of *Torah im derekh eretz,* meaning advocacy of full civic integration and openness to modern education and occupations but without compromising one's strict adherence to the *halakha* (Jewish law and customs). Hirsch's neo-orthodoxy was strongly opposed to the swelling movement of reform Judaism in Germany and had adopted a policy of self-reliance and of separation from what it regarded as the reform-infected bulk of the Jewish community. Following this tradition, the small Adath Jeshurun congregation in Johannesburg maintained a virtually self-contained religious subcommunity for over three decades.[93]

For the first seventeen years of its existence the congregation operated without a rabbi, its spiritual affairs largely handled by one of its founders, Dr. Fritz Homburger, a medical specialist from Frankfurt. It was only in 1953 that a rabbi was brought out from Israel—Pressburg (Bratislava)–born Rabbi Yaacov Salzer. He served the congregation until his death twenty-seven years later in 1980, gaining such widespread recognition as an authority that difficult questions of Jewish law often came to him from sources outside of his own small congregation.[94] But Adath Jeshurun remained aloof from the overall (orthodox) Federation of Synagogues, refusing all overtures aimed at gaining its affiliation. When it sought to establish its own ritual slaughter supervision (*shehita*) in 1959, suppressed resentment flared up. The *Federation Chronicle,* monthly organ of the Federation of Synagogues, attacked the divisiveness of this maverick congregation in a sharply worded editorial. "To listen to them," it stated, "one would think that they have the sole monopoly of the Jewish religion and that in their hands lie the keys to heaven and *Gan Eden* [the Garden of Eden].[95] Nevertheless, Rabbi Salzer took pride in Adath Jeshurun's stand and declared in a manner characteristic of classical neo-orthodox principles that it had "taught South Africa's Jewry that one can stand on both feet in life, being a businessman, a clerk, a student, a typist, having any trade or profession and yet keep up everything which is holy and dear to Judaism." He claimed that the congregation had "smashed the legend" that one could not, and thus need not, carry out the commandments of the Torah in Africa.[96]

In the mid-1960s Adath Jeshurun began to modify its insularity, responding perhaps to the rising public interest in Jewish education. Its afternoon Talmud Torah school, which employed only strictly religious teachers and offered a more demanding standard of religious instruction than did the day schools, attracted some religious families who were not themselves members of the congregation. The potential for a more intense religious schooling was anticipated by Rabbi Norman Bernhard. As has already been mentioned in an earlier context, an unusual combination of attributes made Rabbi Bernhard a particularly appealing innovator in the South African rabbinate. Although he was a graduate of the modern orthodox Yeshiva University and had taken part in some civil rights work in the United States, he also had a strong personal affinity to the very traditionalist Habad Hasidic movement. Indeed, the Lubavitcher Rebbe, Menahem Mendel Schneerson, had himself encouraged Bernhard to take up the position in South Africa. Within a year of his arrival Rabbi Bernhard initiated the creation of a day school at the primary level, named Menorah, in spirit and curriculum compatible with the strictly observant preferences of Adath Jeshurun. He succeeded in this enterprise in the teeth of considerable opposition from community leaders dedicated to the day school movement who charged him with introducing harmful divisiveness into the Jewish educational system.

The responsiveness of a small but energetic section of the community to intensification of religious education at all levels became increasingly evident with the founding in 1966, largely on Adath Jeshurun's initiative, of a boys' high school called Yeshivas Toras Emes. Its ultraorthodox orientation stood in contrast to the more moderate religious-Zionist character of the Yeshiva high school. The founding of a strictly religious girls' high school, Beth Yaakov, followed a decade later. But the most significant of all Adath Jeshurun's emanations was the founding in 1970 of a *kollel,* the first of its kind in South Africa. A *kollel* is a group dedicated to full-time study of Talmud whose members include married men provided with a living stipend from communal funds. Named Kollel Yad Shaul, its nucleus was a group of young men especially brought out from England. Within a few years this *kollel* developed into the center of a small but magnetic subcommunity whose effect on the religious life of the entire Johannesburg community was, in the words of Rabbi Bernhard, "like water hitting parched soil."[97]

Whereas Adath Jeshurun had been a self-contained community, the *kollel* actively set about bringing young Jews, illiterate in Judaism or alienated from it, back to religious observance. It offered part-time talmudic classes for adult men, began running Torah lectures (*shiurim*) on the university campus, and at its medical school organized seminars, hosted Jewish national servicemen, sent personnel to conduct services for isolated country communities, and ran a flourishing bookshop of Torah literature in English. These initiatives met with an enthusiastic response. Scores of families and individuals, many of them university students, accepted the yoke of Jewish religious observances with an alacrity that surprised even the founders of the *kollel.* It also introduced a new phenomenon into Jewish practice—worship in a small *shtiebel* (the Yiddish term for this off-synagogue venue, usually in a small home or study hall) rather than in a large formal synagogue.

By the mid-1980s *shtieblech* (plural of *shtiebel*) were mushrooming all over Johannesburg and also beginning to appear in Cape Town, peopled mainly by newly observant Jews. Some of the well-established, large synagogue congregations were driven to adopting the fashion by forming their own *shtiebel* offshoots.[98] That the ideological ambience of the *kollel* fostered ultraorthodox reservations, if not active hostility, in relation to the community's normative Zionism was demonstrated in several incidents that aroused public controversy. One erupted in 1972 when a *kollel* member deputizing as prayer leader at the Oxford Street synagogue declined to read the prescribed version of the prayer for the welfare of the State of Israel.[99] On the other hand, the *kollel* subcommunity actively encouraged many of its adherents to pursue further studies in Israeli yeshiva institutions, and many in fact settled there.

The potential for growth of religious observance in South African Jewry that had been proven by these developments drew the attention of the greatest of all contemporary movements of orthodox outreach, the Hasidic Habad. As a consequence of Jewish migration to South Africa having been overwhelmingly Litvak, hence belonging to the *misnagdi* religious tradition that stood in opposition to Hasidism, there had never been more than two small synagogues of Hasidic character in the country, one short-lived synagogue in turn-of-the-century Cape Town and another, known as the Hasidic Shul, in Johannesburg. But the Habad movement now had a resourceful supporter in the person of Rabbi Bernhard, and with his encouragement Habad sent Rabbi Mendel Lipskar in 1972 to serve the newly founded Lubavitch Foundation of South Africa. A corresponding bifurcation of orthodox religious and educational institutions ensued, those with an affinity for the outreach program of Lubavitcher Habad Hasidism gravitating toward Rabbi Lipskar and the Habad congregations, five of which had mushroomed in Johannesburg, one in Cape Town, and one in Durban by the mid-1990s. The Lubavitch Foundation also attracted a section of strictly observant as well as newly "returned" Jews to a new Lubavitch-inspired high school named the Torah Academy, and to its own yeshiva established in 1984 and later named Yeshivat Ohr Menahem. This yeshiva, much like its coexisting antecedent, the *kollel,* maintained a quorum of students brought from overseas for two-year periods. By 1987 it had twenty full-time students, half of whom were local. In Cape Town a small Lubavitch day school, called the Hebrew Academy, was founded as the only strictly orthodox alternative in the city to the "national-traditional" Herzlia schools.[100]

The expansion and variegation of orthodox congregations, *shtieblech,* and educational institutions continued apace throughout the 1980s and 1990s as new purveyors of the worldwide *ba'al teshuva* (religious return) phenomenon staked claims in the newly fertilized religious ground of the South African Jewish community. Several rabbis from abroad, radiating dedication and charisma, splintered the core institutions engaged in religious revival into several small units. One example was the Yeshivas Maharsha, founded in 1982 by a brilliant Israel-born rabbi, Aharon Pfeuffer, and headed by him until a tragic automobile accident took his life in 1994. Like the original *kollel,* Pfeuffer's initiative soon transformed itself into a subcommunity comprising an ultraorthodox congregation-cum–learning center. Similarly, from 1982 to 1989 a new arrival, Rabbi Moshe Sternbuch, who was a *halakha* scholar of considerable repute, led a small breakaway group from the original *kollel* into an institution he named the Vilna Gaon Torah Center. As the name patently indicated, it was of pronounced Litvak-*misnagdi* character.

In 1978 a body styled Torah Chizuk International began to bring visiting speakers who toured South Africa, and in early 1986 the dynamic Ohr Somayach institution centered in Jerusalem, a world leader in the "return to religion" phenomenon, launched its entry into South African Jewry. Sponsoring lecture visits by rousing rabbinical personalities, and drawing in talented and inspiring graduates of the local *kollel* and other yeshiva bodies, Ohr Somayach rapidly established itself as a magnetic force in the Johannesburg community. Within a short time its regular Monday night religious lecture session was attracting young adults and students in their hundreds, and by the mid-1990s at least a hundred men of all ages were involved in its evening learning program. It had also introduced a parallel women's learning program and a marriage guidance course for prospective couples. In 1995 it formed its own Ohr Somayach *kollel.* Sensing that even the activities of Ohr Somayach were not exhausting the return-to-religion phenomenon in South Africa, in August 1996 a branch of another leading international outreach movement based in Jerusalem, Aish Hatorah, established itself in one of Johannesburg's suburbs and set about targeting mainly unaffiliated, alienated Jews through lecture and seminar programs.

It is noteworthy that the religiosity to which increasing numbers of Jews were thus turning was primarily centered in Johannesburg[101] and entirely of the orthodox religious variety. By contrast, progressive (reform) Judaism not only failed to attract new adherents but also suffered a distinct decline. To be sure, it had never claimed to encompass more than about 18 to 20 percent of the total number of Jews affiliated to synagogues, and objective research estimates were considerably lower.[102]

The beginnings of progressive Judaism in South Africa were briefly described in the first chapter of this book. Its founding rabbi, Moses Cyrus Weiler, led the movement from 1933 until he settled in Israel in 1958. From its birth the progressive movement had encountered vigorous resistance from the orthodox rabbinate. As in other parts of the world, the conflict had deep theological and social roots, but in South Africa it came to center symbolically on matters as seemingly trivial as the question whether progressive rabbis should be accorded any official role in the opening and closing religious blessings customarily rendered at all communal gatherings. Particularly sensitive and controversial were the annual ceremonies in commemoration of the victims of the Holocaust.

The orthodox majority always had the upper hand. Yet Weiler and the orthodox chief rabbis, Judah Leib Landau and his successor, Louis Rabinowitz, maintained a mutually amicable modus vivendi throughout the period of their contemporaneous ministries.[103] But relations between the two streams took a turn for the worse after Weiler left the scene. In 1963 the orthodox Beth Din in Johannesburg imposed a stringent boycott on reform rabbis, prohibiting even orthodox laymen from entering any reform institution and orthodox rabbis from being present at any activity attended by a reform rabbi.[104] With great difficulty the Jewish Board of Deputies endeavored to mediate in the interests of communal unity.[105] Finally, in June 1965, orthodox Chief Rabbi Bernard Casper and Rabbi Arthur Super, senior rabbi of the United Progressive Jewish Congregation of Johannesburg, reached an understanding, piquantly dubbed by the Jewish press "the concordat." Its terms reflected Rabbi Super's willingness to make concessions for the sake of communal harmony. While declaring that "from the religious point of view there is an unbridgeable gulf between Orthodoxy and Reform," the agreement affirmed that "in social, welfare and other non-religious matters" the two should cooperate in the general communal interest. Hence, at the annual memorial meeting for victims of the Holocaust and all public gatherings of a nonreligious nature, both a reform and an orthodox minister might be seated on the platform. But Rabbi Casper's compromise did not extend beyond this. For the agreement stated that at public communal functions and at the annual memorial meeting for victims of the Holocaust, only an orthodox cantor would recite prayers. Moreover, the customary prayer at the opening of both the Board of Deputies' and the Zionist Federation's conferences would remain the prerogative of the orthodox chief rabbi.[106]

Not surprisingly, Rabbi Super's generous compromise was regarded within his own movement as a capitulation and sharply contested. Indeed, the administrative committee of the South African Union of Progressive Judaism promptly dissociated itself from the "concordat," declaring that Super spoke for no more than his Johannesburg constituency. The relationship between the orthodox and the progressive movements thus continued to be uneasy, periodically erupting into public acrimony. In October 1979 even Johannesburg's progressive Jewish congregations, which had endorsed Rabbi Super's actions, formally declared the "concordat" void. Nevertheless, both the Board of Deputies and the Zionist Federation chose to conduct their activities as if its provisions still applied.[107]

In addition to its woes over relations with the orthodox rabbinate, the progressive movement suffered a series of blows to its morale and membership in the 1980s and 1990s as a result of disruptive inner tensions and rifts revolving around some of its most prominent rabbinical personalities. One was the irrepressible Rabbi Ben Isaacson, who, as has been mentioned earlier, had started out as an orthodox rabbi, left the pulpit in 1965, settled in Israel where he became disenchanted with orthodoxy, and then returned in 1974, this time to take up a position as a progressive rabbi in Johannesburg. But after some eight years of practice in the progressive movement, disillusionment set in. He now became sharply critical of what he considered the progressive movement's superficiality and stagnation. "I have learnt that *halakha* poses problems but the destruction of *halakha* poses even more," he declared.[108] In 1983 he led a nucleus of loyal congregants out of the progressive movement to form an independent congregation called Harel, which veered close to the model of American conservative Judaism without actually seeking affiliation.[109]

In 1984 the progressive movement suffered another major disruption when one of its longest-serving rabbis, Walter Blumenthal, fell out with his congregation, Temple Shalom. The abrupt manner of his dismissal, allegedly for dereliction of duty, was a cause of bitter acrimony and had severe repercussions for progressive Judaism in Johannesburg.[110] After trying in vain to go it alone by forming what was styled a "Fellowship of True Judaism," Blumenthal left South Africa altogether. Even more injurious to progressive Judaism's position was the rebellious disaffection of the charismatic Rabbi Ady Assabi, who had arrived in 1985 and revitalized the local progressive movement. Assabi attained a high public profile, in part by dint of his theological articulateness,[111] and in part because he was more outspoken than most in criticism of apartheid's evils. But he grew increasingly dissatisfied with local standards of the progressive movement. He objected to the "slack and inconsistent application of Jewish customs, particularly those related to marriage, divorce and conversion."[112] The integrity and morale of the progressive movement suffered severe damage when Assabi finally led part of his congregation out of the Union of Progressive Judaism in May 1992. Under Assabi the Shalom Independent Congregation, not unlike Isaacson's short-lived Har-El some years earlier, approximated to the American conservative model. But in late 1998 Rabbi Assabi returned to Israel, leaving the congregation without a rabbi and depleted in membership and funds.

Overall, these schismatic developments greatly weakened the camp of progressive Judaism in South Africa at the very time when orthodoxy was becoming exponentially more appealing and gaining new adherents. It is also noteworthy that some of the developments described above point to a tendency within progressive Judaism, paralleling that of the orthodox Jews, to become more traditional—in this case by adopting a mode akin to that of conservative Judaism in America. A striking symbolic illustration of the transformation that was taking place in the religious character of the community as a whole, especially in Johannesburg, is the fact that Rabbi Assabi's former congregation found it necessary to sell its spacious Shalom Temple building. None other than the ultraorthodox Lubavitch Foundation purchased the property.

Data provided by social scientists, an advantage enjoyed by the practitioner of contemporary history, is sorely lacking when one seeks to account analytically for the turn toward orthodox religiosity that has been chronicled above. An obvious hypothesis that springs to mind would attribute the phenomenon to a sense of dejection, dislocation, and insecurity consequent on the radical transformation of the entire South African social order and the accompanying epidemic of terrifying crime. In this context, the turning of Jews to greater religiosity might be explained as an escape into the warmth of communal seclusion—the spiritual solace and orderly life that comes with submission to the authority of rabbinical mentors and immersion in the all-embracing orthodox code of living.

The historical context certainly lends much credence to this hypothesis: the transformation from white domination to a democratic South Africa, although recognized by many Jews as a great triumph of human justice and welcomed as a relief for their troubled Jewish conscience, now left them—a mere 0.3 percent of all South Africans—with a sense of extreme marginality. The improved sense of rapport with the all-white government authorities, in regard to relations with Israel and Jewish day school education, now gave way to fears of imminent antipathy, if not hostility, toward such Jewish communal allegiances. These were compounded by suspicion that the private interests of all whites would be harmed by affirmative action favoring the formerly underprivileged. Above all, chronic anxiety gripped Jews together with other whites as a horrendously violent crime wave began to spread in the transition years and reached uncontrollable epidemic proportions in the new democratic South Africa. Less able than ever to influence, let alone shape, the South African societal environment upon which their lives depended, many chose rather to change themselves through immersion in as self-sufficient a Jewish communal ambience as was possible.

It is noteworthy that also the Christian churches of South Africa experienced something of a revival among whites in the same period. There was a falloff from the established denominations, such as the Anglican, Methodist, Catholic, and Dutch Reformed Churches, and a contrasting growth of "community churches." This change was most evident among young families in newer suburbs of some major cities, as was also the case in the Jewish community. Also similar was the role of charismatic preaching or teaching that characterized the "community churches," their drawing of rigid boundaries against the secular world and outsiders (comprising both fellow Christians and non-Christians alike), and the churches' heightened caring for the individual members' need to cope with a sense of insecurity in a radically changing social order. In the words of the Reverend Dr. William Domeris, a senior lecturer in the University of the Witwatersrand's department of religious studies: "In an environment where crime is rampant and life cheap, many thousands of South Africans hunger for a sense of security. While they may continue to be victims of crime, those attending Community Churches see themselves as recipients of a unique system of community caring."[113]

Without doubting the impact of these circumstances and hence the validity of the hypothesis that this specifically South African predicament has had a strong bearing on the phenomenon of the turn to religiosity, it must be noted that it fails to constitute a complete explanation. For, as the developments traced above clearly show, the beginnings of the turn long preceded the radical transformation of South Africa itself. Rather, they were contemporaneous with similar developments that already began to appear in the late 1960s in other communities of the Jewish Diaspora. Anecdotal evidence, oral interviews, and the observations of informed participants in the process all indicate much the same motivations and influences upon *ba'alei teshuva* (the returnees or newly religious).[114] These include a search for existential meaning in life, spiritual sustenance that reaches beyond the purely rational, value alternatives to purely materialist interests, and a yearning for the comforting embrace of a caring community.

Characteristic of these motifs is the evidence—albeit largely anecdotal—provided by Rabbi Akiva Tatz, one of the most articulate of the South African–born rabbis who were generated by the local swing to religiosity and in turn influenced it. In his book *Anatomy of a Search,* published in 1987, Rabbi Tatz addresses what he describes as the existential anxiety and "lack of sense of purpose and direction" that characterizes the contemporary generation. He argues that "a Torah framework provides the structure and stability for approaching life in general and particularly life's problem and traumas in a meaningful and organized way." Tatz describes his own typically South African Jewish upbringing, leading to his equally typical entry into medical school: "I had grown up in the lap of South African luxury and lacked nothing: money, servants who did everything from polishing shoes to serving breakfast in bed, weekends on the tennis court and by the pool. . . . I owned three motor cycles before I was eighteen, and an Italian convertible." He describes a sense of deepening existential unease that began to engulf him and some of his contemporaries, a personal crisis that made him wonder whether even the supposedly noble practice of medicine—he was at the time a medical student—provided a meaningful life's compass.[115]

Typically, too, Tatz's first exposure to the inspiring alternative offered by orthodox revival came through a series of outreach *shiurim* (religious lectures) on medical *halakha* given by a rabbi from the *kollel* subcommunity of Johannesburg. Tatz was drawn into increasing religious observance, and after qualifying as a medical practitioner and completing his compulsory military service in that capacity, he proceeded to Jerusalem's Ohr Somayach yeshiva, where he began "to learn" (the yeshiva-world term meant to contrast with "to study," used in a secular context). Tatz describes his own path to orthodox observance and complete faith that does not stop short of the fundamentalist belief that the Talmud "in its original form was given at Sinai, orally, at the same time as the written law."[116] In addition to his own experience he traces similar transitions to "Torah living" typical of South African "returnees," female as well as male, all of which match what is known of the same but far more extensively documented phenomenon in other Diaspora Jewish communities.

Particularly illuminating of the transition from purely Zionist allegiances to more compelling religiosity is Tatz's account of the defection (one of several in those years) of a young man named Rael, a prodigy of the major Zionist youth movement (obviously Habonim, although not specified by Tatz). Typically, he was a bright medical student, whose deep commitment to the youth movement led him to undertake the demanding role of general-secretary, that is to say, effectively the leader of the entire Habonim movement. Tatz spells out the process of disillusionment undergone by Rael. He felt that values to which he had been exposed when he joined the movement as a child had been eroded. For example, what used to be healthy boy-girl relationships at camps had lost all semblance of reserve. Moreover, the level of commitment had dropped, and of those who had fulfilled the act of *aliya* in recent years, few were left in Israel, and even fewer in the kibbutz form of settlement, which represented the ultimate goal of the movement. Disillusioned, they had returned to South Africa or moved on to seek their personal and professional fulfillment in places such as Los Angeles or Boston. Against this background of self-doubt, exposure to the *kollel* ambience in Johannesburg and its compelling outreach activities touched the nerve of traditional, "non-observant orthodox," Jewishness implanted during Rael's childhood upbringing in a small-town Jewish family in the Transvaal. He now saw the light of Torah life and learning. He left Habonim but did go to Israel to join the Ohr Somayach "Torah community," where he worked as the community doctor at night and "learned" in the yeshiva by day.[117]

It is evident that the personal existential motives of the newly religious were much the same in all communities of the Jewish Diaspora. Even so, it remains arguable that the sociological preconditions for religious revival were decidedly more favorable in South Africa. This has been the impression of all the rabbis who came out to South Africa to stoke the fires of religious revival after experience in other places.[118] Praising the remarkable receptivity of South African Jews to their labors, rabbinical outsiders have generally attributed it to the homogeneous Litvak origins of the local Jews and the pervasiveness of a basic affinity to orthodox tradition even if practiced mostly in the breach. It seems that although severely disapproving of the "non-observant orthodox" norms prevalent in South Africa, most visiting rabbis found this to be a distinctly advantageous baseline for their work of religious revival. Hence, too, once they had succeeded in creating new models of strictly observant orthodoxy, this had a ripple effect on the norms of the community as a whole.

By the 1990s not only had compliance to strict orthodox standards become normative, but also otherwise unobservant Jews tended increasingly to conform. Such conformity became evident, for example, in their private wedding arrangements, not only in adherence to strictly kosher catering but also in following observances formerly ignored, such as the bride's mandatory immersion in the *mikveh* (ritual bath) or in eschewing men and women dancing together (at least as long as the officiating rabbi was present). In this context, the congeries of intensely orthodox subcommunal entities nourished by the various schools, yeshivas, and *shtieblech* did not take on the appearance of a religious "cult," that is to say, an illegitimate entity in relation to the consensus in society. Rather, they became models, which progressively influenced the norms of the community as a whole. Indeed, to be *frum* (a Yiddish term, meaning religiously pious) became not only feasible but also even fashionable. This is not to say that the South African community was immune to the disruption of family relationships ofttimes caused by the *ba'alei teshuva* phenomenon. In South Africa, as elsewhere, this has been felt. However, as is corroborated by some recent comparative research on the relationships of "newly religious returnee" daughters with their mothers, South African Jewish parents appear to cope with the problem considerably better than Americans.[119]

An important study of the *ba'alei teshuva* phenomenon in America and Israel by Herbert Danzger may serve as a comparative yardstick for illuminating the sociological context specific to the South African scene.[120] Danzger traced the phenomenon in America back to the rise of Jewish ethnic consciousness in the wake of the civil rights struggle of the 1960s and in conjunction with the 1967 Six Day

War's dramatic arousal of Jewish identification. Attendant countercultural and antiestablishment tendencies paved the way for a renewed interest in orthodox Judaism. Ethnicity became muted, and religion became the dominant theme. He found that the case of Israeli *ba'alei teshuva* was different. They were not propelled by a search for ethnic identity, because for them this was taken for granted. Nor were they the products of a primarily countercultural movement. Theirs was a more personal search for purpose and direction, an escape from intolerable existential realities of life in beleaguered Israel or from a hedonistic to a religiously ordered style of living.

If this explanation is valid, then it may be hypothesized that the South African case falls somewhere between the American and Israeli cases, but rather closer to the latter. For the segmented structure of South African society had long enabled a stable ethnic identification, expressed primarily in Zionism. The decline of organized Zionism, owing to factors discussed earlier in this work, left a vacuum in the still essentially ethnic identity of Jews. It seems that this has been filled by the appeal of return to religious observance and faith, prompted by the dedicated nucleus of local orthodox Jews whose activities we have traced, and dramatically promoted by charismatic newcomers to the communal scene. South Africa's radical transformation and convulsive crime epidemic in turn have given rise to grave existential anxieties, which all the material affluence still available to Jews fails to allay. This has no doubt greatly accelerated the turn to religiosity.

It is no coincidence that the transition from a mode of ethnic identity expressed in Zionism to a mode anchored in religious observance was mediated largely by the religious segment of the Zionist movement in South Africa. As we have seen, it was the creation of the Yeshiva College stream of education by the Mizrahi party and its Bnei Akiva youth movement that set the process in motion. Retaining its Zionist orientation despite the non-Zionist tendencies of the new orthodox forces that burst onto the scene, Bnei Akiva indeed expanded its influence into the centrist King David and Herzlia day school network. In the mid-1970s these schools greatly enhanced their ability to shape their pupils' Jewish identity by introducing informal extracurricular programs. Initially these were implemented by teams of students from Yeshiva University in New York, especially brought out on short visits to South Africa. Called Counterpoint programs, they took the form of intense fun-filled exposures to Judaism in seminar retreats away from the formal school environment.

In 1986 the Board of Jewish Education localized this activity under a professional director of informal Jewish education. Now called the Encounter program, local youth movement leaders conducted it. These were drawn primarily from seniors in the ranks of Bnei Akiva, because they were particularly suited to the program's purpose of providing an experiential encounter infused with Jewish observances and values—"a concentrated injection of 'fun Judaism'" and "touching them with Shabbat," in the words of a director of the Board's informal education department.[121] This, in turn, resulted in a flow of King David day school pupils into the Bnei Akiva movement itself at a time when all the other Zionist youth movements, especially the longtime predominant Habonim movement, were undergoing rapid decline. It was symptomatic of the change in community norms that the very same religious Zionist movement that had created the minority Yeshiva College educational network, because it considered the majority King David schools to be defective, now came to exert a penetrating influence also on the latter, larger school network.

By 1997 Bnei Akiva was the dominant viable remnant of the extraordinarily ubiquitous youth movement phenomenon that had been so formative a factor in the life of the Jewish community. This demonstrates the process of change that had taken place—gradual displacement of the community's preoccupation with largely secular Zionist activity and issues, leaving a vacuum to be filled by a turning to religiosity. To be sure, the Bnei Akiva youth movement continued to balance its local religiosity with encouragement of study and settlement in Israel, thereby still serving as one of the linchpins holding together the old and the new norms that characterized South African Jewry. As we have noted, also the other, newer religious groups, although veering toward non-Zionist ultraorthodoxy, directed their adherents mainly to mother institutions such as Ohr Somayach in Israel. Hence the change may perhaps be better summed up thus: a growing religiosity that subsumed the community's Zionist orientation, rather than completely displacing it. It is noteworthy that much of the highly successful methodology deployed by Ohr Somayach as well as by the informal education programs of the day schools virtually replicated the tried and true techniques that had characterized the various Zionist youth movements in their heyday—such as seminar retreats for study, socially stimulating activities, and emotionally experiential visits to Israel. Much as enthusiastic, dedicated local youth leaders and imported emissaries from Israel had inspired and orchestrated these youth movement activities, so young rabbis possessed of quite the same talents and idealism were now propelling and animating organizations like Ohr Somayach. These charismatic rabbis were fast becoming the new role models for young Jews in search of meaningful content for their natural sense of Jewish ethnicity.

The growth of religiosity was reflected in Allie Dubb's 1991 sociodemographic survey. It showed increased levels of religiosity since the earlier population survey of the mid-1970s. The proportion of very frequent attendance at synagogue had increased significantly, particular in Johannesburg. The proportion of those who attended services during the week had risen from 2.5 percent to 8.4 percent, and of those who attended at least the weekly Sabbath service, from 14 percent to 21.7 percent. Moreover, it showed that the younger age-groups, eighteen to twenty-nine and thirty to forty-four, were attending synagogue at least twice as frequently as their counterparts had done in 1974. The survey also confirmed that the ratio between orthodox and progressive membership had risen in orthodoxy's favor—in 1974 it had been 4.8 to 1, whereas in 1999 it was 6.6 to 1.[122]

An illuminating comparison with levels of religious observance in the Jewish community of Britain was provided by the 1998 national survey of South African Jews conducted jointly by the Institute for Jewish Policy Research, London, and the University of Cape Town's Kaplan Centre for Jewish Studies and Research.[123] It found that of its sample of respondents 14 percent were strictly orthodox (in the

U.K. 10 percent), 61 percent were "traditional," that is, not strictly orthodox (U.K. 15 percent), and 6 percent were nonpracticing, that is, secular (U.K. 23 percent). The comparable U.K. survey reported that 28 percent of all respondents had not attended a synagogue in the past year, whereas in South Africa the figure was only 9 percent. In South Africa 72 percent reported current affiliation to orthodox synagogues and 39 percent said they attended synagogue on a regular basis; 93 percent were found to observe a seder meal, and 75 percent to light Sabbath candles in the home every Friday night. In sum, the survey showed that percentage levels of religious practice in South Africa are not only higher than those in Britain but also "exceed those of the Jewish populations of all other countries including Israel."

Notwithstanding these significant changes, a major caveat is necessary: although they are significant in relative perspective, the extent of transformation in the character of South African Jewry should not be exaggerated. Instructively, Allie Dubb's 1991 sociodemographic survey found that 74.4 percent still rated themselves as moderately observant, 11.3 percent rated their level of observance as low, and only 14.3 percent said they were highly observant. Overall, even at the turn of the twenty-first century, the majority of South African Jews may still be characterized by the pattern of "non-observant orthodoxy."

CHAPTER 6

After Apartheid

Adapting to Apartheid's Demise

The explanation for the erosion and collapse of apartheid, like that of all mammoth political transformations, will no doubt engage many generations of historians and social scientists. Some of the earliest accounts of journalists have been colored by the "Cleopatra's nose" genre of history, highlighting personality traits of the actors and the role of fascinating coincidences and chance encounters.[1] Although the current consensus among academic analysts has readily identified the major explanatory factors involved, evaluation of their relative importance defies agreement.[2] Changing economic reality certainly was one fundamental structural factor, but whether the apartheid system at some point ceased to be, or indeed ever was, functional for primary capitalist interests remains a moot point.[3] There is less disagreement in regard to the assessment that inexorable demographic processes and interlocking economic necessities frustrated all "grand apartheid" social engineering aimed at stemming permanent urbanization of the black population through massive relocation to the so-called "homelands." Another fundamental factor that has engaged the attention of most analysts is the regime's declining capacity effectively to govern the country in the face of escalating revolutionary eruptions within the black townships. Most analysts agree that by 1990 an impasse had been reached. On the one side, the forces of resistance were far from being able to overthrow the white regime. On the other side, the government was barely able to control the internal unrest and enforce its rule, much less implement visionary apartheid strategies that would assure the white minority's entrenched political supremacy. Another factor of indisputable importance is dynamic change within the Afrikaner ethnic group's elites. These made it possible to question former ideological dogmas and rationally confront the realities of the political impasse. Yet another factor that certainly enters the explanatory equation, but whose relative importance remains contested, is the cumulative impact of international sanctions and particularly the more immediate effect of their intensification after the mid-1980s. Although by all accounts trade and military sanctions were far from effective, there is considerable agreement among analysts that the ultimate denial of access to international capital had a critically damaging impact on the South African economy.

All analysts recognize the radically new international constellation resulting from the contemporaneous collapse of Soviet communism as a crucial precipitative factor. It set off the strategic decision of President de Klerk's government finally to abandon apartheid and embark on negotiation for a nonracial democratic dispensation. Even on this point, however, there are different evaluations of the role of this factor in shaping the tactical considerations of the government on the one side and the ANC on the other.[4] At any rate, by most accounts the interplay of considerations predicated on the simultaneous elimination, or at least diminution, of the communist specter from the whites' perspective, and of Soviet support and economic dogma from the ANC's perspective, not only facilitated entry into negotiations but also contributed greatly to their ultimate outcome in the form of a majoritarian polity ensuring the ANC's overwhelming hegemony, rather than a consociational system that would somehow entrench white "group rights."

Be the causes what they may, on 2 February 1990 State President Frederik Willem de Klerk, who had replaced Botha only a few months earlier, made a sensational announcement in the South African parliament. Its truly historic import was the lifting of the ban on the ANC and an array of other repressed opposition organizations, release of persons imprisoned on the grounds of being associated with this opposition, and the government's intention to enter into negotiations for a new democratic political dispensation for all of South Africa's inhabitants. This announcement inaugurated what many have described as the sudden "miracle" of South Africa's peacefully negotiated transformation from a white supremacist polity and racist society to a nonracial democracy. It is now known, however, that this historic moment had been generated through profound internal policy revision within Afrikaner intellectual and political leadership circles and multifaceted behind-the-scenes feelers and negotiations, not only with ANC leaders in exile, but also with Nelson Mandela in prison. The metaphorical miracle, moreover, was far from being devoid of violence and civil disruption. It has been estimated that eruptions of violence in the transition process from February 1990 to May 1994 took a toll of close to 15,000 deaths.[5]

For most South Africans, white and black, this was a period of great promise but equally of tremendous uncertainty and anxiety. Four suspense-filled years of volatile conflict and precarious negotiations were to pass before the first nonracial general election took place on 27 April 1994. As promised, the government released Nelson Mandela unconditionally. On 11 February 1990, the most famous political prisoner of the century, a dignified gray-haired man of seventy-one, incarcerated for twenty-seven years, returned to lead his people to a negotiated emancipation. Mandela addressed tumultuous gatherings of welcome and met with his ANC comrades in and outside of South Africa, but the negotiation process was halting, difficult, and at times acrimonious. The initial "talks about talks" repeatedly broke down as a result of eruptions of violence in the country, mainly bloody clashes in the KwaZulu region between the Zulu Inkatha movement led by Chief Mangosuthu Buthelezi and the ANC. Although on 2 May 1990 talks were resumed in the government's Groote Schuur manor house in the Cape where, inter alia, conditions were laid down for the safe return of resistance movement exiles, it was not until June that the government lifted the state of emergency. Excepted from this relief was Natal, where ANC-Inkatha conflict continued to rage. In August the ANC for its part finally announced that it was suspending the armed struggle.

The progress of negotiations was halted in the wake of a spate of vicious hit-squad murders that appeared to be perpetrated by an unidentified "third force." The ANC accused the government of secretly directing this "third force" and fomenting intrablack divisiveness. Later disclosures revealed that the South African Defense Force had indeed set up a covert operation involving a small band of trained killers who sought out persons marked for elimination as a risk to state security. At the time de Klerk denied the ANC's accusations but, bowing to pressure, appointed a Supreme Court judge to probe murders and acts of violence allegedly committed with political motives. Later he set up a Commission of Inquiry on the Prevention of Violence and Intimidation chaired by Judge Richard Goldstone. As has been mentioned in the previous chapter, Goldstone was an identifying Jew, active in some communal organizations and known for his record in defense of human rights.

Notwithstanding all difficulties and acrimony, in December 1991 a "declaration of intent" to bring about a new nonracial political settlement, free from any form of discrimination or domination, was signed by the parties, with the conspicuous exception of the white Conservative Party and the Pan-Africanist Congress, and the stage was set for the assemblage of a Convention for a Democratic South Africa (CODESA). In March 1992 the government held a referendum of whites to test support for de Klerk's new policy. De Klerk got his mandate to go ahead; the turnout of eligible voters ran to 80 percent, 68.7 percent voting yes.

But violent eruptions continued, and on 17 June 1992 at Boipatong in the Transvaal, residents of an Inkatha-dominated hostel perpetrated a massacre of ANC supporters. CODESA negotiations broke down, and a phase of rolling mass action and strikes ensued, in the course of which the ANC also attempted to undermine the already corrupt and unstable "homeland" regimes that owed their existence to the grand apartheid program. In September 1992 the ANC launched a march across the Ciskei border toward the capital, Bisho. Ciskeian troops opened fire on a column of marchers led by Ronnie Kasrils, the former Umkhonto we Sizwe leader, killing twenty-nine and wounding some two hundred.

Throughout this period, violent attempts to disrupt the negotiation process were also made by the die-hard right-wing whites. Some Afrikaner nationalists raised the far-fetched notion of creating a separate, exclusively Afrikaner ministate. In June 1990 the police arrested eleven extremists allegedly plotting to assassinate de Klerk, Mandela, and other leaders. But volatile provocation continued. In April 1993 Chris Hani, secretary-general of the Communist Party and former chief of staff of Umkhonto we Sizwe, was assassinated, to the shock of the whole country. At a later stage, the Afrikaner Weerstandsbeweging (Afrikaner Resistance Movement), led by Eugene Terre'blanche, staged a demonstrative incursion by driving an armored vehicle through the plate glass doors of the World Trade Centre, in which negotiations were taking place. Overall, however, the resistance mustered by the

Afrikaner radical right proved to be surprisingly weak and ineffectual, and the manifestly implausible notion of a separate Afrikaner *volk* (people's) state came to naught. It is a curious fact that the Jewish journalist Henry Katzew had for many years advocated this notion in all seriousness as a moral survival strategy for the Afrikaner people—a subject discussed in an earlier chapter of this book.

Notwithstanding all obstacles, the signing in September 1992 of a Record of Understanding between the government and the ANC brought the parties back to negotiation, during which agreement was reached, largely on the initiative of Communist Party leader Joe Slovo, on a "sunset clause" that promised a transitional government of national unity for a period, later fixed at five years from the date of the election of a new parliament. A new constitution would be drafted and come into effect after approval by a two-thirds parliamentary majority.

On 27 April 1994, after Buthelezi's Inkatha movement had agreed to participate at the eleventh hour, the first democratic nonracial election at last took place, watched by an applauding world. South Africa had made the transition from pariah to paragon. On 10 May 1994, Nelson Mandela was inaugurated as president, with Thabo Mbeki and F. W. de Klerk as deputy presidents, heading a government of national unity. The newly elected parliament doubled as a constitutional assembly, whose task of drafting a new highly progressive constitution incorporating a bill of fundamental human rights was completed by December 1996. Absent from this constitution was the entrenchment of "group rights," which had been an initial aim of de Klerk's government. A new Constitutional Court of eleven judges was instituted under the presidency of advocate Arthur Chaskalson. In mid-1996 the National Party, which had itself meanwhile become nonracial, left the government of national unity. De Klerk came under fire from Afrikaner ranks for his failure to secure the promised group rights guarantees. In August 1997 he resigned from parliament and as leader of the National Party.

Jews in South Africa shared with all whites the anxiety-filled experience of mingled promise and uncertainty that attended the erratic ups and downs of the transition process. The mood was well described in a speech by Professor Harold Rudolph, a former mayor of Johannesburg, in his capacity as chairman of the Transvaal Council of the Jewish Board of Deputies: "Our future rests on a knife edge balancing precariously between hope for a peaceful democratic non-racial future and the equal possibility of sliding into the abyss of civil war."[6] The apprehensions of many Jews were further compounded by a general sense, rooted in Jewish experience, of vulnerability under any conditions of social upheaval. At the national congress of the Board of Deputies in March 1989—the last congress before de Klerk replaced Botha—deeply ingrained fears of right-wing Afrikaner nationalist antisemitism were reflected in a session devoted to "the South African political scene." Harry Schwarz delivered a paper in which he forecast that Nelson Mandela would soon be released, although negotiations leading to a new constitutional settlement were still a long way off. But even so experienced and perceptive a politician as Schwarz found it very difficult to gauge the potential for a radical Afrikaner backlash. He opined that "in the longer term the risk of right-wing white reactions is real, but not in the short term," a view that proved to be inversely correct.[7]

Jewish fears were heightened when, in the general election of September 1989, the National Party, then led by de Klerk, was badly mauled. It lost seventeen seats to the Conservative Party. On the other extreme of the political spectrum there loomed the specter of hostility on the part of the African National Congress and its satellites within the country, especially their Muslim elements. As events rapidly unfolded in the aftermath of de Klerk's dramatic announcement in February 1990 and the release of Mandela, the generally pervasive identification of Jews with the forces of change was significantly dampened by anxieties on this score. The signs seemed to indicate that should a new political dispensation put the power of government partly or wholly in the hands of the ANC, its jaundiced view of Zionism and animosity toward Israel would result in vindictive denial of the Jewish community's right to identify actively with Israel. Nor did it help that many Jews themselves had a bad conscience about Israel's recent record of cooperation with the white government.

In this charged atmosphere of doubt and fear some sagacious assessments of what was in store for Jews issued from the pen of a particularly well-qualified analyst of the political scene—Steven Friedman of the Center for Policy Studies at the University of the Witwatersrand.[8] Friedman expressed the view that the change South Africa was undergoing lay somewhere between revolution, in which the existing order would be totally replaced, and a process of reform, in which society would remain essentially the same. Deducing that the contemporary white government had all but given up its initial attempt to negotiate for a constitutionally guaranteed protection of the white group, Friedman predicted that the outcome would almost certainly be rule by a black majority as represented by the ANC. He pointed to the difference between developments in South Africa and Eastern Europe. The latter was also undergoing a revolutionary transformation, but there ethnic group rights were seen as an important freedom after years of undemocratic rule and the artificial suppression of ethnic differences. By contrast, in South Africa, where an undemocratic government had artificially enforced ethnic group separation and inequalities, the new democratic dispensation would be opposed in principle to any perpetuation of group rights. However, opined Friedman reassuringly, "one of the few sure predictions which can be made about our future is that there is little chance that majority government will have any effect on Jews' cultural or religious rights."

Friedman acknowledged the presence within the liberation movement of hostility toward Israel and Zionism. He therefore anticipated that an ANC government would remove any privileges enjoyed by the Jews in relation to support for Israel. But he added that the ANC's attitude was moderate; it had already spelled out its position, stating that it recognized Israel's right to exist within secure borders but equally supported demands for a Palestinian state, and was urging Israel to negotiate with the PLO. On the other hand, he warned that the new order would undoubtedly bring great changes to people's lives, not least of all to Jews as part of the white minority. It would no longer be possible for them to live in isolation, cushioned from the poverty that until then had been hidden from their view. There would be affirmative action to promote black personnel; standards would drop; the big cities would look more like those in the third world, schools and hospitals would no longer be privileged services for whites. Within a few years all of these projections were to prove remarkably correct, with the addition of an uncontainable epidemic of crime, a factor underemphasized in this otherwise prescient analysis.

The Jewish community, according to Friedman, had the choice of responding to the change in one of two ways. The first approach—that which the community had, in his view, traditionally followed—would be to evaluate events purely in the light of their effect on Jews as an interest group. The second would be to declare that Judaism had a specific message in regard to the evils of the old order and the shaping of a better society. In his judgment, this approach would require a major shift in the traditional policy of the communal leadership.

In March 1992 a meeting of the national executive council of the Board of Deputies debated the question whether the Jewish community was under threat in South Africa. The discussion still reflected much uncertainty and a sense that the community "was in for a rough ride," in the words of Harold Rudolph. While some claimed that "there was no separate agenda" for the Jewish community, the tenor of the discussion in fact belied this. Indeed, opinions were so divided that the Board's president, Gerald Leissner, is on record saying that he was disappointed and "found it inconceivable that so many people had implied that they preferred the shameful situation of the past forty years to the current initiatives."[9] The main specifically Jewish anxiety was that the PLO would be allowed an embassy, and an African National Congress government would cultivate close relations with countries that were the implacable enemies of Israel. Additional concerns related to the question whether the community could cope with anticipated withdrawal of government subsidies for Jewish education. Moreover, there was also a palpable fear that if the pending referendum on de Klerk's dramatic new course resulted in a yes vote but only by a narrow margin, the right wing would target the Jews.

The Jewish communal leadership thus felt itself caught between the Scylla of possible right-wing Afrikaner scapegoating of Jews and the Charybdis of the resistance movement's hostility to the inherent Zionist identification of South African Jewry. Yet, it had by now freed itself of the self-imposed inhibitions and constraints encapsulated in the "political non-involvement" policy formula. In striking contrast to the timorous neutral posture that had been adopted in the 1961 referendum on South Africa's constitution as a republic, in 1992 Jews as a community and not only as individual citizens rallied to support de Klerk's call for the white electorate's approval of his intention to advance beyond apartheid reforms to negotiation of a new nonracial dispensation. Indeed, in an unprecedented act of "political" intervention, Chief Rabbi Cyril Harris issued a call for announcements to be made in all synagogues urging Jews to vote yes.[10] Even the rabbis of the generally isolationist and self-centered ultraorthodox sector of the community saw fit to call for a yes vote. For most Jews, the alternative was more clear-cut than it had ever been. To deny a mandate for de Klerk's policy would not only be unconscionable from a Jewish point of view, as most Jews by now perceived the issues, but would also be grist to the mill of potential antisemitic forces in South African politics. These included the Conservative Party, which denied being antisemitic but upheld apartheid and openly espoused privilege for white Christians, or worse still the reactionary right-wing Afrikaners associated with Eugene Terre'blanche's patently antisemitic Afrikaner Weerstandsbeweging.

When the matter was discussed at meetings of the Jewish Board of Deputies, it appeared that the only exception to support for de Klerk's policy was, not unpredictably, the small rural remnants of what were called "country community" Jews. Rabbi Zaiden, the Board's professional country communities' rabbi, reported that most Jews in the communities had indicated to him that they would be voting no. He suggested that the chief rabbi issue a message to the communities in question to counter this. Still, some participants in the discussion cautioned against setting a dangerous precedent for direct political intervention that might embarrass the Board. A vote was taken, leading to the decision to issue a statement but to phrase it so as not to highlight the Jews as such. It would urge all South Africans to support the reform process and vote yes in the forthcoming referendum. At the same time it was understood implicitly that unofficially each member of the Board of Deputies would do "everything in his power" to canvass a yes vote.[11]

Within the core of the Jewish community throughout this period there was simmering tension caused by a small section of Jews who reacted assertively, and at times even aggressively, to what they perceived as self-demeaning deference to defamers of Zionism and Israel just because they were paragons of the struggle for a postapartheid South Africa. We have already noted in an earlier chapter such reaction to some of the views of Archbishop Tutu in the late 1980s. When, after Nelson Mandela's release from prison, one of his first internationally significant acts on a visit to ANC comrades in Lusaka was his warm embrace of Yasser Arafat, a shiver of apprehension ran through the Jewish community at large. It was reported, moreover, that when asked at a press conference whether he risked alienating South Africa's influential Jewish community by meeting Arafat and comparing Arafat's struggle to that of the blacks in South Africa, Mandela replied: "If the truth alienates the powerful Jewish community in South Africa, that's too bad."[12]

Whatever disappointment and concern this elicited was overshadowed by the tremendous admiration most Jews had for Mandela thanks to his heroically humane and statesmanlike policy of reconciliation despite twenty-seven years of unjust imprisonment. Yet a vocal minority vented bitter resentment. When progressive rabbi Ady Assabi, at the time the senior rabbi of the combined Emanu-Shalom congregation, invited Mandela to address it in September 1990—the first such invitation—the rabbi faced not only the resignation of some members but even numerous death threats from anonymous callers.[13] Indignant reaction to Mandela's support of Arafat and exaggerated reports of his criticism of Israel were echoed also in American Jewry. In the wake of his visit to the United States in early 1990, Mandela was the object of considerable flak from parts of the Jewish community. One Jewish newspaper featured an editorial criticizing the fad of "Mandelamania." It deplored Jewish fawning over Mandela. "His agenda is not our agenda," it said, "at least not of Jews who understand that Zionism is the national liberation movement of the Jewish people and that the State of Israel is critical to Jewish survival."[14]

In all respects bar the Palestinian question, Mandela's words and deeds were universally appreciated in the Jewish community. He never missed an opportunity to laud the admirably disproportionate role of the Jews in the struggle against apartheid. "As a movement, the African National Congress recognizes the particularly outstanding contribution that the South African Jewish community has made to the struggle for freedom and social justice," he wrote in a typical greeting for the Passover festival, also noting that "despite its relatively small numbers, the Jewish community in this country has made a contribution second to none . . . in the arts, in science, in scholarship, in law and as employers in the economy."[15] Indeed, it is ironic that such generous praise was bestowed on Jews as a whole despite the organized community's past record of dissociation from Jewish radicals and the mutual alienation that marked their relationship.

Throughout this period of South Africa's transition, no single individual did more to assuage Jewish apprehensions and to encourage a positive attitude toward the transformation of South Africa than Chief Rabbi Cyril Harris. Harris was born in Glasgow and came to South Africa after a distinguished ministry in some of London's largest synagogues. His coming to South Africa to assume the important position of chief rabbi of the Union of Orthodox Congregations in 1988 was a veritable gift to the Jewish community. He rapidly won recognition as the right person in the right place. Almost from the moment of his arrival, he identified in the name of Judaism with the struggle peacefully to bring about the abandonment of apartheid and the transformation of South Africa into a nonracial democracy. It was a role for which he was admirably suited, not only by virtue of his strong conviction that Jewish ethics commanded it, but also by dint of his extraordinary personal charisma and rhetorical flair. The record of his ministry in South Africa did much to redeem Judaism's uninspiring profile in the eyes of Jews who had battled apartheid, although Harris himself was fully cognizant of his good fortune in coming to serve the community in the period of apartheid's demise rather than in its heyday. Journalist Susan Belling chose aptly to dub him "the conscience of the community," while Mark Gevisser, writing in the liberal-left *Mail and Guardian,* went so far as to call him "the Desmond Tutu of S.A. Jewry."[16] Harris not only preached the utter inconsistency between Jewish ethics and apartheid, as had other rabbis before him, but also engaged himself in the drive toward change and established a warm relationship with many black religious and political leaders. Above all, he became a very good friend, and in some matters even a confidant, of Nelson Mandela himself. When Mandela made a visit to Israel in October 1999, he asked Harris to join him there, calling him affectionately "my rabbi." Cyril Harris's wife, Ann, a lawyer by profession, was no less active in her own right. She ran a law clinic at the University of the Witwatersrand, headed the social action program of the Oxford Synagogue center, and even ventured to join the Jews for Social Justice delegation that went with the Five Freedoms Forum to Lusaka to meet with ANC leaders in July 1989.

If Rabbi Harris was fortunate to come to South Africa at a time of transition out of apartheid, rather ironically he was perhaps less fortunate in that, as we have seen, the orthodox observant Jews of South Africa under his ministry were at that very time becoming ever more insular and inward looking. Fighting an uphill battle, Harris tirelessly exhorted the community to look outward to its obligations toward society at large and promoted practical projects to that end. "The essence of Judaism is that you are not allowed to ignore the world around you," he preached; "you cannot live on an island . . . in some area called religion, where you just have your prayers, rituals and ceremonies." Indeed, in striking contrast to the past record of most rabbis in South Africa, he taught also that on *halakhic* grounds "it is insufficient to keep apart from violations of human rights. Disassociation is inadequate where vocal protest is called for and positive steps are urgently needed to try to rectify the injustice."[17]

In these endeavors, Rabbi Harris had a loyal if rather small ally in the Jews for Justice and Jews for Social Justice groups. They too campaigned actively for a positive and optimistic attitude toward the forces for radical change in the country. Franz Auerbach, both in his personal capacity and as a spokesperson for Jews for Social Justice, repeatedly tried to disperse the clouds of confusion and rumor surrounding the specter of ANC anti-Zionism.[18] Various opportunities to sound out ANC views gave him grounds for calling on members of the South African Jewish community to accept the goodwill of Mandela and the ANC leadership.

In November 1989 a very encouraging exchange of views took place through the efforts of Jews for Social Justice activists Franz Auerbach and Howard Sackstein, a former chairman of the South African Union of Jewish Students. They brought together some leading personalities in the Mass Democratic Movement, notably Eric Molobi, Murphy Morobe, and the Reverend Frank Chikane, and some rabbis and representatives of the Board of Deputies as well as various other Jewish organizations, including the Zionist Federation.[19] In Cape Town a similar meeting took place also with the participation of some Muslim leaders.

In the course of several meetings with Mandela both before and after his election to the presidency, the Jewish leadership's concern at his show of friendship to the sworn enemies of Israel, Arafat and Qaddafi, was allayed, but never entirely dispelled. Mandela repeatedly justified his unswerving loyalty to any leaders who had supported the ANC's struggle irrespective of their political character. To be sure, he tried to adopt a balanced approach to the Israel-Palestinian conflict. On the one hand, he never questioned the right of Israel to a secure existence. But on the other, he identified unreservedly with the Palestinian Liberation Organization. He called on both sides to negotiate, much as he was doing in South Africa. It is perhaps a measure of his apparent evenhandedness that *Muslim Views* in March 1992 reported on an address by Mandela to leaders of the Muslim community with gratification for his reiteration of loyalty to friends such as Qaddafi and Arafat, yet found it necessary to add: "It came as somewhat of a shock when Mandela told the audience that he recognized the right of Israel's existence."[20]

Indicative of Mandela's genuine goodwill toward Jews was the fact that it was on his own initiative that the first meeting with leaders of the Jewish community was arranged. It took place in June 1990, about half a year after his release. He had asked Israel (Isie) Maisels, whose friendship with him harked back to the late 1950s when Maisels led the defense at the famous Treason Trial, to arrange a meeting in order to clear the air. Maisels responded with alacrity and invited Chief Rabbi Cyril Harris, Helen Suzman, Professor Michael Katz, who was the president of the Board of Deputies, and also Solly Sacks and Abe Abrahamson, respectively chairman and vice-chairman of the Zionist Federation. The exchange of views was conducted in a gratifyingly friendly spirit. But when Michael Katz and Thabo Mbeki drew up a statement issuing from the meeting, it skirted controversy on the question of Israel and Zionism, merely recording that "the Jewish leadership explained to Mr. Mandela and Mr. Mbeki the close relationship which has, as a matter of historical fact, existed between the State of Israel and the South African Jewish community."[21] In late 1992, at the request of Mandela, the Board of Deputies arranged another meeting of note, between Mandela and leading Jewish industrialists, in order to discuss the economic future of South Africa. The participants included Eric Samson of Macsteel, Louis Shill of the Sage mutual fund, Morris Kahn of SA Breweries, and Elliot Osrin of the Foschini clothing store chain.[22]

In August 1990 Mandela, replying to a question by a Jewish student at a meeting held at the University of the Witwatersrand, said candidly: "Your enemies are not my enemies." He reiterated that the ANC would continue to determine its attitude to any country on the basis of its record in relation to the ANC's struggle. For some Jews this answer was "disturbing." Even the South African Union of Jewish Students viewed Mandela's statements "in the gravest light."[23] At the Oslo Conference titled "The Anatomy of Hate," which Mandela attended in August 1990, Elie Wiesel asked him to clarify his views on the 1975 United Nations resolution defaming Zionism as a form of racism. Evading an unequivocal dissociation from the notorious United Nations resolution, Mandela said he was against Zionism if it meant refusal to negotiate with the acknowledged leaders of the Palestinians and brutal suppression of the protests by Arabs in the conquered territories.[24] This elicited praise from the Muslim press in South Africa for what it took to be Mandela's outright "condemnation of Zionism" in Oslo.[25]

Several meetings ensued between the Jewish leadership and representatives of the African National Congress. The outcome was reassuring in regard to the ANC's unequivocal commitment to full freedom of religion and acceptance of the continued existence of private community schools, but the meetings repeatedly failed to dispel apprehension over the question of relations with Israel. The ANC representatives stressed their close relations with the PLO and indicated that should current conditions in the Middle East prevail it might become difficult to maintain diplomatic relations.[26]

If the ANC's official policy in regard to the Middle East left Jews with residual anxieties despite reassuring messages from those who spoke to Mandela, this was partly because of uncertainty whether his successors would hold to the same policy, but mainly because, as has been noted in the previous chapter of this book, at this time the Zionist Federation was led by the Mizrahi and Revisionist parties. Solly Sacks of Mizrahi was the chairman during 1990, the critical year of Mandela's reentry to the open political arena. Mizrahi and the Revisionists constituted the right wing of the Zionist movement and as such identified unreservedly with the government of Israel under Prime Minister Yitzhak Shamir, whose policy was uncompromising in regard to settlement in and retention of the West Bank and Gaza territories that had been under Israel's administration since the Six Day War of 1967. Defensive of Israel and on guard against antisemitism in the guise of anti-Zionism, the Zionist Federation tended to be highly suspicious and critical of the views of Mandela and the ANC in regard to the Israel-Arab conflict. By contrast, those South African Jews who consistently applied a liberal outlook as much to the affairs of Israel as to those of South Africa were inclined to identify with the left wing of the Zionist movement (exemplified by the Israeli Labor Party or others further to the left) and thus had less cause to be upset by Mandela's attitude. But the active Zionists of this persuasion had lost influence in the local Zionist Federation. Consequently, Zionism in South Africa was projecting an almost exclusively right-wing public posture. This alienated from the Zionist Federation not a few Jews who held strong and consistent liberal convictions. Such dissonance ruptured the traditional Zionist consensus within the community, thereby quickening the decline of the Zionist Federation's status.

Whether there was a valid distinction between antisemitism and so-called "anti-Zionism" was hotly debated in the community. As in other parts of the world, this was, of course, a distinction much touted by persons and groups hostile to Israel. Most South African Jews of liberal outlook recognized that in practice manifestations of putative anti-Zionism were either a mask for antisemitism or tended sooner or later to coincide with antisemitism in all essentials. But some such Jews, because they harbored reservations about particular policies of the Israeli government (not least of all its record of military cooperation with South Africa), were inclined to allow the distinction to pass, as long as the so-called "anti-Zionism" did not explicitly negate the very right of Israel to exist as a state for the fulfillment of the national needs and aspirations of the Jews.

This approach was evident in the opinion expressed by Steven Friedman, in the article to which we have referred above. His view was that "it was incumbent upon the Jewish community to examine its reaction to perceived anti-Zionism carefully, as it was inaccurate to label all who criticized Israeli policy as anti-Zionist and antisemitic." Friedman recommended that "were organized Jewry here to take a more critical stance to Israeli government policy—or to signal that there is a difference between support for Israel and support for its government—it could engage in a dialogue with the ANC which would soften positions on both sides without compromising on support for Israel or Zionism."[27] Perhaps the most controversial exemplar of the same approach was Rabbi Ady Assabi. He outspokenly applied his liberal-left views as much to South Africa as to questions relating to Israel (in which he still held citizenship). When he invited Mandela to address his congregation in 1990, Assabi himself contended in his introductory comments that "an anti-Zionist is not necessarily an anti-Semite." For this he was severely criticized by the Zionist Federation and also by the South African Association of Progressive Rabbis. The Zionist Federation issued a remonstrative statement: "We totally dissociate ourselves from Rabbi Assabi's assertion that anti-Zionism is distinct from anti-Semitism. We dare never fall into the trap of our arch enemies, who claim that anti-Zionism is not anti-Semitism. They are one and the same thing."[28]

This division of opinion generated tensions not only within the community but also vis-à-vis Israel's ambassador to South Africa at this time, Zvi Gov-Ari, who was an appointee of Israel's current right-wing government. Gov-Ari deemed it necessary to respond sharply to Mandela's statements. In a letter to the press, he chastised Mandela for his display of support for Yasser Arafat, "an arch-terrorist whose hands drip with the blood of countless innocent victims," and for saying that he sincerely believed there were many similarities between his struggle and that of Arafat. What is more, in what sounded like a presumption to speak for South African Jews, he took Mandela to task for his dismissive remark—"If the truth alienates the powerful Jewish community in South Africa, that's too bad."[29] He followed this up with sharp criticism of Mandela in an address to the South African Zionist Federation's 1990 conference. The ambassador's demeanor provoked a rare incidence of clash between some leaders of the local Jewish community and the diplomatic representative of Israel. It brought upon him the private censure of Board of Deputies' chairman, Mervyn Smith, as well as remonstrative words from Chief Rabbi Harris.[30] Abe Abrahamson, who succeeded Sacks as Zionist Federation chairman in 1991 and held that position until 1994, was in Zionist terms a "non-party man" who did not personally identify with the right wing of Zionism. No predecessor as chairman had a record of political experience as great as Abrahamson—in addition to leadership of the Jewish Board of Deputies in Rhodesia he had served as a minister in the government of that country from 1958 to 1962. But he could not override the general disposition of the Zionist Federation's executive, and it was shared by most of the orthodox rabbis in the community.

When Alon Liel replaced Gov-Ari as Israel's ambassador in 1992, he did his best to change this disposition. As we have seen, Liel had been one of the molders of the Israeli Foreign Ministry's volte-face in regard to South Africa. In the late 1980s he had pushed for sanctions in the face of concerted counterpressure from the leadership of the local Jewish community. Now, as ambassador, he saw his crucial task to be repair of past damage and the building of a positive relationship with black organizations and leaders. The peace process launched at Oslo and capped by the famous Rabin-Arafat handshake on the White House lawn in September 1993 greatly facilitated this because it went a long way toward defusing ANC criticism of Israel. Liel afterward made the ironic observation that "the more the status of Arafat rose in the Israeli government's policy, the more my status improved in parallel in the eyes of the ANC."[31] But within the local Jewish community, Liel had an uphill struggle to justify the Israeli government's new policies whether in regard to South Africa or in regard to the Oslo peace process. Doubts, criticism, and fears on both scores gripped a large segment of the Jews active in the Zionist Federation as well as the increasingly influential orthodox rabbis.

Ironically, the new ambassador of Israel found himself virtually campaigning in the Jewish community to legitimize the PLO as a partner for the peace initiative launched by the government of Yitzhak Rabin and Shimon Peres. By contrast, Liel drew encouragement and support from his contact with Jews who had been active in the liberal or radical opposition to apartheid but alienated from Jewish communal affairs. These included some who were prominent in the ANC and in the unity government formed after the 1994 elections—Joe Slovo, who became minister of housing, and Ronny Kasrils and Gill Marcus, respectively deputy ministers of defense and finance. Liel afterward wrote of Slovo: "In his own way Joe was far more Jewish in his (universal) principles than some of the [Jewish] community's leaders who flaunted their contributions and sometimes their investments in Israel."[32] In addition, Liel enjoyed the support of persons actively involved in Jewish affairs, most notably Chief Rabbi Harris and members of the Jews for Social Justice groups. He also found the Jewish Board of Deputies to be supportive, particularly its director Seymour Kopelowitz, chairman Mervyn Smith, and vice-chairman Marlene Bethlehem. Liel's single-minded concentration on initiating a positive relationship with the ANC was consciously made at the cost of skirting the de Klerk government and Inkatha leader Buthelezi, with whom his predecessors had maintained warm relations. Those who tried to curb or slow down his assiduous endeavors to that end, either because they considered them excessive and premature or because they wished to support de Klerk's side in the negotiation process, included some of the wealthiest and most influential businessmen active in the Jewish community.[33]

By the mid-1990s the clouds that had darkened the Jewish community's attitude toward Mandela had been dispersed, and the community was accommodating to the new reality of a government distinctly more sympathetic to the Palestinian Liberation Organization than to Israel, yet nevertheless willing to maintain correct relations with the latter. In August 1993 Mandela, in his capacity as ANC leader, had been asked to address the opening session of the Board of Deputies' congress. (President de Klerk had addressed the previous congress.) He told the conference that the ANC equally recognized the legitimacy of Palestinian nationalism and of Zionism. As on other occasions, he praised the role of Jews in the liberation struggle and called upon the community to become actively involved in rebuilding the nation. Shortly after his victory in the first nonracial elections of April 1994, Mandela addressed the Sabbath service at the Green and Sea Point Synagogue in Cape Town. He appealed to Jews "who had left South Africa because of insecurity to come back and help us to build our country."[34] Soon afterward, in July 1994, the South African Zionist Federation invited Foreign Minister Alfred Nzo to address its conference. At the last moment he was unable to come and deputed Malcolm Ferguson, South Africa's ambassador to Israel, to take his place. Ferguson reassured the gathering that it was the policy of the government "that we recognize and respect the legitimacy of Zionism as the embodiment of Jewish nationalism. Likewise we accept and recognize the State of Israel and assert and insist on its right to exist within secure borders." Moreover, he said that South Africa recognizes that for South African Jews, "support for and solidarity with world-wide Jewish issues, including Zionism and Israel, have the character of an article of faith."[35]

In the ensuing years of Mandela's presidency he unfailingly gave Jewish delegations a friendly and sympathetic reception and showed that he bore no ill will toward Israel and was genuinely concerned that the peace process between Israelis and Palestinians reach a successful conclusion.[36] On receiving a delegation from the Board of Deputies at his Pretoria residence in October 1996, he said that he had stopped a proposed visit of the Palestinian Hamas leader Sheikh Yassin because of the Jewish community's protest and because he understood that hosting the Hamas leader would harm the peace process. He praised the policies of Yitzhak Rabin and Shimon Peres and said that Netanyahu was playing into the hands of radicals such as the Hamas and Iran and contributing toward their ability to undermine Arafat.[37]

It was by now clear that the fate of the erratic peace process between Israel and the PLO was the determining factor in regard to the ANC government's policy. Every advance improved the new South African government's attitude toward Israel, thereby lightening the spirits of the Jewish leadership, and every regression had the opposite effect. Awareness was growing that whereas right-wing whites no longer constituted a force that could threaten Jews in South Africa, hostility and defamation emanating from within the Muslim community was escalating. Concerned that the new and admirably liberal constitution being drafted should provide adequate protection against abuse of freedom of speech, the Jewish Board of Deputies made a detailed submission to the constituent assembly. To its gratification, the ultimate wording of the constitution included the proviso that freedom of expression does not protect against "advocacy of hatred based on race, ethnicity, gender or religion."[38]

Nevertheless, chronic agitation against the Jewish affinity to Israel had become commonplace, fluctuating in intensity to the rhythm of annual commemoration rallies on "Al Quds Day," or in reaction to Jewish celebration of Israel's Independence Day. Tensions became acute and flared up in response to every development in the Middle East that made the headlines. The Gulf War of early 1991 boosted the rabidly anti-Israel Qibla movement that had been founded in 1980 and had all along identified with the Khomeini regime in Iran. It rallied once more to denounce the United States and Israel and now also to support Saddam Hussein, erstwhile enemy of Iran. Qibla's anti-Israel agitation peaked in March 1994 when, roping in the cooperation of the Pan-Africanist Congress, it led a thousand-strong throng through the streets of Cape Town in a demonstration against the Israeli Embassy. Jews were deeply disturbed to hear the fiery chanting of "Death to Israel" and "One Israeli, One Bullet," an echo of the PAC's former slogan "One Settler, One Bullet." In May 1994, when Yasser Arafat visited South Africa, he delivered a highly provocative speech in a Johannesburg mosque, in which he called on South African Muslims to join "the *jihad* to liberate Jerusalem."[39]

Past Jewish experience made it difficult to be sanguine in the knowledge that the anti-Israel militants represented only a small minority of the Muslims in the country, and that some Muslim clerics were sufficiently perturbed by this hate mongering to launch a "Campaign for Religious Tolerance" in 1995 and to enter into some dialogic relations with Jews. As has been related in an earlier chapter, the main arenas for demonstrations against Zionism and Israel were the Western Cape Province and the various university campuses. A major source of concern for Jews was that the agitation of such Muslim groups seemed to be spreading on and off university campuses to mainstream black political movements. However, there were also countersigns indicating that the ANC leadership was averse to such developments. In 1994, when at an anti-Israel demonstration a member of the ANC Cape regional executive, Dawood Khan, was heard shouting, "Hitler should have burned all the Jews," the chairman of the executive, Reverend Alan Boesak, censured this. Khan was temporarily suspended from the executive and ordered to apologize—which he did.

Concern was greatly heightened when a movement called Pagad, an acronym for People against Gangsterism and Drugs, emerged in 1996 in the Western Cape. Purporting to be a grassroots movement of moral resistance to rampant crime and drug traffic within the colored community, Pagad first gained notoriety as an unscrupulous vigilante movement when its activists captured a known gangster, doused him with petrol, and burned him alive in full public view.[40] Particularly disturbing to Jews, in addition to this group's taking the law into its own hands, were rumors that it had links with Hamas and Hezbollah in the Middle East. During 1996 there were also rumors that Qibla had set up several training camps in the Western and Eastern Cape Provinces, where envoys dispatched from Iran and Algeria conducted indoctrination and military training. In July 1997 there was a firebomb attack on a Jewish home in Cape Town that was known to house a Jewish book center, as well as a spate of phone threats to synagogues and the Jewish home for the aged. In May 1998 even the respectable Muslim Judicial Council in Cape Town was involved in a malicious attack on South African Jews for their support of Israel. An "Open Letter to All South Africans" signed by the Council's secretary-general, Sheikh Achmat Sedick, reacted to the Jewish celebration of the fiftieth anniversary of the founding of the State of Israel by declaring that it was "an appalling state of affairs" for any South African to celebrate "illegal occupation of land . . . butchering, maiming and raping innocent civilian women and children . . . a situation we describe more abhorrent than the Holocaust and the Apartheid policy of South Africa."[41] For Jews this kind of agitation greatly exacerbated the already alarming atmosphere produced by the spiraling epidemic of violent crime and attendant failure of law enforcement that marked the transition to the new South Africa.

Independently of the crime-related security problem, the development of a community organization for self-protection against possible physical harm to Jewish schools, synagogues, and other institutions became a high priority. To be sure, South African Jewry's self-security needs were not unique. The Jews of Argentina suffered a devastating terrorist attack in July 1994 on their major communal institution known as AMIA, with massive loss of lives. Although the Argentine authorities never solved the case, it was strongly suspected that the perpetrators were terrorists from within the Muslim or Arab world. Throughout the Jewish Diaspora, Jewish communities found it necessary to take ongoing self-protection measures. Mendel Kaplan was the first to alert the South African community to the need for an effective communal security operation. Situated in the early 1990s at the helm of major transnational Jewish organizations, the World Jewish Congress and the Jewish Agency for Israel, Kaplan was in a position to initiate useful international liaisons for this purpose and to help personally in setting it up and seeing to its local funding.[42] From July 1993 the South African Jewish community operated, in close cooperation with the police, a multifaceted Community Security Organization (CSO) involving college-age volunteers, mostly graduates of the Jewish day schools, especially trained for the task by a team of professionals. Their activities included monitoring of threats to the community and providing security guards for schools and public events. A mode of positive Jewish identity, dedication to the life of the Jewish community, and social camaraderie developed among the hundreds of youths who served over the years in the CSO. In all it amounted to a surrogate for the now waning Zionist youth movements that had formerly been so vibrant a feature of South African Jewry.

New Communal Directions

As we have seen, throughout the period of high apartheid the Jewish Board of Deputies had concentrated its public relations work purely within the context of white politics with special emphasis on relations with the Afrikaner government and public. Only in the late 1980s did it begin to seek contact with black leaders within the country. Not surprisingly, the Board's executive director, Aleck Goldberg, did not find it easy going. The Board's agenda for such connections was to demonstrate Jewish support for the forces of change in South Africa and to promote understanding of the integral place of Zionism and relations with the State of Israel in the identity of Jews and the life of the community. One important leader who accepted the Board's invitation was Archbishop Desmond Tutu. In February 1990 a meeting was arranged in Cape Town, attended also by Chief Rabbi Cyril Harris, frankly to discuss remarks attributed to the Archbishop by the media a few months earlier while he was on a visit to Israel at the invitation of the Anglican Church in Jerusalem. Chairman Leissner told the archbishop that the Board regretted the spreading of false rumors and allegations whose purport was a threat that if the Jewish community did not assist in the struggle against apartheid it would ultimately pay a penalty when a black government came into power. Leissner said that the Board knew these reports were untrue and had been at pains to deny them in South Africa and abroad. He did, however, question Tutu's purported remarks comparing the plight of Arabs on the West Bank with that of black people in South Africa. Tutu responded that the role of Jews in the opposition to apartheid was well appreciated but, when he visited Israel, it had been his clear perception that the Arabs were being oppressed and, as a black South African, he could not but identify with them.[43]

As the process of transition gathered momentum after the release of Mandela, the Board of Deputies' public relations work underwent a far-reaching reorientation. Seymour Kopelowitz, who replaced Aleck Goldberg as director upon his retirement in late 1990, launched a resourceful and energetic effort to initiate contacts and exchanges of views with a wide range of political leaders who now clearly represented the wave of the future. In the new atmosphere created by the onset of negotiated change, he found greater responsiveness to the Board's initiatives. Unofficial contacts with Albie Sachs, Gill Marcus, and Ronnie Kasrils in particular were gratifying. Despite the bitter mutual alienation of the past and their longstanding criticism of the Board's policies, they evinced a Mandela-like reconciliatory spirit and gave every encouragement to the Board's change of course. As Albie Sachs explained, almost as if to his own surprise: "I am so keen to see nonracialism work, for everyone to feel comfortable and to sense themselves free and safe in the new South Africa, that I eagerly accept any invitation to speak to Jewish groups."[44] Nevertheless, when the Board's executive discussed the question whether officially to seek the cooperation of Jews who were prominent in the African National Congress, the feeling was that this would be inadvisable.[45] Instead, a series of direct approaches was made across the spectrum of black leaders and groups. In Durban, the Council of Natal Jewry maintained ongoing contact with Inkatha, which also had some active Jewish supporters. However, when the Board of Deputies and Rabbi Harris were officially invited by Buthelezi to attend a workshop with the Inkatha leadership, it was deemed inappropriate to associate with a particular party.[46]

Criticism of the Board's policy now came from another quarter. Tony Leon, the new leader of the Democratic Party, successor to the Progressive Party and the symbolic leadership role of Helen Suzman, complained that the Board was deliberately ignoring the political camp that was most sincerely committed to principles valued by the Jewish community. Indeed, he argued that Jews should even be encouraged to support his party as a matter of justifiable self-interest.[47] Leon was a rising star in the new political firmament. Born in Durban in 1956 into a secular but identifying Jewish family long associated with the Progressive Party, Leon had been active in student politics while studying law. He had first entered politics in 1986 at the age of thirty when he won a Progressive Federal Party seat on the Johannesburg City Council. Upon Helen Suzman's retirement in 1989, Leon made a controversial "Young Turk" burst into the succession for her solidly progressive Houghton constituency and became a member of parliament representing what now became the Democratic Party. After that party's weak performance in the first democratic election of 1994—it won a mere 1.7 percent of the vote—its leader Zach de Beer resigned, and Leon made a swift and successful bid for the leadership of the party.

In the next election, in 1999, Tony Leon led the Democratic Party to impressive gains. It won 9.5 percent of the national vote, thereby replacing the National Party, the erstwhile rulers of apartheid South Africa, as the official parliamentary opposition. Indeed, in the Western Cape legislature the Democratic and National Parties were able to form a ruling coalition. It was thus an ironic twist of history, but one not uncharacteristic of the remarkable transformation of the country, that some sixty years after the ascendant Afrikaner nationalist party had adopted an antisemitic platform, a Jew all but stood at the helm of that party's rump, now reduced to the role of a weak parliamentary opposition. Tony Leon had become the new exemplar of what has been described as a "muscular liberalism" appealing to an electorate—mainly white—as a vitally needed democratic counterweight to the overwhelming power of the majority ANC party. Research on a representative sample of the Jewish population indicated that in the 1994 elections 56.4 percent voted for the Democratic Party, 30.8 percent for the (New) National Party, and 11.1 percent for the ANC.[48]

The role of Tony Leon and numerous other Jews in the parliamentary opposition, in addition to that of several Jews in the higher echelons of the ANC, in the first two governments of the new South Africa and in various government departments amounted to a salience of Jews in political governance unprecedented in the history of South Africa.[49] Concurrently, the Jewish Board of Deputies was straining to formulate a proactive program geared to building bridges with other communities and to social action aimed at uplifting the majority population that had been so underprivileged under apartheid. Whereas in the past it had always gone to great pains to emphasize that its mandate was limited purely to looking after the legitimate interests of the Jewish community, it now adopted a "mission statement" that spoke not only of protecting "the civil liberties of South African Jews" but also of "work for the betterment of human relations between Jews and all other peoples of South Africa, based on mutual respect, understanding and goodwill." It declared that the Board was "committed to a new South Africa where everyone will enjoy freedom from the evils of prejudice, intolerance and discrimination." In stark contrast to the Board's policy a few decades earlier as a purely defense agency, it was clearly becoming nearly as much an advocacy agency. Chairman Mervyn Smith declared as much to the Board's national congress: "The Board's ethos has undoubtedly become one of participation in the wider community whilst not neglecting its traditional responsibilities as the guardian of the civil liberties of the Jewish community."[50]

Largely on the initiative of Chief Rabbi Cyril Harris and the prominent businessman Bertie Lubner, and with the support of major communal organizations such as the Board of Deputies, the Board of Education, and the Zionist Federation, practical expression was given to the impulse to make a specifically Jewish contribution to the new South African society. It took the form of an umbrella organization aptly named Tikkun, translated as "helping transformation." The Hebrew expression *tikkun olam* has important conceptual significance in Judaism and connotes the obligation to strive for the healing and perfection of life in this world. "As the Jewish community we seek to make a meaningful difference to the upliftment of disadvantaged people in South Africa," became Tikkun's mission statement. The founding directorate of Tikkun was situated within the Jewish Board of Deputies, its early codirectors being Vivienne Anstey, a professional staff member of the Board, and Herbert Rosenberg, formerly the executive director of the Zionist Federation. Rosenberg went on to construct an increasingly ramified network of projects with an impressive list of patrons topped by Nelson Mandela as patron-in-chief.[51]

To be sure, Tikkun's projects were far from being unprecedented innovations in the Jewish community. As we have seen in other sections of this book, the Jewish community had a long tradition of philanthropic social action dedicated to alleviating the plight of the underprivileged in South Africa. Branches of the Union of

Jewish Women conducted manifold activities throughout the apartheid years, ranging from soup kitchens for needy blacks to crèches and night schools for adult education in various black townships. In the late 1980s the Union launched a number of special projects that moved from a charity model to a development model. After consultation with community members in Soweto, it introduced a Home Instruction Program for preschool children (Hippy) modeled on an initiative started by the Hebrew University's School of Education with funds donated by the National Council of Jewish Women of America. Another early childhood program launched by the Union of Jewish Women was called MATAL. It trained a selection of Soweto school principals and teachers to conduct a science-teaching program for kindergarten and elementary schoolchildren, which had been developed at Tel Aviv University's School of Education.[52] A long-established project of educational outreach was the M. C. Weiler Community School for black children in the Alexandra Township of Johannesburg, which, as we have noted earlier, had been founded in 1945 by the United Sisterhood of the reform congregations. Also lodges of the B'nai B'rith funded a range of welfare projects such as soup kitchens and provision of warm clothing and school textbooks. An example of individual acts of philanthropy was the Isaacson Foundation Bursary Fund, established in 1953 with the purpose of helping black pupils to complete their matriculation and continue their university education. The benefactor, Morris Isaacson, had come as an immigrant from Lithuania to South Africa in 1896 and started out as no more than an itinerant trader or "smous." The well-known Jewish philanthropist in Durban, Aaron Beare, established a similar fund.

Tikkun now set out, as a first step, to coordinate all existing Jewish-sponsored initiatives. Building on these, it harnessed community and business resources and engaged volunteers for the development of a wide variety of new projects aimed at uplifting the disadvantaged. Funding and implementation of these projects were facilitated by prudent linkages to government and nongovernmental agencies alike, as well as by the support of private businesses and banks. Emphasis was placed on making Tikkun's projects self-sustaining and promoting empowerment of their beneficiaries. Cooperation was sought particularly with international Jewish organizations and with government agencies in Israel that had rich experience in aiding developing countries.

The range of projects undertaken was wide—from a home instruction project for preschool youngsters drawing on Israeli experience to a science and technology education project in cooperation with the international Jewish organization ORT; and from sponsorship of leadership-training programs in Israel for entrepreneurial and business skills to educational enrichment programs that linked the Jewish day schools in Johannesburg and Cape Town to counterpart schools wholly comprising black pupils. One of the major projects initiated and developed by Tikkun focused on an impoverished black farming area in Rietfontein, south of Johannesburg. A regional development plan was drawn up and implemented with the assistance of Israeli experts. In part based on the principals of the *moshav* (cooperative settlement) in Israel, it created a model region of agricultural and commercial productivity. Another major project of Tikkun was the creation in

1995 of an urban community center in Hillbrow, a Johannesburg suburb containing a high-density population of all races, plagued by high unemployment, street children, and social problems stemming from drug dealing, child abuse, wife battering, and other forms of crime and violence. The Tikkun project utilized Temple Israel, a large place of worship situated in Hillbrow whose progressive Judaism congregation was greatly diminished owing to demographic changes.

Relative to the more limited and disparate efforts of Jewish organizations in the past, Tikkun represented a major new direction of coordinated communal endeavor and won the praise of Mandela and other new political leaders. But it needs to be said that the sum total of these Tikkun projects was a mere drop in the ocean of South Africa's prodigious needs in the sphere of voluntary social action, and engaged only a small stratum of the Jewish population, most of which was intensely preoccupied with its own mundane struggle to adjust economically and socially to the new order. Most Jews were asking what effect the process of change was having on their own lives rather than what they could contribute to the change. Above all, the average Jew was gripped by chronic anxiety and fear in the face of the evidently uncontrollable spread of random violent crime.

The crime epidemic was one of the insufficiently anticipated aspects of the transition to the new democratic South Africa, although its roots clearly lie in the predemocratic past. According to Institute of Race Relations surveys, between 1974 and 1995 murder had already increased by 119 percent and rape by 149 percent, and South Africa had a reported murder rate of about 45 per 100,000 people in 1995, compared with an international average of 5.5 per 100,000 people.[53] Criminal brutality had always been rampant in the segregated black townships, rooted in simmering social problems such as utter disruption of the family unit, grinding poverty, and heavy unemployment. But under apartheid, the task of the police was less to fight this crime than to prevent it from affecting the privileged white population. The new South Africa inherited a police system grossly inadequate for the protection of all citizens on democratic lines. It lacked legitimacy in the eyes of the masses of the black population, and was demoralized and corrupt. The unbearable level of violent crime has had a devastating impact on the everyday conditions of life in South Africa. Although the black population continues to be its main victim, it has also become traumatic for whites accustomed to the cushioning that had formerly been provided by white minority rule. Crime has become the critical social problem affecting the lifestyle of whites in South Africa and undermining confidence in the new order.

Accurate statistical assessment of crime levels is extremely difficult, as are also comparisons between countries and knowing whether the "war against crime" is being won or lost. But all informed accounts leave no doubt that at the turn of the century South Africa ranks among the most crime-ridden societies in the world. This is especially true for crimes of violence such as murder, assault, rape, and armed robbery. An authoritative assessment published in 2001 concluded that even after what was claimed to be a slight decline in the number of murders since January 1994, the "total of roughly 1,500 murders in March 2000 translated into 55.3 incidents for every one hundred thousand citizens during the course of 1999."

It also found that reported cases of serious assault (defined broadly as a physical attack with some kind of weapon) increased steadily since 1994, reaching 595.1 cases per 100,000 citizens in 1999. It further assessed that on average, for 1999, there were 119.1 reported rapes and attempted rapes for every 100,000 citizens.[54]

Yet, much as one should not underestimate the gravity of the crime epidemic, so too one should not underestimate the capacity of people, in the absence of any alternative, to adapt their lives to escalating levels of crime and personal insecurity. In white suburbs of the cities, private security companies police neighborhoods, houses are surrounded by walls and electrified fences, new town houses are built in the form of *laager* fortresses, and residents are permitted to close off roads with security gates and check posts. At the same time, there can be no doubt that for many blacks crime undermines the promise that democracy will bring a better life, and for many whites it erodes confidence in the new democratic order. Government sensitivity led it to place a moratorium on the release of crime statistics, on the grounds that use of flawed and misleading statistics was rife, a measure hardly likely to improve public confidence.

Jews, in common with all middle-class and well-to-do if not affluent whites, have been deeply disturbed by this criminal violence. By the late 1990s there was hardly a Jew whose family or friends had not been affected in one way or another—in some cases as murder victims, but mostly as victims of vicious armed hijackings of motor vehicles or armed robberies and burglaries of homes and businesses. A letter that appeared in the Johannesburg newspaper, the *Star,* in August 1996 may illustrate the pathos of disillusionment and despair experienced by victims of these violent crimes:

> Through your newspaper, allow me to apologise to my three children and the many hundreds that I have taught. Throughout the dark days of South Africa, my dear children, I have stressed the positives: "Stay, you owe South Africa something. This is the dawn of a new and better day." When my sister-in-law was hijacked, again I counselled patience. When my car was stolen, it was just one of those things. Then my son was mugged and I thanked God he wasn't hurt. Soon afterwards my brother was hijacked and I still didn't see the light. Last Friday evening, when my family gathered to enjoy a Sabbath meal together, in my own driveway, just metres from my front door, my children and eleven-month-old granddaughter were accosted by two savages and my son-in-law was shot. Children, forgive me, I have given you poor advice and served you ill. Take your loved ones, wrap them in your arms and go. The barbarians are not at the gate, they are in our midst.[55]

The spiraling of apparently invincible violent crime has caused many South Africans to consider emigration. But this option has been realistic for only a limited socioeconomic stratum of the population: persons possessed of educational and professional qualifications or capital that might enable them to cope with the generally severely restrictive qualifications for acceptance in desirable countries of choice. By virtue of the relatively high proportion of Jews who fall into this category, they have steadily been choosing the emigration option and probably at a higher rate than other whites. To be sure, crime cannot be considered the only factor that enters into the choice of emigration. Other factors may well be deteriorating economic conditions and prospects, fear of political instability, and injury from (or apprehension of) employment and professional discrimination in the name of affirmative action, however morally justifiable. Yet, available evidence supports the overwhelming anecdotally based impression that for Jews crime has been and continues to be the crucial factor. A majority of respondents in a mid- to late 1990s representative sample of the Jewish population who said they were likely to emigrate gave personal safety as their primary concern. Twelve percent said they were "very likely" to emigrate, and another 15 percent that they were "fairly likely" to leave.[56] The latest research analysis of what is described as the "exodus" of South African Jews arrives at the conclusion that "variation in the timing and rate of change of net emigration during the 1990s is best accounted for by changes in exposure to violent crime."[57]

A definitive tracing of changes in the size of the Jewish population in South Africa over the last two decades of the twentieth century has so far proved unattainable, owing to a dearth of relevant statistical data. There can, however, be no doubt that there has been a drastic demographic decline and that emigration has been the major factor in causing this, although the precise scale of the emigration and what percentage Jews constitute out of total white emigration remain conjectural. Even more conjectural and open to debate is the question whether the trend of emigration casts serious doubt on the long-term viability of the Jewish community itself. The most scientifically thorough demographic analysis of the South African Jewish population to date is still Allie Dubb's *1991 Sociodemographic Survey* published in 1994, to which we have referred in other sections of this book. It showed that after increasing from 104,156 (4.4 percent of whites) to 118,200 (3.1 percent) in 1970, there was a small decline to 117,963 (2.6 percent) in 1980, followed by a sharp decline to an estimated 91,925 (1.8 percent) in 1991. The smallness of the decline from 1970 to 1980 was accounted for largely by immigration and return migration that offset emigration, a factor that has diminished greatly thereafter. Dubb made projections for the year 2001: between 90,700 (on the assumption of low excess emigration) and 86,300 (on the assumption of high excess emigration).[58]

Later estimates made on the basis of a variety of community records including the synagogues, schools, and the burial society as well as the government's statistical services have tended toward confirmation of the higher figure. Although unsubstantiated by scientifically sound analysis of adequate data, and possibly influenced by wishful thinking, in 1998 the conventionally held estimate was of a remaining Jewish population numbering around 90,000. On the basis of the same communal sources, the average annual emigration figure after 1994 was estimated at between 1,500 and 2,000.[59] A paper by two scholars, Shale Horowitz and Dana Kaplan, published by the journal *International Migration* in 2001, came to the conclusion that, owing mainly to emigration no longer offset by new or return immigrants, yearly declines of South African Jewry's population accelerated in the 1990s from between 1 and 2 percent to over 4 percent per annum. They suggested that this trend, "which shows every indication of continuing, calls into question the long-term viability of the Jewish community in anything like its present form."[60]

As has been mentioned in an earlier chapter that traced the decline of the Zionist organization in South Africa, Dubb estimated that in the 1970s Israel was the destination of the largest percentage of emigrants.[61] But this changed in the 1980s when, of about 18,000 emigrants, the percentage going to Israel dropped to 22.6 percent. The United States absorbed 26.9 percent, Australia 22.7, Britain 13.5, and Canada 12.6 percent. Estimates for the mid-1990s were that almost 40 percent were going to Australia, 20 to the United States, 15 to Israel, and about 10 percent each to Britain and Canada. Even the emigrating parents of pupils in the King David schools were mostly choosing Australia rather than Israel. Whereas as late as August 1993 the majority of these were choosing Israel, by 1996 and 1997 their percentage had dropped to only 17.6 and 10.2. By contrast, a comfortable majority of emigrants from the religious day schools (Yeshiva College rightward) continued to choose Israel as a destination (49.4 percent of the combined 1996–97 figure).[62]

Since Australia became the most favored destination of Jewish emigrants, some indication of their numbers relative to those of all South African emigrants may be found there. According to Australian immigration and population statistics, Jews comprised between 12 and 15 percent of the total 49,000 South African–born people living in Australia in 1991. More than half of the South African–born Jews lived in New South Wales, constituting about 20 percent of all South African–born persons in that state. An estimated 10 percent of Sydney Jewry was from South Africa, as was about 4 percent of Melbourne Jewry, and 30 to 40 percent of Perth's 6,000-strong Jewish community. In 1996 there were 55,821 South African–born persons in Australia, 7,535 (13.5 percent) professing Judaism.[63]

Within the Jewish community the topic of emigration was widely discussed. The Jewish Board of Deputies and most of the rabbis, while refraining from adoption of any official policy and constantly on guard to refute the occasional press reports that suggested it was only or mainly Jews who were leaving, conveyed an implicit message of confidence in the future of the new South Africa. The Board took no part in the encouragement of emigration and, at most, joined the Zionist Federation, as did most rabbis, in purveying the slogan "either stay home or go home." This slogan signified the ideological conviction that the only honorable homes were the country that had taken in one's forebears and allowed one to thrive or the Land of Israel, ancestral home of all Jews. It intimated the further unspoken cognition that there was nothing to be proud of in the spectacle of Jews, who had enjoyed the ill-gotten gains of white minority domination over South Africa's resources and people, now choosing to leave rather than face up to the hardships of apartheid's legacy. The ultraorthodox rabbis were the most active in encouraging Jews to stay, for reasons intrinsic to their particular character. In 1999 Rabbi Yossy Goldman, faithful to the exhortation that the Lubavitcher rebbe Menachem Mendel Schneerson had begun to convey as early as the late 1970s, issued a congregational newsletter giving "fourteen reasons to stay in South Africa." The gist of his message was not only that this was where divine providence had placed one but also that, thanks to the now flourishing religious amenities available, there was no other place where Jews could in fact enjoy as satisfying a Jewish life.[64]

At the same time, a stratum of consistently idealistic liberal-minded Jews, who had always opposed apartheid, was accommodating with understanding to the difficult conditions of personal insecurity as well as to the affirmative action and lowering of public service standards. They believed these to be the inevitable unfortunate legacy of the country's past; its gross inequalities caused by white racism, domination, and selfish self-aggrandizement. Postapartheid conscience was the compass that guided the behavior of such Jews.

Community and Conscience

Of all the mantras that the personality and policy of Nelson Mandela imprinted on the new South Africa, perhaps the most profound was "reconciliation." Among other effects, it produced an atmosphere of introspection and soul-searching in white intellectual circles of the liberal kind. It was as if a public postmortem or confessional was being held on the faults of commission and omission perpetrated by different segments of the white population that had benefited in one way or another from the evil fruits of white minority domination and apartheid. Above all, it was the Truth and Reconciliation Commission (TRC) that nourished this atmosphere, as night after night over a period of years television viewers were exposed to heartrending testimonies of shameful indignities and abominable murders and tortures perpetrated during the apartheid years.

The TRC had been launched by a formal act of parliament in December 1995. It was to have seventeen members headed by former Archbishop Desmond Tutu. The aim was to probe gross violations of human rights in order to arrive at the truth and initiate a process of reconciliation and healing, without which it was assumed it would be impossible to create a healthy future for the transformed society of South Africa. One facet of the commission's mandate that aroused bitter controversy was its power to grant amnesty to those who made full disclosure of what they had done, provided that the motivation was shown to be other than patently criminal in nature. Amnesty was applicable only if the acts in question were shown to have been politically motivated. The TRC investigated gross violations of human rights perpetrated between 1960 and 1994, and recorded in its public hearings over twenty thousand statements by victims. The applications of over seven thousand people for amnesty were heard. It also advised the government on reparations and rehabilitation for victims.

This atmosphere of soul-searching and contrition reverberated within intellectual circles in the Jewish community. In 1996 a few young Jews who sought to bridge their Jewish identity with involvement in the building of a new nonracial, democratic, and just society formed a group that they named Gesher (Hebrew for bridge). The group's chairman was Geoff Sifrin, by profession an architect and town planner turned writer and journalist, and its members included Steven Friedman, whose contributions to Jewish thinking over the transition out of apartheid were discussed earlier. Describing itself as a Jewish movement for social action, Gesher was in a sense a successor of the Jews for Justice and Jews for Social Justice groups that had disbanded by 1994. One of the group's activities was the formulation of a submission to the TRC, made in January 1997, in which it expressed a specifically Jewish perspective on contrition and reconciliation as concept and process. Gesher did not purport to represent all Jews; it claimed only to offer a Jewish view as understood by the authors of the submission, but in so doing it attempted to draw upon the finest Jewish religious traditions relating to the concept of reconciliation. Its submission stated that reconciliation is a significant Jewish value for which Jewish tradition prescribes clear guidelines and that "all South Africans were part of the society in which apartheid atrocities were committed, and all bear a responsibility to participate in the process of reconciliation."[65]

According to Gesher's understanding, in Jewish law repentance requires that an individual go through a number of steps: the individual admits to having done wrong, shows genuine regret for having done wrong, attempts to make appropriate reparation, and commits to a firm change of heart and to not repeating the wrong in future. Citing "The Laws of Repentance" from the *Mishneh Torah* of Maimonides, the submission explained that according to Jewish tradition reconciliation cannot be achieved purely by divine intervention; the person or group that has committed a wrong must make peace with the person or group wronged. Furthermore, in terms of Jewish teaching, repentance is required not only from those who implemented the evil system of apartheid but also from "those who consider themselves to be neither victims nor perpetrators, but innocent bystanders." This meant the Jewish community was implicated. Gesher's submission emphasized that Jews themselves had a long history of being persecuted while surrounding populations stood by and later claimed that they were merely innocent bystanders. "In the South African situation people who have thought of themselves as bystanders must ask themselves how they ought to have acted, or in what ways they implicitly supported the apartheid system or failed to carry out their moral duty."[66] Although the bystander was not to be held to the same standard of justice as the perpetrator, he too was obliged to participate in the process of reconciliation. Indeed, even the victims of apartheid had to acknowledge that certain of their actions were a violation of moral standards requiring contrition and reconciliation. Thus, noted Gesher's submission, "suppressing human rights in detention camps during the guerrilla war against apartheid is one illustration. Necklacing of suspected collaborators is another." ("Necklacing" was the murder of victims inside a burning tire, a notorious vigilante practice usually perpetrated against suspected police accomplices in periods of black township unrest.)

One of the effects of the public debate over peace and reconciliation that affected Jews was the invocation of comparisons with the Holocaust and the post–World War Nuremberg trials. Facile use was made of the metaphor of the Holocaust in relation to South African apartheid in a number of works arising from the work of the TRC.[67] In a workshop discussion on Jewish perspectives held by Gesher with the participation of some members of the TRC itself, the subject was earnestly debated.[68] On the one hand, the incomparable horror and bestiality of the Holocaust, unprecedented in its calculated intentionality, rendered comparison with the apartheid regime unacceptable. On the other hand, at least in regard to the processes of truth revelation, punishment, and conciliation in the aftermath of the Holocaust, some conspicuous points of comparison could not be overlooked. As Geoff Sifrin noted: "From the Jewish point of view, when Jews watch or participate in the current discussions of the Truth Commission, there is a parallel sub-text running through their psyches that calls to mind the Holocaust and the Nuremberg trials of Nazi leaders which followed."

One of the participants in the debate was Dr. Franz Auerbach. As in the past, Auerbach pointed to parallels between the role of white bystanders in South Africa and that of Gentiles during the persecution of the Jews in Nazi Germany and the mass slaughter in all of eastern Europe in the war years. He held that in either case the least one should expect of those who were bystanders was the moral duty now "to listen to what actually happened and not to say, 'We didn't know.'" Steven Friedman observed that the TRC process was predicated more on the Christian view of repentance than on that of Judaism in that it allowed for vicarious repentance and absolution, whereas in Judaism, "nobody can right a wrong for you—the only one who can right that wrong is you yourself." He added that Jewish tradition also allowed for circumstances in which it would be impossible for the wronged party to forgive. He said that just as learned rabbis had argued "that it is impossible for us to forgive the Holocaust because we are not direct victims of it, one has to ask whether it was really realistic to expect a Commission process in South Africa to enable people who have lost husbands, wives, children or parents in appalling circumstances to forgive."

Gesher's submission reflected the sorely troubled conscience of, at best, a section of the Jewish community but did not directly impugn the communal leadership. However, there were others in the community who were prompted to place past leaders in the dock of Jewish morality to face retroactive charges of complicity in the apartheid system. This was largely a matter of generational differences. Those who were too young to have borne responsibility for the Jewish communal stance in the worst years of apartheid tended more to a sense of shame and to pointing an accusing finger at their seniors. In a characteristic outcry, one young student who participated in the Gesher discussion declared: "Most of the rabbis on the pulpit now did nothing to stand up against apartheid. Why aren't we saying to them, 'Repent!' Why aren't we saying that we're not prepared to accept you until you say to us 'I have failed to teach you the message of my tradition?'"[69]

In early 1997 Claudia Braude, a young Jewish journalist brought up in an observant Jewish home and educated in a Jewish day school, issued a challenge of this sort in a scathing article she submitted to *Jewish Affairs*. When the journal's editorial committee—of which Braude herself was a dissenting member—rejected the article because it contained possibly libelous statements, she resigned and proceeded to publish her views in the general press.[70] Braude's protest was triggered by her viewing of a television documentary that showed Mandela drinking tea with Betsy Verwoerd, widow of Hendrik Verwoerd, the architect of grand apartheid, and also in amiable conversation with Percy Yutar, state prosecutor in the

Rivonia Trial, the very trial whose judgment exiled Mandela to Robben Island for twenty-seven years. This characteristically conciliatory and forgiving gesture of Mandela failed to allay Braude's personal pain and anger at, in her words, "what Yutar did in the name of Jewish communal interests." She was appalled that a Jew, and a notable lay leader of an orthodox congregation to boot, "could have played the persecutory role he did in the political trial of the apartheid state." In Braude's view, Yutar's behavior epitomized the shameful complicity of the organized Jewish community in apartheid, complicity rooted in cowardly fear of reprisals from the awesome Afrikaner nationalist powers that were. She charged not only that Yutar was never criticized but also that the Jewish press drew thinly disguised relief from the fact that so patriotically zealous a Jewish state prosecutor counterbalanced the embarrassing prominence of so many Jews in the ranks of the accused. Yutar, earning the unstinting praise of Minister of Justice Jimmy Kruger, as "the official with the highest sense of loyalty he had ever found in a public servant," was rewarded with appointment as a provincial attorney general. For this, charged Braude, he was publicly congratulated by the chairman of the Jewish Board of Deputies as well as from the pulpit of his synagogue.

Claudia Braude's judgmental posture reflected the retrospective postapartheid view of one who had grown up well after the period of high apartheid, when the intimidating legacy of Afrikaner nationalist antisemitism had been a determinative factor in the behavior of the Jewish leadership and outweighed all liberal pangs of conscience. Braude not only called to account the entire Board of Deputies' policy of "political non-involvement" and the quiescence of the rabbinate, but also drew broader accusatory conclusions concerning the Jewish education she had received:

> My Jewish education was the direct product of the desire of the apartheid state to promote ethnic separatism. In spite of critical distance from the pressures and imperatives of the apartheid state, the South African Jewish establishment, like much of white South Africa, internalized the values and ideology of apartheid and ethnic separatism. The terms and discourse of apartheid fast became appropriated within all areas of Jewish life and consciousness.[71]

Indeed, she went further, attributing also to Zionism an apartheid-conditioned influence upon both the rabbinate and the community's lay leaders, on the grounds that it induced "the denial of a politically meaningful space for Jews in the Diaspora" and a "deferral away from South Africa to Israel." According to Braude, this made Zionism "arguably one collusional tool in Jewish consciousness under apartheid. It functioned to discourage South African Jews from opposing the racist policies of the National Party and the government."[72]

It is indicative of a confused ambivalence in Braude's judgmental stance that although fully cognizant that this Jewish behavior was, in her own words, "the result of a fearful confrontation with Afrikaans [*sic*] nationalism," she could not bring herself to exonerate the record of the community's leaders, lay and rabbinical. Braude seemed to be dividing blame inconclusively between the Jews, for allowing themselves to be intimidated, and the intimidating Afrikaner nationalists, for causing the Jews to betray their ethical values. In the eyes of other Jews who were not inclined to be so judgmental, Braude's views, however well intentioned, appeared to be no more than the self-righteous harangue of a postapartheid youngster insufficiently mature to appreciate the universal phenomenon of minority-group behavior.[73]

Jews were not the sole white minority ethnic group in South Africa. There were also communities of Germans, Dutch, Greeks, Italians, and Portuguese. A documented historical comparison of the political behavior of these communities suggests itself, but is neither within the scope of the present study nor within the competence of this author. In any case, what one might learn from such a comparison with the Jewish experience would be limited, since none of these other white ethnic groups was as cohesively organized and consistently salient in the South African context. The Portuguese alone exceeded the Jews in numbers, being roughly estimated at over 500,000 by the 1990s. However, as late as 1961 there were only an estimated 10,000 in South Africa. The growth in their numbers is thus very recent, dating mainly from the withdrawal of Portuguese colonial rule from Angola and Mozambique in 1975.[74] The Italian community too reached significant proportions much later than the Jewish community. It numbered only a few thousand until the Second World War, after which a considerable number of former prisoners of war settled in the country. (During the war about 94,000 had been held in South Africa, mainly in the large Zonderwater prisoner of war camp near Pretoria.) The Italian community's numbers were estimated at 41,300 in 1970 and were believed to be about 72,000 by 1993.[75]

Of all other minority communities the Greeks are probably the most comparable to the Jews by dint of the near complete congruence of their ethnicity and the Greek Orthodox religion. It is noteworthy that at least one famous son of that community personifies the type of leader who was concurrently very prominent in his own ethnic community and in the struggle against the apartheid system. He is the brilliant advocate George Bizos, a man cast in much the same mold as the Jewish community's Israel Maisels.[76] However, the Greek (Hellenic) community was careful to take no collective stand against the apartheid policy of the government. Although, comparably to the Jews, it was cohesive and possessed of newspapers and a school of its own, it had nothing like the prominence of the Jews in the South African context. In 1916 there were only some 2,292 members of the Greek Orthodox Church (at about the same time there were about 59,000 Jews), and their roughly estimated numbers had reached no more than 40,000 by 1971, the main increment being after the Second World War and partly from Cyprus.[77]

For our purposes, a sounder and more fruitful basis for comparative examination of Jewish minority-group behavior in the political sphere is provided by studies of the Jews in the United States. The behavior of South Africa's Jews in relation to apartheid certainly bears comparison with that of the Jews in the American South during the civil rights struggle of the 1950s and 1960s. There too Jews were a tiny minority, only a fraction of 1 percent of the total population,[78] and were beneficiaries of the privileged status of whites in a society that discriminated systematically against blacks. There too the leadership of the Jewish community, lay and clerical, had to grapple with a dilemma of conscience, torn between the conviction that Jewish ethics and experience commanded support of equal civil rights, on the one hand, and the responsibility of leadership not to endanger the safety and welfare of the Jewish community by defying the white consensus, on the other hand. The following concluding assessment—made in the most recent and comprehensive study of the record of southern Jews, a fine work by Clive Webb—could well be applied to South African Jewry with only minor adjustments of detail:

> During the desegregation crisis, southern Jews were torn between two contradictory instincts. A historical experience of persecution sensitized Jews to the plight of other oppressed minorities. Southern Jews were therefore more supportive of desegregation than the rest of the white community. At the same time it is precisely because of that experience of persecution that Jews have as an act of self-protection striven to adapt to the laws and customs of their adopted homelands. In the American South, that meant more than anything else an acceptance of racial segregation. Fear of anti-Semitic reprisals forced many southern Jews into an uneasy silence during the civil rights struggle.[79]

In both cases, fear of provoking anticipated retribution overwhelmed the impulse to take a brave stand against the prevailing white consensus. Exactly what Jews had to fear differed according to the variant macrocosmic situation of the two communities. In the South African case, it was the wrath of the powers that stringently controlled and regimented the polity as a whole. For Jews there was the additional extremely problematic complication of Israel's vacillating relations with South Africa, which profoundly affected their integrally Zionist identity. As we have seen in an earlier chapter of this book, the capacity of the Jewish community to stand up to the anticipated ire of the government and the progovernment public was further enfeebled by its being in a sense hostage to Israel's policy toward South Africa. By contrast, the Israel factor figured not at all in the concerns of southern American Jews. Their major fear became that the actions of the national Jewish organizations and northern civil rights activists would identify all Jews with the integrationist movement, thereby activating the antisemitic potential of their southern white neighbors. As in South Africa, any collaborative relationship between Jews and blacks was out of the question. In the United States whatever such relationship existed was confined to the level of national Jewish leadership.[80] The awareness of Jewish southerners, gauged by the Jewish press in the 1950s and 1960s, that South African Jews were in a comparable situation, is also of interest. It appears that in defending their passivity from northerners' criticism, they drew encouragement from the example of South African Jewry's apparent success in coping with similar dilemmas of conscience.[81]

Most historical writings on southern Jews in the United States concur that, overall, the Jews conformed to the norms of the white population and complied with the southern system of discriminatory race relations.[82] As in the case of South African Jewry the assessment that the average Jew was significantly more liberal-minded than members of other white ethnic or religious groups is plausible, but rests on evidence that can hardly be said to be empirically sufficient and conclusive. Much as was true in South Africa, research on southern American Jews shows that even if Jews more than others acknowledged either the principle or the inevitability of equal civil rights and integration, most favored only gradual and controlled change. Not local southerners but liberal northern Jews were the ones who participated in the civil rights movement's assertive incursions into the South with a salience disproportionate to the scale of the Jewish population in the United States. In this respect, there can be no doubt that the role of individual local Jews in the struggle against apartheid, clear across the spectrum from liberal parliamentary opposition to communist agitation and underground resistance movements, exceeds by far the record of resistance evinced by southern Jews of the United States.

This point of contrast extends also, on the other side, to the prominence of individual Jews who enrolled actively in the reactionary political camp. It was far higher in southern American Jewry, in some cases such prosegregation Jews achieving great political prominence. As we have seen, South African Jewry had a few active political advocates for apartheid or for the National Party, such as Joseph Nossel, Mendel Levin, Abe Hoppenstein, and Sam Bloomberg, but they were only of marginal significance. There were no defenders of apartheid comparable to an important political personage such as Charles Bloch in the United States. Bloch applied to great effect his sharp legal expertise in the political battle against desegregation in the state of Georgia, clashing legal swords at one stage with the civil rights lawyer Morris Abrams (later to become national president of the American Jewish Committee). Nor did South African Jewry produce a fervent opponent of integration as prominent as Solomon Blatt, Speaker of the House in the South Carolina legislature of the 1960s, or Sol Tepper, a major advocate of continued segregation in Selma, Alabama.[83]

The situation and behavior of southern American Jews in general may most appropriately be likened to that of the relatively small segment of South African "country Jews," who lived in close economic and social proximity to Afrikaner farmers and small-town people.[84] Their perceived vulnerability to defamation, ostracism, and overt hostility far exceeded that of Jews in South Africa's major cities, which provided a mainly English-speaking and moderately liberal social environment. It is noteworthy that throughout the period of apartheid South African Jews were subjected to few incidents involving violence. By contrast, the experience of southern Jews in the United States was marked by more serious and numerous incidents of unrestrained intimidation and violence, the most infamous and traumatic for the community being the bombing of the synagogue of Rabbi Jacob Rothschild of Atlanta in 1958.

This distinction in regard to fear of violent reprisal is indicative of a major difference in the social situation of these two Jewish communities. The roots of the Jewish community in the history of the American South reached deeply into the pre–Civil War period, whereas in South Africa the community only began to sink generative roots after the 1880s wave of eastern European immigration. Although in the final analysis an abiding sense of being alien to the Christian white majority was the common experience of both communities, Jews were more intimately integrated into the socioeconomic fabric of the white South—a population among the most ethnically homogeneous in all of America—than they ever could be into the rigidly multisegmented society of South Africa. The far more assimilated and less cohesively organized southern Jews of the United States proved to be more intimidated or vulnerable, and consequently even more compliant.

In comparing the two cases qua communities, one important difference was that the southern Jews had no central representative organization equivalent in authority and function to the South African Jewish Board of Deputies. Whereas in South Africa one may speak of a specific, official communal policy in relation to involvement in politics, this is not quite applicable in the case of southern Jews. Since the responsibilities of communal leadership in the southern United States were thus less concentrated, it seems they were also less vulnerable to governmental pressure. In regard to the rabbinate, however, comparison may well be more pertinent. Although more recent historical research on southern American Jewry has modified earlier accounts that depicted rabbis as being universally conformist, quiescent, and compliant, the mixed record of their behavior appears to be much the same as in South Africa.[85] The composition of the rabbinate was, however, very different in the two places. Of the estimated two hundred rabbis who occupied southern pulpits at the time of the segregation crisis, over half were reform,[86] whereas reform (progressive) Judaism never exceeded about 18 percent of South African Jewry and the percentage of reform rabbis was therefore tiny. In southern Jewry, almost all those who had the conviction and courage to take a stand against the white segregationist consensus were reform rabbis. The most notable cases included Rabbis Jacob Rothschild of Atlanta; Perry Nussbaum of Jackson, Mississippi; Charles Mantinband of Hattiesburg, Mississippi; Ira Sanders of Little Rock, Arkansas; and Milton Grafman of Birmingham, Alabama.[87] Overall, the record of their brave opposition to the dominant public consensus against equal civil rights for African-Americans was not matched by the rabbis of progressive Judaism or for that matter also of orthodox Judaism in South Africa. In accounting for this difference note should be taken of the fact that South Africa's rabbis were subject to a more centralized and representative communal authority. Also there was no overarching rabbinical structure, such as the northern-based American synagogue and rabbinical organizations provided for southern rabbis, to boost the moral fortitude of South African rabbis.

On balance, if one is to indulge in moral judgment, the minority-group behavior of South African Jews was certainly not worse than that of southern American Jews. It was left to Chief Rabbi Cyril Harris to formulate perhaps the most balanced exposition of the South African Jewish community's moral conscience when he was obliged to make an official submission to the religious communities' section of the Truth and Reconciliation Commission in November 1997.[88] His submission must be appreciated in the context of others representing the Christian majority. All the churches made contrite apologies for what was described as strategies of disengagement, which contributed to a climate that allowed human rights abuses to take place. Some admitted that by evading involvement in politics they gave the status quo tacit support. Others also were contrite over failure to give sufficient support to activists against apartheid in their midst, or even suppressing their own dissidents. A shameful example of this was the case of Reverend Frank Chikane of the Apostolic Faith Mission (and later general-secretary of the South African Council of Churches), who was rejected by his own church and even subjected to torture with the complicity of a white elder of the church. However, no church group apologized for active complicity in human rights abuses or admitted to having actively supported the policies of apartheid as they were actually implemented by the state. Even the Dutch Reformed Church, although confessing to having "misled" its flock "on apartheid as a biblical instruction," held on to a distinction between bad apartheid, as it were, and good apartheid benignly applied with justice and "Christian love."[89]

Chief Rabbi Harris, in his submission on behalf of the Jewish "faith community," characterized the record of the Jewish community in these words:

> The Jewish community did not initiate apartheid. Many in the Jewish community did not agree with apartheid. Almost everyone in the Jewish community had a kind of awkward tension about apartheid. But most members of the Jewish community benefited in one way or another from apartheid.

Harris submitted that no Jew who lived in South Africa during the apartheid period could possibly claim that his or her present circumstances were not in some measure a result of apartheid. "Anyone who succeeded in business benefited from a right to economic activity which was denied others. Anyone who received a professional qualification, enjoyed a place at school, college or university which was denied to the majority on racial grounds alone." Hence, Rabbi Harris acknowledged, "in that the Jewish community benefited from apartheid an apology must be given to this commission." He submitted, furthermore, that the Jewish community also confessed to a collective failure to protest against apartheid, especially since "the entire thrust of Jewish moral teachings, together with the essential lesson of Jewish historical experience," should have commanded them to do so. He did not enter into a justification of the policy formula of political noninvolvement that had been adopted by the representative leadership of the community, but focused instead on the silent bystander position adopted by the official community. On the one hand, he offered an explanation. He suggested that in part desensitization and the stifling of conscience was one of the evil effects of apartheid itself, and cowardice too was involved. But, he added: "Fear played a very large part—it shouldn't have done, but it did." He said it had to be appreciated that "given the fact that this was a post-Holocaust generation which remembered the record of antisemitism also in South Africa in recent decades, there was always the fear of antisemitism raising its head again should the Jews become too bold in their opposition." Harris did not, however, treat this explanation as a basis for exoneration. Nor did he stage a facile appropriation for Judaism of the universally acknowledged fact that there were proportionately more opponents of the system from among the Jews. He admitted "that these individuals were not all practising Jews," but suggested that "they were moved by either Jewish and more often than not, humanitarian motivations, to speak out."

Notwithstanding the objective causes and reasons for the record of Jewish behavior in the face of the apartheid system and the partially redeeming role of individual Jews who had actively resisted it, Harris did not vindicate the Jewish community as a collective. He averred that, whatever the circumstances, "distancing one's own interests can never be morally justified." "Because of the evil of indifference which so many in the Jewish community professed," he stated, "we confess that sin today before this Commission and we ask forgiveness for it." On the positive side, outlining the various welfare and educational projects encompassed by the Tikkun program, he gave a promising assurance of the community's present commitment to help in the formidable task of uplifting the underprivileged in the new South African society.

It is difficult to know how representative the chief rabbi's affirmation of the TRC process and his implied self-criticism of the community's behavior were of the views and sentiments prevalent among Jews in the country. Judging by the strenuous efforts Rabbi Harris himself had to muster in order to relieve the pessimistic and partly resentful mood of the Jewish public, his admissions of Jewish moral culpability probably went beyond what most ordinary Jews felt. At least one other rabbi publicly expressed reservations about the value or desirability of the TRC in the first place. He was Rabbi Ivan Lerner, the senior minister of the orthodox Claremont Hebrew congregation in Cape Town. Lerner argued that the TRC "will only serve to divide and distract" South Africans from the real task of building a common future.[90] Asked by a commission member how Jews at large viewed the truth and reconciliation process, Harris ventured the opinion that there was a dichotomy: "Those who are over the age of 60 have difficulty with many things including the TRC. We have no difficulty with those who are under 30. There are some difficulties with those in the middle group." It is also instructive that Harris ruffled the feathers of some leading Jewish businessmen when, in answer to another question concerning the advisability of imposing a wealth tax, he responded that he "would put his weight behind the suggestion."

In 1997 the journal *Jewish Affairs*, edited by Professor Joseph Sherman of the University of the Witwatersrand, devoted an issue to a symposium of papers on "Jews and Apartheid."[91] Since the participants were all deeply identifying Jews actively committed to the life of the Jewish community, the symposium did not encompass the views of the alienated type of radical Jew who was known to be harshly condemnatory of the community's record. With this reservation in mind, it may be said that the symposium constituted an illuminating exposure of the Jewish communal conscience. Opinions ranged from shame at the failure of the community to have taken a clear moral stand to indignant rejection of "moral grandstanders" and practitioners of self-flagellation "with neither historical sense nor understanding of the marginalised condition of the Jews in South Africa."[92]

A pivotal question was whether the community (meaning in effect the Board of Deputies) had reasonable cause to anticipate damaging retribution had it adopted a collective stand of opposition to the government's apartheid policy. Broaching the question head-on, Aleck Goldberg posed a putative scenario in which all the Board's officeholders had unanimously agreed to satisfy the passionate and morally correct arguments of those Jews who urged it openly and unequivocally to oppose the government's apartheid policy from its outset. How would the National Party government have reacted? Of course, in the absence of any evidence that might indicate the contingency intentions of the government or its security agencies—if such intentions existed at all—in relation to the behavior of the Jews qua community, Goldberg could answer this question only on the basis of the Board leadership's own perception of the situation. Few persons were in a better position to attest to this perception throughout the apartheid period than Goldberg, who had worked for over thirty years in the South African Jewish Board of Deputies, serving as its executive director from 1981 to 1991. His answer was: "Although Nazi-style antisemitism had been discredited throughout the world after World War II, and the South African government was having enough difficulty trying to justify its race policies, there can be little doubt that it would have reacted with anger against the South African Jewish community." He added that the Board's actions "would undoubtedly have created misgivings and unhappiness in the very community whose interests it was charged to defend." Goldberg argued that, "sensing all these potential repercussions, the Board consciously desisted from adopting what would have been construed as an openly party-political stance."[93]

A similar analysis was offered by Jocelyn Hellig, a professor of religious studies in the University of the Witwatersrand, who served on the executive of the Board of Deputies but only in the latter phase of apartheid rule. Hellig too drew the conclusion that "confronted with the possibility of state-sponsored antisemitism from an avowedly antisemitic party . . . the Jewish community as a community had little option but to respond to apartheid as it did." At the same time, she held that it must be acknowledged that this policy "was bought at an enormous price." It amounted to "the surrender of the Jewish ethic."[94] Franz Auerbach concurred with this assessment:

> First, most members of the Jewish community would have rejected such a stand. . . . Secondly, and more critically, there can be little doubt that if, during the rule of Verwoerd and Vorster, the representative body of the South African Jewish community had spoken in the way it did after 1980, a powerful antisemitic agitation would have been unleashed and this would assuredly have endangered the security of the Jewish community.[95]

Auerbach reasoned that as late as 1972 adoption of a resolution explicitly condemning the government's policy would certainly have been repudiated by a majority of Jews and "would have been treated by the government in power as proof of collective Jewish disloyalty. The proposition that the government would have accused the community of disloyalty is not hypothetical."

Addressing the same question from a different tangent, much the same assessment was made by two well-informed academics, Dr. Sally Frankental and Professor Milton Shain, respectively the former and current director of the Kaplan Centre for Jewish Studies at the University of Cape Town. "Given the anti-Jewish record of the National Party, together with its pro-Hitler and anti-war stance," they opined, "Jewish leadership may justifiably have believed it irresponsible to protest vehemently and publicly. . . . Once the degree of the new government's authoritarianism and the reach of its repressive legislation became evident, it was increasingly dangerous to confront the state."[96] They too noted that the leadership's policy was "a reflection of the bystander quietism of the community-at-large," and pointed to the fact that there was no groundswell of support for a more explicitly critical antiapartheid Jewish position such as could have bolstered those leaders wishing to play a more activist role.

By most accounts, then, it may be said that refraining from direct collective opposition to the government was seen to be the will of Jews at large at least as much as it was the policy of the Board of Deputies' leaders. Of course, one might reasonably charge that it was their duty to lead rather than to follow their public's opinion. But it is equally reasonable to conjecture that were the Board's leaders to have presumed to act against the obvious will of their public, their authority would have been challenged. The community would have split, and in all likelihood an alternative representative type of organization would have emerged. In such a case, the new organization would doubtless have gained the exclusive recognition of the government, and the Board of Deputies would have been marginalized if not wholly suppressed.

Given this assessment of the context in which the leadership of the Board of Deputies had to function and its primary purpose as defender of the Jewish community's safety, welfare, and interests, the policy adopted was in essence responsible and sagacious, despite the heavy price paid in terms of moral values. Nor can it justifiably be said that the Board's policy was an absolutely unqualified moral failure. After all, from the outset it did consistently criticize racial discrimination and all the related evils that were the inherent ingredients of the apartheid system, even if it did so timorously. That its statements constituted an implicit rejection of all that apartheid signified was obvious to Jews and progovernment circles alike. It was not unreasonable of the Board's leadership to assume that it could go no further than this without risking self-damaging consequences, thereby betraying its basic responsibility. As we have seen, after the mid-1970s, as the process of "reformed" apartheid unfolded and the restraints on public criticism loosened, the Board did in fact sharpen the focus of its statements until finally condemning apartheid outright by the mid-1980s. It is, however, cogently arguable that this change of gear could have been made earlier and more boldly without endangering the Jewish community. For, by the early 1970s, the mending of Israel–South Africa relations and the growing cooperation between them, in conjunction with the intensification of the international opposition to the South African government, would probably have made penalization of the Jewish community far less likely.

It is also arguable that the Board of Deputies failed by its own standards consistently to maintain its avowed principle of defending the right and duty of the individual Jew to act politically in accordance with Jewish ethical values. By adding to its policy formula a rider to the effect that this duty should be performed with "a due sense of public responsibility," the Board introduced an unmanageable ambiguity and marred the defensibility of its policy. It is undeniable that the Board, and even more so the majority of the community's rabbis, not only actively dissociated themselves from radical Jews (who were mainly, although not only, communists) but also preferred to obscure the visibility of every form of active resistance to apartheid by Jews. This stood in stark contrast to the conventional celebration of Jewish prominence in all walks of life that conformed with the status quo, not to speak of the lionization of the pantheon of Jewish resisters after the demise of the apartheid regime. In the 1990s the Jewish press abundantly featured interviews with Jewish radical returnees to South Africa, and a highly impressive exhibition, "Jews in the Struggle for Democracy and Human Rights in South Africa," was put on display in 1998 at the University of Cape Town's Kaplan Centre for Jewish Studies.[97] In a sense the very fact that today, in the newly constructed democratic South Africa, the Jewish Board of Deputies is committed to an advocacy role that goes beyond its primary role as defensive communal caretaker is an implicit indictment of its past record.

Most detached and objective observers would agree: although there is nothing in this record deserving of moral pride, neither does it warrant utter self-reproach. From a coldly objective historical perspective, this was characteristic minority-group behavior—a phenomenon of self-preservation, performed at the cost of moral righteousness. The record also shows that on the whole the community's leaders, lay and religious, acted consciously but with deep pangs of conscience, although whether this at all qualifies as a morally redeeming factor will no doubt remain a point of contention.[98]

Notes

Archives frequently cited have been identified by the following abbreviations:

BD	Archives of the South African Jewish Board of Deputies, Johannesburg
BJE	Archives of the South African Board of Jewish Education, Johannesburg
CZA	Central Zionist Archives, Jerusalem
IA	State Archives of Israel, Jerusalem
SA	South African National Archives, Pretoria
UCT	University of Cape Town Manuscripts Department
UJW	Archives of the South African Union of Jewish Women, Johannesburg
ZF	Archives of the South African Zionist Federation, Johannesburg

Introduction: The Jewish Community in South African Society

1. Jews are known to have been among the earliest circumnavigators of the Cape, but only Protestants were allowed to settle there during the rule of the Dutch East India Company (1652–1795). In the brief period of Batavian rule (1803–6) Jews were allowed in, and this continued to be the case under British rule after 1806. On the origins of the Jewish community, see Louis Herrman, *A History of the Jews in South Africa from the Earliest Times to 1895,* Johannesburg, SA, Jewish Board of Deputies, 1935; Israel Abrahams, *Birth of a Community: The History of Western Province Jewry from the Earliest Times to the End of the South African War, 1902,* Cape Town, Cape Town Hebrew Congregation, 1955; Gustav Saron and Louis Hotz, eds., *The Jews in South Africa: A History,* London and Cape Town, Oxford University Press, 1955; Milton Shain, *Jewry and Cape Society,* Cape Town, Historical Publication Society, 1983. See also Markus Arkin, ed., *South African Jewry: A Contemporary Survey,* Cape Town, Oxford University Press, 1984. An illuminating contribution to the economic history of the community is Mendel Kaplan, *Jewish Roots in the South African Economy,* Cape Town, Struik, 1986. See also Veronica Belling, *Bibliography of South African Jewry,* Cape Town, Kaplan Centre for Jewish Studies and Research, University of Cape Town, 1997.

2. Allie Dubb, *The Jewish Population of South Africa: The 1991 Sociodemographic Survey,* Cape Town, Kaplan Centre for Jewish Studies and Research, University of Cape Town, 1994, table i.i, p. 7. See also Gustav Saron, "The Making of South African Jewry," in Leon Feldberg, ed., *South African Jewry 1965,* Johannesburg, Fieldhill Publishing Co., 1965, p. 13; Saron and Hotz, *The Jews in South Africa,* pp. 100, 377–81; Sergio DellaPergola and Allie A. Dubb, "South African Jewry: A Sociodemographic Profile," in David Singer and Ruth Seldin, eds., *American Jewish Yearbook* 88 (1988): 59–140.

3. Well into the period of apartheid, whites were labeled "Europeans." All who were not white were "non-Europeans." In more recent times the designation "blacks" has come to be

used equally comprehensively for all "non-whites." According to official government statistics, in 1946 the total population was 11,418,349, of which 2,372,690 were Europeans and 9,045,659 were non-Europeans. "Non-Europeans" was composed of: Natives (Bantu), 7,831,915; Asiatics, 285,260; Coloreds, 928,484. Home languages of the whites were estimated as: English 933,812 (39.36 percent); Afrikaans, 1,359,691 (57.31 percent); English and Afrikaans, 29,823 (1.26 percent). See *Official Yearbook of the Union,* No. 24, 1948, Pretoria, Union of South Africa, Union Office of Census and Statistics, 1949–50, pp. 1078, 1086.

4. See Gideon Shimoni, *Jews and Zionism: The South African Experience 1910–1967,* Cape Town, Oxford University Press, 1980, p. 17. An insightful analysis of the entire Jewish communal structure and dynamics as it had evolved by the midapartheid period is Steven E. Aschheim, "The Communal Organization of South African Jewry," *Jewish Journal of Sociology* 12, no. 2 (1970): 201–31.

5. Litvak in the singular, Litvakes in the plural. In South Africa, as in Lithuania itself the self-designation most used was "Litvishe yidn." Lithuanian Gentiles were called "Litviner" in Yiddish.

6. The provinces of the northwestern region were Kovno, Vilna, Grodno, and northern Suwalki, whose ethnic composition was mainly Lithuanian and Polish, and Vitebsk, Minsk, and Mogilev, which were mainly Byelorussian and Russian in character.

7. Dov Levin, ed., *Pinkas ha-kehilot: Lita,* Jerusalem, Yad Vashem, 1996 (Hebrew), p. 26. See also Masha Greenbaum, *The Jews of Lithuania,* Jerusalem, Gefen, 1995. Adequate explanation for the remarkably concentrated flow of this Litvak migration to South Africa still awaits definitive historical research, although some major factors have been identified. Its beginnings can be traced back to transitory migration via Britain. See Chaim Gershater, "From Lithuania to South Africa," in Saron and Hotz, *The Jews in South Africa,* pp. 59–84; Shimoni, *Jews and Zionism,* pp. 7–11; Gideon Shimoni, "From One Frontier to Another: Jewish Identity and Political Orientation in Lithuania and South Africa," in Sander L. Gilman and Milton Shain, eds., *Jewries at the Frontier: Accommodation, Identity, Conflict,* Urbana and Chicago, University of Illinois Press, 1999, pp. 129–54. An illuminating contribution to understanding the process of emigration is Aubrey Newman, "Why Did Our Lithuanian Grandparents Come to South Africa?" *Jewish Affairs* 49, no. 2 (winter 1994): 9–12.

8. The pejorative "kaffir" like the slightly less offensive "native" was as common among Jews as all other whites. As it happens, its etymology is Semitic—from the Arabic (and Hebrew) word for "infidel."

9. However, Jews in the South African Republic, which lost its independence after defeat in the Anglo-Boer War of 1899–1902, did suffer from civic disabilities as part of the *uitlander* (alien) population. See Saron and Hotz, *The Jews in South Africa,* pp. 179–212; Shimoni, *Jews and Zionism,* pp. 61–65.

10. On early religious life and institutions in South Africa, see John I. Simon, "A Study of the Nature and Development of Orthodox Judaism in South Africa up to 1935," unpublished M.A. dissertation, University of Cape Town, 1996.

11. See Jocelyn Hellig, "South African Judaism: An Expression of Conservative Traditionalism," *Judaism* 35, no. 2 (spring 1986): 233–42; also idem, "Religious Expression," in Arkin, *South African Jewry,* pp. 95–116.

12. The expression is that of the doyen of South African Jewish historiography, Gustav Saron. See Saron, "The Making of South African Jewry."

13. Prior to 1919, when a truncated Lithuanian state gained independence, the northwestern region of the Pale contained about 15 million inhabitants, of which 30 percent (4,500,000) were ethnic Lithuanians and another 30 percent were Byelorussians. The Jews were the third largest ethnic group, constituting 15 percent and numbering 2,500,000. See

Greenbaum, *The Jews of Lithuania,* p. 208. In the independent state of Lithuania, according to the 1923 census, out of a total population of 2,028,971, the Lithuanians constituted 83.9 percent. The Jews were the next largest national group, constituting 7.6 percent. See Levin, *Pinkas ha-kehilot: Lita,* pp. 26, 46–47.

14. See Ezra Mendelsohn, *On Modern Jewish Politics,* New York, Oxford University Press, 1993, esp. pp. 42–44.

15. On the Zionism of reform or progressive Judaism and the minor manifestations of orthodox rabbinical opposition to Zionism, see Shimoni, *Jews and Zionism,* pp. 50–52.

16. ZF, *Reports and Accounts of the Executive to 21st Conference, November 1945 to April 1947,* p. 17; *Report to 23rd Conference, July 1952,* p. 16.

17. The U.S. total was $16,113,852; South Africa's, $3,898,985. Although Europe taken as a whole contributed more than South Africa ($8,943,654), western countries with far larger Jewish communities raised much less. England and Canada, for example, raised $2,135,789 and $1,131,482, respectively. South African Jewry's contribution continued to be second only to that of U.S. Jewry until the late 1940s. See Shimoni, *Jews and Zionism,* pp. 35–36.

18. Ibid., pp. 43–47; Gideon Shimoni, "Jan Christiaan Smuts and Zionism," *Jewish Social Studies* 39, no. 4 (fall 1977): 269–98.

19. See Leibl Feldman, *Yidden in Johannesburg,* Johannesburg, SA, Yiddish Cultural Federation, Pacific Press, 1956 (Yiddish), pp. 243–44; Michael Pesah Grossman, "A Study of the Trends and Tendencies of Hebrew and Yiddish Writing in South Africa since Their Beginnings in the Early Nineties of the Last Century to 1930," unpublished Ph.D. dissertation, University of the Witwatersrand, 1973, pp. 347–49.

20. See the poignantly insightful analysis of Joseph Sherman, "Serving the Natives: Whiteness as the Price of Hospitality in South African Yiddish Literature," *Journal of Southern African Studies* 26, no. 3 (September 2000): 506–21.

21. On Gandhi's Jewish associates, see Mohandas Karamchand Gandhi, *Satyagraha in South Africa,* trans. V. G. Desai, Stanford Academic Reprints, 1954, esp. pp. 177, 180, 247; also Gideon Shimoni, *Gandhi, Satyagraha and the Jews,* Jerusalem, Leonard Davis Institute of International Relations of the Hebrew University, 1977; Margaret Chatterjee, *Gandhi and His Jewish Friends,* London, Macmillan, 1992; Isa Sarid and Christian Bartolf, *Hermann Kallenbach: Mahatma Gandhi's Friend in South Africa,* Berlin, Gandhi-Information-Zentrum, 1997; George D. Paxton, "Sonia Schlesin, Gandhi and South Africa," *Jewish Affairs* 56, no. 1 (Pesach 2001): 13–19.

22. See Shimoni, *Jews and Zionism,* pp. 81–84.

23. Ibid.

24. It should also be noted, however, that Gandhi himself did not link the cause of the Indians with that of Africans. Convergence of legislation that might have prejudiced Jews as well as Indians occurred also in 1911–13 and 1924. See Shimoni, *Jews and Zionism,* pp. 76–80, 90. On immigration legislation and the Jews, see Edna Bradlow, "Immigration to the Union, 1910–1948: Policies and Attitudes," unpublished Ph.D. dissertation, University of Cape Town, 1978.

25. See Enid Alexander, *Morris Alexander: A Biography,* Cape Town, Juta, 1953; Baruch Hirson, *The Cape Town Intellectuals: Ruth Schechter and Her Circle, 1907–1934,* Cape Town, Merlin Press, 2001.

26. On the occupations of Jewish immigrants, see Louis Hotz, "Jews Who Arrived Here Sixty Years Ago," *Jewish Affairs* 18, no. 2 (February 1963): 4–11; Milton Shain, *Jewry and Cape Society,* pp. 84–86. On early trade union activity of Jews, see Evangelos A. Mantzaris, *Labour Struggles in South Africa: The Forgotten Pages 1903–1921,* Durban, Collective

Resources Publications, 1995, pp. 1–28, 29–48. On the seamy side of life and work in the Jewish immigrant generation, see Charles van Onselen, *Studies in the Social and Economic History of the Witwatersrand 1886–1914,* vol. 1: *New Babylon,* London, Longman, 1982.

27. See Shimoni, *Jews and Zionism,* pp. 159–60.

28. See Emil S. Sachs, *Rebel Daughters,* London, MacGibbon & Kee, 1957.

29. See Feldman, *Yidden in Johannesburg,* pp. 137–41.

30. Ibid., pp. 166–169; Evangelos Mantzaris, "Bund in dorem afrika," *Unser Zeit,* no. 6 (1981): 44–46 (Yiddish); and idem, "Sergei Riger (Baron) in dorem afrika," *Unser Zeit,* no. 9 (September 1983): 42–43 (Yiddish).

31. See E. A. Mantzaris, "Radical Community: The Yiddish-Speaking Branch of the International Socialist League, 1918–1920," in Belinda Bozzoli, ed., *Class, Community and Conflict: South African Perspectives,* Johannesburg, Ravan Press, 1987, pp. 160–76.

32. See Mark Israel and Simon Adams, "'That Spells Trouble': Jews and the Communist Party of South Africa," *Journal of Southern African Studies* 26, no. 1 (March 2000): 145–62.

33. See Eddie and Win Roux, *Rebel Pity: The Life of Eddie Roux,* London, Rex Collings, 1970, pp. 96–97; H. J. and R. E. Simons, *Class and Colour in South Africa: 1850–1950,* London, Penguin, 1969, esp. chapters 17 and 19; Allison Drew, *Discordant Comrades: Identities and Loyalties on the South African Left,* Aldershot, Ashgate, 2000, pp. 94–111.

34. In the late 1930s Bach went to the Soviet Union on party business, where he is believed to have died while in prison after being accused of ideological deviation of one kind or another. See Drew, *Discordant Comrades,* p. 195, n.83: Eddie Roux, *S. P. Bunting: A Political Biography,* Bellville, Mayibuye Press, 1993, pp. 191–92.

35. Document relating to a special meeting of the Communist Party's Johannesburg District Committee, held on 14 February 1946, in SA, J. C. Smuts Papers, CLXVIII.

36. See Leibl Feldman, *Yidden in Dorem Afrike,* Vilna and Johannesburg, Kleckina, Wilno, 1937, pp. 85–101 (Yiddish). According to Feldman, Poalei Zion's participation in the newly founded Communist Party was conditional on the agreement of the Comintern. (This was never given.)

37. See Taffy Adler, "Lithuania's Diaspora: The Johannesburg Jewish Workers' Club, 1928–1948," *Journal of Southern African Studies* 6, no. 1 (October 1979): 70–92; Feldman, *Yidden in Dorem Afrike,* pp. 113–16.

38. See Eddie and Win Roux, *Rebel Pity,* pp. 109–10.

39. Dr. Henry Sonnabend, "Survey of Johannesburg Jewry," ms. produced by South African Jewish Board of Deputies, Bureau of Jewish Statistics and Research, 1936.

40. Allie A. Dubb, *Jewish South Africans: A Sociological View of the Johannesburg Community,* Grahamstown, Institute of Social and Economic Research, Rhodes University, 1977, p. 20.

41. See Shimoni, *Jews and Zionism,* pp. 56–57.

42. Geserd is an abbreviation of the Yiddish name Gezelshaft far aynordnen oyf erd arbetndike yidn in FSSR (Society for Settling Jewish Workers on the Land in the USSR), and it existed in various countries.

43. On Jews in politics and the political attitudes and voting of Jews in the period prior to the creation of the Union of South Africa in 1910, see Saron and Hotz, *The Jews in South Africa,* esp. pp. 179–212. For the period after union, 1910 to 1948, see Shimoni, *Jews and Zionism,* pp. 61–96.

44. *Immigration Quota Act (no. 8 of 1930), Together with Regulations (Government Notice No. 545 of 1930),* Govt. Printer, 1930. The new Immigration Quota Act's central feature was severe restriction of immigration from all countries other than Britain and the Commonwealth, the United States of America, and the countries of western Europe. The restric-

tion was expressed in a universal annual quota of not more than 50 immigrants per restricted country. Provision was made for an additional unallocated quota of up to 1,000 immigrants per year, allowed at the discretion of a board whose terms of reference directed it only to accept immigrants "likely to become assimilated with the inhabitants of the Union."

45. *House of Assembly Debates,* vol. 14, 10 February 1930, cols. 558ff.

46. See Shimoni, *Jews and Zionism,* pp. 100–103.

47. See Milton Shain, *The Roots of Antisemitism in South Africa,* Charlottesville and London, University Press of Virginia, 1994.

48. *Johannesburg Times,* 1 April 1896. My own pet theory is that "Peruvian" originated among Jews as a Yiddish corruption of the word "parvenu."

49. See Shain, *The Roots of Antisemitism in South Africa,* pp. 62–63.

50. See also Milton Shain, "Perceptions of the Smous and Pioneer Jewish Traders in South Africa before 1914: A Critical Appraisal," in Moshe Sharon, ed., *Judaism in the Context of Diverse Civilizations,* Johannesburg, Maksim Publishers, 1993, pp. 207–19. Boer farmers called the familiar Jewish peddler a "smous." One conjecture is that smous derives from the known German pejorative epithet for Jewish trader, Mauschel; another that it is a corruption of Moses; yet another, that it is connected with the Yiddish word *shmuss,* meaning chat or patter. As well as smous, the Jewish peddlers themselves also used the term *tocher,* probably a Yiddish corruption of the Dutch-Afrikaans *toeganger,* roughly meaning one who comes by (to peddle his wares). See the usage of N. D. Hoffman, in an article on the Jews in South Africa sent to *Hatzfira* in 1891, quoted in Shimoni, *Jews and Zionism,* p. 11.

51. Ibid., pp. 105–6.

52. Examples of early works that drew a strong comparison between Afrikaner nationalist ideology and praxis and German national socialism are William H. Vatcher, *White Laager: The Rise of Afrikaner Nationalism,* London, Pall Mall Press, 1965; and Brian Bunting, *The Rise of the South African Reich,* Harmondsworth, Penguin, 1969. Resourceful research in German and South African archives has rendered several more authoritative works on the influence of the Third Reich on South African political developments. See F. J. van Heerden, "Nasionaal-Sosialisme as Faktor in die Suid-Afrikaanse Politiek 1933–1948," unpublished Ph.D. dissertation, University of the Orange Free State, 1972; Albrecht Hagemann, *Südafrika und das "Dritte Reich": Rassenpolitische Affinität und machtpolitische Rivalität,* Frankfurt and New York, Campus Verlag, 1989; idem, "Very Special Relations: The 'Third Reich' and the Union of South Africa, 1933–1939," *South African Historical Journal* 27 (1992): 127–47. The most conclusive is Patrick J. Furlong, *Between Crown and Swastika: The Impact of the Radical Right on the Afrikaner Nationalist Movement in the Fascist Era,* Johannesburg, Witwatersrand University Press, 1991.

53. See G. Saron, *Nazi Models and South African Institutions,* SA, Jewish Board of Deputies, c. 1940; *Nazi Propaganda in South Africa* (reprint from *Common Sense,* January, February, and March numbers, 1940), Johannesburg, The Society of Jews and Christians, n.d.

54. See *The Anti-Jewish Movements in South Africa: The Need for Action,* SA, Jewish Board of Deputies, 1936, pp. 3–5. A pioneering study of these developments and their effect on South African Jewry is Michael Cohen, "Anti-Jewish Manifestations in the Union of South Africa in the Nineteen Thirties," unpublished B.A. hons. thesis, University of Cape Town, 1968; see esp. pp. 18–46. See also Furlong, *Between Crown and Swastika,* pp. 16–45.

55. Saron and Hotz, *The Jews in South Africa,* p. 379.

56. *House of Assembly Debates,* vol. 27, 16 June 1936, cols. 6268ff.

57. See E. F. Sichel, *From Refugee to Citizen: A Sociological Study of the Immigrants from Hitler-Europe Who Settled in South Africa,* Cape Town, Balkema, 1966, pp. 13–25.

58. SA, J. B. M. Hertzog Papers, vol. 62 (viii). Also, E. H. Louw to Dr. Malan, 2 February 1936, D. F. Malan Papers, Manuscripts Department, University of Stellenbosch.

59. It vested the decision in a selection board, which would judge not on racial grounds but on criteria such the "good character of the applicant," his occupational suitability, and his "likelihood of ready assimilation with the European population and of becoming a desirable citizen." *House of Assembly Debates,* vol. 28, 13 January 1937, col. 112.

60. Ibid., cols. 9ff. To ensure wider circulation the National Party's statements were reproduced in a booklet: *The National Party and Jewish Immigration,* Cape Town, National Party, 1937.

61. Party correspondence was made public in *Transvaler,* 3 November 1937; see also Furlong, *Between Crown and Swastika,* pp. 40–41, citing letter from Erasmus to Loubscher, 25 October 1937, from Greyshirts Records.

62. BD, *Press Report,* 15 October 1936, citing *Vaderland,* 29 October 1936.

63. See van Heerden, "Nasionaal-Sosialisme as Faktor," pp. 88–89, 378.

64. *Transvaler,* 1 October 1936.

65. *Burger,* 23 April 1938.

66. Eric Louw's parliamentary speech also appeared as a booklet: *Die Jodevraagstuk in Suid Afrika* (The Jewish Question in South Africa), Cape Town, Nasionale Pers, 1939.

67. See M. Roberts and A. E. G. Trollip, *The South African Opposition, 1939–1945,* London, Longmans, 1941, pp. 90ff; Furlong, *Between Crown and Swastika,* pp. 138–60; Christoph Marx, "The Ossewabrandwag as a Mass Movement," *Journal of Southern African Studies* 20, no. 2 (1994): 195–219.

68. BD, *Report of Executive Council, June 1940 to July 1942,* p. 8.

69. See O. Pirow, *Nuwe Orde vir Suid-Afrika,* Pretoria, Christelike Republikeinse Suid Afrikaanse Nasionaal-Sosialistiese Studiekring, 1940.

70. BD, *Die Nuwe Orde Correspondence Course,* Lecture no. 14, "The Jewish Question" (mimeographed).

71. Furlong, *Between Crown and Swastika,* esp. pp. 66, 208–18.

72. Hagemann concludes that it is "only in the area of countering South African Jewry that there is clear evidence that South Africans planned secret co-operation with the Reich." Hagemann, "Very Special Relations," p. 131.

73. *Transvaler,* 3 and 5 December 1940. The Programme of Principles and Constitution of the party in the Transvaal [Clause 4: Membership] stated: "Any white person settled in the Transvaal, except Jews, may be permitted membership of the party."

74. See Shimoni, *Jews and Zionism,* pp. 152–53.

75. *Jewish Affairs* 9, no. 1 (January 1948).

76. See, e.g., Leslie Rubin, "South African Jewry and Apartheid," *African Report* (February 1970): 22–24.

77. G. Saron, "The Jew in the South African Scene," *Jewish Affairs* 5, no. 6 (June 1945): 9.

Chapter 1: The Jewish Community and the Afrikaner Regime

1. An example of ideological justification of apartheid is N. J. Rhoodie, *Apartheid and Racial Partnership in Southern Africa,* Pretoria, Academica, 1969. Cf. André du Toit, "Ideological Change, Afrikaner Nationalism, and Pragmatic Racial Domination in South Africa," in Leonard Thompson and Jeffrey Butler, eds., *Change in Contemporary South Africa,* Berkeley and Los Angeles, University of California Press, 1975, pp. 19–50.

2. Perhaps the best ongoing contemporary summaries of apartheid legislation and

implementation were provided by the South African Institute of Race Relations, e.g., Muriel Horrell, ed., *Legislation and Race Relations,* Johannesburg, Institute of Race Relations, 1963; idem, *Action, Reaction and Counteraction,* Johannesburg, Institute of Race Relations, 1971.

3. See, e.g., Hermann Giliomee, "The Growth of Afrikaner Identity," in William Beinart and Saul Dubow, eds., *Segregation and Apartheid in Twentieth Century South Africa,* London and New York, Routledge, 1995, pp. 189–205.

4. Arthur Keppel-Jones, *When Smuts Goes,* Cape Town, African Bookman, 1947, p. 71.

5. J. Nossel to Dr. Malan, 28 January 1947, and reply of same date. D. F. Malan Papers, Manuscripts Department, University of Stellenbosch. Also correspondence June and July 1947 between I. Frank and Dr. Malan in *Jewish Times,* 5 October 1951; BD, Report of Executive Council, August 1947 to May 1949, p. 13.

6. E.g., Louw's letter to *Cape Times,* 15 October 1947.

7. Letter, E. Louw to Dr. Malan, 26 October 1947, D. F. Malan Papers, Manuscripts Department, University of Stellenbosch. See also P. F. van der Schyff, "Eric Louw in die Suid Afrikaanse Politiek tot 1948" (Eric Louw in South African Politics until 1948), unpublished D.Litt. dissertation, Potchefstroom University, 1974, pp. 694–701.

8. *Burger,* 30 October 1947; Onderhoud oor Joodse Vraagstuk Party-beleid Verduidedlik: Vrae en Antwoorde (Interview on the Jewish Question, Party-Policy Clarified: Questions and Answers), ms. in Dr. Malan's handwriting, D. F. Malan Papers, Manuscripts Department, University of Stellenbosch.

9. Confidential Report of Interview with the Prime Minister, 1 July 1948, BD, Public Relations Files.

10. Letters to Provincial Secretaries, 5 July 1948, BD, Public Relations Files.

11. In November 1948 the South African government issued a statement in which it said that Jewish organizations had asked for de jure recognition of Israel but the government did not intend to grant this "before the Palestine problem has been definitely settled." It explained that the government's policy was "one of strict neutrality." *Star,* 9 November 1948. See also Walter Eytan, *The First Ten Years: A Diplomatic History of Israel,* New York, Simon & Schuster, 1958, p. 13.

12. ZF, Memo. by Bernard Gering on interview with the Prime Minister, 12 July 1948.

13. *Jewish Affairs* 3, no. 11 (November 1948); Karl Lemeer (pseudonym of Henry Katzew), "The Political Scene," *Zionist Record,* 23 December 1948.

14. BD, *Report of Executive Council August 1947 to May 1949,* p. 15.

15. *Burger,* 29 November 1948.

16. See Patrick J. Furlong, *Between Crown and Swastika: The Impact of the Radical Right on the Afrikaner Nationalist Movement in the Fascist Era,* Johannesburg, Witwatersrand University Press, 1991, pp. 243–48.

17. A separate vote was not held on the Jewish Question at the last Transvaal congress of the Herenigde National Party, which took place in September 1951. However, discussion on the ban took place in committee, and when the congress approved the new qualifications for membership it was implicit that the ban on Jews had been lifted. *Vaderland,* 18 September 1951; *Transvaler,* 19 September 1951. Cf. the editorial comments in *Zionist Record,* 21 September 1951.

18. ZF, Speech by Dr. D. F. Malan, P.M. of South Africa at Banquet in his Honour, Cape Town, August 1953.

19. Neither the Board of Deputies nor the Zionist Federation was responsible for this honoring of Dr. Malan. It was purely the private initiative of Nossel and his associates. The right to honor someone by making a donation to the Jewish National Fund and inscribing

him in the JNF's Golden Book can be exercised by any Jew. See *Jewish Times,* 21 January 1955; *Zionist Record,* 21 January 1955.

20. See also Dr. Malan's foreword in Israel Abrahams, *The Birth of a Community,* Cape Town, Cape Town Hebrew Congregation, 1955. Cf. D. F. Malan, *Afrikaner Volkseenheid en my Ervarings op die Pad daarheen* (National Unity and My Experiences on the Path to It), Cape Town, Nasionale Boekhandel, 1959, chap. 7.

21. See Karl Lemeer, "The Afrikaner's Interest in Israel," *Zionist Record Annual,* September 1953, p. 61.

22. *Volksblad,* 7 July 1956.

23. E.g., S. W. Pienaar, "Natuurlik Staan die Afrikaners by Israel in sy Krisis" (Naturally the Afrikaners Stand by Israel in its Crisis), *Barkai,* December 1955, pp. 20ff. The monthly *Barkai,* edited by J. Rubik, was South African Jewry's sole Hebrew journal, but it published the article in Afrikaans.

24. S. W. Pienaar, "Afrikaners en Joode," *Jewish Affairs* 11, no. 6 (June 1956). Also, e.g., G. J. Claasen, "'n Nuwe Alliansie Tussen Jood en Boer" (A New Alliance between Jew and Boer), *Jewish Herald New Year Annual,* 1954.

25. Melamet's article appeared in the magazine sections of *Die Burger, Die Oosterlig,* and *Die Volksblad* in May 1956. An English translation was published in *Jewish Chronicle,* 25 May 1956.

26. E.g., article by M. Broughton, "South Africa Could Be Seen as the Israel of the South," *Argus,* 9 February 1957; editorial in *Transvaler,* 10 October 1958.

27. This statement, one of many in this period, appeared in a regular column titled "Nationalist Point of View," *Cape Times,* 1 May 1958. See also H. J. Rooseboom, "A Nationalist Looks at South African Jewry," *Jewish Times New Year Annual,* September 1950.

28. *Jewish Chronicle,* 28 November 1952; cf. *Zionist Record,* 18 November 1955; *Jewish Herald,* 10 February 1956.

29. See Henry Katzew, *Solution for South Africa: A Jewish View,* Cape Town, Nasionale Boekhandel, 1955; idem, *Apartheid and Survival: A Jewish View,* Cape Town, Simondium, 1965.

30. The delegation consisted of E. J. Horwitz, B. A. Ettlinger, N. Philips, and G. Saron. Memo of Interview with Dr. Verwoerd, 21 October 1958, BD, Public Relations Files.

31. BD, *Report of Executive Council April 1958 to August 1960,* p. 9.

32. A number of perceptive contemporary analyses of the Jewish community's policy dilemmas over apartheid saw publication. Noteworthy examples are Bernard Sachs, "South Africa, Life on a Volcano: The Jewish Community in a Caste Society," *Commentary* 9, no. 6 (June 1950): 530–37; Edward Feit, "Community in a Quandary: The South African Jewish Community and Apartheid," *Race* 4 (April 1967): 395–408; Henry Katzew, "Jews in the Land of Apartheid," *Midstream* 8 (December 1962): 65–78; Robert G. Weisbord, "The Dilemma of South African Jewry," *Journal of Modern African Studies* 5 (September 1967): 233–41.

33. BD, *Report of Executive Council, April 1958 to August 1960,* p. 9.

34. BD, *Report of Executive Council, August 1947 to May 1949,* p. 15.

35. *Jewish Affairs* 13, no. 1 (January 1958).

36. BD, *Report of Executive Council, September 1955 to March 1958,* pp. 5–8.

37. BD, *Report of Executive Council, April 1958 to August 1960,* p. 9.

38. BD, Public Relations Files.

39. E.g., BD, *Report of Executive Council, September 1962 to June 1965,* p. 9.

40. E.g., Address of Arthur Suzman, Chairman of the Public Relations Committee, to 24th Congress of the Jewish Board of Deputies, June 24–27, 1965, BD, Public Relations Files.

41. As reported in BD, Board of Deputies Meeting, Minutes, 29 June 1975.

42. UJW, Union of Jewish Women of South Africa, 12th National Conference, Johannesburg, 16–20 April 1964, Minutes, p. 2.

43. BD, *Report of Executive Council April 1958 to August 1960,* p. 10.

44. See Johann Kinghorn, "Modernization and Apartheid: The Afrikaner Churches," and John W. De Gruchy, "Grappling with a Colonial Heritage: The English-Speaking Churches under Imperialism and Apartheid," in Richard Elphick and Rodney Davenport, eds., *Christianity in South Africa: A Political, Social and Cultural History,* Cape Town, David Philip, 1999, pp. 135–72.

45. *Eastern Province Herald,* 30 July 1955; *Port Elizabeth Evening Post,* 13 November 1956; *Transvaler,* 15 November 1956.

46. Letter from A. M. Spira (chairman of the Eastern Province Committee of the S.A. Jewish Board of Deputies) to Gus Saron, 1 August 1955, BD, Public Relations Files.

47. The quotations are respectively from *Port Elizabeth Evening Post,* 20 December 1956, 21 December 1956, 18 December 1956.

48. Ibid., 17 December 1956.

49. Statement of Eastern Province Committee of the S.A. Jewish Board of Deputies, BD, Public Relations Files. Also *Port Elizabeth Evening Post,* 14 December 1956; *Oosterlig,* 18 December 1956.

50. BD, Executive Council Minutes, 12 December 1956. For Ungar's embittered views on South African Jewry, see André Ungar, "The Abdication of a Community," *Africa South* 3, no. 2 (January–March 1959): 29–38.

51. The Board of Deputies' general-secretary, Gus Saron, is on record as saying: "I know that the people of the Board and others were perfectly happy to see Ungar go because they thought that young fellow, who doesn't know South Africa, is speaking in a language and in a tone which is not compatible with what the situation calls for." Interview with Gus Saron, by Simon Herman and Geoffrey Wigoder, 4 and 5 August 1961, Oral Records Center, Institute of Contemporary Jewry, Hebrew University of Jerusalem, p. 42.

52. BD, Biographical Files: André Ungar.

53. See *Jewish Chronicle,* London, 29 April 1956, 17 August 1956. In 1955 the apartheid laws obliged the progressive congregation to hand over the management of the school it sponsored in Alexandra to the government. But the congregation continued to provide the school with scholarships and other services.

54. Arthur S. Super, "A Rabbi's Viewpoint: Judaism and Racial Issues," *Jewish Affairs* 27, no. 4 (April 1972): 14–16.

55. Consul-General Dov Sinai to Director-General British Department, 19 December 1963, IA, Foreign Ministry, 3388/6.

56. See, e.g., on protest against university apartheid, *Jewish Times,* 19 December 1956; on participation of Rabbis I. Abrahams, B. Casper, and D. Sherman against 90-day detentions, *Jewish Chronicle,* London, 8 May 1964; on Abrahams's attitude, see his letter in *Jewish Observer and Middle East Review,* 17 January 1964.

57. Rabbi Rabinowitz made these statements in March 1958 in the course of a sermon at the Great Synagogue attended by delegates to the Board of Deputies' 21st Congress, BD, Biographical Files.

58. See Gerald Mazabow, *To Reach for the Moon: The South African Rabbinate of Rabbi Dr. L. I. Rabinowitz,* Johannesburg, Union of Orthodox Synagogues of South Africa, 1999, p. 172.

59. *S.A. Observer,* April 1958.

60. "A Rabbi Speaks Out," *Counter Attack* (Bulletin of the South African Congress of Democrats), November 1959.

61. Quoted in Mazabow, *To Reach for the Moon,* p. 165.

62. *Jewish Chronicle,* London, 22 September 1961.

63. E.g., B. A. Ettlinger (President of the Board of Deputies) to Rabbi Rabinowitz, 14 October 1959; General-Secretary G. Saron to the editor, *Jewish Chronicle,* London, 29 September 1961, BD, Public Relations Files.

64. Quoted in Mazabow, *To Reach for the Moon,* pp. 180–81.

65. *Zionist Record,* 8 April 1960.

66. *Jewish Chronicle,* London, 22 September 1961.

67. Mimeographed text of Rabbi Rabinowitz's Yom Kippur Sermon, October 1959, in BD, Biographical Files.

68. Rabbi Dr. L. I. Rabinowitz, "Meg Zein Apartheid Loyt der Halakha?" (Is Apartheid Permissible According to Jewish Law?), *Afrikaner Yiddishe Zeitung, New Year Annual,* September 1960 (Yiddish).

69. S. Rappaport, *Rabbinic Thoughts on Race,* Johannesburg, C.N.A., 1951; idem, *Jewish Horizons,* Johannesburg, C.N.A., 1959.

70. *Jewish Chronicle,* London, 8 January 1965.

71. Ibid., 22 January 1965; *Zionist Record,* 29 January 1965, 5 February 1965; *Rand Daily Mail,* 30 January 1965.

72. *Star,* 26 October 1961.

73. Copies of correspondence dated 16 April, 25 April, 1 May 1961, BD, Public Relations Files.

74. Copies of letters dated 28 October 1961, 25 November 1961, circular letter 24 July 1962, undated letter to Board of Deputies postmarked 6 August 1962, BD, Public Relations Files.

75. Ben Isaacson, "What Is Wrong with S.A. Jewry: An Outspoken Article by a Local Minister Who Has Gone on *Aliyah,*" *Jewish Times,* 5 October 1965.

76. See Joel Peters, *Israel and Africa: The Problematic Friendship,* London, British Academic Press & Tauris, 1992.

77. Salmon to British Dept., 22 November 1960 and 21 February 1961, IA, Foreign Affairs, 3300/15.

78. See *UN General Assembly, Official Records,* 16th Session, Plenary Meetings: 1033rd and 1034th Meetings, 11 October 1961, pp. 387–405. Also H. S. Aynor, "Israel versus Apartheid at the United Nations," *The Jerusalem Journal of International Relations* 8, no. 1 (1986): 34–41.

79. Speech by Eric Louw, 20 October 1961, Radio South Africa; *Sunday Express,* 22 October 1961.

80. Memoranda on the sequence of events by G. Saron, 12 and 23 November 1961, BD, Public Relations Files.

81. BD, Executive Council, Minutes, 23 October 1961; *Zionist Record,* 20 October 1961.

82. Pratt to A. Levavi (Deputy Director-General, Foreign Ministry), 24 October 1961, IA, Foreign Affairs, 3300/15.

83. *Burger,* 17 November 1961.

84. See *UN General Assembly, Official Records,* 16th Session, Special Political Committee, 276th Meeting, 2 November 1961, pp. 85 ff.

85. Edgar Bernstein to David Ben-Gurion, 15 November 1961, IA, Foreign Affairs, 3300/15.

86. Exchange of correspondence with Jock Isacowitz, 31 October 1961, BD, Public Relations Files.

87. Copy of letter to *Rand Daily Mail,* 1 February 1962, in BD, Public Relations Files.

88. Author's interview with Michael Comay, Jerusalem, May 1977.

89. See Michael Brecher, *The Foreign Policy System of Israel*, London, Oxford University Press, 1971, pp. 234ff.

90. *Divrei Ha-Knesset* (Knesset Protocols), 27 November 1961, p. 450.

91. Ibid., pp. 447–48.

92. Cited by Brecher, *The Foreign Policy System*, p. 234. See also Charles S. Liebman, *Pressure without Sanctions: The Influence of World Jewry on Israeli Policy*, Rutherford, N.J., Fairleigh Dickinson University Press, 1977, pp. 161–64.

93. Cited by Brecher, *The Foreign Policy System*, p. 232.

94. BD, *Press Digest*, nos. 20, 21, 22, 24, November 1961.

95. Letter of Dr. S. Fielding, 4 November 1962, BD, Public Relations Files; also letter from Mendel and Aubrey Levin to *Vaderland*, 12 November 1962.

96. Memorandum of S.A. Congress of Democrats to S.A. Board of Deputies, 5 December 1961, BD, Public Relations Files.

97. *Sondagblad*, 26 November 1961.

98. See Gideon Shimoni, *Jews and Zionism: The South African Experience*, Cape Town, Oxford University Press, 1980, p. 317.

99. ZF, Honorary Officers, Minutes, 2 February 1962.

100. ZF, Minutes of Meeting, Honorary Officers of the Zionist Federation and Board of Deputies, 21 March 1962.

101. *Transvaler*, 9 November 1962; *Dagbreek*, 11 November 1962.

102. Memos. 11 & 12 October 1963, SA, Foreign Affairs, 1/8/3 vol. 2, Old Series.

103. Telegram, Pratt to Foreign Affairs Ministry, 12 September 1963, IA, Foreign Affairs, 3387/16.

104. *Vaderland*, 26 September 1963; *Burger*, 26 and 27 September 1963.

105. The Zionist ideological response to this crisis as elaborated in the Zionist Federation's "enlightenment campaign" is analyzed in Shimoni, *Jews and Zionism*, pp. 342–45.

106. Record of Meeting Held at the Foreign Office, Jerusalem, 14 February 1962; also Meeting of Sub-Committee of Government Jewish Agency Coordinating Committee, Jerusalem, 12 February 1962, ZF, Tel Aviv Office Archives.

107. Minutes of Meeting held in the Prime Minister's Office, Jerusalem, 23 November 1963, ZF, Tel Aviv Office Archives.

108. *Jewish Herald*, 24 October 1961, 6 November 1962.

109. ZF, Honorary Officers, Minutes, 23 July 1968.

110. See BD, *Press Digest*, nos. 21–24, June and July 1967, and a review of the South African press reaction, Afrikaans and English, in *Jewish Affairs* 22, no. 6 (June 1967). Also Milton Shain, "Consolidating the Consolidated: The Impact of the Six Day War on South African Jewry," in Eli Lederhendler, ed., *The Six Day War and World Jewry*, Bethesda, Md., University Press of Maryland, 2000, pp. 205–16.

111. ZF, Aide Mémoire of Interview between Prime Minister and Foreign Minister of South Africa and Messrs. I. A. Maisels, E. J. Horwitz and M. Porter, 8 June 1967.

Chapter 2: The Political Behavior of Jews

1. The sample encompassed 2,302 pupils of which 372 (16.2 percent) were Jewish. H. Lever and O. J. M. Wagner, "Ethnic Preferences of Jewish Youth in Johannesburg," *The Jewish Journal of Sociology* 9 (June 1967): 34–47; Henry Lever, *Ethnic Attitudes of Johannesburg Youth*, Johannesburg, Witwatersrand University Press, 1968. Other research indicating that

Jewish people were less prejudiced than other whites includes T. F. Pettigrew, "Personality and Sociocultural Factors in Intergroup Attitudes: A Cross-National Comparison," *Journal of Conflict Resolution* 2 (1958): 29–42; idem, "Social Distance Attitudes of South African Students," *Social Forces* 38 (1960): 246–53.

2. Allie A. Dubb, *Jewish South Africans: A Sociological View of the Johannesburg Community*, Grahamstown, Institute of Social and Economic Research, Rhodes University, 1977, p. 97.

3. See the critical discussion of the significance and limitations of studies in this field: J. W. Mann, "Attitudes towards Ethnic Groups," in Heribert Adam, ed., *South Africa: Sociological Perspectives*, London, Oxford University Press, 1968.

4. See Henry Lever, "The Jewish Voter in South Africa," *Ethnic and Racial Studies* 2, no. 2 (October 1979): 428–40; idem, *The South African Voter: Some Aspects of Voting Behaviour*, Cape Town, Juta, 1972.

5. In the provincial elections of 1954, 17 Jews were elected, all United Party; in 1959, 16, again all U.P. (a Jewish candidate who stood as a Liberal in Houghton was not successful); in 1965, 9, all U.P. (2 Jewish candidates who stood as Progressives failed to be elected); in 1970, 7, all U.P. BD, Files on Jews in Politics.

6. E.g., in Johannesburg: in 1950 there were 8 Jewish members of the City Council of which 7 were U.P. and one Labor. In 1954 all 11 Jewish councillors were U.P. In 1957 all 10 were U.P., while 3 Jewish candidates who stood for the Liberal Party and another candidate who stood for the Congress of Democrats were unsuccessful. In the 1962 election there were 20 Jews among the candidates (14 U.P. and 6 Progressive) of whom 13 were elected, all U.P. In the 1967 elections 16 Jewish candidates stood for the U.P., of whom 14 were elected; 7 Jews stood, all unsuccessfully, for a new group called the Citizens Group, and one stood, also unsuccessfully, for the National Party. BD, Files on Jews in Politics.

7. See Max Melamet "Lessons of the General Election," *Jewish Times*, 25 April 1958. It was said that Jews cast many of the 1,600 votes polled by Gordon, but some observers noted that a large proportion of these voted for Gordon the man rather than for Gordon the Liberal Party candidate.

8. See, e.g., editorial (in Yiddish) in *Afrikaner Yiddishe Tzeitung*, 24 March 1961.

9. Max Melamet, "South African Jewish Leadership," BD, typescript, September 1966; *Jewish Chronicle* (London), 14 May 1965.

10. Levin's opponent was also a Jew, Alf Widman of the U.P. See *Rand Daily Mail*, 3 March 1967.

11. In the 1953 general elections L. Hirschson, standing for the National Party in Hospital, Johannesburg, was thoroughly defeated by a United Party candidate. Similarly, in the 1954 provincial elections, a Jewish National Party candidate, C. Zeff, lost to the United Party in the Johannesburg City constituency. *Star*, 16 April 1953; *Jewish Times*, 27 August 1954.

12. E.g., in 1961, Bernard Friedman and Abe Einstein lost to the United Party in Johannesburg North and Orange Grove respectively by only 872 and 517 votes. *Star*, 20 October 1961.

13. An example was the Houghton provincial by-election of 1965, when the United Party's Dave Epstein was able to defeat the Progressive candidate, Kenny Gross. *Star*, 24 February 1965.

14. E.g., in Cape Town's Sea Point, the narrow victory—by a mere 231 votes—of the United Party's A. L. Basson, a Gentile, was attributed to "the Jewish vote." *Cape Times*, 23 April 1970. Another example was Johannesburg's Parktown North, in which the United Party's S. Emdin, a Jew, defeated his Progressive Party rival, H. Brigish, also a Jew.

15. The quotations are from a mid-1960s statement by the United Party leader Sir de

Villiers Graaff: "The United Party's Policy of Race Federation," in N. J. Rhoodie, ed., *South African Dialogue,* Johannesburg, McGraw-Hill, 1972, pp. 211–26.

16. See, e.g., Helen Suzman, "The Progressive Party's Programme for a Multi-Racial South Africa," in Rhoodie, *South African Dialogue,* pp. 228–44.

17. See Randolphe Vigne, *Liberals against Apartheid: A History of the Liberal Party of South Africa, 1953–1968,* London, Macmillan, 1997, p. 89.

18. See, e.g., *House of Assembly Debates,* 22 July 1970, vol. 29, cols. 201–12, reproduced in Phyllis Lewsen, ed., *Helen Suzman's Solo Years,* Johannesburg, Jonathan Ball, 1991, pp. 149–52.

19. The Black Sash was an organization of white women founded in 1955. Its members stood in silence in public places carrying placards and wearing white dresses crossed by broad black sashes, a symbol of mourning for the government's violations of civil rights.

20. Examples of Jews who played roles in the development of the Liberal Party are Leslie Rubin, Jack Unterhalter, Jock Isacowitz, Ruth Hayman, Leo Kuper, Marion Friedmann, Gerald Gordon, and Leslie Cooper. See the list of members of the Interim Council and National Committee Members, 1953–68, in Vigne, *Liberals against Apartheid,* pp. 233–35.

21. See Anthony Sampson, *The Treason Cage,* London, Heinemann, 1958; Lionel Forman and E. S. Sachs, *The South African Treason Trial,* London, Calder, 1956; Muriel Horrell, ed., *A Survey of Race Relations in South Africa 1959–60,* Johannesburg, S.A. Institute of Race Relations, 1961, pp. 37–39. See also David Y. Saks, "The Jewish Accused in the South African Treason Trial," *Jewish Affairs* 52, no.1 (autumn 1997): 43–47. For examples of the prominence given to the list of arrested people in the press, see, e.g., *Transvaler,* 20 December 1956; *Sunday Times,* 9 December 1956.

22. Memorandum, circa November 1962, and cuttings from *Daily Dispatch,* 17 November 1962; Memorandum on Government Gazette 25 August 1967, BD, Public Relations Files.

23. E.g., Hugh Lewin, although not a Jew (indeed the son of a priest), was persistently subjected to crude antisemitic abuse. See Hugh Lewin, *Bandiet: Seven Years in a South African Prison,* Cape Town, David Philip, 1989, p. 36. Similarly, the liberal activist Ernie Wentzel was often regarded as a Jew, although he was of "pure" Afrikaner stock.

24. *Transvaler,* 11 September 1956.

25. These examples are culled from *Transvaler,* 21 August 1954, 5 September 1956, 22 August 1956, 31 August 1956.

26. See, e.g., *House of Assembly Debates,* vol.102, 17 June 1959, cols. 8237–8301.

27. *Burger,* 27 July 1958.

28. See, e.g., Karl Lemeer (Henry Katzew), "The South African Scene," in *Zionist Record,* 5 September 1956, and correspondence in *Transvaler,* 30 August 1956.

29. "Jode as Volksgroep en die Afrikaners" (Jews as an ethnic-national group and the Afrikaners), *Burger,* 23 October 1956; *Volksblad,* 27 October 1956. See also the defiant response in *Zionist Record,* 2 November 1956.

30. See Janet Robertson, *Liberalism in South Africa 1948–1963,* Oxford, Oxford University Press, 1971; Vigne, *Liberals against Apartheid.*

31. See Muriel Horrell, ed., *A Survey of Race Relations in South Africa, 1963,* Johannesburg, S.A. Institute of Race Relations, 1964, pp. 54–55; H. H. W. de Villiers, *Rivonia: Operation Mayibuye,* Johannesburg, Afrikaanse Pers, 1964; Miles Brokensha and Robert Knowles, *The Fourth of July Raids,* Cape Town, Simondium, 1965; Hilda Bernstein, *The World That Was Ours: The Story of the Rivonia Trial,* London, SA Writers, 1989.

32. *Sunday Chronicle,* 29 August 1965.

33. *Jewish Times,* 12 September 1958; Bernard Sachs, *South African Personalities and Places,* Johannesburg, Kayor, 1959, p. 170.

34. See, e.g., Joel Joffe, *The Rivonia Story,* Cape Town, Mayibuye Books UWC, 1995, esp. p. 181.

35. *Rand Daily Mail,* 10 June 1976.

36. See Glenn Frankel, *Rivonia's Children: Three Families and the Cost of Conscience in White South Africa,* New York, Farrar, Straus and Giroux, 1999, pp. 8–9, 192.

37. Joffe, *The Rivonia Story,* pp. 1–2.

38. See Jeffrey M. Marker, "The Jewish Community and the Case of Julius and Ethel Rosenberg," *The Maryland Historian* 3, no.2 (fall 1972): 105–21; Deborah Dash Moore, "Reconsidering the Rosenbergs: Symbol and Substance in Second Generation American Jewish Consciousness," *Journal of American Ethnic History* 8, no. 1 (fall 1988): 21–37; Stuart Svonkin, *Jews against Prejudice: American Jews and the Fight for Civil Liberties,* New York, Columbia University Press, 1983.

39. Reported in Pinshaw (Board of Deputies, Cape Town) to Rich (Board of Deputies, Johannesburg) 28 August 1963. UCT, Jewish Board of Deputies Records, Box 57.

40. See Brokensha and Knowles, *The Fourth of July Raids.*

41. *Sunday Times,* 27 September 1964.

42. *Star,* 20 November 1964; *Transvaler,* 8 December 1964. Eisenstein was released after two and a half years in prison and left for England.

43. *Star,* 23 November 1964 and 15 April 1965; *Transvaler,* 24 November 1964; *Rand Daily Mail,* 1 July 1965.

44. See Brokensha and Knowles, *The Fourth of July Raids,* pp. 84, 85.

45. See Adrian Leftwich, "I Gave the Names," *Granta* 78 (June 2002): 11–31.

46. *Sunday Times,* 29 November 1964; Karl Lemeer's column in *Zionist Record,* 4 December 1964; *Sunday Express,* 6 December 1964.

47. Examples of press reports highlighting their Jewish background are in *Rand Daily Mail,* 11 February 1965 and 19 February 1965.

48. Finkelstein was a paraplegic. He was sentenced to 18 months, 15 suspended.

49. *Star,* 11 March 1964; *Burger,* 16 June 1964; and see *House of Assembly Debates,* vol. 10, 23 March 1964, cols. 3499–3504.

50. *Dagbreek en Sondagnuus,* 17 May 1964.

51. *Burger,* 14 September 1962 and 11 October 1962.

52. *Jewish Times,* 28 September 1962 and 12 October 1962; *Burger,* 29 September 1962. That the journalist Bernard Sachs, brother of trade unionist Solly Sachs, had a hand in the formulation of these *Jewish Times* editorials is evident from the almost verbatim repetition of this line of argument in his article "How the Jews Stand in the South African Political Scene," *Sunday Chronicle,* 7 February 1965.

53. *Dagbreek,* 1 September 1963.

54. BD, *Report to South African Jewry, September 1962 to June 1965,* p. 7.

55. Gus Saron, "The Background to Anti-Semitic Propaganda in the Republic" (1964); idem, "Anti-Semitism in South Africa" (31 October 1962); idem, "Memorandum on Anti-Semitic Propaganda in South Africa" (3 December 1964), BD, Public Relations Files.

56. See BD, *Report of Executive Council, April 1958 to August 1960,* pp. 15ff; *Report to South African Jewry, July 1965 to November 1967,* p. 7.

57. See, e.g., Noel Crown, *Persecution of South Africa—a Boomerang Publication* (n.d.); *World Opinion, Fact or Fiction: A Boomerang Publication* (n.d.); *Chance or Conspiracy, Boomerang Publications* (n.d.), BD, Public Relations Files.

58. *Anti-Com Newsletter* 2, no. 8 (August 1964).

59. E.g., editorial titled "Are We Anti-Jewish?" in *Kerkbode,* 18 November 1964.

60. *Anti-Com Newsletter* 2, no. 13 (October 1965) and no. 14 (February 1966); also BD, *Report to South African Jewry, September 1962 to June 1965,* pp. 8, 9.

61. See BD, *Report to South African Jewry, July 1965 to November 1967,* pp. 10, 29; also "Report on the International Symposium on Communism," in *Pretoria News,* 30 September 1966.

62. *South African Observer* (April 1966 and December 1962).

63. Correspondence in *Burger,* 20 September 1963.

64. Dirk Richard, "Waar Staan die Jood in Blanke Bestaansryd" (Where Does the Jew Stand in the White Struggle for Survival) *Dagbreek en Sondagnuus,* 26 September 1965; BD, *Report to South African Jewry, 1965 to 1966,* pp. 5, 6.

65. The number of Jews who were involved in the radical resistance is very difficult to estimate. In a study that focuses primarily on the Communist Party of South Africa, the Springbok Legion, and the South African Congress of Democrats from the late 1940s to the early 1960s, Joshua Lazerson estimates the total number of whites involved throughout this period as no more than 200 to 300 and notes that "many of these whites were Jewish." See Joshua N. Lazerson, *Against the Tide: Whites in the Struggle against Apartheid,* Boulder, Colo., Westview Press and Mayibuye Books, 1994, p. 3. I am much indebted to the biographical information derived from interview sources in this groundbreaking study. I am also indebted to the biographical information provided in Thomas Karis and Gwendolen M. Carter, eds., *From Protest to Challenge: A Documentary History of African Politics in South Africa 1882–1964,* vol. 4: *Political Profiles,* Stanford, California, Hoover Institute Press, 1977.

66. Passes were obligatory identity papers (officially named Reference Books) designed to control the movement of blacks. They recorded personal data and details of employment.

67. See, e.g., Albie Sachs, *The Soft Vengeance of a Freedom Fighter,* Cape Town, David Philip, 1990; Ronnie Kasrils, *Armed and Dangerous: My Undercover Struggle against Apartheid,* Oxford, Heinemann, 1993; AnnMarie Wolpe, *The Long Way Home,* Cape Town, David Philip, 1994; Joe Slovo, *Slovo: The Unfinished Autobiography,* Randburg, Ravan Press, 1995; Baruch Hirson, *Revolutions in My Life,* Johannesburg, Witwatersrand University Press, 1995; Rusty Bernstein, *Memory against Forgetting: Memoirs from a Life in South African Politics 1938–1964,* London, Viking, 1999.

68. See Ezra Mendelsohn, *On Modern Jewish Politics,* New York, Oxford University Press, 1993, pp. 93–103. Also Arthur Liebman, *Jews and the Left,* New York, J. Wiley, 1979; Nathan Glazer, *The Social Basis of American Communism,* Westport, Conn., Greenwood Press, 1961.

69. A trendsetting exposition of this view is Lawrence Fuchs, *The Political Behavior of American Jews,* Glencoe, Ill., Free Press, 1956. See esp. pp. 177–84. Fuchs, drawing on research by Werner J. Cahnman into the cultural consciousness of Jewish youth in America, placed great store by the concept and practice of *tzedakah* (literally "charity" but implying the principle of social justice) as a value inhering in the Jewish subculture.

70. See Immanuel Suttner, ed., *Cutting through the Mountain: Interviews with South African Jewish Activists,* London, Viking, 1999, pp. 602–5, 620. I am much indebted to this invaluable collection of interviews. A superb account of resistance to apartheid by Jewish radicals and the effect it had on their personal lives and families is Glenn Frankel, *Rivonia's Children.*

71. See, e.g., the objections to Fuchs's theory in Charles S. Liebman, *The Ambivalent American Jew: Politics, Religion and Family in American Jewish Life,* Philadelphia, Jewish Publication Society, 1973, pp. 139–44, and also in Werner Cohn, "Jewish Political Attitudes: Their Background," *Judaism* 8, no.4 (fall 1959): 312–22.

72. See Ben Halpern, "The Roots of American Jewish Liberalism," *American Jewish Historical Quarterly* 66 (December 1976): 190–214; Werner Cohn, "Jewish Political Attitudes"; idem, "The Politics of American Jews," in Marshall Sklare, ed., *The Jews: Social Patterns of an American Group,* Glencoe, Ill., Free Press, 1958, pp. 614–26.

73. Peter Medding, "Toward a General Theory of Jewish Political Interests and Behavior in the Contemporary World," in Daniel J. Elazar, ed., *Kinship and Consent: The Jewish Political Tradition and Its Contemporary Uses,* Ramat Gan, Turtledove Publishing, 1981, p. 321.

74. Suttner, *Cutting through the Mountain,* p. 351.

75. Albie Sachs, "Being the Same and Being Different," *The Jewish Quarterly* 40, no. 1 (spring 1993): 13.

76. Suttner, *Cutting through the Mountain,* pp. 60, 59, 70.

77. Hirson, *Revolutions in My Life,* pp. 94, 97.

78. Percy Cohen, *Jewish Radicals and Radical Jews,* London, Academic Press, 1980, esp. p. 213. Cohen's analysis focuses primarily on phenomena in 1960s Europe and the United States. It should be noted that the kinds of outsider marginality that were characteristic of the social situation of those Jews, especially in the United States, are not necessarily of the same nature and complexity as the outsider marginality of South African Jews.

79. Slovo, *Slovo,* p. 3.

80. The author of this book can attest to this, as he was himself a pupil at this school, although belonging to a later generation.

81. Miriam Basner, *Am I an African: The Political Memoirs of H. M. Basner,* Johannesburg, Witwatersrand University Press, 1993, pp. 3–4.

82. Ibid., p. xvi.

83. Slovo, *Slovo,* p. 22.

84. Quoted in Suttner, *Cutting through the Mountain,* p. 602.

85. Barney Simon told an interviewer: "A clear influence on me was being a member of Habonim, which I was from about ten to about seventeen." Ibid., p. 122.

86. Rabbi Harris's eulogy is reproduced in Slovo, *Slovo,* pp. 201–5.

87. Suttner, *Cutting through the Mountain,* pp. 361–62.

88. Cf. Geoffrey Brahm Levey, "Toward a Theory of Disproportionate American Jewish Liberalism," in Peter Y. Medding, ed., *Studies in Contemporary Jewry* 11 (1995): 64–85.

89. Suttner, *Cutting through the Mountain,* pp. 23–47.

90. See Pauline Podbrey, *White Girl in Search of the Party,* Pietermaritzburg, Hadeda Books, 1993.

91. Author's interview with Eli Weinberg, Johannesburg, 28 June 1971; *Rand Daily Mail,* 11 February 1965.

92. Lazerson, *Against the Tide,* p. 97.

93. On the Barsels, see Immanuel Suttner's article based on an interview: "48 Regent Street," in the Israeli newspaper *Ha'aretz* (English edition), 19 September 1999, and Lazerson, *Against the Tide,* p. 92, drawing on an interview by J. Frederikse in South African History Archive, Johannesburg.

94. Cuttings from *Rand Daily Mail,* 4 and 10 November 1962, 1 May 1963, 12 August 1963, in BD, Personality Files.

95. Lazerson, *Against the Tide,* p. 87.

96. Ibid., pp. 37–39.

97. See Hilda Bernstein, *The World That Was Ours;* idem, *The Rift: The Exile Experience of South Africans,* London, Jonathan Cape, 1994.

98. Author's communication with Norman Levy, 15 November 2001; Lazerson, *Against the Tide,* p. 50.

99. See Don Pinnock, *Voices of Liberation,* vol. 2: *Ruth First,* Pretoria, HSRC Publishers, 1997.

100. Suttner, *Cutting through the Mountain,* p. 467.

101. *New Outlook* (April 1985): 32.

102. Suttner, *Cutting through the Mountain,* p. 466.

103. Ibid., p. 374.

104. Ibid., p. 245.

105. "Speaking to Jews in the ANC: 'Hold on for the Next Two Years,' an Interview with Ronnie Kasrils," *Jewish Affairs* 49, no. 1 (autumn 1994): 17.

106. Suttner, *Cutting through the Mountain,* p. 507.

107. Ibid., p. 514. See also "A Question of Identity: An Interview with Raymond Suttner," *Jewish Affairs* 49, no. 1 (autumn 1994): 25–27.

108. Suttner, *Cutting through the Mountain,* p. 500.

109. *House of Assembly Debates,* 24 May 1949, col. 6414, and see D. Saks, "Sam Kahn and the Communist Party," *Jewish Affairs* 51, no.1 (autumn 1996): 25–29.

110. Hirson, *Revolutions in My Life,* p. 125.

111. Author's interview with Arthur Goldreich, Jerusalem, 15 February 1972, in Oral Records Center, Institute of Contemporary Jewry, Hebrew University of Jerusalem.

112. For this information I am indebted to an interview with Harold Wolpe, conducted on the author's behalf by Steven Aschheim, London, 1 June 1971.

113. See interview with Taffy Adler in Suttner, *Cutting through the Mountain,* pp. 8–21, and also with Maxine Hart (pp. 520–34), Irwin Manoim and Anton Harber, who launched the antiapartheid *Weekly Mail* (pp. 143–65).

114. Rusty Bernstein, *Memory against Forgetting,* pp. 2, 10.

115. Ibid., pp. 14–15.

116. Norma Kitson, *Where Sixpence Lives,* London, Chatto & Windus, 1986, pp. 9, 29, 68.

117. Ibid., p. 54.

118. David Kitson had a Jewish mother and a gentile father.

119. As reported in *Friend,* 8 March 1966, in BD, Personality Files: Helen Suzman.

120. Suttner, *Cutting through the Mountain,* pp. 425–28.

121. Ibid., p. 427.

122. Ibid., pp. 108–16; "A Conversation between Nobel Prize Winner Nadine Gordimer and Natan Sharansky," *Jerusalem Report.* 24 October 1991, pp. 5–7. See also article in Hebrew by Yossi Gamzu on interview with Gordimer, *Yediot Ahronot* (Hebrew), 11 October 1991.

123. Suttner, *Cutting through the Mountain,* p. 112.

124. For an analysis of images of the Jew in Gordimer's fiction in terms of postulated "Jewish self-rejection," see Marcia Leveson, *People of the Book: Images of the Jew in South African English Fiction 1880–1992,* Cape Town, Witwatersrand University Press, 2001, pp. 174–90.

125. "A Conversation between Nobel Prize Winner Nadine Gordimer and Natan Sharansky."

126. E.g., the antisemitic taunts of Senator Weichardt, the former Greyshirt leader. *South African Senate Debates,* 29 January 1959, cols. 78–79.

127. Phyllis Lewsen, *Reverberations: A Memoir,* Cape Town, published in association with the Kaplan Centre, 1996, pp. 15, 41.

128. Phyllis Lewsen authored the finely nuanced political biography *John X. Merriman: A Paradoxical South African Statesman,* New Haven and London, Yale University Press, 1982.

129. Lewsen, *Reverberations,* p. 56.

130. Ibid., p. 136.

131. Ibid., p. 151, and Vigne, *Liberals against Apartheid,* p. 21.

132. Janet Levine, *Inside Apartheid: One Woman's Struggle in South Africa,* Chicago, Contemporary Books, 1988, p. 34.

133. Ibid., pp. 47–48.

134. Ibid., pp. 261–62.

135. Author's interview with Selma and Jules Browde, Johannesburg, 16 September 2000.

136. Author's interview with Benjamin Pogrund, Jerusalem, 28 August 1999. And see Benjamin Pogrund, *War of Words: Memoir of a South African Journalist,* New York, Seven Stories Press, 2000.

137. See Benjamin Pogrund, *How Can Man Die Better: Sobukwe and Apartheid,* London, Peter Halban, 1990.

138. Esther Levitan, *The Book of Esther,* Tel Aviv, privately published, 1993, p. 227.

139. Ibid., p. 83.

140. Ibid., p. 191.

141. See Hilda Bernstein, *The Rift,* pp. 271–78.

142. One striking example is Hosea Jaffe, a seminal South African Trotskyist who ultimately went to England. His younger brother, Meyer Jaffe, a leader of the Habonim Zionist youth movement, went to Israel to settle in a Habonim kibbutz; another is Amy Thornton (née Reitstein), who, after being in Hashomer Hatza'ir, became an activist in the Congress of Democrats and later in trade unions and the United Democratic Front. Her brother, Baruch Reitstein (Radyan), settled on a Hashomer Hatza'ir kibbutz in Israel.

143. One pertinent social psychological study known to the author is Heather M. Jones Petersen, "Whites in the Struggle: A Social-Psychological Study of White Left-Wing Political Activists in South Africa," unpublished Ph.D. dissertation, De Paul University, Chicago, 1995. However, it barely touches on the specific case of Jewish radicals.

144. Sam Kahn, "Nats Blackmail Jews on Israel Issue: Zionists Told to Accept Racialism," *New Age,* 1 December 1955.

145. *Rand Daily Mail,* 9 June 1961.

146. *Jewish Times,* 1 December 1961.

147. "Invitation to National Protest Day, 26 June 1950," 13 June 1950; "Memorandum to the S.A. Jewish Board of Deputies in Connection with Recent Statements by the Board," 5 December 1961, UCT, Jewish Board of Deputies Records, Box 809.

148. The Jewish Board of Deputies refused to meet a deputation from the Congress of Democrats. See "Let Board of Deputies Fight Race Discrimination—C.O.D.," *New Age,* 21 December 1961.

149. Editorial in *S.A. Patriot* (September 1962), BD, Public Relations Files.

150. See, e.g., the sympathetic personality profiles of Leslie Rubin: *Jewish Times,* 11 March 1955 and 15 March 1959.

151. Hirson, *Revolutions in My Life,* p. 56. Cf. the similar experience of Raymond Suttner, who relates that even while he was in solitary confinement he did not relish Rabbi Katz's visits. Interview in Suttner, *Cutting through the Mountain,* p. 510.

152. Podbrey, *White Girl in Search of the Party,* pp. 130–31.

153. AnnMarie Wolpe, *The Long Way Home,* p. 227.

154. Suttner, *Cutting through the Mountain,* p. 392.

155. See, e.g., *Jewish Chronicle,* London, 22 April 1960 and 26 April 1963, and esp. "Apartheid and South African Jewry—An Exchange," *Commentary* 24, no. 5 (November 1957): 424–28.

156. The same argument from self-interest was used by other liberals (as also by radicals). See, e.g., Leslie Rubin, "Afrikaner Nationalism and the Jews," *Africa South* 1, no.3 (April–June 1957): 28–34.

157. *Jewish Chronicle* (London), 25 April 1958, 30 April 1958, 4 May 1958, 23 May 1958.

158. *Jewish Observer and Middle East Review,* 8 April 1964, p. 11; *Jewish Times,* 24 April 1964.

159. Leslie Rubin, "South African Jewry and Apartheid," *Africa Report* 15, no. 2 (February 1970): 22–24; cf. Henry Katzew, "South African Jews and Politics, Another View," *Africa Report* 15, no.5 (May 1970): 22–23.

160. *Jewish Opinion: A Newsletter,* July 1954. This newsletter appeared from April 1954 to 11 June 1962.

161. Letter signed "Jewish Conservative" in *Rand Daily Mail,* 4 May 1964.

162. Author's interview with Ellen Hellmann, Johannesburg, 18 June 1971; also her address to a meeting of the national executive of the United Communal Fund Campaign, *Jewish Times,* 10 February 1961. See also her statements in *Sunday Express,* 31 January 1954, and *Zionist Record,* 3 March 1961.

163. *Zionist Record,* 5 May 1961.

164. Suttner, *Cutting through the Mountain,* p. 431.

165. See "Apartheid and South African Jewry—an Exchange," *Commentary* 24, no.5 (November 1957): 428–31.

166. Bernard Sachs, "Apartheid and Board of Deputies: A Reply to Mr. Henry Katzew," *Zionist Record,* 10 July 1970.

167. M.P. Leo Lovell to Chairman, Jewish Board of Deputies, 17 October 1956, BD, Public Relations Files.

168. Suttner, *Cutting through the Mountain,* pp. 231–32.

169. See Rubin, " South African Jewry and Apartheid," 22–24; *Star,* 7 February 1970.

170. By 1965 Fritz Flesch had obsessively accumulated a vast quantity of documentation on South African Jewry and apartheid, which he abstracted and distributed gratis all over the United States in condemnation of South African Jewry and of world Jewry's failure to join his crusade. The material appeared as a random series of abstracted documentation distributed by Fritz Flesch, Detroit, Mich.

171. *Jewish Ledger* (Connecticut), 8 December 1966.

172. Memorandum to President of the B'nai B'rith, USA on South African Jewry and Apartheid, 28 February 1966, BD, Files on World Jewish Organizations.

173. Copy of Minutes of Executive Committee of World Jewish Congress, Jerusalem, July 1964, BD, ibid.

174. S.A. Federation of Students Jewish Associations, Resolutions Adopted at 7th Conference, Durban, July 1959 (mimeographed), ZF, Files on Students Jewish-Zionist Associations.

175. S.A. Federation of Students Jewish Associations, Correlated Resolutions, 1965 (mimeographed), ZF, ibid.

176. *Zionist Record,* 6 September 1968; *Jewish Times,* 6 September 1968.

177. By 1970 it was estimated that 28.6 percent of Jews, as compared with 15.5 percent of all whites, had completed secondary school matriculation; 7.3 percent, compared with 2.9 percent of all whites, had a university degree. *South African Population Study, Advance Report No. 6: Educational Attainment and Languages,* Institute of Contemporary Jewry, Hebrew University of Jerusalem, 1976, p. 1.

178. On the Zionist youth movements and *hachshara* training farms, see Gideon Shimoni, *Jews and Zionism: The South African Experience,* Cape Town, Oxford University Press, 1980, esp. pp. 33–34, 261–64.

179. Ichud Habonim, South Africa, Tochniet le-Shichvat Hashomrim (Programme for the Shomrim Age-Group), booklet 2: "Guide to Discussions on the Platform of Ichud Habonim, Southern Africa," 1960. The author of the present book drafted the wording of the Habonim platform and planned the educational program for the senior age-group of Habonim.

180. *Aleh* (March–April 1959; bimonthly journal of the Habonim senior age-group, the *shomrim*).

Chapter 3: Adapting to Reformed Apartheid

1. On these changes in the Afrikaner sector, see Heribert Adam and Hermann Giliomee, *The Rise and Crisis of Afrikaner Power,* Cape Town, D. Philip, 1979, pp. 104–27, 217–21; Hermann Giliomee, "Apartheid, Verligtheid, and Liberalism," in Jeffrey Butler, Richard Elphick, and David Welsh, eds., *Democratic Liberalism in South Africa: Its History and Prospect,* Middletown, Conn., Wesleyan University Press, 1987, pp. 363–83.

2. *Sunday Express,* 22 March 1970.

3. The elections results in Cape Town's Sea Point constituency and Johannesburg's Parktown North were cases in point. See chap. 2, note 14.

4. Twelve Jewish Johannesburg city councillors resigned from the United Party and joined the Reform Party, only 5 Jews remaining with the United Party.

5. *Oggenblad,* 28 July 1975.

6. Allie A. Dubb, *Jewish South Africans: A Sociological View of the Johannesburg Community,* Grahamstown, Institute of Social and Economic Research, Rhodes University, 1977, p. 141. At the time of publication the Liberal Party had disbanded, but the research, having been conducted earlier, had shown that only 2 percent supported that party. It should be noted that 37 percent of Dubb's sample said they did not know, were undecided, indifferent, or refused to answer.

7. The author is grateful to Professor Hermann Giliomee (correspondence in September 1998) for drawing attention to these polls.

8. Henry Lever, "The Jewish Voter in South Africa," *Ethnic and Racial Studies* 2, no. 2 (October 1979): 428–39.

9. BD, Political Files: A. Hoppenstein.

10. *Jewish Times,* 26 October, 9 November, 23 November 1977. Hoppenstein returned to the South African Foreign Service. In 1979 he was appointed consul general in Washington, D.C., and in 1980 took charge of the South African consulate in New York.

11. This was a three-cornered contest; the third candidate was of the short-lived Republic Party and gained only 391 votes. BD, Political Files.

12. See, e.g., Nathan Mendelow, "Johannesburg's Eighteen Jewish Mayors," *Jewish Affairs* 21, no. 7 (July 1966): 18–31. Also BD, Political Files.

13. At that stage, the name was Progressive Reform Party. The United Party had not yet disbanded, and 9 out of 31 of its candidates in the municipal elections were Jews. BD, Political Files; *Jewish Herald,* 8 February 1977.

14. BD, Political Files.

15. The quotations in this and the following paragraphs are from pamphlets and brochures issued by the parties during the election campaign of May 1987, e.g., *Why You Should Vote NP,* n.d; *NP Position Paper No. 1: Power-Sharing,* compiled by Dr. Stoffel van der Merwe, MP, July 1986; *PFP Constitutional Policy: A Realistic Plan for the Future,* issued by J. Heming, Progressive Federal Party, Cape Town, n.d; *PFP Constitution Plan for a New South Africa,* n.d.

16. *Jewish Herald,* 27 November 1984. Also, author's interview with I. Pinshaw, Johannesburg, September 1986. The State President's Council functioned as an advisory body under terms of the reformed constitution. It had 60 members, 41 of whom were white, 13 colored, and 6 Indian. Pinshaw was its only Jewish member until 1987, when he was joined by another Jewish appointee, S. Spilken.

17. Four electoral districts had major concentrations of Jewish voters: Houghton, Yeoville, and Bezuidenhout in Johannesburg, and Sea Point in Cape Town. Only in Bezuidenhout was the Progressive Party candidate defeated. *Jewish Times,* 1 May 1987; *Cape Times,* 8 May 1987.

18. Another Jew, Theo Aronson, had preceded Bloomberg as a member of parliament for the National Party. However, he was not an elected member. Having suffered defeat when he stood for election in 1981 as a National Party candidate, he was later appointed to parliament under terms of the new constitution. BD, Political Files.

19. *Star,* 11 June 1987; BD, Jews for Social Justice File.

20. Letter to *Star,* 27 June 1988; *Star,* 30 June 1988; *Sunday Star,* 28 August 1998.

21. BD, Political Files.

22. *Herald Times,* 26 May 1988.

23. *Weekly Mail,* 27 October 1988.

24. BD, Management Committee, Minutes, 27 October 1988; "Chairman's Report," in National Executive Council, Minutes, 27 November 1988.

25. BD, Political Files and esp. cuttings from *Herald Times,* 25 August and 15 September 1989.

26. Flyer titled: "The Conservative Party of South Africa," Hillbrow, August 1989, BD, Public Relations Files.

27. "Extracts of Speech by Dr. Andries Treurnicht," Johannesburg City Hall, 13 March 1990, BD, Public Relations Files.

28. Quoted in the *Zionist Record and S.A. Jewish Chronicle,* 6 February 1987.

29. BD, *Report to South African Jewry, 1967–1970,* p. 8.

30. BD, *Towards a Responsible Community,* Johannesburg, SA Jewish Board of Deputies, 1978 (mimeographed address to the 26th National Congress of the Board of Deputies, May/June 1970), pp. 75–83.

31. Ibid., p. 91.

32. BD, *Report to South African Jewry 1972–1974,* p. 5.

33. The Board of Deputies itself instituted a pension scheme for its black employees. BD, *Report to South African Jewry 1972–1974,* p. 5.

34. Ibid.

35. Address to the 29th National Congress, May 1976, in BD, *Towards a Responsible Community,* pp. 120–23.

36. Resolution adopted at the Jewish Board of Deputies' 29th Biennial Congress, May 29–31, 1976, cited in BD, *Report to South African Jewry 1976–78,* p. 10.

37. *Jewish Affairs* 31, no. 5 (May 1976): 12.

38. Inter-Provincial Consultation, Heerengracht Hotel, Cape Town, 28 November 1976, Minutes; Cape Board of Deputies Council, Committee Meeting, 12 May 1978. Solly Kessler and Archie Shandling led the initiative at this meeting. UCT, Jewish Board of Deputies Records, BC 792B, Box 33. Also author's interviews with Mervyn Smith, Cape Town, 4 September 1997; Michael Katz, Johannesburg, 18 February and 8 September 1997; Denis Diamond, Jerusalem, 2 January 2000.

39. These developments are fully documented in Atalia Ben-Meir, "The South African Jewish Community and Politics, 1930–1978, with Special Reference to the South African

Jewish Board of Deputies," unpublished Ph.D. Dissertation, University of Natal, 1995. See chapter 24: "The Board Comes out of the Closet," pp. 450–65.

40. BD, *Report to South African Jewry 1976–1978,* p. 9.

41. BD, *Report to South African Jewry 1978–1980,* p. 9.

42. BD, *Report to South African Jewry 1976–1978,* p. 11.

43. BD, *Report to South African Jewry 1983–1985,* p. 11.

44. See the resolutions adopted at the 34th National Congress, April 1987, in *Jewish Affairs* 42, no. 4 (April 1987): 28–29.

45. BD, Management Committee, Minutes, 19 March 1987, 29 September 1987; National Executive Council, Minutes, 1 November 1987.

46. BD, *Report to South African Jewry 1985–1987,* p. 9.

47. UJW, 40th Anniversary (18th National) Conference of the Union of Jewish Women, 17–20 May 1976, Minutes, pp. 10–15.

48. UJW, Union of Jewish Women, 19th National Triennial Conference, 10–14 June 1979, Minutes, pp. 6, 23.

49. See, e.g., "The Total Zionist Onslaught on South Africa," *South African Observer* (February 1986).

50. An example is Rabbi Pfeuffer, who is reported to have said that helping black people to power in South Africa would be like giving guns to a kindergarten. See BD, Press Items of Jewish Interest, no. 23, 11 December 1986, citing *Star,* 4 December 1986. An earlier example is Rabbi Solomon Poupko, who in 1966 praised what he called the government's "realistic" race relations policy and offered his services as a lecturer on the dangers of communism. He was at the time rabbi of the Sydenham-Highlands North congregation in Johannesburg. See *Beeld,* 1 May 1966.

51. Noam Zohar, ed., *The Price of Equality: A Halachic Critique of Racism,* Jerusalem, Shalom Hartman Institute, 1986, pp. 14, 26. This analysis also concluded that the State of Israel should be halakhically prohibited from extending any aid to the South African government.

52. See, e.g., Rabbi Casper's speech at a public meeting to protest detention without trial, Darragh Hall, Johannesburg, on 26 May 1970 in Bernard Moses Casper, *Broadcasts and Papers* (prepared by Moshe Kahan), Jerusalem, Keren Bernard Moses Casper, 1992, pp. 37–38.

53. Interview in Tzippi Hoffman and Alan Fischer, eds., *The Jews of South Africa: What Future?* Cape Town, Southern Book Publishers, 1988, p. 327.

54. *Zionist Record and S.A. Jewish Chronicle,* 6 March 1987, and various documents in BD, Biographical Files: Chief Rabbi Casper.

55. Interview in Hoffman and Fischer, *The Jews of South Africa,* p. 360.

56. See, e.g., "Rabbi Prof. Weiss Joins in Student Protest," *South African Jewish Times,* 30 June 1972.

57. Author's interview with Rabbi Abner Weiss, Jerusalem, 23 May 2001.

58. *Argus,* 2 April 1976; *Strike* (May 1976); *Jewish Times,* 11 February 1977.

59. E.g., letter from Norman Shandling, 14 December 1977, UCT, Jewish Board of Deputies Records, BC 792, Box 69.

60. Author's interview with Rabbi David Rosen, Jerusalem, 26 November 2001.

61. Reported in the *Citizen,* 22 April 1982. See also *Jewish Affairs* 37, no. 5 (May 1982): 55.

62. Cuttings from the *Cape Times,* August 1985, BD, Biographical Files.

63. Author's interview with Rabbi Selwyn Franklin, Jerusalem, 18 January 2002. See also the interview with Rabbi Selwyn Franklin in Hoffman and Fischer, *The Jews of South Africa,* pp. 329–40.

64. A full report appeared in *Sunday Express,* 7 November 1976.

65. Author's interview with Rabbi Richard Lampert, Jerusalem, 4 February 2000.

66. *Sunday Star,* 8 October 1986.

67. *Jewish Times,* 31 July 1986.

68. The heading of the report of Rabbi Isaacson's sermon is "Jews Should Know Better: Rebel Rabbi Slams Establishment for Not Speaking Out against Apartheid Exploitation," *Sunday Star,* 15 September 1985. This and the following quotations are from newspaper cuttings in BD, Biographical Files: Rabbi B. Isaacson.

69. "Rabbi Raps Rabbi: You've Got It Wrong—Most Jews Are Eroding Apartheid," from newspaper cuttings, September 1986, BD, ibid.

70. See interview in Immanuel Suttner, ed., *Cutting through the Mountain: Interviews with South African Jewish Activists,* London, Viking, 1999, p. 585.

71. E.g., "South African Jews Are Called 'Sick' by Johannesburg Rabbi," *Jewish Floridian,* 6 March 1987.

72. *Jewish Times,* 20 September 1985; *Herald Times,* 10 October 1986.

73. See David Sherman, "My Encounter with Apartheid: A Reform Rabbi's Viewpoint," *Jewish Affairs* 52, no. 1 (autumn 1997): 74–75.

74. Press cuttings (esp. *Star,* 27 May 1996) in BD, Biographical Files: Rabbi A. Assabi.

75. *Zionist Record and S.A. Jewish Chronicle,* 25 July 1986; *Sunday Times,* 16 September 1990.

76. Evidence of these threats is in BD, Biographical Files: Rabbi A. Assabi.

77. E.g., the reports of Chairmen Morris Porter and Teddy Schneider and General-Secretary Gus Saron in BD, Deputies Meetings, Minutes, 29 April 1962, 30 August 1964, 28 August 1966.

78. As reported by Saron in BD, Deputies Meetings, Minutes, 26 February 1967. Similarly, the Board of Deputies' executive director in the 1980s, Aleck Goldberg, persuasively represented the community's position during an extensive lecture tour to the United States under the aegis of the American Jewish Committee.

79. The Board of Deputies' records are replete with repudiations of such overseas perceptions. E.g., Gus Saron's response to a banner headline in *New York Herald Tribune,* 30 March 1964: "Anti-Semitism Joins Apartheid in South Africa"; Chairman David Mann's criticism of an American Jewish Committee survey of world antisemitism, BD, Deputies Meeting, Minutes, 27 May 1973.

80. BD, Transcript of address by Denis Diamond to plenary assembly of the World Jewish Congress, February 1975, in S. A. Board of Deputies Meeting, Minutes, 23 February 1975.

81. BD, Transvaal Regional Conference, Minutes, 1 May 1977.

82. See Chaim Bermant's column in *Jewish Chronicle* (London), 23 March 1979, and the response of Denis Diamond in *Jewish Affairs* 34, no. 5 (May 1979): 24–25.

83. As reported in the World Jewish Congress's publication *News and Views* (February/March 1980): 7.

84. *Cleveland Jewish News,* 16 June 1978, 30 June 1978.

85. As reported in *News and Views* (summer 1983): 3.

86. "Confidential memo on liaison with Jewish organizations outside of South Africa and certain current problems," presented by Harry Schwarz, BD, Management Committee, Minutes, 15 May 1985.

87. BD, International Affairs Committee, Minutes, Confidential Meeting with AJC, 17 October 1985.

88. BD, Report in Management Committee, Minutes, 9 April 1991, 1 July 1991.

89. The National Council of Jewish Women in the United States was also party to

NJCRAC's policy. Letter from Rhoda Berman, National President, Union of Jewish Women of South Africa, to Joan Bronk, National President of National Council of Jewish Women, 8 August 1991, BD, Public Relations Files.

90. BD, US Correspondence Files, 1988; National Executive Committee, Minutes, 10 August 1988.

91. Memorandum dated 5 August 1988: "South Africa: Apartheid and Sanctions—The Attitude of the South African Reform Movement"; letter from Leslie Bergman, Vice-Chairman of SAUPJ, to Michael Katz, President of Board of Deputies, 23 August 1988, BD, Public Relations Files.

92. Letter from Union of Orthodox Congregations of America to Chief Rabbi Harris, 26 September 1989, BD, Public Relations Files.

Chapter 4: Dissonance and Change

1. *Burger,* 24 June 1968.

2. *Vaderland,* 14 April 1969.

3. The military matériel involved was probably related to the Mirage planes used by both Israel and South Africa at the time, spare parts for which were being withheld by France. Some conjectures in this regard are made in James Adams, *The Unnatural Alliance,* London, Quartet Books, 1984, p. 32.

4. Joel Peters, *Israel and Africa: The Problematic Friendship,* London, British Academic Press, 1992, pp. 69–70, citing *Foreign Trade Statistics,* Central Bureau of Statistics, Israel.

5. "Minutes of Meeting between Dr. Hilgard Muller and Mr. Abba Eban, 3 June 1970," SA, Foreign Affairs, 1/8/3, vol. 2A (2/12/68–21/7/71).

6. See Edgar Bernstein, "Israel, the O.A.U. and South Africa: What to Do When Interests Differ," *Jewish Affairs* 26, no. 1 (July 1971): 8–11.

7. Statement by Minister of Finance 30/8/71 in SA, Cabinet Minutes 1/1/4 1971, and correspondence in SA, Foreign Affairs, 1/8/3, vol. 2A (B2/12/68–E21/7/71).

8. E.g., *Ha'aretz,* 1 December 1967 (Hebrew); Henry Katzew, "O.A.U.: Israel's Reaction to the Contribution," *Jewish Affairs* 26, no. 1 (July 1971): 2–14.

9. "Consul-General Fincham to Secretary for Foreign Affairs, Cape Town and Pretoria, 25 May 1972," SA, Foreign Affairs, 1/8/3, vol. 3 (1/8/71–6/12/72). Fincham noted that there was "considerable relief in the Israeli Foreign Ministry that the threatened opposition to our presence in Israel did not materialize."

10. See Susan A. Gitelson, *Israel's African Setback in Perspective,* Jerusalem, Hebrew University, 1974; Ron Kochan et al., "Black African Voting Behavior in the U.N. on the Middle East Conflict 1967–1973," in Michael Curtis and Susan A. Gitelson, eds., *Israel and the Third World,* New Brunswick, N.J., Transaction Books, 1976, pp. 289–317. The most objective and thorough analysis is Peters, *Israel and Africa.*

11. Quoted in Curtis and Gitelson, *Israel and the Third World,* p. 347, and in Peters, *Israel and Africa,* p. 58.

12. Telegraphic report of speech by Defense Minister P. W. Botha at George, 14 October 1973, SA, Foreign Affairs, 1/8/3, vol. 5 (4/12/73–30/4/76).

13. Peters, *Israel and Africa,* pp. 69–70, citing Central Bureau of Statistics, Israel.

14. An example was Ambassador Unna's refusal to attend a performance of the play *Golda* in a Pretoria theater on the grounds that it was not open to all races. See BD, Press Digest, no. 12 (22 May 1978); no. 13 (7 June 1978).

15. Peters, *Israel and Africa,* p. 155.

16. SA Secretary of Commerce to Secretary Foreign Affairs, 24 September 1976, "The Arab Countries and Trade with South Africa," SA, Foreign Affairs, 1/8/3, vol. 6 (4/5/76–24/11/76).

17. SA Ambassador to Secretary Foreign Affairs, 27 October 1976, SA, Foreign Affairs, 1/8/3, vol. 6 (4/5/76–24/11/76).

18. "SA Embassy Tel Aviv, Mid-Year Report to Secretary for Foreign Affairs," 30 August 1977, SA, Foreign Affairs, 1/8/3, vol. 8 (3/8/77–26/1/78).

19. Embassy Report, "Discussion with Mr. Chiechenover, Director-General of Israel's Foreign Ministry," 15 October 1979, SA, Foreign Affairs, 1/8/3, vol. 1, new series (B29/9/63–E30/4/86).

20. The United Nations' *International Trade Statistics Yearbook* gave the following figures for South African trade in 1984 (in millions): with Israel—imports $83, exports $129; with U.S.A.—imports $2,375, exports $1,458; with U.K.—imports $1,660, exports $742; with West Germany—imports $2,339, exports $676. *International Trade Statistics Yearbook* 1, New York, UN Publishing Division, 1986. According to *Statistics of Foreign Trade* 18, Jerusalem, Central Bureau of Statistics, 1986 (in Hebrew), in 1985 Israel's imports from South Africa reached $174,654,000 and its exports $63,896,000. This was still under 1 percent of Israel's total trade. For a balanced inquiry into South Africa's relations with Israel in the comparative context of Israel's relations with African states see Kunirum Osia, *Israel, South Africa and Black Africa: A Study of the Primacy of the Politics of Expediency,* Washington, D.C., University Press of America, 1981.

21. "SAW Memorandum vir die Buitelandse Handelsbetrekkinge Komitee," 27 February 1978, SA, Foreign Affairs, 1/8/3, vol. 1, new series (B29/9/63–E30/4/86).

22. See Aaron S. Klieman, *Israel's Global Reach: Arms Sales as Diplomacy,* Washington, D.C., Pergamon, 1985, esp. pp. 151–54.

23. It is known that Israeli scientists made visits, notably Amos Horev, and there is documentary evidence, e.g., "Relations between South Africa and Israel in the Field of Nuclear Development," 3 February 1983, SA, Foreign Affairs, 1/8/3, vol. 1, new series (B29/9/63–E30/4/86).

24. Far-reaching conjectures are made in Adams, *The Unnatural Alliance.* However, no firm evidence has yet come to light confirming such conjectures. See Gerald M. Steinberg, "The Mythology of Israel–South African Nuclear Cooperation," *Middle East Review* 19, no. 3 (spring 1987): 31–38.

25. Ambassador Fincham to Secretary for Foreign Affairs, 10 November 1978, SA, Foreign Affairs, 1/8/3, vol.10 (21/9/78–29/5/79).

26. See Alon Liel, *Tzedek shachor: ha'mahapakh ha'drom afrikai* (Black Justice: The South African Upheaval), Tel Aviv, Hakibbutz Hameuchad, 1999, p. 26.

27. Naomi Chazan, "The Fallacies of Pragmatism: Israeli Foreign Policy towards South Africa," *African Affairs* 82, no. 327 (April 1983): 169–99. See also idem, "Israel and South Africa: Some Preliminary Reflections," *New Outlook* (June 1988): 8–11. Chazan's cogent critique contrasts greatly with the bitterly self-reproachful conspiratorial view vented in Benjamin Beit-Hallahmi, *The Israeli Connection: Who Israel Arms and Why,* New York, Pantheon Books, 1987.

28. See the investigative reports by Peta Krost in Johannesburg and Judy Herbstein in Tel Aviv, "Revealed: Israel's Secret Aid to Enemies of Apartheid," *Sunday Independent,* 6 April 1997.

29. See the investigative report by Tom Nugend, *Jerusalem Post,* 18 April 1986.

30. In 1992 the tie with the Los Angeles Center for Foreign Policy Options ended when the ICIC was incorporated as a nonprofit organization in Israel. Concurrently it established

a South Africa–based trust and developed new training programs within South Africa itself. The author is indebted to communications from Dr. Shimshon Zelniker in Jerusalem, January 2002.

31. "Reshamim mi-yachasei Israel–Drom Afrika le-eit krisat ha-apartheid" (Notes on Israel–South African Relations at the Time of the Collapse of Apartheid), unpublished essay by David Ariel, May 1999, p. 12.

32. See the reports by Amos Ben-Vered in *Ha'aretz,* 19 June 1986 (in Hebrew), and by Roy Isacowitz in *Jerusalem Post,* 11 July 1986; and *Knesset Debates,* no. 21, session 309, 19 March 1987, 2250–64.

33. See Naomi Chazan, "Israeli Perspectives on the Israel–South Africa Relationship," *Research Report,* nos. 9 and 10, London, Institute of Jewish Affairs, December 1987. Cf. the defense of existing Israel–South Africa relations by Eliahu Lankin, Israel's Likud-appointed ambassador to Pretoria from 1981 to 1985, in *Jerusalem Post,* 10 October 1986, and 8 April 1987, and the contrary views of Professor Shlomo Avineri in *Jerusalem Post,* 2 August 1985, and in *Ma'ariv,* 13 February 1987 (in Hebrew). Right-wing Knesset member Raphael Eitan in a lecture at Tel Aviv University in 1987 went so far as to express sympathy for the white minority and to favorably compare its rightful struggle for survival to that of the Jews in the Middle East, *Yediot Ahronot,* 25 December 1987 (in Hebrew).

34. Israel Ministry of Foreign Affairs Information Division, briefings, 27 March 1987; 16 September 1987.

35. BD, Press Items of Jewish Interest, no. 6, 26 March 1987.

36. *Zionist Record and S.A. Jewish Chronicle,* 27 March 1987.

37. See Liel, *Tzedek shachor,* pp. 52–84.

38. Melville L. Edelstein, *What Do Young Africans Think?* Johannesburg, Institute of Race Relations, 1972; also "The Urban African Image of the Jew," *Jewish Affairs* 27, no. 2 (February 1972): 6–8.

39. Martin E. West, *Divided Community: A Study of Social Groups Racial Attitudes in a South African Town,* Cape Town, Balkema, 1971, p. 79.

40. Henry Lever, *South African Society,* Johannesburg, Jonathan Ball, 1978, pp. 182–206. One of the studies discussed by Lever was S. Buxbaum, "The Social Distance Attitudes of a Sample of South African and Coloured Matriculation Pupils," unpublished hons. dissertation, University of the Witwatersrand, 1970.

41. Marcia Leveson, *People of the Book: Images of the Jew in South African English Fiction, 1880–1992,* Johannesburg, Witwatersrand University Press, 1996, esp. pp. 208–15.

42. Bloke Modisane, "An African Writer Looks at the Jew in South Africa," *Jewish Quarterly* 11, no. 4 (39) (winter 1963–4): 38–41.

43. Lewis Nkosi, *Home and Exile,* London, Longmans, 1983, p. 17.

44. Tzippi Hoffman and Alan Fischer, eds., *The Jews of South Africa: What Future?* Johannesburg, Southern Book Publishers, 1988.

45. Ibid., pp. 48, 39, 41,33, 34, in that sequence.

46. *The Jewish News* (London), 19 March 1987.

47. Hoffman and Fischer, *The Jews of South Africa,* pp. 15–16.

48. BD, Press Items of Jewish Interest, no. 3, 13 February 1987; no. 4, 26 February 1987; *Herald Times,* 20 February 1987; *Jerusalem Post,* 11 March 1987.

49. See *Herald Times,* 22 November 1989.

50. Hoffman and Fischer, *The Jews of South Africa,* p. 66.

51. *NUSAS Talks to the ANC* (report on meeting between the National Union of South African Students and the African National Congress, held from Sunday, 31 March, to Tuesday, 2 April 1986, in Harare, Zimbabwe), p. 28.

52. Hoffman and Fischer, *The Jews of South Africa*, pp. 71–79.

53. On these contacts with blacks, see BD, *Report to South African Jewry, 1980–1983*, p. 17; *Report to South African Jewry, 1985–1987*, pp. 11, 64.

54. Marcus Arkin, *South African Jewry: A Contemporary Survey*, Cape Town, Oxford University Press, 1984, p. 142.

55. "The People of South Africa: Population Census 1996, Primary Tables: The Country as a Whole, Report Number 03–01–19 (1996)," *Statistics South Africa*, Pretoria, p. 44. Since 16.7 percent chose not to state their religion, this is probably an underestimate. The total was probably close to 650,000.

56. Christopher Saunders and Nicholas Southey, *A Dictionary of South African History*, Cape Town, David Philip, 1998, pp. 88–89.

57. The Muslim Judicial Council in the Cape Province, the Sunni Jamiat al-Ulama of Natal, Transvaal, and Cape Town, the Jamiat al-Ulama in Natal, and the ultratraditional Majlis al-Ulama in Port Elizabeth.

58. See Ebrahim Moosa, "Islam in South Africa," in Martin Prozesky and John de Gruchy, eds., *Living Faiths in South Africa*, Cape Town, David Philip, 1995, pp. 129–54; Abdulkader Tayob, *Islamic Resurgence in South Africa: The Muslim Youth Movement*, Cape Town, UCT Press, 1995.

59. E. Bernstein, "Indian Passive Resistance: A Personal Viewpoint," *Jewish Affairs* 1, no. 7 (December 1946): 34–37. Other examples are Dr. B. Friedman, "The Indian Bill—and After," *Jewish Affairs* 1, no. 7 (December 1946): 5–8; C. Legum, "The Indian Boycott and Its Implications," *Jewish Affairs* 2, no. 4 (April 1947): 42–45. Opposition to legislation discriminating against Indians by limiting their right to trade and to land ownership was expressed, e.g., in *Zionist Record*, 7 May 1943: "Although Jewry today presents a besieged fortress and is hard pressed to solve its own problems, we are nevertheless conscious of injustice meted out to others."

60. Farid Esack, *Qur'an, Liberation and Pluralism: An Islamic Perspective of Interreligious Solidarity against Oppression*, Oxford, Oneworld Publications, 1997, p. 9.

61. Ibid., p. 41. Also Abdulkader Tayob, "Muslims' Discourse on Alliance Against Apartheid," *Journal for the Study of Religion* 3, no. 2 (September 1990): 31–47.

62. Important studies on Muslim attitudes and hostility in the context of antisemitism in South Africa are Jocelyn Hellig, *Anti-Semitism in South Africa Today*, Tel Aviv, Tel Aviv University, 1996, and Milton Shain, "Muslim Antisemitism and Anti-Zionism in South Africa, 1945–1998," paper presented at international conference of the Vidal Sassoon International Center for the Study of Antisemitism, the Hebrew University of Jerusalem, 13–16 June 1999. See also Margo Bastos, "Muslim Anti-Zionism and Antisemitism in South Africa since the Second World War, with Special Reference to Muslim News/Views," unpublished M.A. dissertation, University of Cape Town, 2002.

63. Hoffman and Fischer, *The Jews of South Africa*, pp. 122–33.

64. Relating his childhood experiences in the autobiographical introduction to his theological work, Esack notes: "Besides Christians, the only recollection I have of the religious Other are of Mr. Frank, a kind debt collector who was a Jew." Esack, *Qur'an, Liberation and Pluralism*, p. 2.

65. Hoffman and Fischer, *The Jews of South Africa*, pp. 134–42.

66. Ibid., pp. 117–18.

67. Ibid., pp. 143–49.

68. Ibid., pp. 150–70.

69. Leaflet titled "Urgent Appeal! Boycott," in the author's possession.

70. Quoted in *Strike* (October 1982): 4.

71. *Wits Student,* vol. 34, no. 18, 11 August 1982; ZF, Honorary Officers Minutes, discussion on "Recent Events at Wits Campus," 10 August 1982. Advocate Israel Maisels was asked to meet with the university's vice-chancellor with a view to finding a mutually satisfactory solution.

72. Hoffman and Fischer, *The Jews of South Africa,* p. 132.

73. See BD, Press Items of Jewish Interest, no. 10, 27 May 1987, and also the exchange of letters in *Cape Times,* 23 May 1987.

74. See *Jewish Affairs* 42, no. 7 (July 1987): 10; "UCT Muslims and Jews Clash on Anti-Zionism," *Cape Times,* 21 May 1987.

75. Copy of "Report on Events on Campus on Wednesday 11 May 1988 by M. Shear, Deputy Vice-Chancellor, 13 May 1988," BD, Files on Students Clashes.

76. *Muslim Digest* (July–October 1986): 3–7.

77. A second version of this vitriolic booklet was widely distributed in the mid-1990s under the title *Arabs and Israel: War or Peace,* and after some scandal regarding misappropriation of funds, the IPCI appeared under an alternative name: The Islamic Arabian Dawah Centre International. Ahmad's son, Yousuf, followed in his father's footsteps.

78. BD, Honorary Officers Minutes, 3 November 1989; 18 January 1990.

79. See Alan M. Tigay, "Xhosa Rabbi," *Jerusalem Post,* 20 September 1974.

80. See Professor M. E. R. Mathivha, *The Basena/Vamwenye/Balemba,* privately published by the author, 1997; also S. E. Moeti, "Lemba Religion and Rituals," *Jewish Affairs* 44, no. 5 (September/October 1989): 43–46; Tudor Parfitt, *Journey to the Vanished City: The Search for a Lost Tribe of Israel,* London, Hodder and Stoughton, 1992.

81. Gina Buijs, "Black Jews in the Northern Province: A Study of Ethnic Identity in South Africa," *Ethnic and Racial Studies* 24 no. 2 (November 1998): 676–82. Also Andrew Beattie, "South Africa's Black Jews," in *Sunday Independent,* 14 September 1997.

82. See A. B. Spurdle and T. Jenkins, "The Origins of the Lemba 'Black Jews' of Southern Africa: Evidence from P12F2 and other Y-Chromosome Markers," *American Journal of Human Genetics* 59, no. 5 (November 1996): 1126–33; Trefor Jenkins, "The Lemba People: Solving a Genetic Puzzle," *Arena* (magazine for alumni of the University of the Witwatersrand) 8, no. 24 (March 2001): 8–11.

83. Parfitt, *Journey to the Vanished City.*

84. See Nicholas Wade, "DNA Backs a Tribe's Tradition of Early Descent from the Jews," *New York Times,* 9 May 1999.

85. Most active is a certain self-styled "Rabbi Marciano ben Yishai of the King David Society International Foundation" in the United States, which was dedicated to bringing back to the fold the lost exiles of the House of Israel. He pretentiously declared the Lemba of southern Africa to be Jews and called for them to be helped financially and reincorporated into Judaism. Another initiative was that of an American Sephardi–based outreach association called "Kulanu" (All of Us), whose representative in Johannesburg, Rufina Bernadetti Silva Mausenbaum, is herself a descendant of Portuguese crypto-Jews who made her way back to the Jewish fold. See correspondence during September 1997 in BD, and "Kulanu" on the Internet.

86. Letter (undated) to "Fellow Jew" signed by Prof. Mathivha, president of the Lemba Cultural Association, filed September 1997 in BD, and BD, Management Committee Minutes, 16 September and 11 November 1997.

87. *Jon Qwelane Show,* Radio 702, 16 August 2000.

88. Professor Buijs has suggested that in the postapartheid political context the Lemba's motivation for a claim to Jewish identity might indeed become less serviceable than a more pan-African identity. Buijs, "Black Jews in the Northern Province," p. 681.

89. The estimate for Natal University in Durban was 140 to 350, Rhodes University 120, Pretoria University 80, The University of Port Elizabeth 30 to 40; and there were 400 to 500 in the Johannesburg Teachers' Training College. "Report to Honorary Officers on Student Affairs," by Prof. Marcus Arkin, Director General of the SAZF, 28 January 1975, ZF, Student Affairs Files. In 1981 a systematic inquiry headed by advocate Morris Friedman arrived at much the same estimates. "Commission of Inquiry into the Students Jewish and Zionist Movements: Report," 1981, ZF, Student Affairs Files.

90. Article by Michael Friedberg in *Ra'ayonot* (annual SAFSJA publication), 1971, p. 4.

91. See, e.g., Gordon G. Kling, "Perspective: South African Jewry Gone Awry," *Hakinor* (SAFSJA organ) (May 1970).

92. Geoffrey Hart, "Jewish Liberals in South Africa," *Bet Hillel* (1970): 10–11. BD, Student Affairs Files.

93. Tony Karon, "South African Jewry: An Alternative to Complicity," *Strike* (May 1985): 4–7.

94. Barbara Meltz, "From African Culture to Jewish Identity," *Hame'orer* (journal of the Movement for Zionist Fulfillment in Israel) 5 (winter 1986): 35.

95. BD, 27th National Congress, 10–14 May 1972, Minutes, p. 100; *Report to South African Jewry, 1972–1974,* p. 4.

96. *Strike* (March 1973).

97. *Jewish Times,* 27 October 1972; *Star,* 27 October 1972.

98. Jonathan Block, "We Weave Blankets but We Can't Afford to Buy Them: A Focus on Phillip Frame," *Strike* (March 1973).

99. *Strike* (April 1973).

100. "Dr Verwoerd and the 'Jewish Question,'" *Strike* (April 1973).

101. *Jewish Times,* 11 May 1973.

102. Cape Jewish Board of Deputies Committee Meeting, 7 September 1973, UCT, Board of Deputies Records, Box 105, File 305B.

103. G. Saron to I. Pinshaw, 19 April 1973, UCT, Board of Deputies Records, Box 105, File 305B.

104. ZF, Executive Council, Minutes, 26 April 1973; Honorary Officers, Minutes, 8 May 1973.

105. Special Meeting, 26 April 1973, UCT, Board of Deputies Records, Box 105, File 305B.

106. *Jewish Times,* November 1972; UCT, Board of Deputies Records, Box 809.

107. "Student Jewish Association Report on Wages Paid by Jewish Communal Institutions in Cape Town to Their Black Employees," reproduced in *Strike* (June 1973). Also "Jewish Students Criticise Black Wages," *Cape Times,* 8 June 1973.

108. Dennis Davis, "Guess Who Came to Dinner," backed by an editorial, in *Strike* (May, 1976). *Strike* also praised David Rosen, rabbi of the Green and Sea Point Congregation, for demonstratively refraining from attendance at the banquet.

109. *Wits Student,* 29 September 1982; *Strike* (October 1982).

110. *Genesis* 3 (organ of SAUJS Johannesburg) (winter 1978).

111. *Strike* (April 1987).

112. *Strike* (April 1987); (September 1983).

113. *Wits Student,* 22 October 1982.

114. Reproduced in *Jews for Justice Newsletter* (August 1987). See also the defense of Israel by liberal youth movement and student leaders, e.g., Paul Smith, "Israel–South Africa: Room for Compassion?" in *Strike* (August 1987).

115. "The South African Jewish Student, by Oz," *Strike* (May 1976). Even earlier, attention

had been drawn to the contrast between the characteristic orientation of Jewish students in Cape Town "towards NUSAS liberalism," on the one hand, and the burgeoning emphasis on religion and close contacts with the orthodox *kollel* in Johannesburg, on the other. See Denis Snitcher, "Jewish Students Verlig or Verkramp?" *Lama* (UCT student magazine) (May/June 1973).

116. See the special "Jews and the Law in South Africa" issue of *Jewish Affairs* 55, no. 2 (winter 2000).

117. *Star,* 23 April 1990.

118. BD, Biographical Files containing, inter alia, Rex Gibson's profile in *Optima* 34, no. 1 (March 1986): 32–35.

119. Immanuel Suttner, ed., *Cutting through the Mountain: Interviews with South African Jewish Activists,* London, Viking, 1999, pp. 326–27. Also the author's personal communication with Arthur Chaskalson.

120. Suttner, *Cutting through the Mountain,* p. 554.

121. Franz Auerbach, "Jewish Humanism: A Personal Voyage," BD, Biographical Files.

122. See F. E. Auerbach's article in *Rand Daily Mail,* 24 February 1971, and his letter to the editor, *Rand Daily Mail,* 15 January 1985, in defense of Archbishop Tutu's comparisons between apartheid and Nazi Germany.

123. *Sunday Star,* 12 November 1989, and F. Auerbach's correspondence with the Department of Home Affairs, 13 and 20 June 1990, BD, Biographical Files.

124. See Joshua N. Lazerson, *Against the Tide: Whites in the Struggle against Apartheid,* Boulder, Colo., Westview Press, and Bellville, Mayibuye Books, 1994, pp. 240ff.

125. Suttner, *Cutting through the Mountain,* pp. 198–99. Audrey Coleman's parents were first-generation South African Jews. Max Coleman's father was born in Lithuania, grew up in Ireland, and married an Irish Gentile. He was therefore not a Jew in terms of Jewish law (*halakha*).

126. Suttner, *Cutting through the Mountain,* p. 412.

127. By 1991 the proportion of Jews in what the state census described as administrative-managerial and professional occupations was 52 percent compared with 30 percent for the whole white population. See Anthony Arkin, "Economic Activities," in Marcus Arkin, ed., *South African Jewry: A Contemporary Survey,* Cape Town, Oxford University Press, 1984, pp. 57–78; idem, "Jewish Economic Activity in Modern-Day South Africa," *Jewish Affairs* 34, no. 1 (autumn 1999): 53–56.

128. See, e.g., the discussion of the literature on this and related questions of race and class in T. R. H. Davenport, *South Africa: A Modern History* (third edition), Macmillan, Johannesburg, 1987, pp. 571–78; F. A. Johnstone, "White Prosperity and White Supremacy in South Africa Today," *African Affairs* 69, no. 274 (1970): 124–40; Merle Lipton, *Capitalism and Apartheid: South Africa 1910–1986,* London, Wildwood House, 1985; Harold Wolpe, "Capitalism and Cheap Labour Power in South Africa: From Segregation to Apartheid," in William Beinart and Saul Dubow, eds., *Segregation and Apartheid in Twentieth Century South Africa,* London and New York, Routledge,1995, pp. 60–90.

129. Tony Bloom, "You Can't Solve Problems by Walking Away," *Sunday Times,* 10 June 1984.

130. *The Federation Chronicle,* September 1985. In 1988 Bloom took up permanent residence in London.

131. See the report prepared by Gus Saron and Aleck Goldberg in June 1973, which provides rather weak evidence in the business field: "Jewish humanitarian work for blacks in South Africa," pp. 7–8, BD, Public Relations Files.

132. These are documented in a private-circulation publication: *Seeking Tzedakah,* with photography by Gerald Hoberman and text by Marian Robertson, published by the Kaplan Kushlick Foundation, Cape Town, 2000.

133. Mendel Kaplan, *Jewish Roots in the South African Economy,* Cape Town, Struik, 1986, pp. 29, 389.

134. *Jews for Social Justice Newsletter* (November 1985).

135. Jews for Justice leaflet calling a protest meeting for 8 June 1986, BD, Jews for Justice File 303.12.

136. *Jews for Justice Newsletter* (April 1987).

137. *Jews for Social Justice Newsletter* (October 1988).

138. Jews for Justice Meeting, 1 November 1989, Minutes, UCT, BC 1030, B4.3.

139. E.g., David Alexander (age 20), head of the Netzer-Maginim youth movement of progressive Judaism in 1987; Mervyn Sloman (19) and Simon Whitesman, matriculates of Herzlia, the latter also a leader in the Habonim-Dror youth movement; Evan Robins (20), matriculate of Herzlia and chairman of Cape Town Bnei Akiva in 1988. See *Jews for Justice Newsletter* (October 1989).

140. Raymond Louw, ed., *Four Days in Lusaka: Whites in a Changing Society,* published by the Five Freedoms Forum, South Africa, 1989, pp. 131–33.

141. *Jews for Justice Newsletter* (April 1987).

142. See Sally Frankental and Milton Shain, "Accommodation, Apathy and Activism: Jewish Political Behaviour in South Africa," *Jewish Quarterly* 40, no. 2 (1993): 5–12.

143. Jews for Justice Meeting (with participation of Rabbi Cyril Harris and Anne Harris), 19 November 1989, UCT, Jews for Justice Archival Files, BC 1030, B4.3.

144. *Jews for Justice Newsletter* (October 1988).

145. *Jews for Justice Newsletter* (September 1988).

Chapter 5: A Transformed Community

1. R 1 million was allowed in cash and R 2 million per year over a six-year period from 1967 to 1972. Accumulated funds waiting for transfer had meanwhile to be held in nonresident bonds. In 1969 another R 18 million was approved under similar conditions over a six-year period (1969–74). "Oorplasing van Fondse na Israel" (Transfer of Funds to Israel), Confidential memo, 20 August 1971, in SA, Foreign Affairs, 1/8/3, vol. 3 (1/8/71–6/12/72).

2. ZF, Honorary Officers, Minutes, 4 November 1986.

3. *A Decade of Freedom: Report on Keren Hayesod–UIA in the First Ten Years of the State of Israel,* Tel Aviv, Keren Hayesod, 1958. This provides the following figures: 1948/9 to March 1958, $14,663,000 from South Africa; England $15,584,000; Canada $14,673,000. The U.S. United Israel Appeal in the same period provided $430,176,000.

4. This statement is based on two separate summaries of yearly income compiled by the head office of Keren Hayesod, to which I am indebted for providing this information: (1) "Keren Hayesod Actual Receipts by the Treasury of the Jewish Agency for Israel from 1970 to 1975" (Hebrew). This shows the following comparative income from the three largest contributing communities: South Africa $82,473,302, Britain $129,177,793, Canada $152,739,533, the Jewish population of Britain and Canada each being more than three times as large as South Africa's. (2) A summary of transfers to the Keren Hayesod from 1973 to 2000, which remains restricted information. This shows that from 1976/7 to 1986/7 Canadian Jewry accounted for 47.49 percent, British Jewry 28.24 percent, and South African

Jewry 24.27 percent; from 1987/8 to 1995: Canada 52.91 percent, Britain 25.36 percent, South Africa 21.73 percent; from 1996 to 2000: Canada 56.50 percent, Britain 27.22 percent, South Africa only 16.28 percent.

5. "IUA Report," in ZF, 32nd S.A. Zionist Federation Conference, 31 August–4 September 1972, Minutes.

6. ZF, *Report of Executive to the 30th S.A. Zionist Federation Conference, 31 August–4 September 1967;* also ZF, S.A. Zionist Youth Council Census, 1966. Census reports of the Zionist Youth Council in 1954, 1960, and 1964 gave membership figures as 5,500, 5,722, and 5,846 respectively.

7. ZF, *Report of Executive to 31st S.A. Zionist Conference, March 1970.* The membership of the other movements was Bnei Akiva, 1,730; Betar, 1,550; Hashomer Hatza'ir, 250; Magen David Adom Youth, 445. Based on the official South African census of 1970 it has been estimated that in the population of 118,120 Jews, 17 percent (20,080) were in the age-group 10–19. This was roughly the age-group encompassed by the youth movements. See *South African Jewish Population Study, Advance Report No. 3: Demographic Characteristics,* Jerusalem, Institute of Contemporary Jewry, Hebrew University, 1978, p. 5.

8. *Jews in the "New South Africa": Highlights of the 1998 National Survey of South African Jews,* JPR Report no. 3, September 1999, Cape Town, Institute of Jewish Policy Research and Kaplan Centre, University of Cape Town, 1999, p. 3.

9. "Report of the Women's Zionist Council," ZF, 42nd Zionist Federation Conference, 29 July–1 August 1993, Minutes, p. 17.

10. ZF, 24th S.A. Women's Zionist Biennial Conference, 16–20 August 1981, Minutes, p. 59.

11. Report on 21st S.A. Women's Biennial Conference in *Zionist Record and S.A. Jewish Chronicle,* 30 May 1975; ZF, 40th South African Zionist Federation Conference, 8–10 October1988, Minutes, p. 69.

12. See Gideon Shimoni, *Jews and Zionism: The South African Experience 1910–1967,* Cape Town, Oxford University Press, 1980, pp. 176–96, 240–52.

13. ZF, Meeting of S.A. Zionist Council, 18 and 19 June 1966, Minutes.

14. ZF, *Report of Executive to 30th S.A. Zionist Federation Conference, September 1967,* pp. 13, 14.

15. ZF, *Report of Executive to 32nd S.A. Zionist Federation Conference, 31 August–4 September 1972,* p. 2.

16. ZF, *Report of Executive to 35th S.A. Zionist Federation Conference, 31 August–4 September 1978,* p. 36.

17. ZF, Executive Council, Minutes, 29 April 1976.

18. E.g., ZF, Executive Council, Minutes, 29 April 1976; 24 June 1976; Meeting of Senior Honorary Officers of the S.A. Zionist Federation and S.A. Jewish Board of Deputies, 6 September 1977; Executive Council, Minutes, 18 August 1997 and 29 September 1977; Honorary Officers, Minutes, 18 August 1987.

19. See, e.g., *Zionist Record,* editorial, 19 November 1976, and the debate on the Zionist Socialist proposal. ZF, 34th Zionist Federation Conference, 2–6 September 1976, Minutes, pp. 171ff.

20. ZF, 43rd S.A. Zionist Federation Conference, 30–31 July 1994, Minutes, p. 9; also *Constitution of the S.A. Zionist Federation as Amended at the 43rd S.A. Zionist Federation Conference, 31 July 1994.*

21. An incisive analysis of the decline of the Zionist Federation is Marcus Arkin, "The Zionist Federation Umbrella," *Jewish Affairs* 53, no. 2 (winter 1998): 25–36.

22. See Ernest Stock, "The Reconstituted Jewish Agency," *American Jewish Yearbook*

1972, vol. 73, pp. 178–93; Charles Liebman, *Pressure without Sanctions: The Influence of World Jewry on Israeli Policy,* Rutherford, N.J., Fairleigh Dickinson University Press, 1977, pp. 131–47; Daniel Elazar, *People and Polity: The Organizational Dynamics of World Jewry,* Detroit, Wayne State University Press, 1989, pp. 134–52.

23. CZA, F24, 31st S.A. Zionist Federation Conference, 31 August–4 September 1978, Minutes, p. 89.

24. CZA, F24, 37th S.A. Zionist Federation Conference, 2–5 September 1982, p. 28.

25. ZF, Honorary Officers, Minutes, 17 July 1984.

26. Acrimony marked the closure of the paper in its last issue. See *Zionist Record–Jewish Chronicle,* 17 December 1993; also Marcus Arkin, "Who Killed the Zionist Record," *Hashalom* (March 1994). From the mid-1980s onward the demographic shrinkage of the community and financial nonviability of the Jewish press had led to a process of amalgamation. In 1986 the weeklies *S.A. Jewish Times* and the *Jewish Herald* merged to form the weekly *Herald Times.* In late 1993 the *Jewish Voice, Herald Times,* and *Zionist Record* merged to form the new bimonthly *S.A. Jewish Times,* but it closed in December 1997. In May 1998 the new weekly *S.A. Jewish Report* was launched.

27. Report and Charts Tabled by Yitzhak (Itz) Stein, Director of Zionist Federation Tel Aviv Office, ZF, Executive Council, Minutes, 20 May 1981.

28. Allie A. Dubb, *The Jewish Population of South Africa: The 1991 Sociodemographic Survey,* Cape Town, Kaplan Centre for Studies and Research, University of Cape Town, 1994, pp. 12, 17–18.

29. According to estimates of *aliya* made at the Jewish Board of Deputies in 1998. BD, Management Committee, Minutes, 5 February 1998.

30. E.g., ZF, 37th South African Zionist Federation Conference, 2–5 September 1982, Minutes, pp. 53–60. Ironically, but not uncharacteristically, the major proponent of this demand at the conference, Habonim leader and chairman of the Zionist Youth Council Johnny Broomberg, never went to live in Israel. On the other hand, the Zionist Federation's chairman who at the time argued for moderation, Itz Kalmanowitz, did settle in Israel during his term of office.

31. Dubb, *The Jewish Population of South Africa,* p. 17.

32. In the period 1986–98 two of the three successive chairmen of the Zionist Federation were Mizrahi leaders, Solly Sacks (1986–91) and Joe Simon (1994–99), both capping their terms of office with *aliya* to Israel. In between their terms (1991–94) Abe Abrahamson, a nonparty Zionist (and a former government minister in Rhodesia), was chairman.

33. Marcus Arkin, "Zionist Ideology: Changing Priorities for the 1980s," in ZF, 26th S.A. Zionist Conference, August/September 1980, Minutes, p. 35. See also Marcus Arkin, *The Zionist Idea: A History and Evaluation,* Publication of the S.A. Zionist Federation, circa 1977, p. 36.

34. See, e.g., ZF [*Report to*] *34th S.A. Zionist Federation Conference, 2–6 September 1976: Zionism Our Badge of Honour,* p. 3. See also [*Report to*] *35th S.A. Zionist Conference, 31 August–4 September 1978: Aliya—Our Pledge of Faith,* p. 3.

35. ZF, Honorary Officers, Minutes, 6 April 1976.

36. ZF, Honorary Officers, Minutes, 13 April 1976.

37. Greenstein told the conference that from 1971 to 1977 an amount of $34 million had been approved for investment. Furthermore, following the visit of Israel's minister of finance, Simha Ehrlich, in 1977 the South African government agreed to a further $36 million for investment at the rate of $12 million a year. CZA, F24, 35th Zionist Federation Conference, 31 August–4 September1978, Minutes, pp. 241–42.

38. CZA, *Protocols of the 29th Zionist Congress, 1978,* pp. 39–48 (Hebrew).

39. I venture this surmise on the strength of interviews with former diplomats who

prefer to remain anonymous. Also M.P. Harry Schwarz, an acknowledged parliamentary expert on military affairs, told the author that the South African authorities kept him in the dark. Author's interview with Harry Schwarz, Johannesburg, 17 February 1998.

40. ZF, Honorary Officers, Minutes, 18 November 1975. Statement dated 22 October 1975.

41. Marcus Arkin, "Israel and South Africa: The Economic Connection," *Supplement to Barclays Business Brief,* May 1979, pp. 1, 2; idem, "The Zionist Dimension," in Marcus Arkin, ed., *South African Jewry: A Contemporary Survey,* Cape Town, Oxford University Press, 1984, p. 89.

42. ZF, Honorary Officers, Minutes, 7 October 1986.

43. ZF, Honorary Officers, Minutes, 29 September 1987.

44. ZF, Executive Council, Minutes , 26 April 1973; Honorary Officers, Minutes, 8 May 1973; similarly the appeal by Habonim's leader, Sam Seligman, in ZF, 37th S.A. Zionist Federation Conference, September 1982, Minutes, pp. 136–45.

45. ZF, 37th S.A. Zionist Federation Conference, September 1982, Minutes, pp. 136–45.

46. See Chaim Shur, *Shomrim in the Land of Apartheid: The Story of Hashomer Hatzair in South Africa 1935–1970,* Kibbutz Dalia, Ma'arechet Publishing House, 1998, p. 15.

47. Personal communications with Dr. Leslie Stein, September 2001.

48. For what appears to this writer to be a rather dramatized account of these events, see Shur, *Shomrim in the Land of Apartheid,* pp. 9–18.

49. ZF, Honorary Officers, Minutes, 2 February 1971; 23 February 1971. The minutes state, "It was questionable whether the Federation was justified in spending so large a sum of money on a movement that had so little potential for growth. . . . If the World Movement of Hashomer Hatza'ir wished to send an emissary at its own expense, there would be no objection from the Federation."

50. ZF, Honorary Officers, Minutes, 12 January 1982; 19 January 1982.

51. ZF, Honorary Officers, Minutes, 9 March 1982; 16 March 1982. See also Esther Levitan, *The Book of Esther,* Tel Aviv, privately published, 1993, p. 191.

52. Dubb also found, however, that this was partly offset by between 7,000 and 10,000 Israelis, an influx from Zimbabwe (whose Jewish population declined from a high of about 8,500 in the mid-1960s to a mere 700 by 1991), and by return immigration of South African Jews. He estimated that of the original 39,000 Jews who had emigrated since 1970, some 4,400 had returned to South Africa by 1991. Dubb, *The Jewish Population of South Africa,* pp. 7, 12–19.

53. See Bernard Steinberg, "Jewish Education in South Africa," *Jewish Education* 39, no. 4 (December 1969): 14–22; idem, "Education as Ethnic Response: The Case of South African Jewry," in Moshe Sharon, ed., *Judaism in the Context of Diverse Civilizations,* Johannesburg, Maksim Publishers, 1993, pp. 239–51; idem, "South Africa: Jewish Education in a Divided Society," in H. S. Himmelfarb and S. DellaPergola, eds., *Jewish Education Worldwide: Cross-Cultural Perspectives,* Lanham, Md., University Press of America, 1989, pp. 357–93; Ronnie Mink, "Education," in Arkin, *South African Jewry,* pp. 117–29.

54. BD, Minute Book of the Fourth Biennial Conference of the South African Board of Jewish Education, Johannesburg, Afternoon Session, 15 March 1936, and see Gus Saron, "The Struggle over 'Religion' in Jewish Education: Early Controversies in the South African Board of Jewish Education," *The Federation Chronicle,* Rosh Hashana 5741/ September 1980, pp. 14–29.

55. BD, Minute Book of the Seventh Conference of the South African Board of Jewish Education, Fourth Session, 4 March 1945.

56. BJE, *Report to the 14th National Education Conference, April 1967,* p. 11. Cf. Prof. A. M. Dushkin's comparative table, "Extent of Jewish Education Received by Children between the Ages of 5 and 17 in the Diaspora 1967," in *Jewish Education in the Diaspora,* Jerusalem,

WZO, 1971, p. 7; also Sergio DellaPergola, *South African Population Study, Advance Report No. 12: Jewish Community Activities*, Jerusalem, Institute of Contemporary Jewry, 1978, p. 4.

57. The 1980 estimate is given in Steinberg, "Education as Ethnic Response," p. 368. The 2000 estimate is based on updated information collated by David Saks, Jewish Board of Deputies, February 2002.

58. Rabbi Kopul Rosen, "The Case for the Jewish Day School," *King David Schools 20th Anniversary Celebration 1948–1968*, Johannesburg, 1968, pp. 16–19.

59. Isaac Goss, "Why Should We Have Jewish Day Schools?" *The Jewish Herald*, Rosh Hashana, 5714/ 1953. See also idem, *Adventure in Jewish Education*, Johannesburg, S. A. Board of Jewish Education, 1961; *Gleanings: Reflections on Judaism and Jewish Education*, Johannesburg, Kayor, 1972.

60. It ought to be noted that the officially formulated principles of CNE did not impose the Afrikaners' Calvinist Articles of Faith upon non-Afrikaners or Jews. The policy stated (italics supplied): "*For Afrikaans-speaking children* this means that they must be reared on the basis of the Christian National Education attitude to life and to the world as held by our nation." See "Christian National Education Policy as Outlined by the Institute for CNE of the FAK," 1948, translated in William H. Vatcher, *White Laager*, London, Pall Mall, 1965, pp. 288–301.

61. *Transvaler*, 10 March 1964.

62. See, e.g., articles in *Common Sense* (June 1941, January 1949, May 1949).

63. See Gus Saron, "Religious Instruction in State Schools," *Jewish Affairs* 28, no. 11 (November 1973): 8–13; also *House of Assembly Debates*, vol. 19, 27 February 1967, col. 2001.

64. E.g., Resolution of the World Zionist Organization's Zionist General Council of December 1953 cited in ZF, *Report of Executive to S.A. Zionist Federation 24th Conference, 8–12 July 1954*, p. 20.

65. Quoted in report on the Zionist Conference in *Jewish Times*, 12 June 1959.

66. ZF, Honorary Officers, Minutes, 29 May 1974, 23 August 1974; Report of Treasurer, Morris Borsuk, in ZF, 34th S.A. Zionist Federation Conference, 2–6 September 1976, Minutes, p. 52.

67. Meyer E. Katz, "The History of Jewish Education in South Africa, 1841–1980," unpublished Ph.D. dissertation, University of Cape Town, 1980, esp. pp. 566, 607.

68. Statement by Ivan Greenstein, Chairman of the Board of Jewish Education, in BD, Meeting of Deputies, Minutes, 2 April 1978.

69. *Jewish Times*, 9 August 1978, and see Norman Sandler, "Can the Schools Survive Drastic Financial Pruning?" in BJE, *Report to 18th National Education Conference, 3–6 August 1978*.

70. BJE, Honorary Officers, Minutes, 23 October 1979; 18 March 1980; 29 July 1980; Executive Council, Minutes, 22 March 1982.

71. BJE, Executive Council, Minutes, 23 August 1982; *Rand Daily Mail*, 16 February 1985; author's interview with Kenny Katz (Board of Education chairman in the period under discussion), Johannesburg, 10 June 1998.

72. In the Cape the private schools received R 140 per pupil, and this alleviated the position of Cape Town's large Herzlia network and of the small school in Port Elizabeth. In Natal 75 percent of the salaries for secular studies were covered. Report of Chairman Kenny Katz in BJE, Executive Council, Minutes, 22 March 1982.

73. Author's interview with Jeffrey Bortz, Johannesburg, 17 June 1998.

74. I am indebted to David Ginsberg, director of finance and administration of the United Herzlia Schools, for providing documentation of these facts in correspondence dated 31 October 2001.

75. BJE, Executive Council, Minutes, 20 January 1986.

76. BJE, Executive Council, Minutes, 7 April 1986.

77. BJE, Executive Council, Minutes, 6 May 1986.

78. BJE, Executive Council, Minutes, 15 March 1989.

79. BJE, Executive Council, Minutes, 8 May 1990.

80. Fees were increased by 17.5 percent, *Herald Times,* 29 May 1987.

81. *Jewish Voice,* special issue on the South African Board of Jewish Education's 22nd conference (April 1990): 12.

82. Interview with Cyril Linde, financial director of the South African Board of Jewish Education, conducted by David Saks, Johannesburg, 20 January 1998.

83. BJE, Correspondence included in National Executive Council Meeting, Minutes, 20 March 1994.

84. *South African Government Gazette,* no. 19387, 12 October 1998, p. 35.

85. See the introductory chapter above and Jocelyn Hellig, "Religious Expression," in Arkin, *South African Jewry,* pp. 95–116; idem, "South African Judaism: An Expression of Conservative Traditionalism," *Judaism* 35, no. 2 (1986): 233–42.

86. Sergio DellaPergola and D. Tal, *South African Jewish Population Study, Advance Report No. 11: Religion and Religious Observance,* Jerusalem, Institute of Contemporary Jewry, 1978, pp. 7–10.

87. Steinberg, "South Africa: Jewish Education in a Divided Society," pp. 375–93; idem, "Jewish Education in South Africa," *Jewish Education* 39, no. 4 (1969): 14–22.

88. See full report in *Zionist Record,* 26 November 1954.

89. *Jewish Herald,* 19 February 1985.

90. *Jewish Times Special Supplement: The Yeshiva Gedola of Johannesburg,* 8 November 1985, in BD, File: Adath Jeshurun.

91. *SA Jewish Observer* (November 1966).

92. Report on the Jewish Board of Education's conference, in *Zionist Record,* 11 April 1967.

93. See Jeremy Hayman, "A Case Study of the Modern Orthodox and Ultra-Orthodox Sectors of Johannesburg Jewry with Special Reference to their Educational Institutions," unpublished Master of Education dissertation, University of Cape Town, 1988, esp. p. 54.

94. *Jewish Times,* 5 November 1980.

95. *Federation Chronicle* (April 1959). See also *Jewish Times,* 22 May 1959.

96. The quotation is from a sermon, Passover 1959, in possession of Rabbi J. M. Salzer, son of Rabbi Yaacov Salzer, who succeeded his father as rabbi in 1983. See also *Adath Jeshurun Golden Anniversary* (1986) in BD, File: Adath Jeshurun.

97. Interview with Rabbi Bernhard conducted by David Saks, Johannesburg, 17 June 1997.

98. See Norman Bernhard, "The Shtiebilisation of the Community: Good or Bad?" *Jewish Affairs* 50, no. 3 (spring 1995): 77–80.

99. *Jewish Times,* 21 April 1972.

100. See Hayman, "A Case Study of the Modern Orthodox and Ultra-Orthodox Sectors," esp. pp. 90, 91, 117.

101. The other major center, Cape Town, was far less affected by this extraordinary transformation. Only the Lubavitch movement made significant progress in Cape Town's community.

102. Dubb, *The Jewish Population of South Africa,* p. 108.

103. On Rabbi Rabinowitz's policy toward progressive Judaism in South Africa, see Gerald Mazabow, *To Reach for the Moon: The South African Rabbinate of Rabbi Dr. L. I. Rabinowitz,* Johannesburg, Union of Orthodox Synagogues of South Africa, 1999, pp. 198–202.

104. *Zionist Record,* 16 August 1963.

105. E.g., correspondence between Rabbi Isaacson, who balked at these strictures, and Gus Saron, 5 and 12 August 1963, BD, Files: Reform and Orthodoxy, 1960–1963; *Jewish Herald,* 20 August 1963; *Jewish Times,* 7 and 21 June 1963.

106. "Orthodoxy and Reform Memorandum, signed by Rabbi B. M. Casper and Rabbi A. S. Super, 23 Sivan 5725/23 June 1965," in BD, 24th Conference of the S.A. Jewish Board of Deputies, 24–27 June 1965), Minutes, p. 113.

107. BD, Executive Council, Minutes, 26 November 1979.

108. *Zionist Record,* 18 February 1983.

109. Rabbi Isaacson now conducted conversions according to *halakha,* performed no remarriages without a *get (halakhic* divorce), and upheld kashrut, but retained mixed seating and equal participation of women in the synagogue service.

110. See *Jewish Times,* 21 September 1984.

111. See Ady Assabi, "Catharsis and Rebirth: The Judaism of the Future," *Jewish Affairs* 50, no. 3 (spring 1995): 81–86. Also Dana Evan Kaplan, "Rabbi Ady Assabi and the Development of Conservative Judaism in South Africa," *Conservative Judaism* 51, no. 1 (fall 1998): 46–62; idem, "Progressive Judaism in the Beloved Country: Religious Thought and Institutional Trends in South Africa Today," *The Journal of Progressive Judaism* 8 (1997): 28–58.

112. *Saturday Star,* 30 May 1992.

113. William R. Domeris, "Revivalist Movements in South African Churches," *Jewish Affairs* 54, no. 1 (autumn 1999): 20.

114. See, e.g., C. K. Harris, "The Baalei Teshuva Phenomenon and South African Jewry," *Jewish Affairs* 54, no. 1 (autumn 1999): 67–68.

115. Akiva Tatz, *Anatomy of a Search: Personal Drama in the Teshuva Revolution,* New York, Mesorah Publications, 1987, pp. 11, 15–17.

116. Ibid., p. 29.

117. Ibid., pp. 102–8.

118. Author's interview with Rabbi Yosef Goldman, 21 June 1999. Rabbi Goldman came to South Africa from America in 1976 with the encouragement of the Lubavitcher rebbe and was the first director of the Habad House in Johannesburg.

119. See Roberta G. Sands and Dorit Roer-Strier, "*Ba'alot Teshuvah–D*aughters and Their Mothers: A View from South Africa," *Contemporary Jewry* 21 (2000): 55–77.

120. See Herbert M. Danzger, *Returning to Tradition: The Contemporary Revival of Orthodox Judaism,* New Haven and London, Yale University Press, 1989.

121. Interview with David Shaw (director of the department of informal Jewish education, South African Board of Jewish Education) conducted by David Saks, Johannesburg, 18 December 1997.

122. Dubb, *The Jewish Population of South Africa,* pp. 108–10.

123. Barry A. Kosmin, Jacqueline Goldberg, Milton Shain, and Shirley Bruk, *Jews of the "New South Africa": Highlights of the 1998 National Survey of South African Jews,* London, Institute for Jewish Policy Research Report no. 3, September 1999, esp. pp. 13, 14.

Chapter 6: After Apartheid

1. Allister Sparks, *Tomorrow Is Another Country: The Inside Story of South Africa's Negotiated Revolution,* Sandton, Struik, 1994; Patti Waldmeir, *Anatomy of a Miracle: The End of Apartheid and the Birth of the New South Africa,* London, Viking, 1997.

2. See Rodney Davenport and Christopher Saunders, *South Africa: A Modern History*

(fifth edition), London, Macmillan, 2000; T. R. H. Davenport, *The Transfer of Power in South Africa,* Cape Town, David Philip, 1998.

3. See, e.g., Merle Lipton, *Capitalism and Apartheid: South Africa, 1910–1986,* Cape Town, David Philip, 1986; Dan O'Meara, *Forty Lost Years: The Apartheid State and the Politics of the National Party, 1948–1994,* Randburg, Ravan Press, 1996.

4. See Adrian Guelke, *South Africa in Transition: The Misunderstood Miracle,* London, I. B. Tauris, 1999.

5. Ibid., p. 45.

6. BD, *Report to Congress, 1990–1992,* p. 10.

7. "Address by MP Harry Schwarz," p. 5, in BD, Jewish Board of Deputies 35th Congress, 25–27 March 1989, Minutes.

8. Steven Friedman, "South Africa in Transition: Implications for Jewry," *Jewish Affairs* 46, no. 1 (March/April 1991): 5–15. Also Steven Friedman's address in BD, Jewish Board of Deputies 36th Congress, 30 May–2 June 1991, Minutes.

9. BD, National Executive Council, Minutes, 8 March 1992.

10. Message from office of the Chief Rabbi: "Urgent to All Colleagues," 12 March 1992, in BD, Public Relations Files.

11. BD, Management Committee, Minutes, 26 February1992 and 8 March 1992.

12. Quoted, e.g., in *Citizen,* 1 March 1990.

13. See, e.g., "Outspoken Rabbi Dons Bullet-Proof Vest," *Sunday Times,* 16 September 1990.

14. *Jewish News,* 28 June 1990.

15. Passover message from Mandela, dated 13 April 1992, in BD, Public Relations Files. See also Nelson Mandela, *Long Walk to Freedom: The Autobiography of Nelson Mandela,* New York, Little, Brown, 1994, pp. 62 ff.

16. *Jewish Times,* Chanukah supplement 1997; "The Mark Gevisser File," *Mail and Guardian,* 29 September–7 October 1996.

17. Cyril Harris, *For Heaven's Sake: The Chief Rabbi's Diary,* Goodwood, Western Cape, 2000, p. 272.

18. E.g., letter to editor, *Star,* 24 September 1990.

19. Reports in BD, Transvaal Council, Minutes, 27 November 1989, and Management Committee, Minutes, 30 November 1989; 13 June 1990.

20. *Muslim Views* (March 1992): 3.

21. Report in BD, Management Committee Minutes, 13 June 1990.

22. BD, National Executive Council, Minutes, 6 December 1992.

23. *Jewish Herald Times,* 17 August 1990; letter to editor, *Citizen,* 31 August 1990.

24. ZF, Jewish Telegraphic Agency and S.A. Zionist Federation Daily News Cables, 30 August 1990.

25. *Al-Qalam* (September 1990): 10. Copy in BD, Public Relations Files.

26. Reports in BD, Transvaal Council, Minutes, 10 December 1990; Transvaal Council, Minutes, 16 September 1991.

27. Friedman, "South Africa in Transition: Implications for Jewry": 13.

28. Jewish Telegraphic Agency, 24 September 1990.

29. "Mandela Can't Compare SA Situation with Israel," *Cape Times,* 7 March 1990.

30. Harris, *For Heaven's Sake,* p. 13; author's interview with Mervyn Smith, Cape Town, 4 September 1997.

31. Alon Liel, *Tzedek shachor: hamahapakh hadrom afrikai* (Black Justice: The South African Upheaval), Tel Aviv, Hakibbutz Hameuchad, 1999 (Hebrew), p. 106, and see also pp. 88–93, 104–9.

32. Ibid., p. 93.

33. Ibid., pp. 66–72.

34. Address by ANC president Nelson Rolihlahla Mandela at the opening of the 37th Congress of the S.A. Jewish Board of Deputies, 21 August 1993, BD, Public Relations Files; *Jewish Herald Times,* 13 May 1994.

35. "Address delivered by His Excellency Mr. Malcolm Ferguson, South Africa's ambassador to Israel on behalf of Mr. Alfred Nzo, Foreign Minister, to the South African Zionist Federation Conference held in Johannesburg on the 31st July 1994," in ZF, 43rd S.A. Zionist Conference, 30–31 July 1994, Minutes.

36. E.g., Memorandum of Meeting with President Mandela , 3 October 1996, BD, Public Relations Files.

37. Memo: "Meeting with President Mandela 22 October 1998 at His Residence in Pretoria," BD, Public Relations Files.

38. Submission and Proposals on Chapter 2 of the Working Draft of the New Constitution, to Hassen Ebrahim, Executive Director Constituent Assembly, 19 February 1996, in BD, National Executive Council, Minutes, 2 June 1996.

39. I am indebted to two surveys of these events and analyses of the problematic Muslim-Jewish relationship in South Africa: Jocelyn Hellig, *Anti-Semitism in South Africa Today,* Tel Aviv, Tel Aviv University, 1996, esp. pp. 23–28, and Milton Shain, "Muslim Antisemitism and Anti-Zionism in South Africa, 1945–1998," paper presented at an international conference, The Dynamics of Antisemitism in the Second Half of the Twentieth Century, The Vidal Sassoon International Center for the Study of Antisemitism, The Hebrew University of Jerusalem, 13–16 June 1999.

40. *Cape Times,* 5 August 1996.

41. Sheikh Achmat Sedick (Secretary-General, Muslim Judicial Council, Cape Town), "An Open Letter to All South Africans," 29 April 1998, in BD, Public Relations Files; also published in *Cape Times,* 5 May 1998.

42. Author's interview with Mendel Kaplan, Jerusalem, 24 September 1998.

43. BD, Management Committee, Minutes, 6 February 1990.

44. Albie Sachs, "Being the Same and Being Different," *Jewish Quarterly* 40, no. 1 (spring 1993): 13.

45. BD, Management Committee, Minutes, 12 August 1991.

46. BD, Transvaal Council, Minutes, 2 July 1990.

47. "Address by Tony Leon," in BD, Management Committee, Minutes, 12 April 1994; circular letter, "To Fellow South Africans, from Tony Leon M.P., Leader of the Democratic Party, 22 March 1994," BD, Public Relations Files.

48. See Tony Leon, *Hope and Fear: Reflections of a Democrat,* Johannesburg, Jonathan Ball Publishers, 1998; Barry A. Kosmin, Jacqueline Goldberg, Milton Shain, and Shirley Bruck, *Jews of the "New South Africa": Highlights of the 1998 National Survey of South African Jews,* London, Institute for Jewish Policy Research Report no. 3, September 1999, p. 23.

49. The most prominent in the ANC were Joe Slovo, Ronnie Kasrils, Gill Marcus, and Raymond Suttner. Examples of lesser-known persons who served at various times in the 1990s as government department heads are Lael Bethlehem, who at age 30 was appointed chief director of forestry in the Department of Water Affairs and Forestry; Lisa Seftel, chief director of the Department of Labor Relations; Carol Steinberg, chief director of Cultural Development; Bernie Fanaroff, head of the National Crime Prevention Strategy (NCPS).

50. This "Mission Statement" appears throughout the 1990s in all reports to the congress of the Jewish Board of Deputies. Smith's speech is in BD, 38th National Congress, 20–22 August 1995, Minutes.

51. See *Tikkun Times* (July 2000).

52. UJW, Union of Jewish Women 1988 Triennial Conference, 7–10 August 1988, Minutes, pp. 98–99.

53. *South Africa Survey 1996–7,* Johannesburg, S.A. Institute of Race Relations, 1997, pp. 63–67.

54. See Mark Shaw and Peter Gastrow, "Stealing the Show? Crime and its Impact in Post-Apartheid South Africa," *Daedalus* 130, no. 1 (winter 2001): 239–41. Also Peter Gastrow and Mark Shaw, "In Search of Safety: Police Transformation and Public Responses in South Africa," ibid.: 259–76. See also William Gutteridge and J. E. Spence, eds., *Violence in Southern Africa,* London, Frank Cass, 1997.

55. Letter signed by Ernie Saks, in *Star,* 16 August 1996. The writer, an educator of note in the Jewish day school system, and a former mayor of the town of Sandton, nevertheless has remained in South Africa to this day.

56. Kosmin et al., *Jews of the "New South Africa,"* pp. 24–25.

57. Shale Horowitz and Dana Evan Kaplan, "The Jewish Exodus from the New South Africa: Realities and Implication," *International Migration* 39, no. 3 (2001): 4.

58. Allie A. Dubb, *The Jewish Population of South Africa: The 1991 Sociodemographic Survey,* Cape Town, Kaplan Centre for Jewish Studies and Research, University of Cape Town, 1994, pp. 7, 9–19.

59. BD, Report on Recent Demographic Trends and Emigration Patterns in the South African Jewish Community, compiled by D. Saks, Research Assistant SAJBD, 15 April 1998.

60. Horowitz and Kaplan, "The Jewish Exodus," p. 7.

61. Of about 21,000 emigrants, 37.5 percent went to Israel, 23.7 percent to the United States, 15.2 percent to Britain, 12.9 percent to Australia, and 9.4 percent to Canada. Dubb, *The Jewish Population of South Africa,* pp. 20–21.

62. D. Saks, Recent Trends in Jewish Emigration from South Africa, 1996/7, tabled in BD, Management Committee, Minutes, 5 February 1998.

63. *Community Profiles 1991 Census: South African Born,* Bureau of Immigration and Population Research, Australian Government Publishing Service, Canberra, October 1994, pp. 1–3; David Lucas, *Community Profiles 1996 Census: South African Born,* Department of Immigration and Multicultural Affairs, Canberra, February 2000, pp. 1–5, 29. See also entry on Australia by Hilary Rubinstein in David Singer and Ruth Seldin, eds., *American Jewish Year Book 1996,* vol. 96, New York, the American Jewish Committee, 1996, p. 347; W. D. Rubinstein, *Judaism in Australia,* Canberra, Australian Government Publishing Service, 1995, p. 32.

64. *Good Shabbos Sydenham,* Published by the Sydenham–Highlands North Hebrew Congregation, Johannesburg, February 1999.

65. "Reconciliation—a Jewish View; a Submission to the South African Truth and Reconciliation Commission, January 1997," p. 2, BD, Public Relations Files.

66. Ibid., p. 4.

67. See, e.g., Kader Asmal, Louise Asmal, and Ronald Suresh Roberts, *Reconciliation through Truth: A Reckoning of Apartheid's Criminal Governance,* Cape Town, Oxford University Press, 1997. See also Steven Robins's rather convoluted personalized exposition in Sarah Nuttall and Colin Coetzee, eds., *Negotiating the Past: The Making of Memory in South Africa,* Cape Town, Oxford University Press, 1998, pp. 120–40.

68. "The Truth Commission: Jewish Perspectives on Justice and Forgiveness in South Africa," *Jewish Affairs* 51, no. 3 (spring 1996): 30–39.

69. Ibid., p. 36.

70. *Mail and Guardian,* 27 March–3 April 1997, p. 22.

71. Claudia B. Braude, "From the Brotherhood of Man to the World to Come: The Denial of the Political in Rabbinic Writing under Apartheid," in Sander Gilman and Milton Shain, eds., *Jewries at the Frontier,* Urbana and Chicago, University of Illinois Press, 1999, p. 283.

72. Ibid., p. 284.

73. This reaction was witnessed by the author when Braude presented these views in a paper at an academic conference of Cape Town University's Kaplan Centre for Jewish Studies in September 1996.

74. See Allistair James McDuling, "Language Shift and Maintenance in the Portuguese Community of Johannesburg," unpublished M.A. (linguistics) dissertation, University of South Africa, 1995. McDuling cites immigrant figures of Portuguese persons from Portugal and Madeira from 1961 to 1992 as, respectively, 34,218 and 5,931. He also describes the Portuguese minority as lacking in cohesion, without even a single community school of its own comparable to the Deutsche Schule or the Greek SAHETI, not to speak of the Jewish King David schools, pp. 8, 139–40, 194.

75. See G. Sani, *History of the Italians in South Africa 1489–1989,* Johannesburg, Isando Press, 1992; David D. Saks, "South Africa's Italian Community," *Africana Notes News* 30, no. 5 (March 1993): 178–85.

76. See George Bizos, *No One to Blame? In Pursuit of Justice in South Africa,* Cape Town, David Philip, 1998.

77. Author's interview with Mr. Lagoudis, chairman of the Hellenic Community of Johannesburg, in Johannesburg, April 1971. On the early development of the Greek community, see Evangelos Anastasios Mantzaris, "Class and Ethnicity: The Politics and Ideologies of the Greek Community in South Africa, circa 1890–1924," unpublished Ph.D. dissertation, department of sociology, University of Cape Town, 1982. It is perhaps indicative of the far greater salience of the Jewish presence in South Africa that the author of this fine study found it appropriate to apply his research focus on the interrelationship of ethnicity and class mainly to a series of published studies on the Jews in South Africa. These are cited in the introductory chapter above.

78. In 1954 the total Jewish population in the twelve southern states was 228,763. Clive Webb, *Fight against Fear: Southern Jews and Black Civil Rights,* Athens and London, University of Georgia Press, 2001, p. 45.

79. Ibid., p. 218.

80. Ibid., p. xiii.

81. See Adam Mendelsohn, "South African Jews Also Face Racial Crisis: American Jewish Newspapers on Apartheid South Africa during the Civil Rights Era," *Jewish Affairs* 56, no. 3 (spring 2001): 19–23.

82. See particularly the seminal study of Leonard Dinnerstein, "Southern Jewry and the Desegregation Crisis, 1954–1970," *American Jewish Historical Quarterly* 62, no. 3 (1973): 231–41; Leonard Dinnerstein and Mary Palson, eds., *Jews in the South,* Baton Rouge, Louisiana State University Press, 1994.

83. See Webb, *Fight against Fear,* pp. 114–46.

84. An extreme example of conformity to norms in the farming community in the 1940s and 1950s was the involvement of several Jewish farmers in notorious abuses related to the use of black convicts as slave-like farm laborers in the Bethal district. These abuses were starkly revealed by the investigative reportage of Ruth First. In 1959 Chief Rabbi Louis Rabinowitz intervened to persuade the Jewish farmers to voluntarily release their convict laborers. See Ruth First, "Bethal Case-Book," *Africa South,* 2, no. 3 (April–June 1958): 14–25; BD, *Press Digest,* 22, 18 June 1959; Gerald Mazabow, *To Reach for the Moon: The South*

African Rabbinate of Rabbi Dr. L. I. Rabinowitz, Johannesburg, Union of Orthodox Synagogues of South Africa, 1999, pp. 153–54.

85. See Mark K. Bauman and Berkeley Kalin, eds., *The Quiet Voices: Southern Rabbis and Black Civil Rights, 1880s to 1990s,* Tuscaloosa, University of Alabama Press, 1997.

86. Ibid., pp. 9–10.

87. See Webb, *Fight Against Fear,* pp. 169–215.

88. "TRC Religious Community Hearings: Oral Submission by Chief Rabbi C. K. Harris to TRC 18/11/1997 and Questions and Answers That Followed," BD, Public Relations Files.

89. See James Cochrane, John de Gruchy, and Stephen Martin, eds., *Facing the Truth: South African Faith Communities and the Truth and Reconciliation Commission,* Cape Town, David Philip, 1999, esp. pp. 32–39.

90. Rabbi Lerner expressed his views in various newspapers in January 1996. See the discussion of the controversy that ensued in Dana Evan Kaplan, "Reconciliation and Healing: A South African Jewish Perspective," *The Reconstructionist* 63, no. 2 (spring 1999): 76–92.

91. *Jewish Affairs* 52, no. 1 (autumn, 1997).

92. Ibid., pp. 80–81.

93. Ibid., p. 50.

94. Ibid., pp. 36–37.

95. Ibid., pp. 34–35.

96. Ibid., p. 55.

97. See the photographic catalogue *Looking Back: Jews in the Struggle for Democracy and Human Rights in South Africa,* compiled by Milton Shain et al., Cape Town, Isaac and Jessie Kaplan Centre for Jewish Studies and Research, University of Cape Town, 2001.

98. See Milton Shain and Sally Frankental, "'Community with a Conscience': Myth or Reality?" in Glenda Abrahamson, ed., *Modern Jewish Mythologies,* Cincinnati, HUC Press, 2000, pp. 57–67.

Index